W9-CFS-677

counseling
american
minorities

a cross cultural perspective

counseling american minorities

a cross cultural perspective

Third Edition

Donald R. Atkinson
University of California at Santa Barbara

George Morten
Loyola Marymount University, Los Angeles

Derald Wing Sue
California State University, Hayward

wcb
Wm. C. Brown Publishers
Dubuque, Iowa

Part Openers
One & Two: © Michael Siluk
Three: © Diane Tong
Four: © Jean-Claude Lejeune
Five: © Steve Takatsuno
Six: © Michael Siluk

Copyright © 1979, 1983, 1989 by Wm. C. Brown Publishers. All rights reserved

Library of Congress Catalog Card Number: 88–070961

ISBN 0–697–05948–0

No part of this publication may be reproduced, stored in a retrieval system, or transmitted, in any form or by any means, electronic, mechanical, photocopying, recording, or otherwise, without the prior written permission of the publisher.

Printed in the United States of America by Wm. C. Brown Publishers
2460 Kerper Boulevard, Dubuque, IA 52001

10 9 8 7 6 5 4 3

Contents

Preface

This third edition of *Counseling American Minorities: A Cross-Cultural Perspective,* like the first two, is designed to help counselors and mental health practitioners maximize their effectiveness when working with a culturally diverse population. A major thesis of this book is that counselors can establish the necessary and sufficient conditions of a counseling relationship with clients who are culturally different. While similarity in race, ethnicity, and culture may be highly correlated with counseling success, we believe that other attributes (ability to share a similar world view, appropriate use of counseling strategies, awareness of own values, etc.) may be equally important factors in cross-cultural counseling.

The purposes of this edition remain the same as those of the earlier editions. First, as a collection of readings, it is intended to sensitize counselors (minority as well as nonminority) to the life experiences of culturally distinct populations. Minority observers have strongly criticized the counseling profession for its lack of attention to the unique needs and experiences of minority individuals. We hope this text can serve as a first step in sensitizing counselors to these needs and experiences. While direct exposure to the environment of the clientele population is perhaps best, reading relevant materials written by and about minority individuals is at least a starting point.

A second major purpose of the book is to examine the traditional counseling role, which has been heavily criticized by minority authors, and to suggest new directions for the counseling profession when dealing with minorities. By combining the present empirical, theoretical, and conceptual work on counseling minorities, it is our purpose to offer direction for future counseling practice, counselor education, and counseling research.

The actual text of this third edition has changed considerably. Chapters 1, 2, 3, and 16 have all been updated and expanded considerably. Perhaps the most significant changes to this edition, however, have been made in parts 2 through 5, which are devoted to minority group readings. In part 2 (The American Indian Client), we have retained the Lewis and Ho reading entitled "Social Work with Native Americans" and added two new readings by Everett, Proctor, and Cartmell ("Providing Psychological Services to American Indian Children and Families") and Edwards and Edwards

("American Indians: Working with Individuals and Groups"). Both the D. W. Sue ("Ethnic Identity: The Impact of Two Cultures on the Psychological Development of Asians in America") and Brower ("Counseling Vietnamese") articles have been retained in part 3 (The Asian American Client), and a new reading by Root ("Guidelines for Facilitating Therapy with Asian American Clients") has been added. In part 4 (The Black Client), we have added new readings by F. Jones ("External Crosscurrents and Internal Diversity: An Assessment of Black Progress, 1960–1980") and Grevious ("The Role of the Family Therapist with Low-Income Black Families") while retaining the A. Jones and Seagull ("Dimensions of the Relationship between the Black Client and the White Therapist") article. And in part 5 (The Latino Client), we have added a new reading by Laval, Gomez, and P. Ruiz ("A Language Minority: Hispanic Americans and Mental Health Care") while retaining the chapters by Padilla, R. A. Ruiz, and Alvarez ("Community Mental Health Services for the Spanish-Speaking/Surnamed Population") and Christensen ("Counseling Puerto Ricans: Some Cultural Considerations").

In revising parts 2 through 5, we have maintained our original design of beginning each part with a historical/sociological overview of the ethnic population followed by two readings that discuss the pragmatics of counseling members of this ethnic group. In selecting new readings for parts 2 through 5, we have attempted to identify articles that reflect the latest theory and research regarding the ethnic group discussed. In retaining readings from the second edition, we have selected those readings that have "withstood the test of time" and for which no more recent article has appeared that does a comparable job.

We have again included the Position Paper on Cross-Cultural Counseling Competencies in the appendix of this edition. This document, which describes eleven cross-cultural competencies that counselors should have in the areas of beliefs/attitudes, knowledges, and skills, is the product of the American Psychological Association's Division 17 Education and Training Committee.

This book of readings originated because each of us saw the need for a book in the counseling field that would treat a broad range of ethnic groups in a single volume. Many books available on counseling minorities are, for the most part, limited in perspective to the problems of a single ethnic group. A few of these texts have demonstrated or at least implied that other minority groups experience similar concerns in an oppressive society. Although this approach is valuable, it runs the risk of glossing over minority differences. This book is designed to foster direct comparison and contrast of various racial/ethnic minority group experiences and concerns that may be similar or dissimilar.

We believe that the current text, as a book of readings, can be used in conjunction with a variety of courses in the broad field of mental health: counseling techniques, theories of counseling, the social worker and urban problems, community psychology, changing roles of the counselor, mental health outreach, and individual and group analysis. Its primary use, however, is likely to be in undergraduate and graduate courses designed specifically to facilitate understanding the minority experience as it relates to such objectives as counseling minority youth, cross-cultural counseling, or multicultural counseling. To this end, it can serve as the principal text for such courses.

Parts 2 through 6 conclude with a number of hypothetical cases which require the reader to assume he or she is interacting with a minority client. Each case is followed by several questions designed to induce the reader to examine his/her own biases and stereotypes, and to explore potential obstacles to minority group/cross-cultural counseling. The most effective use of these cases and questions will probably occur when they serve to stimulate group discussion, preferably in settings where a number of racial/ethnic groups are represented.

It would be pleasing if we could report that in the ten years since the first edition of *Counseling American Minorities: A Cross-Cultural Perspective* appeared in print oppression of minorities had become a thing of the past. Unfortunately, this is hardly the case. Legislative and judicial achievements of the 1960s and 1970s came under attack at the local, state, and federal levels in the 1980s. Minority persons continue to experience discrimination in employment, housing, and education. Physical harassment and abuse of minorities is actually on the rise. The need for counselor knowledge of, and sensitivity to, the minority client experience is greater now than it has been at any time in the past three decades. We hope this text enhances counselor knowledge and sensitivity in this important area.

D. R. A.
G. M.
D. W. S.

Part 1
Why a Cross-Cultural Perspective?

1 Introduction
Defining Terms

The 1960s and 1970s witnessed a sudden increase in the number of articles that related to minority group counseling appearing in the professional counseling literature. A number of these studies identified such diverse groups as the aged, Asian Americans, Blacks, Chicanos, drug users, gays, the handicapped, Native Americans, prison inmates, students, and women as minority groups; this led to some question about what the term *minority* means. To add to the confusion, a number of terms are often used interchangeably with *minority* and/or with each other when their applicability is questionable. Writers, researchers, and practitioners have frequently failed to clearly distinguish between such important concepts as race, ethnic group, culture, and minority. The rhetoric and emotionalism surrounding the field of counseling minorities have distorted communications sufficiently without added confusion arising from undefined terms. Since counseling effectiveness relies so heavily on accurate and appropriate communication, especially in working with a culturally diverse client, it seems imperative that counselors clarify the meaning of these words. The following discussion is offered to define and elucidate certain basic terms and concepts related to minority group/cross-cultural counseling.

Race, Ethnicity, and Culture

Two terms that are often used interchangeably in the counseling literature are race and ethnicity. According to the *Oxford Dictionary of Words,* the term "race" first appeared in the English language less than three hundred years ago. Yet in that brief time race has come to be one of the most misused and misunderstood terms in the American vernacular (Rose, 1964).

The term race, as it is most frequently used today, borrows much of its meaning from a biological conception. As such, race refers to a system by which both plants and animals are classified into subcategories according to specific physical and structural characteristics. As it pertains to the human group, Krogman (1945) defines race as ". . . a subgroup of peoples possessing a definite combination of physical characters, of genetic origin, the combination of which to varying degrees distinguishes the subgroup from other subgroups of mankind" (p. 49). Physical differences involving skin pigmentation, head form, facial features, stature, and the color distribution and texture of body hair, are among the most commonly recognized factors distinguishing races of people. But, as Anderson (1971) points out, this system is far from ideal, in that not all racial group members fit these criteria precisely. While we commonly recognize three basic racial types—Caucasoid, Mongoloid, and Negroid—a great deal of overlapping occurs among these groups. In fact, when we look beneath the superficial characteristics, we find there are more similarities between groups than differences (owing to the fact that all humanoids originate from a single species), and more differences within racial groups than between them. The apparent flexibility of this definition poses little difficulty for biologists, whose major intent is to create a schema for showing genetic relationships. Unfortunately, this same level of functional clarity is not shared by the social sciences.

Most of the confusion surrounding the term race occurs when it is used in social context. As Mack (1968) so adequately points out, race in the biological sense has no biological consequences, but what people *believe* about race has very profound social consequences. Through subtle yet effective socializing influences, group members are taught and come to accept as "social fact" a myriad of myths and stereotypes regarding skin color, stature, facial features, and so forth. Thus, as Mack (1968) contends, "most of men's discussions about race are discussions about their beliefs, not about biological fact" (p. 103).

Ethnicity, on the other hand, refers to a group classification in which the members share a unique social and cultural heritage passed on from one generation to the next (Rose, 1964). Ethnicity is often erroneously assumed to have a biological or genetic foundation. For instance, Jews, as well as numerous other groups, are frequently identified as a racially distinct group. But, as Thompson and Hughes (1958) point out:

> . . . (Jews) . . . are not a biological race because the people known as Jews are not enough like each other and are too much like other people to be distinguished from them. But as people act with reference to Jews and to some extent connect the attitudes they have about them with real and imagined biological characteristics, they become a socially supposed race (p. 67).

If one accepts the view that ethnicity is the result of shared social and cultural heritage, it is apparent that Jews are an ethnic group. Hence, ethnic differences often involve differences in customs, language, religion, and other cultural factors; racial differences may or may not be germane to ethnic differences.

Finally, there is common confusion over the relationship of the term "culture" with race and ethnicity. Moore (1974) hits at the heart of the confusion:

> Sometimes we tend to confuse race and ethnic groups with culture. Great races do have different cultures. Ethnic groups within races differ in cultural

content. But, people of the same racial origin and of the same ethnic groups differ in their cultural matrices. All browns, or blacks, or whites, or yellows, or reds are not alike in the cultures in which they live and have their being. The understanding of the culture of another, or of groups other than our own, demands a knowledge of varied elements within a culture or the variety of culture components within a larger cultural matrix (p. 41).

Numerous definitions of culture have been offered by anthropologists over the years, including Kroeber and Kluckhohn's (1952) attempt to synthesize many of them:

> Culture consists of patterns, explicit and implicit, of and for behavior acquired and transmitted by symbols, constituting the distinctive achievement of human groups, including their embodiments in artifacts; the essential core of culture consists of traditional (i.e., historically derived and selected) ideas and especially their attached values; culture systems may, on the other hand, be considered as products of action, on the other as conditioning elements of further action (p. 181).

Needless to say, the myriad of confusing definitions that Kroeber and Kluckhohn set out to eliminate was only augmented by their earnest efforts. The most succinct and useful definition, for our purposes, is that offered by Linton (1945), who sees culture as, " . . . the configuration of learned behavior and results of behavior whose components and elements are shared and transmitted by the members of a particular society" (p. 32). By virtue of this definition of culture and those concepts of race and ethnicity accepted earlier, it is clear that the various ethnic groups within racial and among racial categories have their own unique cultures. It should also be clear that even within ethnic groups, small groups of individuals may develop behavior patterns they share and transmit, which in essence constitute a form of culture.

Before leaving this discussion of culture, it is important to dismiss two terms that have been widely used in the past to describe minority groups: "culturally deprived" and "culturally disadvantaged." The term "culturally deprived" implies the absence of culture, a (perhaps hypothetical) situation that has no relationship to the groups addressed in this book. Notwithstanding the effects of the larger society's culture on minorities through the mass media, minority groups clearly possess and transmit a culture of their own.

The term "culturally disadvantaged" suggests the person to whom it is applied is at a disadvantage because she/he lacks the cultural background formed by the controlling social structure. The use of "disadvantaged" rather than "deprived" is intended to recognize that the individual possesses a cultural heritage, but also suggests it is not the *right* culture. While less noxious than "culturally deprived," "culturally disadvantaged" still implies a cultural deficiency, whereas the real issue is one of ethnocentrism, with the values of the majority culture viewed as more important than those of minority cultures. A person may be economically disadvantaged because he/she has less money than the average person, or educationally disadvantaged due to inferior formal education. We seriously object, however, to any inference that minority peoples have less culture.

Even the currently popular terms "culturally different" and "culturally distinct" can carry negative connotations when they are used to imply that a minority person's culture is at variance (out-of-step) with the dominant (accepted) culture. The inappropriate application of these two terms occurs in counseling when their usage is restricted to minority clients. Taken literally, it is grammatically and conceptually correct to refer to a majority client as "culturally different" or "culturally distinct" from the counselor if the counselor is a minority individual.

Melting Pot, Cultural Assimilation, and Cultural Pluralism Philosophies

Throughout the early stages of its development, the United States projected an image of the cultural melting pot, a nation in which all nationalities, ethnicities, and races melted into one culture. Many Americans took pride in the melting pot image and a play by British playwright Israel Zangwill, entitled *The Melting Pot,* enjoyed widespread popularity in this country when it was first performed in 1908. Inherent in the melting pot concept was the view that a new and unique culture would continually emerge as each new immigrant group impacted upon the existing culture (Krug, 1976).

Not everyone in the United States, however, subscribed to the melting pot theory and philosophy. The Chinese Exclusion Act passed by Congress in 1882 was the first of a number of federal and state laws established to insure that certain immigrant groups would have minimal impact on the emerging American culture. In 1926 Henry Pratt Fairchild, a noted American sociologist of the time, wrote that the melting pot philosophy and unrestricted immigration were "slowly, insidiously, irresistably eating away the very heart of the United States" (Fairchild, 1926, p. 261). According to Fairchild and others, the "heart of the United States," was an (equivocally defined) American culture that was based primarily on the values and mores of early immigrants, principally English, Irish, German, and Scandinavian groups. Instead of melting all cultures into one, opponents of the melting pot philosophy argued that an effort should be made to culturally assimilate ("Americanize") all immigrant groups. To reduce the effects of the melting pot phenomenon and increase the probability of cultural assimilation, immigration quotas were developed for those countries whose culture diverged most from the American culture. Public education, with its universal use of the English language, was viewed as the primary institution for perpetuating the existing American culture (Epps, 1974).

The growing awareness of civil rights that took place in the 1960s and 1970s led to increased recognition that the melting pot principle had bypassed certain ethnic groups and that the cultural assimilation philosophy was objectionable because it called for relinquishing traditional ethnic values and norms in favor of those of the dominant culture. With the civil rights movement came a growing interest in cultural pluralism. According to the theory of cultural pluralism, individual ethnic groups maintain their own cultural uniqueness while sharing common elements of American culture (Kallen, 1956). Cultural pluralism is often likened to a cultural stew: the various ingredients are mixed together, but rather than melting into a single mass, the components remain intact and distinguishable while contributing to a whole that is richer than its parts alone. Cultural pluralism has enjoyed some popularity and acceptance (although hardly widespread) during the 1970s as evidenced by the passage of the Ethnic Heritage Studies Bill by Congress in 1973 and the implementation of bilingual, bicultural education in many metropolitan school districts. Whether support for bilingual, bicultural education will continue in the 1980s, however, remains to be seen.

Minority, Oppression, and the Third World

The term *minority* is frequently used in counseling literature to refer to racial/ethnic minorities or the nonwhite populations. Other authors have defined minority groups as physically or behaviorally identifiable groups that make up less than 50 percent of the United States population. Included in this definition are racial/ethnic minorities, the aged, the poor, gay people and others of a non-straight sexual orientation, handicapped persons, drug users, and prison populations.

In common usage, however, numerical size alone does not determine minority status. Over 80 percent of the population of South Africa is nonwhite, yet this group is frequently referred to as a minority by individuals within and outside South Africa (Rose, 1964). Prerequisite to an understanding of this use of the term minority is an understanding of the term *oppression.*

Oppression is a state of being that a person is forced to accept with respect to self, others, and society in general (Goldenberg, 1978). It is a state of being in which the oppressed person is deprived of some human right or dignity and is (or feels) powerless to do anything about it. Oppression can manifest itself in many ways. European Jews during World War II and both Black Americans and American Indians throughout much of U.S. history are examples of groups that have experienced oppression in its most extreme form, genocide. Insidious forms of oppression that continue to plague groups of Americans in the 1980s include political, economic, and social oppression. Examples of oppression currently experienced by minority groups include harassment of Vietnamese shrimp fishing boats in Louisiana and Texas, an average life expectancy for American Indians approximately twenty years less than the national norm, and educational and income statistics for Blacks and Hispanics that still trail far behind the national averages.

A definition of minority preferred by the present authors and employed in this book, which incorporates the concept of oppression, has been offered by Wirth (1945):

> . . . a group of people who, because of physical or cultural characteristics, are singled out from the others in society in which they live for differential and unequal treatment, and who therefore regard themselves as objects of collective discrimination (p. 347).

Since we have already established culture as characterized by shared and transmitted behavior, this definition allows us to accept all those groups included in the racial/ethnic and numerical definitions, plus other groups that are oppressed by society *primarily because of their group membership* as minorities. Most importantly, this definition allows us to include women as minorities, a group of oppressed individuals who constitute a numerical majority in this country.

Another term that is frequently used interchangeably with the word "minority" is "Third World." The term Third World is of French derivation (*tiers monde*), which enjoys international acceptance to describe the nonindustrialized nations of the world that are neither Western nor Communist (Miller, 1967). Many of these countries are located in Africa, South America, and Asia, primarily nonwhite portions of the world. In the United States, nonwhite individuals are frequently referred to as Third World persons. The term has certain political connotations, however, and to some degree has been used as a symbol of comradeship among all oppressed people. The misuse of the term occurs when it is used in this broader sense to apply to all oppressed people, since oppressed people live in First World (Capitalist societies), Second World (Socialist societies), and Third World nations, and are not necessarily distinguished by skin color.

Minority Group/Cross-Cultural Counseling

Minority group counseling, then, can be defined as any counseling relationship in which the client is a member of a minority group, regardless of the status of the counselor (who may be a member of the same minority group, a different minority group, or the majority group). To date much of the writing on minority group counseling has dealt exclusively with racial minorities and has examined the majority counselor–minority client relationship to the exclusion of other possibilities. This limited view of minority group counseling has fallen into some disfavor, perhaps because it ignores the special conditions of a counseling relationship in which the counselor is also a minority person. Further, there is concern that the term minority group counseling suggests a minority pathology; this is perceived as analogous to "Black pathology," an attempt to explain Black behavior in terms of White norms.

Cross-cultural counseling, by way of contrast, refers to any counseling relationship in which two or more of the participants are culturally different. This definition of cross-cultural counseling includes situations in which both the counselor and client(s) are minority individuals but represent different racial/ethnic groups (Black-Chicano, Asian American–Native American, Puerto Rican–Black, and so forth). It also includes the situation in which the counselor is a racial/ethnic minority person and the client is White (Black counselor–White client, Chicano counselor–White client, etc.). Additionally, it includes the circumstance in which the counselor and client(s) are racially and ethnically similar but belong to different cultural groups because of other variables such as sex, sexual orientation, socioeconomic factors, and age (White male–White female, Black straight person–Black gay, poor Asian American–wealthy Asian American).

This book is primarily concerned with counseling situations in which the client is a minority group member and culturally different than the counselor. Although the readings selected for inclusion in this volume relate specifically to racial/ethnic (Third World) minorities, the contributions here included are believed to be applicable to all oppressed people. Since the intention is to include counseling relationships defined as minority group counseling *and* cross-cultural counseling, the editors have elected to identify this focus as *minority group/cross-cultural counseling.*

References

Anderson, C. H. (1971). *Toward a new sociology: A critical view.* Homewood, Ill.: The Dorsey Press.

Epps, E. G. (1974). *Cultural pluralism.* Berkeley, Calif.: McCutchan Publishing Co.

Fairchild, H. P. (1926). *The melting pot mistake.* Boston: Little, Brown, & Co.

Goldenberg, I. I. (1978). *Oppression and social intervention.* Chicago: Nelson-Hall.

Kallen, H. M. (1956). *Cultural pluralism and the American idea.* Philadelphia: University of Philadelphia Press.

Kroeber, A. L., and Kluckhohn, C. (1952). *Culture: A critical review of concepts and definitions.* New York: Vintage Books.

Krogman, W. M. (1945). The concept of race. In R. Linton (Ed.), *The science of man in the world crisis.* (pp. 38–62). New York: Columbia University Press.

Krug, M. (1976). *The melting of the ethnics.* Bloomington, Ind.: Phi Delta Kappa Educational Foundation.

Linton, R. (1945). *The cultural background of personality.* New York: Appleton-Century Co.

Mack, R. W. (1968). *Race, class, & power,* New York: American Book Co.

Miller, J. D. B. (1967). *The politics of the third world.* London: Oxford University Press.

Moore, B. M. (1974). Cultural differences and counseling perspectives. *Texas Personnel and Guidance Association Journal, 3*, 39–44.

Rose, P. I. (1964). *They and we: Racial and ethnic relations in the United States.* New York: Random House.

Thompson, E. T., and Hughes, E. C. (1958). Race: *Individual and collective behavior.* Glencoe, Ill.: Free Press.

Wirth, L. (1945). The problem of minority groups. In R. Linton (Ed.), *The science of man in the world crisis.* New York: Columbia University Press.

2 Minority Group Counseling
An Overview

Until the mid-1960s, the counseling profession demonstrated little interest in or concern for the status of racial, ethnic, or other minority groups. Counseling and Guidance, with its traditional focus on the needs of the "average" student, tended to overlook the special needs of students who, by virtue of their skin color, physical characteristics, socioeconomic status, etc., found themselves disadvantaged in a world designed for White, middle-class, physically able, "straight" people. Psychotherapy, with its development and practice limited primarily to middle and upper class individuals, also overlooked the needs of minority populations.

By the late 1960s, however, "The winds of the American Revolution II . . . (were) . . . howling to be heard" (Lewis, Lewis & Dworkin, 1971, p. 689). And as Aubrey (1977) points out, the view that counseling and guidance dealt with the normal developmental concerns of individuals to the exclusion of special groups' concerns could no longer be accepted.

> Events in the 1960's, however, would blur this simple dichotomy by suddenly expanding potential guidance and counseling audiences to include minority groups, dissenters to the war in Viet Nam, alienated hippie and youth movements, experimenters and advocates of the drug culture, disenchanted students in high schools and universities, victims of urban and rural poverty and disenfranchised women (p. 293).

The forces that led to this voluminous, and often emotional, outcry in the professional counseling literature go far beyond the condition of social unrest existing in the United States in the late 1960s and early 1970s. The spark of dissatisfaction was struck when the guidance movement first began and accepted, intentionally or unintentionally, the practically unfulfilled, idealistic promises of the Declaration of Independence as a guideline (Byrne, 1977). As Shertzer and Stone (1974) suggest, "The pervasive concept of individualism, the lack of rigid class lines, the incentive to exercise one's talents to the best of one's ability may have provided a philosophical base . . ." (p. 22) for the dramatic shift in emphasis the profession took almost sixty years after its inception. Fuel for the fire was added when the Civil Rights movement of the 1950s provided convincing evidence that the educational establishment had failed to make provision for equal educational opportunity to all and that the time had come to correct existing discrepancies. The fire of discontent was fanned into a bright flame as the political activism associated with the Viet Nam war touched almost all phases of American life.

Although the intensity of the human rights and social change movements declined somewhat by the mid 1970s, professional psychology, always delayed and reactive in its response to social issues, began to recognize the unique counseling needs of ethnic populations. The American Psychological Association (APA), for example, moved from according ethnic minority issues an ad hoc status in the early 1970s to granting divisional status to ethnic psychologists in 1987. In 1971 APA established the Board of Social and Ethical Responsibility for Psychology to examine ways in which social responsibility can be integrated as a dominant theme in the science and profession of psychology. In 1974 the APA, with funding from the National Institute for Mental Health, established the APA Minority Fellowship Program. The 1973 Vail Conference, the 1975 Austin Conference, and the 1978 Dulles Conference, all examined the need to expand the roles of culturally diverse people in psychology. The APA Office of Cultural and Ethnic Affairs was established in 1978, and the Board of Ethnic Minority Affairs was established in 1980. After considerable lobbying by minority members of APA, the Society for Psychological Study of Ethnic Minority Issues (Division 45) was formally established by APA in January 1987.

Although the APA and other professional organizations have given increased attention to ethnic minority issues, many of the same problems that affected counseling services for diverse groups in the 1960s have persisted. The Dulles Conference, for example, documented in 1978 the underrepresentation of ethnic minorities among psychologists, university faculty, APA members, and APA governing bodies. The Dulles Conference report also cited continued racism in the profession and in society as reasons why inadequate mental health services are still accorded ethnic minorities. The Special Populations Task Force of the President's Commission on Mental Health (1978) similarly concluded that ethnic minorities "are clearly underserved or inappropriately served by the current mental health system in this country" (p. 73). More recently, several reviews of research published in the 1980s conclude that ethnic minorities still may be receiving differential and inferior forms of treatment from counselors and psychologists (Abramowitz & Murray, 1983; Atkinson, 1985).

The Unfulfilled Promise of Counseling for Minorities

Minority group authors, particularly those representing racial/ethnic minority groups, have been vociferous and unequivocal in their denunciations of the counseling profession since the mid 1960s. In a comprehensive review of counseling literature related to racial/ethnic minority groups, Pine (1972) found the following view of counseling to be representative of that held by most minority individuals:

> . . . that it is a waste of time; that counselors are deliberately shunting minority students into dead end non-academic programs regardless of student potential, preferences, or ambitions; that counselors discourage students from applying to college; that counselors are insensitive to the needs of students and the community; that counselors do not give the same amount of energy and time in working with minority as they do with White middle-class students; that counselors do not accept, respect, and understand cultural differences; that counselors are arrogant and contemptuous; and that counselors don't know themselves how to deal with their own hangups (p. 35).

Although Pine's article deals primarily with racial/ethnic minorities, similar views of counseling have been expressed by feminist, gay, pacifist, and other activist minority groups (Counseling and the Social Revolution, 1971).

To some extent minority group unhappiness with counseling reflects disillusionment with all the organized social sciences because of their poor performance as instruments for correcting social ills (Sanford, 1969). Psychology in particular has been criticized for its role as the "handmaiden of the status quo" (Halleck, 1971, p. 30). Frequently minorities see psychology functioning to maintain and promote the status and power of the Establishment (Sue & Sue, 1972).

To a large degree, minority group dissatisfaction with the counseling profession can be explained as disenchantment with unfulfilled promises. As suggested earlier, counseling has at least covertly accepted such ideal rights as "equal access to opportunity," "pursuit of happiness," "fulfillment of personal destiny," and "freedom" as inherent goals in counseling (Adams, 1973; Belkin, 1975; Byrne, 1977). Although these lofty ideals may seem highly commendable and extremely appropriate goals for the counseling profession to promote, in reality they have often been translated in such a way as to justify support for the status quo (Adams, 1973).

While the validity of minority criticisms can and will be argued by professional counselors, there is little doubt that, for whatever reasons, counseling has failed to serve the needs of minorities, and in some cases, has proven counterproductive to their well-being. The fact that various minority groups are underrepresented in conventional counseling programs (Sue, 1973), despite the fact that they experience as much or more stress than do nonminorities (Smith, 1985), suggests these groups perceive counseling as irrelevant to their needs.

There is evidence, for example, that ethnic minorities prefer to discuss emotional and educational/vocational problems with parents, friends, and relatives rather than professional counselors (Atkinson, Ponterotto, & Sanchez, 1984; Webster & Fretz, 1978). The lack of minority counselors in many counseling agencies may be a factor in underutilization and the preference for discussing personal concerns with friends and relatives.

Thompson and Cimbolic (1978) found that Black college students were more likely to make use of counseling center services if Black counselors were available than if only White counselors could be seen for appointments. There is also substantial evidence that Asian Americans, Blacks, Chicanos, and Native Americans terminate counseling after an initial counseling session at a much higher rate than do Anglos (Sue, Allen, & Conaway, 1978; Sue & McKinney, 1975; Sue, McKinney, Allen, & Hall, 1974). Clearly, minorities see the counseling process, as currently implemented, as irrelevant to their own life experiences and inappropriate or insufficient for their felt needs.

When minorities do bother to seek treatment there is evidence that they are diagnosed differently and receive "less preferred" forms of treatment than do majority clients (Abramowitz & Murray, 1983). In the area of diagnosis, Lee and Temerlin (1968) found that psychiatric residents were more likely to arrive at a diagnosis of mental illness when the individual's history suggested lower-class origin than when a high socioeconomic class was indicated. Haase (1956) demonstrated that clinical psychologists given identical sets of Rorschach test records made more negative prognostic statements and judgments of greater maladjustment when the records were identified as the products of lower-class individuals than when associated with middle-class persons. Broverman, Broverman, Clarkson, Rosenkrantz, and Vogel (1970) found sex also to be a factor in diagnosis, with less favorable judgments by clinical psychologists with respect to female clients than for male clients. In a related study, Thomas and Stewart (1971) presented counselors with taped interviews of a high school girl in counseling and found the girl's career choice rated more appropriate when identified as traditional than when identified as deviant (traditionally male attitude). Similar results have been cited by Schlossberg and Pietrofesa (1973). Mercado and Atkinson (1982) found that male counselors suggested sex-stereotypic occupations for exploration by a high school girl.

In the area of treatment, Garfield, Weiss, and Pollack (1973) gave two groups of counselors identical printed descriptions (except for social class) of a 9-year-old boy who engaged in maladaptive classroom behavior. The counselors indicated a greater willingness to become ego-involved when the child was identified as having upper-class status than when assigned lower-class status. Habermann and Thiry (1970) found that doctoral degree candidates in Counseling and Guidance more frequently programmed students from low-socioeconomic backgrounds into a noncollege bound track than a college preparation track. Research documentation of the inferior quality of mental health services provided to racial/ethnic minorities are commonplace (Clark, 1965; Cowen, Gardner, & Zox, 1967; Guerney, 1969; Lerner, 1972; Thomas & Sillen, 1972; Torion, 1973; Yamamoto, James, Bloombaum, & Hattem, 1967; Yamamoto, James & Palley, 1968).

Differential diagnoses and treatment of minorities is presumably a function of stereotypes held by counselors. Evidence that counselors do hold stereotypes of minorities is beginning to accumulate. Casas, Wampold, and Atkinson (1981) found that university counselors tend to group student characteristics into constellations reflective of common ethnic stereotypes. In a study employing an illusory correlation paradigm, Wampold, Casas and Atkinson, (1981) found that nonminority counselor trainees are more likely to be influenced by stereotypes when assigning characteristics to ethnic groups than are minority counselor trainees. Finally, even when attempting to be sensitive to the needs of Mexican American students, university counselors may base their counseling services on stereotypes that are not supported by research (Casas & Atkinson, 1981).

Criticism of the Traditional Counseling Role

Due in part to the unfulfilled promise of counseling for minorities, a great deal of criticism has been directed at the traditional counseling role in which an office-bound counselor engages the client in verbal interaction with the intention of resolving the client's psychological problems. For the most part, this criticism can be summarized as three interrelated concerns: criticism of the intrapsychic counseling model, criticism of how counseling approaches have developed, and criticism related to counseling process variables.

Criticism of Intrapsychic Counseling Model

Perhaps the strongest, most cogent indictment of the traditional counseling role has been criticism of the intrapsychic view of client problems inherent to some degree in all current counseling approaches. According to Smith (1985),

> What has become known as the traditional model of counseling is, in reality, a set of principles that has been extracted from various counseling theories and that is seen to cut across theoretical counseling formulations. Such principles tend to stress that (1) clients' problems are located within the individual (intrapsychically based), rather than in the conditions to which minorities adjust; (2) clients' problems should be resolved internally; (3) clients are familiar with the roles of client and counselor; and (4) talk rather than direct action is the more desirable counseling technique (p. 568).

The intrapsychic model assumes client problems are the result of personal disorganization rather than institutional or societal dysfunctioning (Bryson & Bardo, 1975). Counselors, these critics argue, should view minority clients as victims of a repressive society and rather than intervene with the victim, counselors should attempt to change the offending portion of the client's environment (Banks, 1972; Katz, 1985; Williams & Kirkland, 1971).

The issue of whether one focuses on the *person* or *system* is an important one. Counseling in this country has grown out of a philosophy of "rugged individualism" in which people are assumed to be responsible for their own lot in life. Success in society is attributed to outstanding abilities or great effort. Likewise, failures or problems encountered by the person may be attributed to some inner deficiency (lack of effort, poor abilities, etc.). For the minority individual who is the victim of oppression, the person-blame approach tends to deny the existence of external injustices (racism, sexism, age, bias, etc.).

Pedersen (1976) has suggested that the counselor can help the minority client either adopt, or adapt to the dominant culture. Vexliard (1968) has coined the terms autoplastic and alloplastic to define two levels of adaption; the first, ". . . involves accommodating oneself to the givens of a social setting and structure and the latter involves shaping the external reality to suit one's needs" (Draguns, 1976, p. 6). Thus, critics of the traditional counseling role see cultural adoption and the autoplastic model of adaption as repressive but predictable outcomes of the intrapsychic counseling model. The counseling roles they advocate can be viewed as directed toward the alloplastic end of the auto-alloplastic adaption continuum, and will be discussed in some detail in the final chapter of this book.

Criticism of How Counseling Approaches Have Developed

Minority intellectuals have criticized contemporary counseling approaches which they contend have been developed by and for the White, middle-class person (Edwards, 1982; Jackson, 1985; Katz, 1985; S. Sue & Zane, 1987). Katz (1985) suggests that the counseling profession "has at its core an inherent set of cultural values and norms by which clients are judged" (p. 615) and that these cultural values and norms are the product of White culture. In order to make counseling more responsive to ethnic minority needs, these critics argue, we must develop strategies, theories, and models that are appropriate to specific populations. Using treatment approaches developed for White, middle-class Americans with ethnically diverse clients is illogical and possibly even dangerous (Edwards, 1982).

However, little or no attention has been directed to the need to develop counseling procedures that are compatible with minority cultural values. Unimodal counseling approaches are perpetuated by graduate programs in counseling that give inadequate treatment to the mental health issues of minorities (Ponterotto & Casas, 1987). Cultural influences affecting personality, identity formation, and behavior manifestations frequently are not a part of training programs. When minority group experiences are discussed, they are generally seen and analyzed from the "White, middle class perspective." As a result, counselors who deal with the mental health problems of minorities often lack understanding and knowledge about cultural differences and their consequent interaction with an oppressive society.

Majority counselors who do not have firsthand experience with the minority client's specific cultural milieu may overlook the fact that the client's behavior patterns have different interpretations in the two cultures represented. Behavior that is diagnosed as pathological in one culture may be viewed as adaptive in another (Wilson & Calhoun, 1974). Grier and Cobbs (1968) in their depiction of Black cultural paranoia as a "healthy" development make reference to the potential for inappropriate diagnoses. Thus, the determination of normality or abnormality tends to be intimately associated with a White, middle-class standard.

Furthermore, counseling techniques which are a product of the White, middle-class culture are frequently applied indiscriminately to the minority population (Bell, 1971). In addition, counselors themselves are often culturally encapsulated (Wrenn, 1962), measuring reality against their own set of monocultural assumptions and values, and demonstrating insensitivity to cultural variations in clients (Pedersen, 1976). New counseling techniques and approaches are needed, it is argued, that take into account the minority experience (Gunnings, 1971).

In response to this criticism, mental health associations have begun to recognize the need for specialized training for practitioners who work with ethnically diverse populations. In a position paper that resulted from the APA-sponsored Vail Conference, for example, it was strongly recommended that it be considered unethical for psychologists not trained in cultural diversity to provide services to ethnically diverse groups. Also, both the APA and AACD (American Association for Counseling and Development) have incorporated knowledge of cultural diversity into their training standards.

Unfortunately, however, most training programs have yet to implement training in cross-cultural counseling. A recent survey of counselor education programs found that only one third of the responding programs require courses or practicums in cross-cultural counseling (Ibrahim, Stadler, Arredondo, & McFadden, 1986). Moreover, Bernal and Padilla (1982) reported that only 41 percent (31 of 76) of the clinical psychology programs responding to their survey offered one or more courses "that might contribute to the student's understanding of minority or other cultures" (p. 782). One reason for these statistics may be that the training standards of the APA, AACD, and other mental health professional associations are not specific enough about the training that counselors and psychologists should receive with respect to culturally diverse groups. As Ponterotto and Casas (1987) suggest, "the [counseling] profession has not yet defined culturally competent training" (p. 433).

Although professional mental health associations have not included specific cultural competencies in their training standards, models of cross-cultural competencies do exist. The APA Division 17 Education and Training Committee developed a position paper identifying cross-cultural counseling competencies that was published in *The Counseling Psychologist* (D. Sue, Bernier, Durran, Feinberg, Pedersen, Smith, & Vasquez-Nuttall, 1982) and that is reprinted in Appendix A. Steps for achieving competence in cross-cultural counseling are also outlined in S. Sue, Akutsu, and Higashi (1985). These competencies will be discussed at greater length in Chapter 16.

The issue is perhaps best represented semantically by the emic-etic dichotomy, which was first presented by the linguist, Pike (1954). Draguns (1976) offers the following definition of these two terms:

> Emic refers to the viewing of data in terms indigenous or unique to the culture in question, and etic, to viewing them in light of categories and concepts external to the culture but universal in their applicability (p. 2).

The criticisms relevant to the current discussion, then, focus on what can be called the "pseudoetic" approach to cross-cultural counseling (Triandis, Malpass, & Davidson, 1973): culturally encapsulated counselors assume that their own approach and associated techniques can be culturally generalized and are robust enough to cope with cultural variations. In reality, minority critics argue, we have developed emic approaches to counseling that are designed by and for White, middle-class individuals.

Criticism Related to Lack of Ethnic Diversity among Counselors

In addition to being guided by theories and techniques based on White, middle-class values, the counseling profession has been criticized for being disproportionately composed of White counselors. The underrepresentation of ethnically diverse counselors, critics contend, helps explain why ethnic minorities seldom seek or remain in counseling. Culturally similar counselors, it is argued, are viewed by clients as more credible sources of help. Furthermore, an ethnically similar counselor may be able to identify more directly with his/her client's problems and may therefore be a more effective counselor than would be a nonminority counselor. While several major reviews have found equivocal support for the superiority of ethnically similar counseling dyads over ethnically dissimilar dyads (Atkinson, 1985), ethnic minority underrepresentation in the related field of applied psychology is undeniable. Ethnic group underrepresentation repeatedly has been documented in clinical psychology (Boxley & Wagner, 1971; Kennedy & Wagner, 1979; Padilla, Boxley, & Wagner, 1973; Russo, Olmedo, Stapp, & Fulcher, 1981), counseling psychology (Parham & Moreland, 1981; Russo et al., 1981), and counselor-education programs (Atkinson, 1983; Jones, 1976).

Criticisms Related to Counseling Process Variables— Barriers to Minority Group/Cross-Cultural Counseling

Much of the criticism related to minority group counseling focuses upon the interactions that occur between counselor and client. Counseling is seen as a process of interpersonal interaction and communication which requires accurate sending and receiving of both verbal and nonverbal messages. When the counselor and client come from different cultural backgrounds, barriers to communication are likely to develop, leading to misunderstandings that destroy rapport and render counseling ineffective. Thus, process manifestations of cultural barriers pose a serious problem in minority group/cross-cultural counseling.

Most of the writing on barriers to minority group/cross-cultural counseling has focused on racial/ethnic minorities as clientele with a major portion of these studies examining the White counselor–Black client relationship. It is evident, however, that many of the concepts developed by these authors have relevance to any counseling situation involving an individual from a minority (i.e., oppressed) group. It is equally clear that although presented from a majority counselor–minority client perspective, many of the same barriers may exist between a counselor and client who represent two different minority groups (i.e., two different cultures).

In the present discussion, we make a distinction between cultural barriers that are unique to a minority group/cross-cultural counseling situation (e.g., language differences) and those that are process barriers present in every counseling relationship but are particularly thorny and more likely to occur in a cross-cultural situation (e.g., transference).

Barriers Indigenous to Cultural Differences

In discussing barriers and hazards in the counseling process, Johnson and Vestermark (1970) define barriers as ". . . real obstacles of varying degrees of seriousness . . ." (p. 5). They go on to describe cultural encapsulation as one of the most serious barriers that can affect the counseling relationship. Padilla, Ruiz, and Alvarez (1975) have identified three major impediments to counseling that a non-Latino counselor may encounter when working with a Latino client. Sue & Sue (1977) have generalized these barriers as relevant to all Third World people. We expand the concept further and attempt to relate the three barriers to all minority group/cross-cultural counseling situations. The three barriers are (a) language differences, (b) class-bound values, and (c) culture-bound values. These three categories are used to facilitate the present discussion; it should be pointed out, however, that all three categories are recognized as functions of culture, broadly defined.

Language Differences—Much of the criticism related to the traditional counseling role has focused on the central importance of verbal interaction and rapport in the counseling relationship. This heavy reliance by counselors on verbal interaction to build rapport presupposes that the participants in a counseling dialogue are capable of understanding each other. Yet many counselors fail to understand the client's language and its nuances sufficiently so as to make rapport building possible (Vontress, 1973). Furthermore, educationally and economically disadvantaged clients may lack the prerequisite verbal skills required to benefit from "talk therapy" (Calia, 1966; Tyler, 1964), especially when confronted by a counselor who relies on complex cognitive and conative concepts to generate client insight.

Sue and Sue (1977) have pointed out that the use of standard English with a lower-class or bilingual client may result in misperceptions of the client's strengths and weaknesses. Certainly the counselor who is unfamiliar with a client's dialect or language system will be unlikely to succeed in establishing rapport (Wilson & Calhoun, 1974). Furthermore, Vontress (1973) suggests that counselors need to be familiar with minority group body language lest they misinterpret the meaning of postures, gestures, and inflections. For example, differences in nonverbal behavior are frequently seen in the comparison of Blacks and Whites. When speaking to another person, Anglos tend to look away from the person (avoid eye contact) more often than do Black individuals. When listening to another person speak, however, Blacks tend to avoid eye contact while Anglos make eye contact. This may account for statements from teachers who feel that Black pupils are inattentive (they make less eye contact when spoken to) or feel that Blacks are more angry (intense stare) when speaking.

Similar observations can be made regarding cross-cultural counseling with other, nonracially identified minority groups. For instance, prison inmates have developed a language system that tends to change over a period of time. The naive counselor who enters the prison environment for the first time may find that his/her use of standard English may elicit smiles or even guffaws from clients, to say nothing of what this does to the counselor's credibility. Gays, too, have developed a vocabulary that may be entirely foreign to a "straight" counselor. Anyone who doubts this statement need only visit a gay bar in San Francisco or elsewhere and listen to the public dialogue. Any counselor unfamiliar with gay vocabulary is likely to be perceived as too straight by a gay client to be of any help. Gays, like other minority groups, rely heavily upon their own vernacular to convey emotions and, understandably, they prefer a counselor who can grasp these emotions without further translation into standard English.

Unique language patterns can also be associated with poor Appalachian Whites, drug users, the handicapped, and to some extent almost any category that qualifies as a minority group as defined in this book. Often with political activism, minority groups will develop expressive language that is not common to, or has a different connotation than, standard English. Inability to communicate effectively in the client's language may contribute significantly to the poor acceptance which counseling has received from minorities.

Class-bound Values—Differences in values between counselor and client that are basically due to class differences are relevant to minority group/cross-cultural counseling since, almost by definition, many minority group members are also of a lower socioeconomic class. Furthermore, for the purposes of this book, differences in attitudes, behaviors, beliefs, and values among the various socioeconomic groups constitute cultural differences. The interaction of social class and behavior has been well documented by Hollingshead (1949). The importance of social class for school counseling has been discussed by Bernard (1963). Combining the results of several studies, Havighurst and Neugarten (1962) concluded that at least 50 percent of the American population falls into either the upper lower or lower lower socioeconomic classes, suggesting that a large portion of the counselor's potential clientele may be from these socioeconomic classes. The impact of social class differences on counseling in general acquires added significance if one accepts the statement presented earlier in this chapter, that existing counseling techniques are middle- and upper-class-based.

One of the first and most obvious value differences encountered by the middle-class counselor and the lower-class client involves the willingness to make and keep counseling appointments. As Sue and Sue (1977) point out, ". . . lower-class clients who are concerned with 'survival' or making it through on a day-to-day basis expect advice and suggestions from the counselor . . . (and) . . . appointments made weeks in advance with short weekly 50 minute contacts are not consistent with the need to seek immediate solutions" (p. 424). Vontress (1973) states that Appalachian Whites refuse to be enslaved by the clock and not only refuse to adhere to values of promptness, planning, and protocol, but suspect people who do adhere to these values.

Differences in attitudes toward sexual behavior often enter the counseling relationship between a counselor and client representing different socioeconomic classes. For the most part, open acceptance of sexual promiscuity differs from one socioeconomic level to another, although other factors (e.g., religious beliefs) play heavy roles. Middle-class counselors, whether consciously or unconsciously, often attempt to impose middle-class sexual mores on lower- and upper-class clients.

The fact that the clients' socioeconomic status affects the kind of therapeutic treatment clients receive has been well documented. Ryan and Gaier (1968), for instance, found that students from upper socioeconomic backgrounds have more exploratory interviews with counselors than do students representing other social classes. Middle-class patients in a veterans administration clinic tend to remain in treatment longer than do lower-class patients. And Hollingshead and Redlich (1958) found that the level of therapeutic intensiveness varies directly with socioeconomic background.

Culture-bound Values—Culture, as broadly defined for the purposes of this book, consists of behavior patterns shared and transmitted by a group of individuals. In addition to language and class-bound values already discussed, culture-bound values obviously involve such elements as attitudes, beliefs, customs, and institutions identified as integral parts of a group's social structure.

Counselors frequently impose their own cultural values upon minority clients in ignorance, reflecting an insensitivity to the clients' values. Referring to clients from racial/ethnic minorities as "culturally deprived" is an example of this imposition. "Straight," male counselors sometimes make sexual remarks about females in front of a male client that may be repugnant to the client if he is gay (to say nothing about how it would affect females who overheard it). Nor is the experience reported by Granberg (1967) in which he found himself incorrectly assuming his homosexual client wanted to become "straight" an unusual example of the counselor's cultural values interfering with the counseling relationship. Drug and prison "counselors" often fulfill roles of instilling the values of the larger society upon their clientele without full awareness of their impact.

For some time the role of the counselor's values in the counseling relationship has been a thorny professional issue. The issue becomes even more poignant when a majority counselor and minority client are involved. In this case, ". . . the values inherent in (the) two different sub-cultures may be realistically as diverse as those of two countries" (Wilson & Calhoun, 1974). While the major concern with this issue, in the broader context, centers on the counselor's influence upon the client, class- and culture-bound value differences can impede further rapport building. Cayleff (1986) suggests that "cultural misunderstandings . . . may precipitate difficulties in communication, obscure expectations, affect the quality of care dispensed, and dramatically alter a patient's willingness or ability to maintain a therapeutic program" (p. 346).

For example, many professionals argue that self-disclosure is a necessary condition for effective counseling. Jourard (1964) suggests that people are more likely to disclose themselves to others who will react as they do, implying that cultural similarity is an important factor in self-disclosure. Furthermore, self-disclosure may be contrary to basic cultural values for some minorities. Sue and Sue (1972) have pointed out that Chinese American clients, who are taught at an early age to restrain from emotional expression, find the direct and subtle demands by the counselor to self-disclosure very threatening. Similar conflicts have been reported for Chicano (Cross & Maldonado, 1971) and Native American (Trimble, 1976) clients. Poor clients, of whatever racial or ethnic background, frequently resist attempts by the counselor to encourage client self-exploration and prefer to ascribe their problems, often justifiably, to forces beyond their control (Calia, 1966). In addition, many racial minorities have learned to distrust Whites in general and may "shine on" a majority counselor, since this has proven to be adaptive behavior with Whites in the past. Sue and Sue (1977) suggest that self-disclosure is itself a cultural value and counselors who ". . . value verbal, emotional and behavioral expressiveness as goals in counseling are transmitting their own cultural values" (p. 425).

Related to this last point is the lack of structure frequently provided by the counselor in the counseling relationship. Often, in order to encourage self-disclosure, the counseling situation is intentionally designed to be an ambiguous one, one in which the counselor listens empathically and responds only to encourage the client to continue talking (Sue & Sue, 1972). Minority clients frequently find the lack of structure confusing, frustrating, and even threatening (Haettenschwiller, 1971). Atkinson, Maruyama, and Matsui (1978) found that Asian Americans prefer a directive counseling style to a nondirective one, suggesting the directive approach is more compatible with their cultural values.

Similar results were found in a replication of the Atkinson et al. (1978) study with American Indian high school students (Dauphinais, Dauphinais, & Rowe, 1981). Black students also were found to prefer a more active counseling role over a passive one (Peoples & Dell, 1975).

Process Manifestations of Cultural Differences

Many of the problems encountered in minority group/cross-cultural counseling which have been identified as cultural barriers might better be conceived of as process manifestations of cultural differences, since they may be present to some extent in any counseling relationship but are aggravated by cultural differences. We will briefly discuss five of them: stereotyping, resistance, transference, countertransference, and client expectations.

Stereotyping—Stereotyping is a major problem for all forms of counseling. It may broadly be defined as rigid preconceptions which are applied to all members of a group or to an individual over a period of time, regardless of individual variations. The key word in this definition is *rigidity,* an inflexibility to change. Thus, a counselor who believes that Blacks are "lazy," "musical," "rhythmic," and "unintelligent"; Asians are "sneaky," "sly," "good with numbers," and "poor with words"; or that Jews are "stingy," "shrewd," and "intellectual" will behave toward representatives of these groups as if they possessed these traits. The detrimental effects of stereotyping have been well documented in professional literature (Rosenthal & Jacobsen, 1968; Smith, 1977; Sue, 1973). First, counselors who have preconceived notions about minority group members may unwittingly act upon these beliefs. If Black students are seen as possessing limited intellectual potential, they may be counseled into terminal vocational trade schools. Likewise, if Asian Americans are perceived as being only good in the physical sciences but poor in verbal-people professions, counselors may direct them toward a predominance of science courses. The second and even more damaging effect is that many minorities may eventually come to believe these stereotypes about themselves. Thus, since the majority of stereotypes about minorities are negative, an inferior sense of self-esteem may develop.

Due to stereotyping or attempts to avoid stereotyping by the counselor, majority counselors frequently have difficulty adjusting to a relationship with a minority client. The most obvious difficulty in this area occurs when the counselor fails to recognize the client as an individual and assigns to the client culturally stereotypic characteristics that are totally invalid for this individual (Smith, 1977). In an effort to treat the client as just another client, on the other hand, the counselor may demonstrate "color or culture blindness" (Wilson & Calhoun, 1974). In this case the counselor may avoid altogether discussing the differences between the two participants, thus implying that the client's attitudes and behaviors will be assessed against majority norms. The content of the counseling dialogue may also be restricted by the preoccupation of the majority counselor with fear that the client will detect conscious or unconscious stereotyping on the part of the counselor (Gardner, 1971).

Resistance—Resistance is usually defined as client opposition to the goals of counseling and may manifest itself as self-devaluation, intellectualization, and overt hostility (Vontress, 1976). While it is a potential difficulty in any counseling encounter, the problem becomes particularly acute when the counselor and client are culturally different, since the counselor may misinterpret the resistance as a dynamic of the client's culture.

Transference—Transference occurs when the client responds to the counselor in a manner similar to the way he or she responded to someone else in the past (Greenson, 1964, pp. 151–152), and this may manifest itself as either a liking or disliking of the counselor. Clients may or may not be aware of the transference effect themselves. This phenomenon is particularly problematic in the majority counselor–minority client dyad, ". . . because minority group members bring to the relationship intense emotions derived from experiences with and feelings toward the majority group" (Vontress, 1976, p. 49). Minority clients, for instance—due to their experiences with an oppressive, majority-controlled society—are likely to anticipate authoritarian behavior from the counselor.

Countertransference—Countertransference occurs when the counselor responds to a client as he or she responded to someone in the past (Wilson & Calhoun, 1974, p. 318). Countertransference is particularly difficult for the counselor to recognize and accept since counselors typically view themselves as objective, although empathic, participants in the counseling relationship. It seems highly unlikely, however, that majority counselors in this society are entirely free of the stereotypic attitudes toward minority peoples (Jackson, 1973). An argument can be made that counselors, like everyone else, carry with them conscious and unconscious attitudes, feelings, and beliefs about culturally different people, and that these will manifest themselves as countertransference (Vontress, 1976).

Client Expectation—Closely related to transference, client expectations for success in the counseling relationship can directly affect counseling outcome. When the minority client finds him/herself assigned to a majority counselor, the client's prognostic expectations may be reduced (Wilson & Calhoun, 1974). Prior to the initial counseling session the client may experience feelings of distrust, futility, and anger, which generate an expectation that counseling will not succeed. Such an expectation usually dooms the counseling relationship to failure.

Barriers to Minority Counselor-Minority
or Majority Client Counseling

As used in the counseling literature, minority group counseling frequently implies that the counselor is a member of the dominant culture and the client a minority group member, suggesting that this combination is of greatest threat to effective counseling. A few authors have referred to the problems encountered in counseling when the client and counselor are from the same minority group. Virtually none have discussed the difficulties experienced when the counselor is from a different minority group than the client. Lest the impression be given that culturally related barriers only exist for the majority counselor–minority client dyad, we now turn briefly to difficulties experienced by minority counselors and their clients.

Intra-Minority Group Counseling

Several authors have identified problems that the minority counselor may encounter when working with a client from a cultural background similar to that of the counselor. Jackson (1973) points out that the minority client may respond with anger when confronted by a minority counselor. The anger may result from finding a minority person associated with a majority controlled institution. Some clients may experience anger, on the other hand, because they feel a majority counselor would be more competent, thus enhancing the probability of problem resolution. Or the client's anger may reflect jealousy that the counselor has succeeded through personal efforts in breaking out of a repressive environment. In the case of a Third World counselor, the counselor may also be seen as

> . . . too white in orientation to be interested in helping, as less competent than his colleagues, as too far removed from problems that face the patient, or as intolerant and impatient with the patient's lack of success in dealing with problems (Jackson, 1973, p. 277).

The minority counselor may respond to minority client anger by becoming defensive (Jackson, 1973), thus impeding the counseling process. Minority counselors may also either deny identification with or over-identify with the client (Gardner, 1971). Sattler (1970) has suggested that minority counselors may have less tolerance and understanding of minority clients and view the contact as low status work compared with counseling a majority client.

Calnek (1970) points out the danger that Third World counselors too often adopt stereotypes that Whites have developed concerning how minority clients think, feel, and act. The counselor may deny that the client is also a minority person, for fear the common identification will result in a loss of professional image for the counselor. Over-identification, on the other hand, may cause the counseling experience to degenerate into a gripe session. Calnek also refers to the danger of the counselor projecting his/her own self-image onto the client because they are culturally similar.

While the foregoing comments are, for the most part, directed at the Black counselor–Black client dyad, it is easy to see that the problem could be generalized to include other intra-minority group situations.

Inter-Minority Group Counseling

Counselors representing one minority group who find themselves working with a client representing a different minority group often face the problems associated with both the majority counselor–minority client and the intra-minority group counseling situations. Although the camaraderie of Third World peoples that results from awareness of shared oppression helps to bridge cultural differences on college and university campuses, in the nonacademic world these differences are often as intense or more intense than those between the dominant and minority cultures. One need only observe Chicano students and parents in East Los Angeles or Black students and parents in Bedford-Stuyvesant to gain an appreciation of ethnocentrism and the difficulty which culturally different minority counselors can perceive in these situations. Furthermore, the counselor representing a different minority than the client may be suspect to the client, for the same reasons counselors of similar minority backgrounds would be suspect.

Potential Benefits in Cross-Cultural Counseling

Almost no attention has been given in the counseling literature to identifying the benefits of cross-cultural counseling. In reference to the minority counselor–majority client dyad, Jackson (1973) suggests that the client may find it easier to, ". . . share information that is looked on as socially unacceptable without censor from the therapist" (p. 275), suggesting self-disclosure, at least of some materials, may be enhanced. Students who are rebelling against the Establishment, for instance, may prefer a minority counselor, feeling that the counselor's experience with oppression qualifies him/her to acquire empathy with the client (Gardner, 1971). Gardner (1971) also suggests majority clients may prefer minority counselors if they are dealing with material that would be embarrassing to share with a majority counselor. Jackson (1973) points out that there is a tendency in this situation to perceive the counselor more as another person than as a superhuman, notwithstanding those cases where the counselor is perceived as a "super-minority." In the latter case, the client may view the minority counselor as more capable than his/her majority counterpart, owing to the obstacles the counselor had to overcome. The net effect in this case may be a positive expectation. The possibility that minority counselors are less likely to let secrets filter back into the client's community is also cited by Gardner (1971) as a positive variable in cross-cultural counseling.

Several authors (Draguns, 1975, 1976; Trimble, 1976), while referring in part to national cultures, have suggested that cross-cultural counseling is a learning experience to be valued in and of itself. The counseling process, with its intentional provision for self-disclosure of attitudes, values and intense emotional feelings, can help the counselor and client gain a perspective on each other's culture, frequently in a way never experienced outside of counseling. Cross-cultural counseling also offers an opportunity to both counselor and client to expand their modes of communication, to learn new ways of interacting. Rather than being viewed as a deficit, client (and counselor) bilingualism should be viewed and treated as a strength.

Again it seems apparent that much of the foregoing can be generalized to apply to nonracially or ethnically identified minorities. It also seems evident that further research and discussion are needed regarding both the barriers and benefits of cross-cultural counseling. Those discussed above, along with several proposed by the current authors, are outlined in table 2.1. In addition to citing positive and negative aspects of cross-cultural situations, the authors have attempted, as shown in table 2.1, to identify their counterparts when counselor and client are culturally similar.

Editors' View

The editors of this book of readings are in agreement with those earlier writers who have suggested that cross-cultural counseling can not only be effective for resolving client difficulties, but can also serve as a forum for a unique learning experience. That barriers to cross-cultural counseling exist is not at issue here. Clearly, cultural differences between counselor and client can result in barriers that are, in some instances, insurmountable. However, the results of a recent study support the hypothesis that cultural sensitivity on the part of the counselor can help overcome some of the barriers that exist when the counselor and client are ethnically different. Pomales, Claiborn, and LaFromboise (1986) found that Black college students rated a counselor who acknowledged and showed interest in the role of culture in the client's problem more positively than they did a "culture blind" counselor (one who minimized the importance of culture and shifted the conversation to other factors).

As suggested earlier, we believe cross-cultural counseling can involve benefits to both client and counselor that may not be possible in intra-cultural counseling. Furthermore, it is our contention that the primary barrier to effective counseling and one which underlies many other barriers is the traditional counseling role itself. No one has yet offered conclusive evidence that differences in status variables (e.g., race, ethnicity, sex, sexual orientation) alone create barriers to counseling. The fact that one person in a counseling dyad is born Black and one White, for instance, should not negate the possibility of their working together effectively. From our perspective, it is how we perceive and experience our and our client's Blackness and Whiteness that creates barriers to constructive

Table 2.1
Culturally Relevant Barriers and Benefits in Inter- and Intra-Cultural Counseling

Inter-Cultural Counseling	
Barriers	*Benefits*
—client resistance	—client's willingness to self-disclose some material
—client transference	—client less likely to view counselor as omniscient
—client cultural restraints on self-disclosure	
—client expectations	—client expectation for success may be enhanced
—counselor countertransference	—potential for considerable cultural learning by both client and counselor
—counselor maladjustment to the relationship	
—counselor misdirected diagnosis	—increased need for counselor and client to focus on their own processing
—counselor patronization of client's culture	—potential for dealing with culturally dissonant component of client problem
—counselor denial of culturally dissonant component of client problem	
—counselor "missionary zeal"	
—language differences	
—value conflicts	

Intra-Cultural Counseling	
Barriers	*Benefits*
—unjustified assumption of shared feelings	—shared experience may enhance rapport
—client transference	—client willingness to self-disclose some materials
—counselor countertransference	—common mode of communication may enhance process

communication. For the most part, our perceptions and experiences are shaped by a socialization process that begins at birth. We feel that the traditional counseling role (nonequalitarian, intrapsychic model, office-bound, etc.) often helps to perpetuate the very socialization process that creates a barrier between culturally different individuals.

Some critics will argue that differences in experiences are paramount, that a counselor who experiences being Black will understand the Black client's perspective better than any White counselor ever can. We agree to a point. There is simply no conclusive evidence, however, that a counselor must experience everything his/her client does. Carried to the extreme, the similarity of experience argument suggests that all counseling is doomed to failure since no two individuals can ever fully share the same life experiences. Furthermore, while cultural differences do result in unique experiences for both the client and the counselor, our experiences as human beings are remarkably similar. This view—that we are more alike than different—is perhaps best expressed by the sociobiologist De Vore (1977):

> Anthropologists always talk about crosscultural diversity, but that's icing on the cake. The cake itself is remarkably panhuman. Different cultures turn out only minor variations on the theme of the species—human courtship, our mating systems, child care, fatherhood, the treatment of the sexes, love, jealousy, sharing. Almost everything that's importantly human—including behavior flexibility—is universal, and developed in the context of our shared genetic background (p. 88).

In chapter 3 we propose an identity development model that assumes a panhuman response *across* minority groups to the experience of oppression. A primary purpose of the model, however, is to suggest that attitudes and behaviors vary greatly *within* the various minority groups and are reflective of stages in identity development. One of the great dangers of attempting to study minority groups, despite the best of intentions, is that old stereotypes are replaced by new ones. The Minority Identity Development model is presented prior to the minority group reading to minimize the development of new stereotypes by suggesting that, even within cultural groups, attitudes and behaviors vary greatly.

References

Abramowitz, S. I., & Murray, J. (1983). Race effects in psychotherapy. In J. Murray & P. R. Abramson (Eds.), *Bias in psychotherapy* (pp. 215–255). New York: Praeger.

Adams, H. J. (1973). The progressive heritage of guidance: A view from the left. *Personnel and Guidance Journal, 51,* 531–538.

Atkinson, D. R. (1983). Ethnic minority representation in counselor education. *Counselor Education and Supervision, 23,* 7–19.

Atkinson, D. R. (1985). A meta-review of research on cross-cultural counseling and psychotherapy. *Journal of Multicultural Counseling and Development, 13,* 138–153.

Atkinson, D. R., Maruyama, M., & Matsui, S. (1978). The effects of counselor race and counseling approach on Asian Americans perceptions of counselor credibility and utility. *Journal of Counseling Psychology, 25,* 76–83.

Atkinson, D. R., Ponterotto, J. G., & Sanchez, A. R. (1984). Attitudes of Vietnamese and Anglo-American students toward counseling. *Journal of College Student Personnel, 25,* 448–452.

Aubrey, R. F. (1977). Historical development of guidance and counseling and implications for the future. *Personnel and Guidance Journal, 55,* 288–295.

Banks, W. (1972). The Black client and the helping professionals. In R. I. Jones (Ed.) *Black psychology.* New York: Harper & Row.

Belkin, G. S. (1975). *Practical counseling in the schools.* Dubuque, Iowa: William C. Brown Publishers.

Bell, R. L. (1971). The culturally deprived psychologist. *Counseling Psychologist, 2,* 104–107.

Bernal, M. E., and Padilla, A. M. (1982). Status of minority curricula & training in clinical psychology. *American Psychologist, 37,* 780–787.

Bernard, H. W. (1963). Socioeconomic class and the school counselor. *Theory into Practice, 2,* 17–23.

Boxley, R., & Wagner, N. N. (1971). Clinical psychology training programs and minority groups: A survey. *Professional Psychology 2,* 75–81.

Broverman, I., Broverman, D. M., Clarkson, F. E., Rosenkrantz, P. S., & Vogel, S. (1970). Sex role stereotype and clinical judgments of mental health. *Journal of Consulting and Clinical Psychology, 34,* 1–7.

Bryson, S., & Bardo, H. (1975). Race and the counseling process: An overview. *Journal of Non-White Concerns in Personnel and Guidance, 4,* 5–15.

Bryne, R. H. (1977). *Guidance: A behavioral approach.* Englewood Cliffs, N.J.: Prentice-Hall.

Calia, V. F. (1966). The culturally deprived client: A re-formulation of the counselor's role. *Journal of Counseling Psychology, 13,* 100–105.

Calnek, M. (1970). Racial factors in the countertransference: The Black therapist and the Black client. *American Journal of Orthopsychiatry, 40,* 39–46.

Casas, J. M., & Atkinson, D. R. (1981). The Mexican American in higher education: An example of subtle stereotyping. *Personnel and Guidance Journal, 59,* 473–476.

Casas, J. M., Wampold, B. E., & Atkinson, D. R. (1981). The categorization of ethnic stereotypes by university counselors. *Hispanic Journal of Behavioral Sciences, 3,* 75–82.

Cayleff, S. E. (1986). Ethical issues in counseling gender, races, and culturally distinct groups. *Journal of Counseling and Development, 64,* 345–347.

Clark, K. B. (1965). *Dark ghetto: Dilemmas of social power.* New York: Harper and Row.

Counseling and the Social Revolution. (1971). *Personnel and Guidance Journal, 49* (9).

Cowen, E. L., Gardner, E. A., & Zox, M. (Eds.) (1967). *Emergent approaches to mental health problems.* New York: Appleton-Century-Crofts.

Cross, W. C., & Maldonado, B. (1971). The counselor, the Mexican American, and the stereotype. *Elementary School Guidance and Counseling, 6,* 27–31.

Dauphinais, P., Dauphinais, L., & Rowe, W. (1981). Effects of race and communication style on Indian perceptions of counselor effectiveness. *Counselor Education and Supervision, 21,* 72–30.

De Vore, I. (1977). The new science of genetic self-interest. *Psychology Today, 10* (9), 42–51, 84–88.

Draguns, J. G. (1975). Resocialization into culture: The complexities of taking a worldwide view of psychotherapy. In R. W. Brislin, S. Bochner, & W. J. Lonner (Eds.), *Cross-cultural perspectives in learning.* New York: John Wiley & Sons, Halsted.

Draguns, J. G. (1976). Counseling across cultures: Common themes and distinct approaches. In P. B. Pedersen, W. J. Lonner, & J. G. Draguns (Eds.), *Counseling across cultures.* Honolulu: The University of Hawaii Press.

Edwards, A. W. (1982). The consequences of error in selecting treatment for Blacks. *Social Casework, 63,* 429–433.

Gardner, L. H. (1971). The therapeutic relationship under varying conditions of race. *Psychotherapy: Theory, Research and Practice, 8,* (1), 78–87.

Garfield, J. C., Weiss, S. L., & Pollack, E. A. (1973). Effects of the child's social class on school counselor's decision making. *Journal of Counseling Psychology, 20,* 166–168.

Granberg, L. I. (1967). What I've learned in counseling. *Christianity Today, 2,* 891–894.

Greenson, R. R. (1964). *The technique and practice of psychoanalysis* (Vol. 1). New York: International Universities Press.

Grier, W. H., & Cobbs, P. M. (1968). *Black rage.* New York: Bantam Books, Inc.

Guerney, B. G. (Ed.) (1969). *Psychotherapeutic agents: New roles for nonprofessionals, parents, and teachers.* New York: Holt, Rinehart & Winston.

Gunnings, T. S. (1971). Preparing the new counselor. *The Counseling Psychologist, 2* (4), 100–101.

Haase, W. (1956). *Rorschach diagnosis, socio-economic class and examiner bias.* Unpublished doctoral dissertation, New York University.

Habermann, L., & Thiry, S. (1970). *The effect of socio-economic status variables on counselor perception and behavior.* Unpublished master's thesis, University of Wisconsin.

Haettenschwiller, D. L. (1971). Counseling black college students in special programs. *Personnel and Guidance Journal, 50,* 29–35.

Halleck, S. L. (1971). Therapy is the handmaiden of the status quo. *Psychology Today, 4,* 30–34, 98–100.

Havighurst, R. J., & Neugarten, B. L. (1962). *Society and education* (Second edition). Boston: Allyn & Bacon, Inc.

Hollingshead, A. B. (1949). *Elmtown's youth: The impact of social classes on adolescents.* New York: John Wiley and Sons, Inc.

Hollingshead, A. B., & Redlich, F. C. (1958). *Social class and mental health.* New York: John Wiley & Sons, Inc.

Ibrahim, F. A., Stadler, H. A., Arredondo, P., & McFadden, J. (1986). Status of human rights issues in counselor education: A national survey. Paper presented at the meeting of the American Association for Counseling and Development, Los Angeles.

Jackson, A. M. (1973). Psychotherapy: Factors associated with the race of the therapist. *Psychotherapy: Theory, Research and Practice, 10,* 273–277.

Jackson, G. G. (1985). Cross-cultural counseling with Afro-Americans. In P. Pedersen (Ed.), *Handbook of cross-cultural counseling and therapy.* Westport, Conn.: Greenwood Press.

Johnson, D. E., & Vestermark, M. J. (1970). *Barriers and hazards in counseling.* Boston: Houghton Mifflin Co.

Jones, L. K. (1976). A national survey of the program and enrollment characteristics of counselor education programs. *Counselor Education and Supervision, 15,* 166–176.

Jourard, S. M. (1964). *The transparent self.* Princeton, N.J.: D. Van Nostrand Co.

Katz, J. H. (1985). The sociopolitical nature of counseling. *The Counseling Psychologist, 13,* 615–624.

Kennedy, C. D., & Wagner, N. N. (1979). Psychology and affirmative action: 1977. *Professional Psychology, 10,* 234–243.

Lee, S., & Temerlin, M. K. (1968). *Social class status and mental illness.* Unpublished doctoral dissertation, University of Oklahoma.

Lerner, B. (1972). *Therapy in the ghetto: Political impotence and personal disintegration.* Baltimore: Johns Hopkins University Press.

Lewis, M. D., Lewis, J. A., & Dworkin, E. P. (1971). Editorial: Counseling and the social revolution. *The Personnel and Guidance Journal, 49,* 689.

Mercado, P., & Atkinson, D. R. (1982). Effects of counselor sex, student sex, and student attractiveness on counselor's judgments. *Journal of Vocational Behavior.*

Mitchell, H. (1971). Counseling black students: A model in response to the need for relevant counselor training programs. *The Counseling Psychologist, 2* (4), 117–122.

Padilla, E. R., Boxley, R., & Wagner, N. N. (1973). The desegregation of clinical psychology training. *Professional Psychology, 4,* 259–264.

Padilla, A. M., Ruiz, R. A., & Alvarez, R. (1975). Community mental health services for the Spanish-speaking/surnamed population. *American Psychologist, 30,* 892–905.

Parham, W., & Moreland, J. R. (1981). Nonwhite students in counseling psychology: A closer look. *Professional Psychology, 12,* 499–507.

Pedersen, P. B. (1976). The field of intercultural counseling. In P. B. Pedersen, W. J. Lonner, & J. G. Draguns (Eds.), *Counseling across cultures.* Honolulu: The University of Hawaii Press.

Peoples, V. Y., & Dell, D. M. (1975). Black and white student preferences for counselor roles. *Journal of Counseling Psychology, 22,* 529–534.

Pike, K. L. (1954). *Language in relation to a unified theory of the structure of human behavior.* Part 1: Preliminary edition. Summer Institute of Linguistics.

Pine, G. J. (1972). Counseling minority groups: A review of the literature. *Counseling and Values, 17,* 35–44.

Pomales, J., Claiborn, C. D., & LaFromboise, T. D. (1986). Effects of Black students' racial identity on perceptions of white counselors varying in cultural sensitivity. *Journal of Counseling Psychology, 33,* 57–61.

Ponterotto, J. G., & Casas, J. M. (1987). In search of multi-cultural competence within counselor education programs. *Journal of Counseling and Development, 65,* 430–434.

Rosenthal, R., & Jacobson, L. (1968). *Pygmalion in the classroom: Teacher expectation and pupils' intellectual development.* New York: Holt, Rinehart & Winston.

Russo, N. R., Olmedo, E. L., Stapp, J., & Fulcher, R. (1981). Women and minorities in psychology. *American Psychologist, 36,* 1315–1363.

Ryan, D. W., & Gaier, E. L. (1968). Student socio-economic status and counselor contact in junior high school. *Personnel and Guidance Journal, 46,* 466–472.

Sanford, N. (1969). Research with students as action and education. *American Psychologist, 24,* 544–546.

Sattler, J. M. (1970). Racial "Experimenter Effects" in experimentation, testing, interviewing and psychotherapy. *Psychological Bulletin, 73,* 137–160.

Schlossberg, N. K., & Pietrofesa, J. J. (1973). Perspectives on counseling bias: Implications for counselor education. *The Counseling Psychologist, 4,* 44–54.

Shertzer, B., & Stone, S. C. (1974). *Fundamentals of counseling* (2nd ed.) Boston: Houghton Mifflin.

Smith, E. J. (1977). Counseling Black individuals: Some stereotypes. *Personnel and Guidance Journal, 55,* 390–396.

Smith, E. M. J. (1985). Ethnic minorities: Life stress, social support, and mental health issues. *The Counseling Psychologist, 13,* 537–579.

Special Populations Task Force of the President's Commission on Mental Health (1978). Task panel reports submitted to the President's Commission on Mental Health: Vol. 3. Washington, D.C.: U.S. Government Printing Office.

Sue, D. W. (1973). Ethnic identity: The impact of two cultures on the psychological development of Asians in America. In S. Sue & N. N. Wagner (Eds.), *Asian Americans: Psychological perspectives.* (pp. 140–149.) Ben Lomand, Calif.: Science and Behavior Books, Inc.

Sue, D. W., Bernier, J. E., Durran, A., Feinberg, L., Pedersen, P., Smith, E. J., & Vasquez-Nuttall, E. (1982). Position paper: Cross-cultural counseling competencies. *The Counseling Psychologist, 10(2),* 45–52.

Sue, D. W., & Sue, S. (1972). Counseling Chinese-Americans. *Personnel and Guidance Journal, 50,* 637–644.

Sue, D. W., & Sue, D. (1977). Barriers to effective cross-cultural counseling. *Journal of Counseling Psychology, 24,* 420–429.

Sue, S., Akutsu, P. O., & Higashi, C. (1985). Training issues in conducting therapy with ethnic-minority-group clients. In P. Pedersen (Ed.), *Handbook of cross-cultural counseling and therapy* (pp. 275–280). Westport, Conn.: Greenwood Press.

Sue, S., Allen, D., & Conaway, L. (1978). The responsiveness and equality of mental health care to Chicanos and Native Americans. *American Journal of Community Psychology.*

Sue, S., & McKinney, H. (1975). Asian Americans in the community mental health care system. *American Journal of Orthopsychiatry, 45,* 111–118.

Sue, S., McKinney, H., Allen, D., & Hall, J. (1974). Delivery of community health services to Black and White clients. *Journal of Consulting Psychology, 42,* 794–801.

Sue, S., & Zane, N. (1987). The role of culture and cultural techniques in psychotherapy: A critique and reformulation. *American Psychologist, 42,* 37–45.

Thomas, A., & Sillen, S. (1972). *Racism and psychiatry.* New York: Brunney Mazel.

Thomas, A. H., & Stewart, N. R. (1971). Counselor response to female clients with deviate and conforming career goals. *Journal of Counseling Psychology, 18,* 352–357.

Thompson, R. A., & Cimbolic, P. (1978). Black students' counselor preference and attitudes toward counseling center use. *Journal of Counseling Psychology, 25,* 570–575.

Torion, R. P. (1973). Socioeconomic status and traditional treatment approaches reconsidered. *Psychological Bulletin, 79,* 263–270.

Triandis, H. C., Malpass, R. S., & Davidson, A. R. (1973). Psychology and culture. *Annual Review of Psychology, 24,* 355–378.

Trimble, J. E. (1976). Value differences among American Indians: Concern for the concerned counselor. In P. Pedersen, W. J. Lonner, & J. G. Draguns (Eds.), *Counseling across cultures.* Honolulu: The University of Hawaii Press.

Tyler, L. (1964). The methods and processes of appraisal and counseling. In A. S. Thompson & D. E. Super (Eds.), *The professional preparation of counseling psychologists.* New York: Bureau of Publications, Teachers College, Columbia University.

Vexliard, A. (1968). Temperament et modalites d'adaptation. *Bulletin de Psychologie, 21,* 1–15.

Vontress, C. E. (1973). Counseling: Racial and ethnic factors. *Focus on Guidance, 5,* 1–10.

Vontress, C. E. (1976). Racial and ethnic barriers in counseling. In P. Pedersen, W. J. Lonner, & J. G. Draguns (Eds.), *Counseling across cultures.* Honolulu: The University of Hawaii Press.

Wampold, B. E., Casas, J. M., & Atkinson, D. R. (1981). Ethnic bias in counseling: An information processing approach. *Journal of Counseling Psychology, 28,* 498–503.

Webster, D. W., & Fretz, B. R. (1978). Asian American, Black, and White college students' preferences for help-giving sources. *Journal of Counseling Psychology, 25,* 124–130.

Williams, R. L., & Kirkland, J. (1971). The white counselor and the black client. *Counseling Psychologist, 2,* 114–117.

Wilson, W. & Calhoun, J. F. (1974). Behavior therapy and the minority client. *Psychotherapy: Theory, Research and Practice, 11,* 317–325.

Wrenn, C. G. (1962). The culturally encapsulated counselor. *Harvard Educational Review, 32,* 444–449.

Yamamoto, J., James, Q. C., Bloombaum, M., & Hatten, J. (1967). Racial factors in patient selection. *American Journal of Psychiatry, 124,* 630–636.

Yamamoto, J., James, Q. C., & Palley, N. (1968). Cultural problems in psychiatric therapy. *Archives of General Psychiatry, 19,* 45–49.

3 A Minority Identity Development Model

One of the most promising approaches to the field of cross-cultural counseling has been the renewed interest in racial/cultural identity development (Parham & Helms, 1981; Helms, 1985; D. W. Sue & D. Sue, in press). While it is undeniable that each minority group has a unique cultural heritage that makes it distinct from other groups, this fact has erroneously been interpreted as evidence of cultural conformity—a monolithic approach which views all Asians, Blacks, Hispanics, American Indians, and other minorities as possessing the same group attitudes and behaviors.

Clearly, uniformity of attitudes and behaviors is no more true for minority individuals than it is for members of the dominant culture. With regard to the very issue of cultural distinction, minority attitudes may vary from desire for total assimilation into the dominant culture to total rejection of the dominant culture and immersion in the minority culture (Parham & Helms, 1981).

D. Sue and S. Sue (1972) provide evidence of the disparate ways in which Chinese Americans respond to cultural conflict. Some reject their Chinese background entirely and try to assimilate into the dominant society. Others adhere to traditional cultural values and attempt to resist assimilation. Still others stress pride in their racial identity while refraining from the conformity inherent in both the traditional Chinese practices and assimilation into the mainstream culture. Ruiz and Padilla (1977) suggest there is a danger inherent in trying to isolate the "true nature" of the Hispanic character since each person's attitudes and behaviors are a function of his/her degree of acculturation. Furthermore, these writings suggest that not only do intragroup differences exist, but attitudes and behaviors within individuals can fluctuate greatly as their identification with one culture or another changes.

The purpose of this chapter is to explicate a model of identity development that acknowledges coincidental identity transformational processes involving minority groups and utilize these processes to help explain individual differences within minority groups.

A number of earlier authors have also attempted to explain individual differences within racial/ethnic groups. Some of these early attempts took the form of simple typologies in which a particular minority group was divided into smaller subcategories or types based on their degree of ethnic identification. As Hall, Cross, and Freedle (1972) point out, these subgroups generally included both "conservative" and "militant" types and one or two categories in between. Vontress (1971), for instance, theorized that Afro-Americans conformed to three distinct subgroups: (1) Colored, (2) Negro, and (3) Black. Briefly, these subcategories represented decreasing levels of dependence upon White society and culture as the source of self-definition and worth, and an increasing degree of identification with Black society and culture. As another example, Mayovich (1973) typed Japanese Americans according to four separate categories: (1) Conformists, (2) Anomic, (3) Liberal, and (4) Militant. Mayovich (1973) hypothesized that as a result of their acceptance or rejection of traditional values and their involvement or detachment from social issues, all Japanese Americans (at least those of the Sansei generation) fell into one of these four types.

This method of "typing" minority individuals has come under heavy criticism in recent years, however (Parham & Helms, 1981; Helms, 1985; Atkinson & Schein, 1986; Ponterotto & Wise, 1987). Banks (1972), for instance, contends that these theorists have mistakenly proposed labels that attribute certain fixed personality traits to people, when in fact their behavior is a function of a specific situation. Others (Cross, 1970; Hall, Cross & Freedle, 1972; Jackson, 1975) have suggested that any attempt to define minority "types" must acknowledge movement of individuals across categories. Helms (1985) goes further and states that these models may (a) unintentionally "blame the victim" by placing too much emphasis on individual rather than system change; (b) become obsolete since they are so dependent on societal forces which may have changed; (c) erroneously assume that identity development follows a linear and continuous course; and (d) make us view the "stages" as static, discrete entities rather than a dynamic and evolving process. In spite of such criticisms, it is important to recognize the early topologies as pioneering attempts that paved the way for more sophisticated models of identity development.

A second major approach has viewed minority attitudes and behavior as a product of an identity development continuum. This approach differs from earlier topologies in that minority attitudes and behaviors are viewed as flexible and a function of the individual's stage of identity development. Rather than type the individual, stages of development through which any minority person may pass are described. Attitudinal and behavioral attributes, therefore, are not viewed as fixed characteristics but as related to identity development.

These early attempts to define a process of minority identity development were almost exclusively the work of Black intellectuals who were obviously influenced in their thinking by the impact of social, psychological, and cultural events in the sixties. Hall, Cross, and Freedle (1972) describe how these events highlighted the process of Black identity transformation:

> We have seen a change in the nature of black-white relations in America. To be sure, this change has produced many consequences, one of which has been an identity transformation among American blacks. The transformation has been from an older orientation whereby most blacks viewed themselves as inadequate, inferior, incapable of self-determination, and unable to cope with the intricacies of life in a complex society, to one of feeling adequate, self-reliant, assertive, and self-determinative (p. 156).

The most highly developed models of Black identity transformation have been offered by Cross (1970, 1971) and Jackson (1975). Each of these men, independent of the other, developed a multistage identity development process, although each acknowledges the influence of earlier writers (Crawford & Naditch, 1970; Sherif & Sherif, 1970; Thomas, 1971; Wallace, 1964).

Cross (1971) described his model as "Negro-to-Black Conversion Experience," consisting of preencounter, encounter, immersion, and internalization stages. According to the model, Blacks at the preencounter stage are "programmed to view and think of the world as being nonblack, anti-black, or the opposite of Black" (Hall, Cross, & Freedle, 1972, p. 159). At the next stage, the Encounter stage, the Black individual becomes aware of what being Black means and begins to validate him/herself as a Black person. During the Immersion stage, the Black person rejects all nonblack values and totally immerses him/herself in Black culture. Finally, in the Internalization stage, the Black person gains a sense of inner security and begins to focus on ". . . things other than himself and his own ethnic or racial group" (Hall, Cross, & Freedle, 1972, p. 160). Although there is considerable debate about the validity of the model and the existence of several stages, tentative exploratory studies provide support, if somewhat mixed (Hall, Cross, & Freedle, 1972).

Jackson (1975) identifies a similar four-stage process as the Black Identity Development Model. In stage one, Passive Acceptance, the Black person accepts and conforms to White social, cultural, and institutional standards (p. 21). In stage two, Active Resistance, the Black person rejects all that is White and attempts to remove all White influences upon his/her life (p. 22). In stage three, Redirection, the Black individual no longer admires or despises what is White but rather considers it irrelevant to Black Culture (p. 23). Finally, in stage four, Internalization, the Black person acknowledges and appreciates the uniqueness of the Black culture and comes to accept and reject various aspects of American culture based on their own merits.

Although these identity development models pertain specifically to the Black experience, the editors of the present text believe that some of the basic tenets of these theories can be generalized and applied to other minority groups, due to their shared experience of oppression. Several earlier writers (Stonequist, 1937; Berry, 1965) have also observed that minority groups share the same patterns of adjustment to cultural oppression. Parallels are most easily drawn between Blacks and other racial/ethnic groups. The fact that other minority groups such as Asian Americans (S. Sue & D. W. Sue, 1971; Mayovich, 1973), Hispanics (Szapocznik & Associates, 1980), and women (Downing & Roush, 1985) have proposed similar models may indicate experiential validity. During the past two decades, the social and political activity of Hispanics, Asian Americans, and American Indians has resulted in an identity transformation for persons within these groups similar to that experienced by Black Americans. A Third World consciousness has emerged, with the common experience of oppression clearly serving as the unifying force.

Parallels between the Black experience and those of other minority groups have also been suggested. Women, gays, the aged, the handicapped, and other oppressed groups have become increasingly conscious of themselves as objects of oppression, and this has resulted in changed attitudes toward themselves, their own minority groups, other minority groups, and members of the dominant culture. Based on views expressed by earlier writers and our own clinical observation that these changes in attitudes and subsequent behavior follow a predictable sequence, we propose a five-stage Minority Identity Development (MID) model.

The MID model we propose is not presented as a comprehensive theory of personality development, but rather as a schema to help counselors understand minority client attitudes and behaviors within existing personality theories. The model defines five stages of development that oppressed people may experience as they struggle to understand themselves in terms of their own minority culture, the dominant culture, and the oppressive relationship between the two cultures. Although five distinct stages are presented in the model, the MID is more accurately conceptualized as a continuous process in which one stage blends with another and boundaries between stages are not clear.

It is our observation that not all minority individuals experience the entire range of these stages in their lifetimes. Prior to the turbulent 1960s— a decade in which the transition of many individuals through this process was accelerated and, therefore, made more evident—many people were raised and lived out their lives in the first stage. Nor is the developmental process to be interpreted as irreversible. It is our opinion that many minority individuals are raised by parents functioning at level five, but in coming to grips with their own identity, offsprings often move from level five to one of the lower levels. On the other hand, it does not appear that functioning at lower levels of development is prerequisite to functioning at higher levels. Some people born and raised in a family functioning at level five appear never to experience a level-one sense of identity.

At each level we provide examples of four corresponding attitudes that may assist the counselor to understand behaviors displayed by individuals operating at or near these levels. (It is our contention that minority behavior, like all human behavior, can only be fully understood within the context of the attitudes that motivated it.) Each attitude is believed to be an integral part of any minority person's identity or of how he/she views (a) self, (b) others of the same minority, (c) others of another minority, and (d) majority individuals. It was not our intention to define a hierarchy with more valued attitudes at higher levels of development. Rather, the model is intended to reflect a process that we have observed in our work with minority clients over the past three decades.

Minority Identity Development Model

Stage One—Conformity Stage

Minority individuals in this stage of development are distinguished by their unequivocal preference for dominant cultural values over those of their own culture. Their choices of role models, life-styles, value system, etc., all follow the lead of the dominant group. Those physical and/or cultural characteristics that single them out as minority persons are a source of pain and are either viewed with disdain or are repressed from consciousness. Their views of self, fellow group members, and other minorities in general are clouded by their identification with the dominant culture. Minorities may perceive the ways of the dominant group as being much more positive, and there is a high desire to "assimilate and acculturate." The attitudes which minorities may have about themselves in this stage are ones of devaluation and depreciation on both a conscious and subconscious level. For example, Asians may perceive their own physical features as less desirable and their cultural values and Asian ways as a handicap to successful adaptation in White society. Their attitudes towards members of their own group tend to be highly negative in that they share the dominant culture's belief that Asians are less desirable. For example, stereotypes portraying Asians as inarticulate, good with numbers, poor managers, and aloof in their personal relationship are believed. Other minority groups are also viewed according to the dominant group's system of minority stratification (i.e., those minority groups that most closely resemble the dominant group in physical and cultural characteristics are viewed more favorably than those less similar). Attitudes toward members of the dominant group, however, tend to be highly appreciative in that the members are admired, respected, and often viewed as ideal models.

It is quite obvious that in the Conformity stage of development Asian Americans and other minorities view themselves as deficient in the "desirable" characteristics held up by the dominant society. Feelings of racial self-hatred caused by cultural racism may accompany this type of adjustment (S. Sue & D. W. Sue, 1972).

A. *Attitude toward self: Self-depreciating attitude.* Individuals who acknowledge their distinguishing physical and/or cultural characteristics consciously view them as a source of shame. Individuals who repress awareness of their distinguishing physical and/or cultural characteristics depreciate themselves at a subconscious level.
B. *Attitude toward members of same minority: Group-depreciating attitude.* Fellow minority group members are viewed according to dominant-held beliefs of minority strengths and weaknesses.
C. *Attitude toward members of different minority: Discriminatory attitude.* Other minorities are viewed according to the dominant group's system of minority stratification (i.e., those minority groups that most closely resemble the dominant group in physical and cultural characteristics are viewed more favorably than those less similar).
D. *Attitude toward members of dominant group: Group-appreciating attitude.* Members of the dominant group are admired, respected, and often viewed as ideal models. Cultural values of the dominant society are accepted without question.

Stage Two—Dissonance Stage

The movement into the Dissonance stage is most often a gradual process, but as Cross (1971) points out a monumental event such as the assassination of Martin Luther King may propel the Black person into the next stage. In this case, since denial seems to be a major tool used by Conformity-stage persons, minorities in the Dissonance stage begin to experience a breakdown in their denial system. A Latino who may feel ashamed of his/her cultural upbringing may encounter a Latino who seems proud of his/her cultural heritage. A Black who may have deceived himself/herself into believing that race problems are due to laziness, untrustworthiness, or personal inadequacies of his/her group, suddenly encounters racism on a personal level.

A. *Attitude toward self: Conflict between self-depreciating and self-appreciating attitudes.* With a growing awareness of minority cultural strengths comes a faltering sense of pride in self. The individual's attitude toward distinguishing physical and/or cultural characteristics is typified by alternating feelings of shame and pride in self.
B. *Attitude toward members of same minority: Conflict between group-depreciating and group-appreciating attitudes.* Dominant-held views of minority strengths and weaknesses begin to be questioned, as new, contradictory information is received. Cultural values of the minority group begin to have appeal.

C. *Attitude toward members of different minority: Conflict between dominant-held views of minority hierarchy and feelings of shared experience.* The individual begins to question the dominant-held system of minority stratification and experiences a growing sense of comradeship with other oppressed people. Most of the individual's psychic energy at this level, however, is devoted to resolving conflicting attitudes toward self, the same minority, and the dominant group.

D. *Attitude toward members of dominant group: Conflict between group-appreciating and group-depreciating attitude.* The individual experiences a growing awareness that not all cultural values of the dominant group are beneficial to him/her. Members of the dominant group are viewed with growing suspicion.

Stage Three—Resistance and Immersion Stage

In this stage of development, the minority individual completely endorses minority-held views and rejects the dominant society and culture. Desire to eliminate oppression of the individual's minority group becomes an important motivation of the individual's behavior.

D. W. Sue and D. Sue (in press) believe that movement into this stage seems to occur for two reasons. First, the person begins to resolve many of the conflicts and confusions in the previous stage. As a result, a greater understanding of societal forces (racism, oppression, and discrimination) emerges, along with a realization that he/she has been victimized by it. Second, the individual begins to ask him/herself the following question: "Why should I feel ashamed of who and what I am?" The answers to that question will evoke both guilt and anger (bordering on rage): guilt that he/she has "sold out" in the past and contributed to his/her own group's oppression, and anger at having been oppressed and "brainwashed" by the forces in the dominant society.

A. *Attitude toward self: Self-appreciating attitude.* The minority individual at this stage acts as an explorer and discoverer of his/her history and culture, seeking out information and artifacts that enhance his/her sense of identity and worth. Cultural and physical characteristics which once elicited feelings of shame and disgust at this stage become symbols of pride and honor.

B. *Attitude toward members of same minority: Group-appreciating attitude.* The individual experiences a strong sense of identification with, and commitment to, his/her minority group, as enhancing information about the group is acquired. Members of the group are admired, respected, and often viewed as ideal models. Cultural values of the minority group are accepted without question.

C. *Attitude toward members of different minority: Conflict between feelings of empathy for other minority experiences and feelings of culturocentrism.* The individual experiences a growing sense of camaraderie with persons from other minority groups, to the degree that they are viewed as sharing similar forms of oppression. Alliances with other groups tend to be short-lived, however, when their values come in conflict with those of the individual's minority group. The dominant group's system of minority stratification is replaced by a system which values most those minority groups that are culturally similar to the individual's own group.

D. *Attitude toward members of dominant group: Group-depreciating attitude.* The individual totally rejects the dominant society and culture and experiences a sense of distrust and dislike for all members of the dominant group.

Stage Four—Introspection Stage

In this stage of development, the minority individual experiences feelings of discontent and discomfort with group views rigidly held in the Resistance and Immersion stage, and diverts attention to notions of greater individual autonomy.

What occurs at this stage is very interesting. First, the minority individual may begin to feel progressively more comfortable with his or her own sense of identity. This security allows the person to begin to question some of the rigidly held beliefs of the Resistance stage that all "Whites are bad." There is also a feeling that too much negativism and hatred directed at White society tends to divert energies from more positive exploration of identity questions. This stage is characterized by greater individual autonomy. During this stage the person may begin to experience conflict between notions of responsibility and allegiance to his/her own minority group, and notions of personal autonomy. There is now a belief that perhaps not everything in the dominant culture is bad and that there are many positive as well as negative elements within it.

A. *Attitude toward self: Concern with basis of self-appreciating attitude.* The individual experiences conflict between notions of responsibility and allegiance to minority group and notions of personal autonomy.

B. *Attitude toward members of same minority: Concern with unequivocal nature of group appreciation.* While attitudes of identification are continued from the preceding Resistance and Immersion stages, concern begins to build up regarding the issue of group usurpation of individuality.

C. *Attitude toward members of different minority: Concern with ethnocentric basis for judging others.* The individual experiences a growing uneasiness with minority stratification that results from culturocentrism and placing a greater value on groups experiencing the same oppression than on those experiencing a different oppression.

D. *Attitude toward members of dominant group: Concern with the basis of group depreciation.* The individual experiences conflict between an attitude of complete distrust for the dominant society and culture, and an attitude of selective trust and distrust according to dominant individuals' demonstrated behaviors and attitudes. The individual also recognizes the utility of many dominant cultural elements yet is uncertain whether or not to incorporate such elements into his/her minority culture.

Stage Five—Synergetic Articulation and Awareness Stage

Minority individuals in this stage experience a sense of self-fulfillment with regard to cultural identity. Conflicts and discomforts experienced in the Introspection stage have been resolved, allowing greater individual control and flexibility. Cultural values of other minorities as well as those of the dominant group are objectively examined and accepted or rejected on the basis of experience gained in earlier stages of identity development. Desire to eliminate *all* forms of oppression becomes an important motivation for the individual's behavior.

A. *Attitude toward self: Self-appreciating attitude.* The individual experiences a strong sense of self-worth, self-confidence, and autonomy as the result of having established his/her identity as an individual, a member of a minority group, and/or a member of the dominant culture.

B. *Attitude toward members of same minority: Group-appreciating attitude.* The individual experiences a strong sense of pride in the group without having to accept group values unequivocally. Strong feelings of empathy with the group experience are coupled with an awareness that each member of the group is an individual.

C. *Attitude toward members of different minority: Group-appreciating attitude.* The individual experiences a strong sense of respect for the group's cultural values coupled with awareness that each member of the group is an individual. The individual also experiences a greater understanding and support for all oppressed people, regardless of their similarity or dissimilarity to the individual's minority group.

D. *Attitude toward members of dominant group: Attitude of selective appreciation.* The individual experiences selective trust and liking for members of the dominant group who seek to eliminate repressive activities of the group. The individual also experiences an openness to the constructive elements of the dominant culture.

Table 3.1
Summary of Minority Identity Development Model

Stages of Minority Development Model	Attitude toward self	Attitude toward others of the same minority	Attitude toward others of different minority	Attitude toward dominant group
Stage 1— Conformity	self-depreciating	group-depreciating	discriminatory	group-appreciating
Stage 2— Dissonance	conflict between self-depreciating and appreciating	conflict between group-depreciating and group-appreciating	conflict between dominant-held views of minority hierarchy and feelings of shared experience	conflict between group-appreciating and group-depreciating
Stage 3— Resistance and Immersion	self-appreciating	group-appreciating	conflict between feelings of empathy for other minority experiences and feelings of culturo-centrism	group-depreciating
Stage 4— Introspection	concern with basis of self-appreciation	concern with nature of unequivocal appreciation	concern with ethnocentric basis for judging others	concern with the basis of group depreciation
Stage 5— Synergetic Articulation and Awareness	self-appreciating	group-appreciating	group-appreciating	selective appreciation

Implications of the MID Model for Counseling

As suggested earlier, the MID model is not intended as a comprehensive theory of personality, but rather as a paradigm to help counselors understand minority client attitudes and behaviors. In this respect, the model is intended to sensitize counselors to (1) the role oppression plays in a minority individual's identity development, (2) the differences that can exist between members of the same minority group with respect to their cultural identity, and (3) the potential which each individual minority person has for changing his/her sense of identity. Beyond helping to understand minority client behavior, the model has implications for the counseling process itself.

The general attitudes and behaviors that describe minority individuals at the Conformity stage (e.g., denial of minority problems, strong dependence on and identification with dominant group, etc.) suggest that clients from this stage are unlikely to seek counseling related to their cultural identity. It is more likely that they will perceive problems of cultural identity as problems related to their personal identity. Clients at this stage are more inclined to visit and be influenced by counselors of the dominant group than those of the same minority. Indeed, clients may actively request a White counselor and react negatively toward a minority counselor. Because of the client's strong identification with dominant group members, counselors from the dominant group may find the conformist client's need to please and appease a powerful force in the counseling relationship. Attempts to explore cultural identity or to focus in on feelings may be threatening to the client. This is because exploration of identity may eventually touch upon feelings of racial self-hatred and challenge the client's self-deception ("I'm not like other minorities"). Clients at the Conformity stage are likely to present problems that are most amenable to problem solving and goal-oriented counseling approaches.

Minority individuals at the Dissonance stage of development are preoccupied by questions concerning their concept of self, identity, and self-esteem; they are likely to perceive personal problems as related to their cultural identity. Emotional problems develop when these individuals are unable to resolve conflicts which occur between dominant-held views and those of their minority group. Clients in the Dissonance stage are more culturally aware than Conformity clients and are likely to prefer to work with counselors who possess a good knowledge of the client's cultural group. Counseling approaches that involve considerable self-exploration appear to be best suited for clients at this stage of development.

Minority individuals at the Resistance and Immersion stage are inclined to view all psychological problems (whether personal or social in nature) as a product of their oppression. The likelihood that these clients will seek formal counseling regarding their cultural identity is very slim. In those cases when counseling is sought, it will tend to be only between members of the same minority group, and generally in response to a crisis situation. Therapy for Stage Three clients often takes the form of exposure to, and practice of, the ways and artifacts of their cultures. An example of this might be a woman who experiences a release of tension and anxiety because of her involvement in a class concerning women's liberation. Clients at this stage who do seek counseling are likely to prefer group process and/or alloplastic approaches to counseling. In addition, approaches that are more action-oriented and aimed at external change (challenging racism) are well received. D. W. Sue and D. Sue (in press) believe that most counselors find minorities at this stage difficult to work with. A counselor (even if a member of the client's own race) is often viewed by the culturally different client as a symbol of the oppressive establishment. A great amount of direct anger and distrust may be expressed toward the counselor. The counselor will be frequently tested and challenged as to his/her own racism and role in society.

Clients at the Introspection stage are torn between their preponderant identification with their minority group and their need to exercise greater personal freedom. When these individuals are unable to resolve mounting conflict between these two forces, they often seek counseling. While Introspective clients still prefer to see a counselor from their own cultural group, counselors from other cultures may be viewed as credible sources of help if they share world views similar to those of their clientele and appreciate their cultural dilemmas. Counselors who use a self-exploration and decision-making approach can be most effective with these clients.

Clients at the fifth stage of identity development have acquired the internal skills and knowledge necessary to exercise a desired level of personal freedom. Their sense of minority identity is well balanced by an appreciation of other cultures. And, while discrimination and oppression remain a painful part of their lives, greater psychological resources are at their disposal in actively engaging the problem. Attitudinal similarity between counselor and client becomes a more important determinant of counseling success than membership-group similarity.

Discussion of the MID model's implications for counseling is admittedly highly speculative at this point, and the model itself requires empirical verification before more definitive inferences are drawn. We hope the model will stimulate much-needed research with regard to minority identity development and that it will help the reader distinguish and comprehend intragroup differences that are evident in the readings to follow.

References

Atkinson, D. R., & Schein, S. (1986). Similarity in counseling. *The Counseling Psychology, 14,* 319–354.

Banks, W. (1972). The Black client and the helping professional. In R. I. Jones (Ed.), *Black psychology.* New York: Harper & Row.

Berry, B. (1965). *Ethnic and race relations.* Boston: Houghton Mifflin.

Crawford, T. J., & Naditch, M. (1970). Relative deprivation, powerlessness, and militancy: The psychology of social protest. *Psychiatry, 33,* 208–223.

Cross, W. E. (1970). The black experience viewed as a process: A crude model for black self-actualization. Paper presented at the Thirty-fourth Annual Meeting of the Association of Social and Behavioral Scientists, April 23–24, Tallahassee, Fla.

Cross, W. E. (1972). The Negro-to-Black conversion experience. *Black World, 20,* 13–27.

Downing, N. E., & Roush, K. L. (1985). From passive acceptance to active commitment: A model of feminist identity development for women. *The Counseling Psychologist, 13,* 695–709.

Hall, W. S., Cross, W. E., & Freedle, R. (1972). Stages in the development of Black awareness: An exploratory investigation. In R. I. Jones (Ed.), *Black psychology* (pp. 156–165). New York: Harper & Row.

Helms, J. E. (1985). Cultural identity in the treatment process. In P. Pedersen (Ed.), *Handbook of cross-cultural counseling and therapy.* Westport, Conn.: Greenwood Press.

Jackson, B. (1975). Black identity development. *MEFORM: Journal of Educational Diversity & Innovation, 2,* 19–25.

Maykovich, M. H. (1973). Political activation of Japanese American youth. *Journal of Social Issues, 29,* 167–185.

Parham, T. A., & Helms, J. E. (1981). The influence of black students' racial identity attitudes on preference for counselor's race. *Journal of Counseling Psychology, 28,* 250–257.

Parks, R. E. (1950). *Race and culture.* Glencoe, Ill.: The Free Press.

Ponterotto, J. G., & Wise, S. L. (1987). Construct validity study of the racial identity attitude scale. *Journal of Counseling Psychology, 34,* 123–131.

Ruiz, R. A., & Padilla, A. M. (1977). Counseling Latinos. *Personnel and Guidance Journal, 55,* 401–408.

Sherif, M., & Sherif, C. (1970). Black unrest at a social movement toward an emerging self-identity. *Journal of Social and Behavioral Sciences, 15,* 41–52.

Stonequist, E. V. (1937). *The marginal man.* New York: Charles Scribner's Sons.

Sue, D. W., & Sue, D. (in press). *Counseling the culturally different: Theory and practice.* New York: John Wiley & Sons.

Sue, S., & Sue, D. W. (1971). Chinese-American personality and mental health. *Amerasia Journal, 1,* 36–49.

Szapocznik, J., Kurtines, W. M., & Fernandez, T. (1980). Bicultural involvement and adjustment in Hispanic-American youths. *International Journal of Intercultural Relations, 4,* 353–365.

Thomas, C. W. (1971). *Boys no more.* Beverly Hills, Calif.: Glencoe Press.

Vontress, C. E. (1971). Racial differences: Impediments to rapport. *Journal of Counseling Psychology, 18,* 7–13.

Wallace, A. F. C. (1964). *Culture and personality.* New York: Random House.

Part 2
The American Indian Client

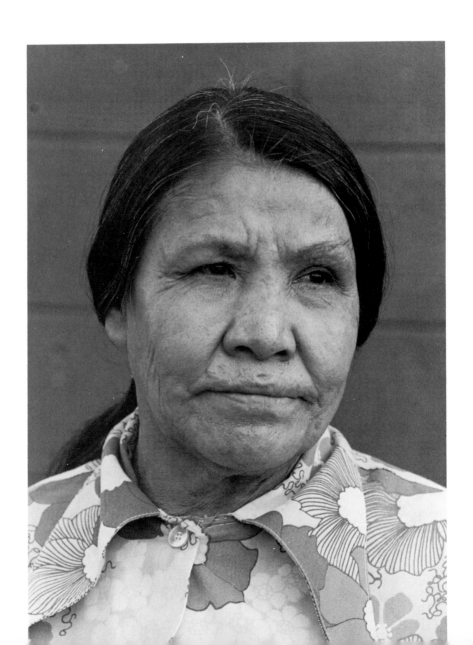

We are not free. We do not make choices. Our choices are made for us; we are the poor. For those of us who live on reservations these choices are made by federal administrators, bureaucrats, and their 'yes men,' euphemistically called tribal governments. Those of us who live in non-reservation areas have our lives controlled by local white power elites. We have many rulers. They are called social workers, 'cops,' school teachers, churches, etc. , . . .
(Warrior, 1967, p. 72)

For nearly five hundred years, American Indians have been fighting a defensive war for their right to freedom, their lands, their organization, their traditions and beliefs, their way of life, and their very lives. American Indians have experienced massacres by the U. S. Army, have seen the Bureau of Indian Affairs systematically destroy their leadership and way of life, have known promises broken, have had their land taken from them, and have watched their children die because of inadequate health care, poverty, and suicide. By almost every measure of impoverishment and deprivation, the American Indian is the poorest of the poor (Farb, 1967). Their population has decreased from a high of three million to above one million. In the past Indians were killed in massacres, but cultural genocide continues to operate through institutional racism. The following statistics are provided by Josephy (1971) and Richardson (1981):

- The average annual income of American Indians ($1,500) is 75 percent below that of the national average and $1,000 less than that of Blacks.

- The unemployment rate for American Indians is nearly 40 percent (ten times the average).

- The life expectancy of American Indians is forty-four years.

- Approximately 50 percent of American Indians live on reservations.

- Infant mortality for Native Americans after the first month of life is three times the national average.

- Fifty percent of Indian school children (double the national average) fail to complete high school.

- The suicide rate of Indian teenagers is one hundred times that of Whites.

- Until 1975, the Bureau of Indian Affairs was run by non-Indians.

It is ironic that many of the Whites who created these problems refer to them as "Indian problems" and have tried a variety of White-imposed methods to solve them. In essence, the attempts to solve the problems have consisted of imposing White solutions on the Indian; turn the Indian into a White and the problem will go away! The U. S. government has also imposed a legal definition of their identity: An individual must have an Indian blood quantum of 25 percent to be considered an Indian. Such an arbitrary definition has caused problems both in and out of the community.

Such attempts are not only manifestations of cultural oppression, they have marked a failure on the part of Whites to understand that the twenty-five hundred years of Indian histories and cultures have little in common with European-based cultures.

In "Providing Psychological Services to American Indian Children and Families," Everett, Proctor, and Cartmell mention how this history of treatment has made American Indians mistrust of Anglos a major obstacle in cross-cultural mental health service delivery. Major differences in communication styles, cultural values, and attitudes and expectations between Indians and Anglos also are discussed. The authors provide valuable insight into how non-Indian psychologists may better understand and work with their Indian clients. E. Edwards and M. Edwards in "American Indians: Working with Individuals and Groups" deal with another dimension of American Indian life. Like the previous authors, they believe in the use of culture-specific techniques when working with Indian clients. However, they bring in the importance of understanding how groups in American Indian culture affect our mental health practices. The concept of "consensus" in American Indian communities is crucial for effective cross-cultural work. Some very interesting case studies will aid the reader in grasping their central ideas.

The fact that the helping professions (counseling, psychotherapy, social work) as practiced in the United States may be instruments of cultural oppression is indirectly discussed by Lewis and Ho in their article "Social Work with Native Americans." They point out how social work and other mental health approaches and strategies arise from the milieu of direct intervention. Native American cultural concepts of noninterference are at odds with such a therapeutic orientation. In addition, certain Native American values revolving around sharing, time perspectives, patience, and nonverbal communication may also cause problems for the prospective, well-meaning counselor.

Counselors must not only recognize the historical American Indian experience of oppression and exploitation but also be alert to how their conventional training in mental health practices may be inappropriate for the life-styles and values of American Indians. To impose them blindly is to perpetuate oppression of the most damaging kind.

Farb, P. (1967). The American Indian: A portrait in limbo. *Saturday Review,* October 12, 26–29.

Josephy, Jr., A. M. (Ed.) (1971). *Red power.* New York: McGraw-Hill Book Co.

Richardson, E. (1981). Cultural and historical perspectives in counseling American Indians. In D. W. Sue (Ed.), *Counseling the culturally different: Theory and practice.* New York: John Wiley & Sons.

Warrior, C. (1971). We are not free. In A. M. Josephy, Jr. (Ed.), *Red power.* New York: McGraw-Hill.

4 Providing Psychological Services to American Indian Children and Families

Frances Everett, Noble Proctor, and Betty Cartmell

Some children in any culture exhibit psychological or psychiatric disturbances that interfere with their normal growth and development. American Indian children may present a myriad of psychological disturbances that merit mental health attention and care (Green, Sack, & Pambrum, 1981). However, numerous barriers to effective service delivery to American Indian populations have been identified, and Indian children and families remain an underserved population (Center for Social Research and Development, 1976; President's Commission on Mental Health, 1978; Slaughter, 1976).

Although the American Indian population is increasing, there is a continuing shortage of Indian mental health professionals. The 1980 census (Bureau of the Census, 1981) reported that 1,418,195 American Indian and Alaska natives were living in the United States. The American Psychological Association (APA) estimates, however, that only 76 of its members (.2%) are American Indians and that only 27 of these members have subspecialties in the clinical and counseling areas (Russo, Olmedo, Stapp, & Fulcher, 1981). Such trends are also not changing or, at best, are changing very slowly. Of the 3,098 doctoral degrees conferred in psychology in 1980, only 9 were to American Indians and only 4 of these were in clinical and counseling psychology (Russo et al., 1981). Thus, many of those providing mental health services to American Indians will continue to be non-Indians.

Although non-Indian psychologists are becoming increasingly involved in mental health service delivery to American Indians, they are, unfortunately, typically not prepared to work effectively with Indian clientele. The non-Indian psychologist may not be aware of the cultural values, life-styles, family practices, developmental progressions, and needs of their American Indian clients. This lack of cultural awareness typically

Everett, F., Proctor, N., and Cartmell, B. (1983). Providing psychological services to American Indian children and families. *Professional Psychology, 14,* 588–603. Copyright 1983 by the American Psychological Association. Reprinted by permission of the publisher and author.

results in conflicts and frustrations for both the psychologist and his or her Indian clients; ultimately, American Indian children and families may not receive appropriate mental health services.

Psychologists who work with Indian children and families must become sensitized to the issues inherent in service delivery to this population. The National Institute of Mental Health (NIMH; Fields, 1979), the APA (Korman, 1974), the President's Commission on Mental Health (1978), and others have acknowledged the need and ethical responsibility for psychologists to understand their clients' cultural values before delivering mental health services (Pedersen & Marsella, 1982). We will review a few of the cultural differences considered relevant to the psychologist inexperienced in working with American Indian children and families. Although ideally each culture will strive to understand the other one, the current focus is on helping the non-Indian psychologist relate to his or her Indian clientele.

Basic information regarding American Indians and their culture(s) is essential. One should attempt to gain knowledge and insight into the unique way of life of the population to be served. Although such information is of importance, it must also be cautiously used. While the majority culture frequently perceives of American Indians as a homogeneous group with the same appearance, customs, and language, this is certainly not the reality. In actuality, American Indians are, as a group, a highly diversified people, and they should not be approached stereotypically. General statements regarding them may not be generalizable across individuals, tribes, and regions. In addition to individual differences, there are vast intertribal and interclan differences in customs, practices, family structure and roles, beliefs, and attitudes. American Indians, like all people, are also in transition; all are changing and some are changing faster than others. Indian families vary along a continuum from those that retain and are only comfortable with traditional ways to those that are completely assimilated and acculturated and have accepted the life-style of the dominant culture. More recent transitions also include a trend for some American Indians to try to recapture lost or nearly lost traditional cultural values. With these cautions in mind, we can review aspects of traditional American Indian culture(s) that may be relevant to service delivery.

Attitudes and Expectations Relevant to Psychological Service Delivery

One of the most immediate problems encountered in service delivery is the attitude of the American Indian toward psychologists. The American Indian client and non-Indian psychologist may approach one another with apprehension, mistrust, and perhaps even hostility (Good Tracks, 1973; Jilek-Aall, 1976; LaFromboise & Dixon, 1981; Lewis & Ho, 1975; Lockart, 1981; Slaughter, 1976; Spang, 1965). Historical reviews show years of culture conflict and clash that can carry over to contemporary service delivery. Throughout history, the nature of interventions experienced by American Indians has been that of attempts by various groups to change the customs, practices, and beliefs of the Indian population. As early as the 1600s, various religious groups attempted to persuade Indians to allow their children to be "adopted" by majority culture families (Slaughter, 1976). This purportedly was to enable the children to be reared in a "proper" or "superior" environment complete with the "right" attitudes and religious beliefs in order that they might be elevated from their "savagery." Groups have sent missionaries to the Indians to persuade them that religions, other than those held by the tribes, were in some way better. The federal government, under the policy of Manifest Destiny, has intervened repeatedly, often with disastrous results for Indians. Whole nations of people have been uprooted from their homes and lands and transported to places that were often so different in geography and ecology as to be virtually incapable of supporting life as the tribes knew it. Indian memories are also long, and the past is not forgotten.

It should, thus, come as no surprise to find Indians today whose feelings toward mental health service providers range from caution to open hostility. These feelings may cause psychologists to encounter what they may see as massive delays and resistance to their genuine offers of aid. It may not be easy for the psychologist to avoid personalizing these feelings. Hostility and anger directed toward the service provider may be especially frustrating to the one genuinely concerned with service delivery or helping. Perhaps studying the history of the particular group one is working with will aid in understanding the group's feelings.

The American Indian's mistrust of Anglos is a major obstacle in cross-cultural mental health service delivery. The counselor attribute of trust is especially valued by American Indians (LaFromboise, Dauphinais, & Rowe, 1980; La Fromboise & Dixon, 1981; Trimble, 1976). Problems with trusting thus contribute to American Indians underutilizing mental health services. A disproportionately high percentage of those who do seek out services also do not continue. Of those American Indians who approach conventional mental health centers, 55% do not return after the first interview, compared with 30% for the general population (Sue, Allen, & Conaway, 1978).

The establishment of trust is always essential to the success of a psychotherapy or counseling relationship. Relationships will build slowly when American Indians suspend trust until the mental health service provider proves that he or she is trustworthy. Although a mental health service provider cannot make up for all injustices of past and present, he or she can understand a hostile client's feelings. Historic or cultural distrust may also need to be acknowledged and dealt with as one tries to provide the optimal conditions for mental health care (Lockart, 1981).

The attitudes of American Indians toward mental health service providers is also affected by legislative and jurisdictional policies. As citizens of the United States and members of sovereign tribes, American Indians maintain a dual citizenship (President's Commission on Mental Health, 1978; Slaughter, 1976). As citizens of the United States, they are entitled to all the rights, benefits, and responsibilities from local, state, and federal governments to which all other citizens are entitled. In addition, on the basis of treaties, the federal government specified the services that would be provided to American Indians in exchange for vast and extensive land, water, and mineral rights. Federal provision of human services for American Indians was included in these contracts. Such treaties, then, established some resources for which only Indian people are eligible and some protections to which Indian people are entitled.

Indian people expect that rights guaranteed in treaties will be honored, and they may approach a mental health service provider expecting that their services have been guaranteed. In contrast, the psychologist may be unaware of (or interpret differently) the legal and jurisdictional issues relevant to service delivery to American Indians. Indeed, confusion regarding jurisdictional responsibility for service delivery has been a major barrier to the delivery of human services to American Indians (Center for Social Research and Development, 1976; President's Commission on Mental Health, 1978). Such confusion may well give rise to differing expectations on the part of the non-Indian psychologist and his or her client(s). Although the Indian client may perceive receipt of services as his or her guaranteed right, the psychologist may not concur and may mistakenly believe that the appropriate action to take with American Indian clients is to transfer the responsibility for serving the family to the Indian Health Service or the nearest urban Indian center. Although the Indian Health Service does provide a variety of mental health services to Indian people (Beiser & Attneave, 1978), this does not exempt other agencies and service providers from also delivering services.

Non-Indian mental health providers and their Indian clients may also have differing expectations of their respective roles. Clarification of the traditional Indian expectation of the service provider, or healer, may be illuminating. For the traditional American Indian, disease may be seen as a phenomenon of the supernatural and full of moral implications. The patient, in turn, entrusts much faith in the medicine man and woman, believing that the healer is endowed with supernatural power (Jilek-Aall, 1976; President's Commission on Mental Health, 1978). It is accepted that the healer or medicine man or woman will know what the problem is and how to treat it. The patient is relatively passive during the healing ceremony, again, assuming that the healer will know what is needed. The patient's role is mainly that of presenting self for treatment. The Indian healing ceremony traditionally involves other family members, relatives, neighbors, and friends, all of whom may support the patient. Although there are intertribal differences, in some tribes the families of the patient will explain the presenting complaint to the healer. Traditional healing procedures may be lengthy, but improvement is expected quickly (Jilek-Aall, 1976). In contrast, traditional Anglo beliefs hold that disease is a phenomenon of nature and that treatment should be scientifically based. The Anglo faith resides in science, and the patient faces treatment alone.

Such differences in attitudes regarding sickness and treatment have obvious implications for cross-cultural service delivery. The American Indian client may approach the psychologist passively and be affronted by the asking of too many questions. Direct interrogation may be perceived as rude or may convey diagnostic incompetence and lack of healing power. Problems could well be encountered by a psychologist and his or her client who might be very reluctant to describe symptomatology but who expects to be treated. Treatment in isolation may remove the natural support systems of the patient. And services or treatments that span weeks or even months before anything is achieved may quickly lose credibility with the American Indian client.

These differences in attitudes can compound the problems of service delivery; effective cross-cultural service delivery is a formidable task. Mental health service providers would do well to acknowledge the natural support systems and healing systems of American Indians. The importance of traditional medicine and the beliefs of American Indians should be considered as a vital part of a total treatment plan (Bergman, 1973; President's Commission on Mental Health, 1978).

Patience is also essential to cross-cultural service delivery. The non-Indian psychologist can best be effective after he or she is accepted by his or her clientele. Such acceptance may take time, particularly since academic credentials and degrees need not signify power and status to the American Indian. The psychologist may be seen as an outsider who must undergo some rite of passage to gain access to the Indian community (Good Tracks, 1973; Lewis & Ho, 1975). This trial period may well require an inordinate amount of patience from the psychologist. Most important to passing the test is the quality of the interaction and the sensitivity of the psychologist in interacting with the Indian client or community. Sensitivity and respect for social mores are especially important at this point. Initial successes are also important, since they can increase one's credibility in the Indian community; word travels quickly through close-knit Indian communities.

Communication Styles Relevant to Psychological Service Delivery

Communicating with American Indian clients may be complicated because of language differences. There is no universal, traditional Indian language. Although there are linguistic groups, each tribe is likely to have its own language. Intratribal dialects are also possible and add to linguistic variability. Just as they differ in their traditional languages, American

Indians differ in their abilities to use the English language. As with any bilingual group, these abilities range from a very articulate command of English to that of a limited receptive vocabulary and little or no expressive vocabulary. Although American Indians do show a diversity of English competence, most Indian clients are fluent enough in English to communicate with the non-Indian mental health service provider. However, in more isolated areas, language differences are more likely to be a problem. At times, problems with communication may also be reflecting other issues. One "full-blood" Cherokee, for example, refused to speak in English during an attempt interview with an Anglo service provider. Although he had the language skills to communicate, his reluctance to relate to Anglos prevented him from doing so.

Other differences in communicating styles may also be noted. One apparent difference is the amount of eye contact made and maintained. To many traditional Indians, direct eye contact is considered disrespectful; so, one must not engage in it or expect it. Avoidance of eye contact, in turn, is a gesture of respect (Lewis & Ho, 1975; Youngman & Sadongei, 1974). In contrast, Anglos expect and maintain more eye contact and may interpret its absence as rude, disrespectful, and hostile as well as conveying disinterest. Such differences have resulted in numerous misunderstandings. One unfortunate incident documents the inappropriate use of behavior modification techniques to increase the amount of eye contact exhibited by an 8-year-old Navajo girl (Goldstein, 1974). Following a behavior modification workshop, a counselor selected eye contact as an initial behavior in shaping a Navajo child to pay attention. Such a process did not acknowledge the cultural aspects of this child's behavior. The Navajo creation myth talks of a terrible monster called He-Who-Kills-With-His-Eyes. Navajo children hear of this monster and are taught to avert their eyes to avoid bringing harm to others (Moss & Goldstein, 1973). To a Navajo, a stare can then imply aggressive assault. The counselor was thus asking this child to exhibit a behavior inconsistent with her culture. The shaping of this culturally inappropriate behavior created additional problems for the Navajo child.

Social mores regarding touching may also vary. Cultural differences in handshaking may, unfortunately, interfere with the initiating of effective communication. The Anglo culture praises the use of a firm, aggressive handshake in greeting and decries the use of a weak one. One's inner strength may be evaluated on the basis of the strength of one's grip (within reason). In contrast, the American Indian culture views the firm handshake as aggressive and very disrespectful. These differences may also be transferred to touching in general. Although an Anglo may view a pat on the back or head or a hug as friendly behavior which may facilitate rapport, these same behaviors may be interpreted by an Indian client as inappropriate, aggressive, and disrespectful.

Differences in self-disclosing styles may also be apparent. Anglo mental health service providers are typically concerned, especially early in an interview, with collecting information about their clients. Traditional training in interviewing frequently results in the psychologist at some point asking a series of detailed and personal questions. The collection of social histories and other relevant information comes close to interrogations in which the psychologist asks for much information from the client and discloses little or nothing of himself or herself. Such an interviewing style is not consistent with traditional Indian styles of communicating.

To the American Indian, direct interrogation may be perceived as rude or, as acknowledged previously, may convey diagnostic incompetence and lack of healing power (Jilek-Aall, 1976). Instead, the American Indian may be much more comfortable if the psychologist shares some of himself or herself. Self-disclosing on the part of the psychologist may well generate more useful information than direct interrogation. If one is concerned, for example, about the family composition of a traditional American Indian, one might begin by sharing something about one's own family. The American Indian client may then feel more comfortable describing his or her own family. It should be acknowledged that such a style may initially be uncomfortable to the non-Indian mental heath provider. The non-Indian psychologist most likely has a history of one-sided interviewing and may interpret personal self-disclosures as a waste of time or as inappropriate. Nevertheless, it is a style that may at times be more productive. Particularly when one begins with a directive interviewing style to discover that it is not working (i.e., they may be met with much silence), it may be time to try an alternate style. Additional research efforts such as those of Dauphinais, Dauphinais, & Row (1981) are necessary to further clarify patterns of communication that are effective when working with American Indians.

The timing of communications may also vary across cultures. American Indian clients might approach non-Indian mental health service providers slowly. Silence may ensue and can be very appropriate. Cross-cultural service delivery may take more time, and taking things slowly may well be needed. Additionally, for some traditional people, the actual timing of events and/or discussions can be very important. There may be culturally specific rules that affect communication such as "One should not grieve or cry after dark," and so forth.

Mental health service providers experienced in working with American Indian clients also suggest that nonverbal communication may play different roles for Indians and Anglos. American Indians may be particularly aware of nonverbal communication. Perhaps because of some avoidance of both eye contact and direct questioning in interactions, they may be especially attuned to nonverbal aspects of communication. An Indian client may rapidly become aware if you are sending mixed messages, that is, if your body language, actions, tone of voice, facial expressions, and so forth do not match the verbal message that you are trying to get across. One should consider that the American Indian to whom one is talking is closely observing and testing the quality, feeling-tone, and correctness of the interaction. Sincerity and patience, although always important, may be especially so when working with traditional American Indians.

Cultural Values Relevant to Psychological Service Delivery

Cultural values potentially structure and impact all aspects of mental health service delivery. Comparisons of Anglo and Indian culture(s) reveal possible differences in a myriad of beliefs, perceptions, and interpretations of events. Although knowledge is insufficient to provide an absolute, definitive statement of all of the differences between Anglos and Indians, we can begin by acknowledging an amalgam of cultural differences that, at this point in time, seem relevant to the psychologist inexperienced in working with traditional American Indians.

Family Structure

Traditionally, Indian people lived within extended family networks. Members of the extended family have responsibilities to and for one another. This large network developed out of Indian traditions regarding blood relatives and the extended family system. Historically, the extended family and clans functioned as social units with the welfare of each individual being shared by all (Lewis, 1970; Locklear, 1972; Slaughter, 1976). Traditions vary from tribe to tribe as to who is considered a member of one's extended family, and the relationships can be quite complicated. Although the structure varies from tribe to tribe, the function is similar. Across tribes the relationships are meaningful to those involved.

Today, the extended family is a resource network for many Indian people. The extended family can give a member many relatives whose responsibilities are clear because of their place and position within the individual's social context. Family members are interdependent, and needs are met in many ways. For the Indian child in an extended family, many supports will be available.

The structure of the family is relevant to the structure of intervention or mental health service delivery (Attneave, 1969). Individual families may have a protocol for dealing with important issues and problems. Specific people are designated as important to seek out, involve, and listen to. For an American Indian with an existent, strong, extended family, seeking help from outside the family may be difficult. Needs are to be met by family members or by those within the tribe. Mental health service providers may be outsiders who are, therefore, hard to or even not to be approached. Even if services are sought out or requested from an outsider, the extended family may well continue to play an important role in intervention or treatment plans. Individual clients may wish to review information with and inform specific others. A psychologist unfamiliar with family protocol might be frustrated with an Indian client who does not commit him- or herself to decisions and courses of action. Decision making may take time and may need to involve many people.

When extended families provide a major source of support for Indian people, intervention strategies might involve the entire relevant network. The usefulness of involving the entire family in any sort of treatment situation has, as acknowledged, long been recognized by American Indians. More recently, the relevance of involving the extended family in treatment plans has been recognized by others as well. Mental health service providers should keep in mind this very effective technique in dealing with what appears to be individual problems (Attneave, 1969; Jilek-Aall, 1976; Lewis & Ho, 1975; President's Commission on Mental Health, 1978; Slaughter, 1976).

For some American Indians, however, extended families are not intact or available to provide primary supports. As acknowledged previously, much diversity exists among Indian people. Some American Indians are transitional or semiacculturated, and the family and tribal structures may provide varied assistance. And, for some American Indians, traditional ways have no (or little) impact on their behavior. Extended families are not intact and available to offer assistance. For individuals with weak or nonexistent family supports, other or new support systems might need to be identified or developed and, when applicable, used in interventions.

Child-Rearing Practices

Familiarization with traditional child-rearing practices may also be relevant to the psychologist working with Indian children and families. Various traditions may affect the Indian child's development. Ceremonies may begin early and play an important role in the life of the child. Indian child rearing is also influenced by the traditional belief that each child is unique from its earliest moments. Children are believed to be born with the power, ability, and right to make important choices or decisions. Noncoercive and noninterfering styles of parenting evolve from such a philosophy. Rearing patterns encourage the child's self-determinism, since freedom of choice is prized and respected (Good Tracks, 1973; Slaughter, 1976). Such parenting styles may at times be perceived as permissive or negligent.

Children traditionally are also allowed to develop freely. There is not a concern and preoccupation with developmental expectations or notions of developmental timing and sequencing. Although non-Indians may be concerned about the scheduling and timing of developmental milestones (e.g., the average or expected age for walking, talking, toilet training), Indian parents may not be. Their attitude instead may be that the child will do these things when he or she is ready, that "when" (within limits) is irrelevant, and that the child should not be pushed. Such an attitude, needless to say, does not fit well with the collection of detailed developmental histories that are frequently required as part of providing mental health services to children.

Traditional management of children is also positive—children enjoy the warmth and support of many. It is deemed a privilege to tend to and play with children. Children occupy a central position in tribal life and represent the renewal and preservation of life. They are taught correct ways to act by the examples of adults and older children, and the extended family provides a wide range of modeling resources (Morey & Gilliam, 1974).

Traditional Indians generally did not use physical punishment as a means of teaching and controlling their children (Freeman, 1968; Lewis, 1970; Morey & Gilliam, 1974; Slaughter, 1976; Wallis, 1954; Hill Witt, Note 1). Many believe(d) that children are especially beloved by the spiritual powers because they have so recently come from mystery. These same traditions hold that striking or punishing a child may cause the child to return to the mystery from which it came (Hill Witt, Note 1). Among traditional people, child abuse was almost nonexistent. Those parents who no longer share this mystic view may nonetheless perpetrate the behavior pattern that prohibits harsh physical or mental punishing of a child. The child who is misbehaving may be ignored or shunned or corrected quietly and verbally (Morey & Gilliam, 1974; Slaughter, 1976).

Although such child management styles sound idyllic, contemporary pressures on Indian people are breaking down such patterns for some families. Unemployment, alcoholism, and edemic poverty are factors that do not enhance parenting in any culture. We must acknowledge that, unfortunately, these problems do adversely affect many Indian children (Center for Social Research and Development, 1976). Additionally, there is much diversity in parenting among Indian people. The child-rearing philosophies and child-rearing techniques operable in the Indian culture may vary from the most traditional to the most acculturated or assimilated.

Noninterference

The American Indian culture has a great respect for individuality. Traditional Indian societies were organized with voluntary cooperation, and force or coercion was generally not employed. It is believed that every person has the right to choose what type of behavior he or she wants to exhibit as long as it does not interfere with the goals of the group. This has been described as the principle of noninterference (Good Tracks, 1973; Wax & Thomas, 1961). Belief in such a principle results in more traditional American Indians feeling that they do not have the right to interfere in others' activities and that others do not have the right to interfere in theirs. An American Indian parent, for example, may respect a young child's decision not to go to school and may perceive enforced school attendance as unnecessarily coercive. Intervention is not allowed or acceptable even when it is to keep the other person from doing something foolish or dangerous (within limits). Noninterference is not compatible with coercive styles of intervention (Good Tracks, 1973; Slaughter, 1976). Indeed, it has been suggested that certain styles of direct intervention are antithetical to the Indian value of noninterference (Good Tracks, 1973; Keller, 1972; Slaughter, 1976). The more traditional or less acculturated the individual, the more important this principle may be. Good Tracks (1973) further observed that "when an Anglo is moved to be his brother's keeper and that brother is an Indian, then almost everything he says or does seems rude, ill-mannered, or hostile" (p. 30).

Providing services may thus be interpreted as inappropriate interference by some American Indians. Intervention strategies should be carefully considered. Authoritarian or highly directing or controlling approaches may be particularly counterproductive. Lecturing, advice giving, and even making suggestions may, for example, be interpreted as intrusive. Again, patience and understanding of cultural differences might minimize the frustrations for both the service providers and their clients.

The Individual Versus the Group

Historically, a unique, complex relationship developed between the Indian individual and the group tribal system (Bryde, 1971). Most tribes respect the rights of all individuals. Each person is given the freedom to assume responsibility for his or her own decisions and behavior. Self-determinism is prized and valued. At the same time, there is a strong group cohesiveness, and individuals are sensitive to those around them. Decisions are ideally made within a larger social context, and group consensus may also be valued (Slaughter, 1976). Decisions may take time; since the rights of all are respected, group consensus is hoped and strived for. When group cohesiveness is strong, group work interventions may be especially effective.

Indian traditions also value modesty and humility in the presence of others. It may be considered ill-mannered to speak of one's accomplishments (Youngman & Sadongei, 1974). In Indian culture(s) modesty is a virtue, and its practice is pragmatic. To be overconfident and a braggart would bring social disapproval on oneself. Although one does not openly brag or try to stand out in front of the group, American Indians are also concerned about not bringing shame on themselves, family, or tribe. Bringing dishonor on oneself or one's people is especially undesirable.

The majority culture may, however, operate with different rules. Such cultural differences may be reflected in cross-cultural misinterpretations. In the classroom, for example, American Indian children may not feel comfortable talking about assets or things done well (Youngman & Sadongei, 1974). Such discomfort may extend to not volunteering answers and information to questions that are asked within the classroom. Such behaviors may pose problems for the Indian child whenever he or she is in an environment that is not sensitive to cultural diversities. The referral of a second-grade Pawnee child to a psychologist illustrates these problems. This

7-year-old boy was referred by his teacher to a psychologist because of his withdrawn, sullen behavior. This child seldom raised his hand in class and avoided eye contact with teachers. He was also reportedly not as competitive in recess play as the teacher thought he should be. The teacher perceived this behavior as depressed and as a sign of psychological disturbance. Such behaviors were not interpreted within the context of this child's more traditional rearing in a rural area of Oklahoma. Fortunately, the psychologist appreciated the role that culture played in this child's behavior. Although this child was not clinically depressed, he was clearly unhappy about the many demands on him that were inconsistent with his culture. Consultation with the teacher was an important part of the intervention, and changing the teacher's expectations and reactions improved this Indian child's affect and school performance and behavior.

An American Indian client may also not readily identify strengths and assets during an interview. Failure to do so may be culturally determined as opposed to being reflective of a poor self-concept or weak ego, or a passive, nonverbal interpersonal style. At times the Indian way of avoiding personal glory and gain has also created problems for service providers trying to gain a foothold or access to a tribe. Seeking out the leader of a group can be deceptive. Often the real authority lies with a person who is never identified as a visible authority to the service provider. The person might be a medicine man or woman or an elder within the tribe. Such a leader may be highly visible to the tribe, but not to an outsider.

Giving, Sharing, and Cooperating

Giving, sharing, and cooperating are all valued by traditional people (Lewis & Ho, 1975; Locklear, 1972; Spang, 1965). A nonmaterialistic view toward life may be held. People are likely to be evaluated personally rather than on the amount of possessions, and wealth may further be measured by one's willingness and ability to share. Thus, the accumulation of material belongings beyond those necessary to life may have little attraction for the traditional person. Those tribal members who do obtain more than is necessary may share this with those who have less than they. This practice of giving and sharing is in contrast to the majority culture. The Anglo culture more highly values the attainment of material possessions and wealth.

Such different cultural perceptions regarding the role of material possessions as well as giving and sharing have at times posed problems. As an example, a psychologist assessing the family background and home environment of an American Indian child as part of a custody or placement evaluation may be unduly influenced by the financial standing and material surroundings of the child. The application of Anglo middle-class standards to child welfare issues has, in particular, been identified as a major problem for Indian children (Center for Social Research and Development, 1976; Slaughter, 1976). Although national statistics are not widely accepted, all statistics do indicate a disproportionately high number of out-of-home placements of Indian children. One widely cited statistic (Unger, 1977) reports that 25% to 35% of all Indian children are taken from their families and placed in foster homes, adoptive homes, and/or institutions. Sensitization to cultural differences is essential if service providers are to make appropriate recommendations. The Indian Child Welfare Bill (P.L. 95-608) now further requires the use of appropriate standards for the removal of Indian children from their families and their subsequent placement in appropriate foster or adoptive homes.

Differences in cultural views on cooperation have also been noted. In the Anglo community, cooperation is viewed as desirable philosophically; however, competition is stressed in everyday life. Anglos compete with one another in many facets of life. To the American Indian, this type of behavior is undesirable, and cooperation is emphasized. Results of studies examining cooperation and competition among Indian children (Miller, 1973; Miller & Thomas, 1972) also suggest that the less acculturated the Indian children, the greater the occurrence of cooperative as opposed to competitive behavior. Once the service provider has gained acceptance into the group, this cooperative behavior can be of great use in almost any type of community work.

Time

Differing concepts of time may be one source of frustration for cross-cultural service delivery. The Anglo person is taught both early and throughout his or her lifetime to view life in a linear-time perspective. Events in history are recorded by their moment in time. Our daily lives are lived in concert with the movements of the hands of a clock and the marking off of days on a calendar. It is time to get up, time for breakfast, time to go to work; we have a 3 o'clock appointment. There are rules for time, such as it is rude to be late for a scheduled meeting but it is more proper to be fashionably late for a party, and so forth. In contrast, the traditional American Indian is not taught the linear view of time and its consequent rules. There is, instead, a spatial view that is difficult, if not impossible, for the non-Indian to grasp. Events, for example, take place at a location rather than at a certain time. The American Indians' temporal concepts have little or nothing to do with the movements of the hands of a clock (Lewis & Ho, 1975; Locklear, 1972, Spang, 1965). Natural phenomena, the occurrence of events, and the location in space of these events, as well as an internal feeling of synchronicity, are the determinants of the passage of time to an American Indian (Deloria, 1973). Therefore, to give a traditional American Indian an appointment to meet with you at 3 o'clock sharp on April 2 might virtually be as meaningless to him or her as the statement, "I will come to see you when the time is right, and the place is right," might be to you.

These differing views of temporal concepts have given rise to much banter among American Indians and Anglos who deal with them. The term typically used is *Indian time*. This is usually given as an explanation for what appears to be chronic lateness on the part of the Indian. Although this term may be jokingly used, its relevance for the service provider should not be minimized. This lateness can be easily misinterpreted by the non-Indian service provider as a lack of politeness, resistance to treatment, laziness, noninvolvement, and so forth. This may, however, simply be the result of a very different view of the concept of time. Unless understanding and patience are employed, the resulting conflicts from these different views can severely damage the relationship between the provider of services and the American Indian.

Aging

Cultural differences are also apparent in views on aging. The American Indian culture places great value on two periods in a person's life— childhood and old age. To the Indian, children are very special and desirable. Pregnancy is likely to be a joyous occasion, regardless of parental circumstances. Child-rearing practices also reflect the American Indian's valuing of children since parental (and family) warmth and permissiveness are characteristic of many Indian homes.

The other time period that is greatly valued is old age (Slaughter, 1976; Spang, 1965). The elder members of tribes have always been seen as valuable resources for the tribes. Their wisdom and experience are actively sought by members of the tribe, and they are often given preferential treatment. This is in contrast to the majority culture that places less value on the elderly and greater emphasis on youth. This difference should be kept in mind by the non-Indian service provider. Knowledge of the mores and history of the tribe or clan with whom one is working can most easily be obtained from the elders. This is one of their natural roles, and the seeking of knowledge from them will be highly condoned by the tribe. Additionally, gaining acceptance from and aligning oneself with respected elders may enhance one's own power and credibility. Interacting with these honored and revered members of the tribe may also be expected. Service providers could unwittingly offend Indian communities by not giving appropriate recognition to or preferential treatment to these elder members of the tribe. More traditional Indians, for example, may expect elder members of the tribe to be treated first. When selecting who is "next" from the waiting room, the traditional Indian may expect that it should be an elder as opposed to who is scheduled or who has waited the longest.

Religion

Religion has played and continues to play an important role in the life of American Indians (Bryde, 1971). Most tribes believe in a supreme force and a related deep reverence for nature. Today there is not an identified or unified American Indian religion, and Indian religion is best characterized as highly diversified. Although Indians now claim membership in most of the major Protestant and Catholic denominations, many of the traditional religions also still exist. For the more traditional, religion is a way life, and it is involved in every activity of the day. There is much mysticism involved, including a belief in spirits, both good and bad, spells, hexes, (termed by many as *being bothered*), anthropomorphism, and reincarnation. Such religious tenets may differ from those of Anglo religions.

How will these differing views of religion held by American Indians affect what a service provider does? If one is dealing with a very traditional American Indian, everything that occurs will be affected by his or her religious beliefs. Religion will pervade all acts, behaviors, social interactions, and so forth. Again, we should acknowledge that the behavior of the Indian population cannot be easily interpreted without some understanding of cultural differences. If an American Indian, for example, were to report seeing a spirit and talking with it to a psychologist who knew nothing of the true beliefs of that tribe, an accurate diagnosis would, in all likelihood, be difficult to make. For some traditional American Indians, spirits may be very much a part of a traditional Indian belief system and not visual or auditory hallucinations. Such information would be essential to a psychologist or other service provider working with such an American Indian client.

A major aspect of Indian religion is a feeling of harmony with nature (Bryde, 1971; Spang, 1965). The land, water, and forests are believed to belong to all and not just to a segment of the population. The mystical view of being at one with the universe may result in some American Indians unquestioningly accepting the position in which they find themselves (Locklear, 1972). An acceptance of things as they are, a harmony with nature, and a belief in noninterference may not be consistent with mental health interventions. As noted previously, more active styles of intervention may be especially problematic when working with traditional American Indians.

Culture Conflict

Culture conflict and clash pose special problems for American Indian children and families. The old Iroquois saying about how one cannot for long have one's feet placed in two canoes is particularly appropriate for these families. To operate effectively in both cultures with a certain level of authenticity in each has been called "controlled schizophrenia," and perhaps it is (Hill Witt, Note 1). In any event, it is difficult, and there are special problems for Indian people who live in or between two cultures.

For some Indian children, adjustment to another culture comes with adjustment to school. Consider the culture shock that surely must be experienced by a young Indian child from a traditional family when he or she enters first grade in a typical Anglo elementary school. Developmental reviews suggest that during middle childhood, indicators of stress begin to increase for American Indian children. Clearly a number of school-related problems begin to emerge during those years.

The split between Indian ways and Anglo ways can also exacerbate the normal adolescent task of identity formation (Allen, 1973). Numerous social indicators clearly signal stress for Indian adolescents, and rates for drug abuse and suicide have rapidly accelerated for Indian youths in recent years (Bynum, 1972; Muskrat, 1973; President's Commission on Mental Health, 1978). Such statistics suggest that adolescence, although typically a critical period, may be especially so for Indian youth.

The case of a 15-year-old Indian adolescent referred for a psychological evaluation illustrates some of the compounded stresses that some Indian youth experience. A serious suicide attempt was the most recent of a series of problems for this adolescent. As a young child she was traditionally reared. However, her family setting was a troubled one, and she was sexually abused by her father. At the age of 12 she was removed from her home. Since then, unfortunately, she has resided in eight different foster homes. At the time of the evaluation, she was experiencing tremendous guilt over her incestuous history. Her anger and guilt over her past pain led her to reject and deny her home "where bad things happened" and the culture of her childhood. As part of renouncing her past, she demanded that the staff treat her as a non-Indian. Her struggles to integrate an acceptable self were intense, and inpatient services were required.

The search for an Indian identity goes in many directions and is compounded by the immediate difficulty of defining an Indian. There is no single definition of an Indian. Individuals vary in degree of blood and level of acculturation. For some purposes one may be an Indian but not for others, and one may be accepted as an Indian by some individuals but not by others. This search for a definition involves both legal and emotional issues.

In a search for identity, the adolescent defines self in relation to culture. Various styles or levels of acculturating have been identified that may be relevant to identity formation (McNickle, 1968; Spindler, 1955). Although some individuals may be lost between two worlds or cultures, others with bicultural capabilities may have unique combinations of skills that can be an advantage in both Indian and Anglo society. Indeed, for some, the problems of the "marginal man" might be seen as advantages rather than liabilities (McFee, 1972). An awareness of varied styles of acculturation is important to the psychologist who wishes to relate across cultures. The structuring of psychological interventions must consider where the American Indian client is along the acculturation continuum. Additional attention to the diversity of American Indians across the acculturation continuum is clearly needed to enhance psychological service delivery to all American Indian children and families.

Our review of cultural values relevant to psychological service providers has necessarily been brief. The state of the art of cross-cultural service delivery is an underdeveloped area. We have presented a number of cultural differences that seem relevant to the psychologist inexperienced in working with traditional American Indians. These, as well as other still-to-be identified values, may well affect many aspects of service delivery. Perhaps with this beginning, we can help initiate the lengthy process of ultimately enhancing psychological service delivery to American Indian children and families. Additional study and research are clearly needed to document, refine, and give new direction to such efforts.

Reference Note

1. Hill Witt, S. Perspectives on Native American families. In V. Seitz (Chair), *Cultural diversity in the international year of the child.* Symposium presented at the meeting of the American Psychological Association, New York, September 1979.

References

Allen, J. R. The Indian adolescent: Psychosocial tasks of the Plains Indian of Western Oklahoma. *American Journal of Orthopsychiatry,* 1973, *43,* 368–375.

Attneave, C. L. Therapy in tribal settings and urban network intervention. *Family Process,* 1969, *8,* 192–210.

Beiser, M., and Attneave, C. L. Mental health services for American Indians: Neither feast nor famine. *White Cloud Journal,* 1978, *1*(2), 3–10.

Bergman, R. L. A school for medicine men. *American Journal of Psychiatry,* 1973, *130,* 663–666.

Bryde, J. F., *Modern Indian psychology.* Vermillion: Institute of Indian Studies, University of South Dakota, 1971.

Bureau of the Census. *1980 census of population: Age, sex, race, and Spanish origin of the population by regions, divisions, and states.* Washington, D.C.: U.S. Government Printing Office, 1981.

Bynum, J. Suicide and the American Indian: An analysis of recent trends. In M. M. Bahr, B. A. Chadwick, and R. C. Day (Eds.), *Native Americans today: Sociological perspectives.* New York: Harper & Row, 1972.

Center for Social Research and Development. *Indian child welfare: A state-of-the-field study.* Denver, Colo.: Denver Research Institute, University of Denver, 1976.

Dauphinais, P., Dauphinais, L., & Rowe, W. Effects of race and communication style on Indian perceptions of counselor effectiveness. *Counselor Education and Supervision,* 1981, *21,* 72–80.

Deloria, V., Jr. *God is red.* New York: Grosset and Dunlap, 1973.

Fields, S. Mental health and the melting pot. *Innovations,* 1979 *6*(2), 2–3.

Freeman, D. Adolescent crisis of the Kiowa-Apache Indian male. In E. D. Brody (Ed.), *Minority group adolescents in the United States.* Baltimore, Md.: William & Wilkins, 1968.

Goldstein, G. Behavior modification: Some cultural factors. *The Psychological Record*, 1974, *24*, 89–91.

Good Tracks, J. G., Native American noninterference. *Social Work*, 1973, *18*, 30–34.

Green, B. E., Sack, W. H., and Pambrum, A. A review of child psychiatric epidemiology with special reference to American Indian and Alaska Native children. *White Cloud Journal*, 1981, *2*(2), 22–36.

Jilek-Aall, L. The western psychiatrist and his nonwestern clientele. *Canadian Psychiatric Association Journal*, 1976, *21*(6), 353–359.

Keller, G. Bicultural social work and anthropology. *Social Casework*, 1972, *53*, 455–465.

Korman, M. National conference on levels and patterns of professional training in psychology: The major themes. *American Psychologist*, 1974, *29*, 441–449.

LaFromboise, T., Dauphinais, P., and Rowe, W. Indian students' perception of positive helper attributes. *Journal of American Indian Education*, 1980, *19*, 13–16.

LaFromboise, T., Dixon, D. American Indian perception of trustworthiness in a counseling interview. *Journal of Counseling Psychology*, 1981, *28*, 135–139.

Lewis, C. *Indian families of the Northwest coast: The impact of change*. Chicago: University of Chicago Press, 1970.

Lewis, R. C., & Ho, M. K. Social work with Native Americans. *Social Work*, 1975, *20*, 379–382.

Lockart, B. Historic distrust and the counseling of American Indians and Alaska Natives. *White Cloud Journal*, 1981, *2*(3), 31–34.

Locklear, H. H. American Indian myths. *Social Work*, 1972, *17*, 72–80.

McFee, M. The 150% man, a product of Blackfeet acculturation. In H. M. Bahr, B. A. Chadwick, and R. C. Day (Eds.), *Native Americans today: Sociological perspectives*. New York: Harper & Row, 1972.

McNickle, D. The sociocultural setting of Indian life. *The American Journal of Psychiatry*, 1968, *125*, 219–223.

Miller, A. G. Integration and acculturation of cooperative behavior among Blackfoot Indian and Non-Indian Canadian children. *Journal of Cross-Cultural Psychology*, 1973, *4*, 374–380.

Miller, A. G., and Thomas, R. Cooperation and competition among Blackfoot Indian and urban Canadian children. *Child Development*, 1972, 43, 1104–1110.

Morey, S. M., and Gilliam, O. L. *Respect for life*. Garden City, New York: Waldorf Press, 1974.

Moss, R. N., and Goldstein, G. S. An encounter experience among the Navajo. *Social Change*, 1973, *3*(1), 3–6.

Muskrat, J. Thoughts on the Indian dilemma. *Civil Rights Digest*, 1973 (Fall), 46–50.

Pedersen, P. B., and Marsella, A. J. The ethical crisis for cross-cultural counseling and therapy. *Professional Psychology*, 1982, *13*, 492–500.

President's Commission on Mental Health, Special Populations Subpanel. *Mental Health of American Indians and Alaskan Natives*. Washington, D.C.: U.S. Government Printing Office, 1978.

Russo, N. F., Olmedo, E. L., Stapp, J., and Fulcher, R. Women and minorities in psychology. *American Psychologist*, 1981, *36*, 1315–1363.

Slaughter, E. L., *Indian child welfare: A review of the literature.* Center for Social Research and Development. Denver, Colo.: Denver Research Institute, 1976.

Spang, A. Counseling the Indian. *Journal of American Indian Education,* 1965, *5,* 10–15.

Spindler, G. D. *Sociocultural and psychological processes in Menomini acculturation.* Berkeley: University of California, 1955.

Sue, S., Allen, D. B., and Conaway L. The responsiveness and equality of mental health care to Chicanos and Native Americans. *American Journal of Community Psychology,* 1978, *6,* 137–146.

Trimble, J. Value differences among American Indians. Concerns for the concerned counselor. In P. Pedersen, W. Lonner, and J. Draguns (Eds.), *Counseling across cultures.* Honolulu: University Press of Hawaii, 1976.

Unger, S. *The destruction of American Indian families.* New York: Association on American Indian Affairs, 1977.

Wax, R. H., and Thomas, R. K. Anglo intervention vs. native noninterference. *Phylon,* 1961, *22* (Winter), 53–56.

Wallis, R. S. The overt fears of Dakota Indian children. *Child Development,* 1954, *25,* 185–192.

Youngman, G., and Sadongei, M. Counseling the American Indian child. *Elementary School Guidance and Counseling,* 1974, *8,* 273–277.

5 American Indians: Working with Individuals and Groups

E. Daniel Edwards and Margie E. Edwards

THERE ARE APPROXIMATELY ONE million American Indians living in the continental United States today.[1] The 1970 census reported that about 80 percent of all American Indians claim to be members of some 250 tribes.[2] In addition, there are an almost equal number of native Alaskan groups located throughout Alaska.[3] Each of these tribes is unique. Many of them continue to maintain their own tribal languages, values, customs, religions, and leadership systems.[4]

The Place of the Group in American Indian Culture

Historically, American Indians developed societies with well-defined roles, responsibilities, government and economic systems, recreational and leisure styles, religious rites and ceremonies, and social behavior in which group involvement, support, and consensus played major roles. Their social, economic, and political traditions reflect a strong emphasis on group involvement and decision making.

Group solidarity was achieved in a number of ways. Many "work" assignments were combined with recreational and leisure activities. Elderly American Indians taught the younger people crafts, narrated myths, gave moral talks, and in other ways instructed the young.[5]

Some tribes utilized "potlatches" to achieve group solidarity. These gatherings were held to bestow titles or other honors, to conduct family rites, to show mourning, to announce a new chief, to save face, and to demonstrate power and wealth. All members of the family group presenting the potlatch participated in the preparation and actual event, which would last for several days and feature huge amounts of food, dancing and singing, and the giving of many gifts.

Group consensus was valued by most Indian tribes. Many meetings, discussions, and "powwows" were lengthy because American Indians strove for group consensus, not majority rule, in their decision-making processes that would affect the majority of Indian people. Each individual's opinion was heard and weighed in arriving at decisions affecting the group.

Edwards, E. D., and Edwards, M. E. (1980). American Indians: Working with individuals and groups. *Social Casework, 61,* 498–506. Reprinted by permission of Family Service America.

Although group consensus was highly valued, so was the Indians' appreciation for each person as an individual. Most tribes respected the individual and allowed each person a great deal of freedom and autonomy, particularly in those areas that would have more repercussions for the individual than for the group as a whole. However, Indian values were repeatedly reinforced. The individual was well acquainted with those values and roles that reinforced group closeness. They were also well aware of areas in which individual decision making was allowed.

Cultural Strengths and Weaknesses

Culturally, American Indians enjoy many group activities. They are energetic, fun-loving people who enjoy sports, games,[6] music, crafts, participation in ceremonies, and a variety of other small and large group recreational and cultural activities. Hospitality, generosity, good humor, and good sportsmanship are values that have been emphasized in their group activities. Self-discipline, self-control, and self-development were emphasized through play. Feelings of pleasure and enjoyment were shared by participants and spectators.[7]

Since the time of Christopher Columbus, many detrimental cultural changes have been imposed on the American Indian people. In 1890, after the massacre of the Sioux at Wounded Knee, South Dakota, all Indians recognized as such by the federal government were relocated on reservations.[8] This disruption of Indian culture, combined with subsequent attempts at forced assimilation, broken treaties, and unfulfilled promises has contributed greatly to the Indian's distrust of Anglos and subsequent poor relationships. Because of these events, American Indians may require a substantial time commitment before they develop professional relationships with non-Indian social workers.

The diversification of American Indian tribes and individuals may also contribute toward blocking of group cohesion. Historically, some tribal groups have competed against one another, and there are carry-overs of past events to present-day relationships that may negatively affect group involvement. Many different lifestyles and philosophies exist among American Indians today, which sometimes lead to feelings of diviseness.

Stereotypes and Myths

A number of stereotypes and myths persist regarding American Indians, many of which are incorrect or short-sighted. Examples of these stereotypes include: Indians are oil-rich, lazy, drunken, unproductive, good with their hands but not with their heads, on the government dole, stoic, long-suffering, warlike, blood-thirsty, debauched, barbaric, unemotional, aloof, and with little hope for the future. Other stereotypes view Indians as proud, controlled, reserved, honest, sharing, and self-sufficient.

American Indians are as individualistic as members of any other group. These stereotypes, however, cannot help but influence their feelings toward themselves as well as their perceptions of the non-Indian's attitude toward the Indian. The National Congress of American Indians felt so strongly about the image of American Indians that they began a national public relations campaign in 1969 to create a "new and true picture" of American Indians that would portray important values and result in an improvement of the Indians' image to Indians and non-Indians alike.[9]

Relationships in Cross-Racial Situations

Dealings with Authority

The historical treatment of American Indians provides some basis for their suspiciousness of Anglo people in "authority" roles. On occasion, Indian clients have been "promised" results that were not obtained, or they may have misunderstood the procedures, "promises," or role of the professional person. These misunderstandings may lead to suspiciousness, mistrust, and reluctance to become involved with other professionals.

Social workers should move slowly, identify problems and procedures clearly, make commitments regarding situations in which they have control, follow through consistently, and use client strengths appropriately in order to help develop feelings of trust and establish professional relationships. For example, an eight-year-old girl was returned from foster care to the care of her mother. A month later, the girl ran away. Her mother located her, spoke with her firmly, and told her that she was wanted and needed and was never to run away again. The daughter complied. The social worker praised the mother for the strength she had shown in locating her daughter and setting the limits for her daughter's behavior.

In working with an American Indian client, the social worker should assume an appropriate authoritarian position that permits the client to assume as much responsibility as possible for his or her activities, discussions, and decision making.

Sociocultural Expectations

Indians have been taught to value themselves, their families, clans, and tribes, and to adhere to values that are revered by their various tribal groups. When working with these clients, social workers should consider the values of each specific tribe.

As social workers learn about the specific Indian tribal group with which they are working, they will be more able to discuss tribal matters, cultural customs, and current areas of concern to the group. This understanding will facilitate a more successful intervention.

It is important for social workers to understand that Indian values are interwoven throughout their culture, lifestyle, religion, and daily activities. In many Indian tribal groups tribal values are reinforced through the use of ceremonies. When ceremonies are held, it is important for family members to participate, even if participation requires traveling long distances or giving up other commitments.

Non-Indian social workers should expect that it will take time before they are trusted and accepted by the Indian people with whom they work. The sometimes rapid turnover of social work staff has contributed to the wariness with which American Indians approach relationships with a new social worker. Social workers can expect that it will take three to six months before they are accepted by the people in traditional Indian communities.

In the "not too distant past," all social workers working with American Indians have been non-Indian. In recent years, a number of professional and paraprofessional American Indian people have been employed to work with Indians. Regardless of the ethnic background, Indian clients will individually and collectively assess the expertise and commitment of any helping person before relationships will develop.

Introspection is often difficult for Indians. Self-evaluations may also be difficult for students involved in professional training programs. Indians reared in the traditional ways of their tribes may have difficulty talking about themselves. Indian tradition dictates that Indians do not exaggerate their abilities or use their own name or the word "I" excessively. Traditionally, Indian people are expected to know their strengths but not to exaggerate them; they are to exhibit confidence, but not flaunt their skills. An Indian client may bring another person with them to an interview so that they will have someone there who can speak on their behalf.

American Indians believe that people should be able to understand one another; it is not necessary to explain one's feelings or problems in detail. The Indian client, therefore, often expects the professional person to be able to understand without the client having to voice concerns in detail.

Many American Indians have learned to relate to new situations by being passive. The pace of the interview must be geared to motivate clients to respond more as an interview progresses. Social workers should strive to feel comfortable in periods of silence, to listen, hear, understand, and respond as an American Indian would as important considerations are discussed. One technique that is helpful in building a relationship with American Indians is helping clients resolve tangible problems. Economic needs, employment referrals, health care, school-related problems, housing, and other tangible needs often bring clients to a social service agency. Helping an Indian client obtain the services desired facilitates the development of a relationship that may continue in subsequent contacts or allow the client to return for services in the future.

Language Problems

Most American Indians are bilingual; however, some Indians, particularly older ones, may not speak English very well or at all. A social worker must assess the client's communication skills and respond appropriately.

Because the bilingual client's vocabulary in English may be limited, verbal messages may be misinterpreted. It is not uncommon for American Indians to ask how long they "have to come" to see a social worker, when what they are really asking is "will this experience be long enough and important enough for me to risk getting involved?" It is also common for young people to ask repeatedly when groups will be held, will they be allowed to attend, and so on. This constant questioning of others about events is a result of past experiences in which many enjoyable activities were cancelled or discontinued. They fear that this enjoyable experience may also not continue. Social workers need to clarify the purposes for social work intervention and the time commitment, and help clients develop positive therapeutic relationships at an appropriate pace.

Clients may also not understand what is being proposed in the case of a group experience. On one occasion, several group members were participating in a group activity collecting pine cones in the nearby mountains. They also went to the local park to add more to their collection. Several group members then asked if they could also go to the cemetery to find more pine cones. One group member did not know what a "cemetery" was; she came from a very traditional Indian family who had a great deal of respect for dead people. Upon entering the cemetery, she became very frightened. Had the group worker told her the group was planning to go to a "graveyard" instead of a "cemetery," the girl would have understood the terminology used and would have been in a better position to express her feelings about this experience.

With some bilingual clients, it is necessary to explain problems that the English-speaking social worker can express in English with one or two words. In some Indian languages there is not a word that means "retarded" or "developmentally disabled." Some words that are closely related are entirely different. For example, one Indian mother was very frightened when she asked, "You don't mean my child is crazy, do you?" when the social worker had tried to explain that her child had some learning problems and would probably be classified as an educably retarded youngster. It therefore requires a great deal of time to work with bilingual clients where language barriers are present.

Using Culture-Specific Techniques

Because of the vast number of individual tribal groups, it is important for the individual and cultural values of each American Indian, individually and as a group, to be considered in social work intervention. Efforts should be directed toward helping clients understand the social work intervention process. It is also important to consider modifying procedures when it would be beneficial to the client.

Sometimes Indian clients' problems are related to someone close who has recently died. In the interview process, when a topic directly relates to the deceased, it is wise to use a term such as sister, brother, father, and so on, other than the person's given name because it is a violation of tradition to use the dead person's name. Moreover, if the social worker feels that he or she may not have the expertise to handle the above topic, a suggestion could be made to involve the skills of a medicine man, should the client desire.

When helping clients solve problems, a social worker may use role-playing techniques that reflect the here and now within the client's culture. The clan system may be utilized to support or implement change. For example, if a male Indian is having problems with his in-laws, and his culture does not allow him to speak directly to his mother-in-law, role playing the use of other clan members as intermediary sources could be helpful.

Eye contact may sometimes cause uneasiness with an Indian client. The worker should develop a technique of looking elsewhere when interviewing or develop an activity or game where worker and client can talk without constant eye contact.

It is important for workers to understand when Indian clients may be experiencing conflicts related to their cultural values. For example, one young adult Indian male had a difficult time identifying goals for his future. It was very difficult for him to verbalize these frustrations when working with a social worker because he had been taught by a very traditional father that "any Indian 'worth his salt' was to handle all of his problems on his own." It was important for the social worker to verbalize this conflict between the client's own personal frustrations and the expectations of his culture. After discussing these verbally, the young man was able to look at his options and plan for his future. However, at the end of the interview he showed evidence of being embarrassed. During the subsequent interview, he was very quiet. The social worker once again verbalized the conflict and identified for the young man the ways in which he was assuming responsibility for himself; the worker also provided feedback that indicated he saw the young man as a valuable, worthwhile, strong, capable person. This feedback was important to the self-esteem of the client. The client terminated shortly after this interview, but would return for counseling on a limited basis.

The setting in which the social work services are provided is important to the success of the treatment. Some young people who have been reared on Indian reservations will be more verbal and responsive in outdoor settings, where the atmosphere is similar to their home environment. Adults may also prefer to work with the social worker on the porch or in an outdoor patio area.

The use of humor, particularly as it relates to being teased and teasing one another about incidents related to everyday living, can help set a positive atmosphere for the Indian client. Indian people tease and use humor as an indication of acceptance and comfort. If social workers can make fun of themselves and the things they do, Indian people often read this as an indication of the social worker's comfort in the experience also.

It is important for social workers to assess the uniqueness of each client, whether the client is seeing the worker as an individual or as a member of a group. In dealing with the Indian client, however, it is also important to assess the degree of affiliation and identification with traditional Indian culture, the conflicts that exist between minority and majority culture values, the willingness to risk, and the real issues with which the Indian client desires help.

A consistency of appointments with clients should be maintained, and appointments should not be broken, unless absolutely necessary. Sessions should be held regularly even if some members are missing. Clients should be given time to warm up to the counseling or group situation, time to think through matters being discussed and possible alternatives, and time to unwind in terminating the sessions.

When a client does not keep an appointment, the worker should make an effort to contact the client to let the client know that he or she was missed, then the appointment should be rescheduled. The worker should avoid imposing any feelings of guilt on the client. Clients should understand what they can expect from the social worker and what the social worker will expect from them. Once the relationship has been developed, it is important to identify goals and to partialize the assignments to be accomplished. Short-range goals often help clients see that something of worth is being accomplished.

Relationships with Indian clients take time. Workers must avoid overestimating a relationship initially. Even though a relationship is developing, and the client's goals are being worked on, the Indian person may still desire distance in the relationship.

Social workers must not underestimate the relationship at termination. Many American Indians develop close working relationships with professional people, both individually and in groups, and may wish to continue the relationship, even though it is necessary to terminate. Clients may become physically ill, avoid final sessions, develop other problems, or negate the benefit of the services they have received. They may, however, respond with appreciation and identification of areas of personal growth.

Because of the Indian's belief in the value of individuality, some of them will consider it inappropriate to discuss the problems of other members of their families in meetings with social workers.[10] Social workers can be helpful by expressing an understanding of this value and the conflict it may cause. The value of individuality also dictates to some Indians that they must resolve individual problems on their own. In such situations, social workers should identify their role as a "sounding board" and help Indian clients develop their own plans for working through the conflicts involved.

Intervention Strategies and Skills with Groups

The value that American Indians place on consensus can readily be used in forming the basis of group work practice.[11] When working with clients in groups, solutions to problems should take into consideration the Indian client's cultural traditions and values. These cultural resources may be seen by the clients as valuable and appropriate resources to use in other times of stress as well.

Working with Indians in task groups may require a long-term investment. Individual citizens and elected or appointed tribal representatives often seek to be involved in decisions that will affect Indian people as a group. Consensus for community activities and programs is still valued by some American Indian tribes.

One of the roles of a professional worker in task groups is to interpret and clarify policies for committees, suggest viable alternatives, help identify leadership and potential leadership among American Indian people, see that programs and policies are enacted at a suitable pace, and support appropriately American Indians who assume leadership roles on policymaking boards and committees. These procedures may be time-consuming, but they will result in more effective policy decisions. For example, one task group assignment on an Indian reservation involved several months of work to establish a boys' home. Members of the Indian community were actively involved in all aspects of this project, from initial planning to implementation. When the home was established, it was accomplished with the support, interest, and sanction of the community.

It is important that practitioners working with groups of American Indians become acquainted with resources available in the community. Once relationships are established, referrals for other community services can be a part of the group experience. The interest and support of the worker and other group members may motivate some participants to seek assistance from other agencies.

Groups led by more than one leader have been a successful technique, especially with groups of children, adolescents, married couples, and families. Co-leaders provide support for one another as well as gain greater insight and awareness into the problems and strengths of group members.

Providing positive reinforcement for clients is particularly important. In the initial stages of a group's development, it may be more appropriate to provide positive reinforcement on an individual basis. Being praised in front of other group members in the initial stages of a group's development may often be embarrassing and culturally inappropriate in working with groups of American Indians. When group cohesiveness is developed, group members may appropriately provide positive support to one another.

Treatment methods with American Indians experiencing alcoholism problems should be task-centered. Social workers should continue to reach out to Indian clients with understanding and sensitivity. Specific tangible goals should be identified for Indian clients that can realistically be achieved.

Family group sessions with Indian families may involve participation from extended family members, members of the clan, and others. These sessions may need to be informal in nature and require longer periods of time to develop relationships and to achieve desired goals. The work accomplished, however, will be with the knowledge and support of a large number of significant people.

Youth Groups

The wide diversification of American Indians lends itself to considerable creativity in programming for Indian groups. Activity groups are especially enjoyed by Indian youths. These groups have been helpful in boarding school settings, because they provide group members with an opportunity to discuss mutual interests and concerns, to develop talents and skills, to enjoy experiences in the community, to develop leadership skills, to discuss future goals and plans, and to enjoy the association of one another.

Leaderships groups with young Indians have been particularly successful. These groups are designed to help group members practice and develop their leadership skills and share their group experiences with others.

Special interest groups may also be developed to meet specific needs of Indian young people. A group may focus on participation in outdoor activities such as hiking, mountain climbing, hunting, or fishing. Other groups may develop special interests such as American Indian dancing, beading, or making dance costumes. A cooking group, where youths learn to cook traditional Indian foods, could provide an appropriate outlet for young people.

Community or school project groups can be developed for Indian youths to choose their own projects. They may ask to have the local gym remain open one night per week. They may develop a volleyball program at the gymnasium or Indian center. Another project may seek to have the school library open one night per week with special help available to Indian students to help them with homework assignments, school papers, or special projects. For example, one young Indian leadership group planned and decorated a float for their high school's homecoming parade. Other Indian classmates were somewhat apprehensive about participating in building or riding on the float until they saw the finished product, which was so attractive that several young Indian people volunteered to ride on the float.

Groups that help to make Indian young people aware of community resources are helpful. Group members could visit employment centers, job service centers, businesses that hire young people for on-the-job training, technical colleges, junior colleges, and four-year colleges. It is important for young Indian people to talk with older Indians who are actively involved in employment, training, or educational programs as they visit various sites.

Groups which focus on increasing positive feelings about one's "Indianness" could also be helpful. The University of Utah's American Indian Social Work Career Training Program staff recently conducted a group experiment with American Indian girls.[12] Group members participated in a number of discussions and activities that were related to traditional and modern-day American Indian activities, including dancing, singing, beading, crafts, foods, and games. Discussions related to historical, cultural, and present-day concerns of American Indians. Everyone involved perceived this group as a positive experience. The use of experimental groups such as this have been successful with Indian young people, who seem to enjoy participating in innovative group experiences.

Groups for the Elderly

Groups for the elderly have been particularly well received. They enjoy participating in crafts and cultural activities specific to their own cultural group and to other tribes as well as doing modern-day crafts that originate in the dominant culture. Excursions of both long and short duration are motivating group activities. Some Indian aged groups have planned fundraising events to provide financial assistance for such excursions. They enjoy sports activities, including bowling and golf. Dinners and special events where food is served are also very popular among American Indian aged. American Indian elderly have keen senses of humor; they enjoy participating in groups, and enjoy one another's company. They tend to be willing to risk and involve themselves in new activities.

What the Worker Can Do

Groups can be organized around clear purposes and goals. Group members should actively participate in the formulation and modification of these goals. Programming for group sessions should tie in directly and specifically to individual and group goals.

An effective group programming method is that of "unit programming." Group workers and members agree to focus on the attainment of two or three goals over a period of four to ten group sessions. These goals may include self-image improvement, development of communication or problem-solving skills, developing better relationships with peers, understanding racial and cultural differences and similarities, or achieving skills in American Indian activities. The repetition involved in unit programming is reinforcing and facilitates the attainment of goals.

Group members should be encouraged to use their new skills in their relationships with people outside of the group. Assignments should be given to group members to assist them to achieve their goals. Assignments should be discussed at each group session with continued encouragement or modification as necessary.

For example, Sharon, a teenage girl who did not have many friends, was given two tickets to a weekend movie at her boarding school. Sharon agreed that she would take a friend with her. The following week Sharon returned to see the group workers with the two movie tickets. Sharon said that she had wanted to go to the movie, but was reluctant to ask a friend to go with her. The assignment was restated for the coming weekend. The next week the group worker met Sharon and the friend who had gone with her to the movie. This "beginning friendship" was then generalized to others at the boarding school.

A group worker should use the communication patterns that are evident in the group. For example, one group of adolescent girls was particularly artistic. The group worker asked each of the girls to draw a picture of something that was causing them some concern or difficulty either at school, home, or with their friends. Every group member willingly participated in this activity. This exercise helped many of the quieter group members to discuss their concerns more freely.

Group workers should reserve time after each group session for group members who would like to stay and talk individually or in subgroups with the worker. A flexible time period for group sessions also allows group members to bring up areas of concern when they are ready to do so. It is not unusual for Indian group members to bring up problems at the end of a group session; this is most often not an avoidance technique.

For example, a young adult alcoholism group was meeting to reinforce the maintenance of their sobriety. After an involved group discussion, one group member indicated that she had a concern that she wanted to share with the group. She then proceeded to discuss a "dry drunk" incident (an experience where a recovering alcoholic has all the symptoms and reactions commonly associated with heavy drinking, when no drinking has occurred). She was very troubled by this experience. The group helped to identify the incident, shared similar experiences, and offered understanding and possible alternatives for ways of handling future episodes. She was most relieved, and expressed her appreciation to the group.

Group workers have alternative methods to offer as many services as possible to clients, thus allowing them choices. The more choices which can be made available to American Indians, the better the opportunities for success. Social work services may be offered to clients individually, with their friends or acquaintances, in subgroups, small groups, leadership groups, or special project groups.

Implications for Education and Practice

Social work education should undertake to prepare American Indians and non-Indians to practice with people from both cultures. Students should be prepared to practice social work with individuals, groups, and communities in a generalist approach. Social work techniques that have the most potential for work with Indians should be emphasized in innovative and creative approaches.

Practicum opportunities should be made available for Indians in agencies serving Indians exclusively, agencies serving non-Indians exclusively, and agencies serving both Indians and non-Indians. All students should have opportunities for choice in terms of their practicum placements and an opportunity to work with clients from a variety of ethnic cultures. Practicum instruction should be highly professional. American Indian professional faculty and consultants should be available in both the academic and practicum settings.

Students should be encouraged to invest themselves in an ongoing learning process. This process should encourage students to develop an interest in continuous learning that will better enable them to meet the unique needs of special populations throughout their social work careers.

Students should gain expertise with several group techniques and how they may be combined and integrated to provide the best possible services for American Indians. Students should acquire both activity skills (including American Indian cultural activities) and discussion approaches to meet the needs of each client and group more effectively. Students should also strive for greater self-awareness and understanding of themselves and their professional roles.

Specific American Indian content should be integrated into the curriculum in such a way as to provide a knowledge base to enhance social work practice with Indians. This knowledge base should include historical, cultural, and present-day concerns. Students should understand that minority people participate within two cultures—the majority culture and their own minority culture—and they must understand the concerns and strengths utilized by American Indians as they negotiate relationships within both the majority and their minority cultures.

Reference Notes

1. Jamake Highwater, *Fodor's Indian America* (New York: David McKay, 1975), p. 61.
2. Mary Ellen Ayers, "Counseling the American Indian," *Occupational Outlook Quarterly* (Washington, D.C.: U.S. Department of Labor, Spring 1977), p. 24.

3. Ibid.

4. Ibid.

5. Clark Wissler, *Indians of the United States* (New York: Anchor Books, 1966), p. 274.

6. Stewart Cullen, *Games of the North American Indians* (New York: Dover Publications, 1975).

7. Brad Steiger, *Medicine Talks: A Guide to Walking in Balance and Surviving on the Earth Mother* (New York: Doubleday, 1975), p. 67.

8. Sar A. Levitan and William B. Johnston, *Indian Giving: Federal Programs for Native Americans* (Baltimore: Johns Hopkins University, 1975), p. 7.

9. Howard M. Bahr, Bruce A. Chadwick, and Robert C. Day, eds., *Native Americans Today: Sociological Perspectives* (New York: Harper and Row, 1972), pp. 48–49, 524.

10. Ronald G. Lewis and Man Keung Ho, "Social Work with Native Americans," *Social Work* 20 (September 1975), 380–81.

11. Charles E. Farris and Lorene S. Farris, "Indian Children: The Struggle for Survival," *Social Work* 21 (September 1976): 388.

12. E. Daniel Edwards et al., "Enhancing Self-Concept and Identification with 'Indianness' of American Indian Girls," *Social Work with Groups* 1 (Fall 1978): 309–18.

6 Social Work with Native Americans

Lewis, Ronald G.
Ho, Man Keung

*If social workers are to serve Native
Americans effectively, they must
understand their distinctive
characteristics and vary their
techniques accordingly.*

In the past, the social work profession has failed to serve effectively an important segment of the population—the Native Americans. Although social workers are in sympathy with the social problems and injustices long associated with the Native American people, they have been unable to assist them with their problems. This lack of success on the part of social workers can be attributed to a multitude of reasons but it stems, in general, from the following: (1) lack of understanding of the Native American culture, (2) retention of stereotyped images of Native Americans, (3) use of standard techniques and approaches.

Currently, the majority of social workers attempting to treat Native Americans are whites who have never been exposed to their clients' culture. Even when the social worker is a Native American, if his education and training have been in an environment that has completely neglected the Native American culture, there is still the possibility that he has drifted away from his people's thinking. Social workers with no understanding of the culture may have little or no sympathy for their Native American clients who fail to respond quickly to treatment.

Furthermore, Native Americans continue to be stereotyped by the current news media and often by the educational system. In all likelihood, the social worker will rely on these mistaken stereotypes rather than on facts. As Deloria explained, "People can tell just by looking at us what we want, what should be done to help us, how we feel, and what a 'real' Indian is like."[1] If a worker wishes to make progress in helping a Native American, he must begin by learning the facts and discarding stereotypes.

The ineffectiveness of social workers in dealing with Native Americans can often be attributed directly to the methods and techniques they use. Naturally, social workers must work with the tools they have acquired, but

Reprinted with permission from *Social Work*, Vol. 20, No. 5 (September 1975), pp. 379–382.

these may have a detrimental effect on a Native American. For example, the concept of "social work intervention" may be consistent with much of the white man's culture, but it diametrically opposes the Native American's cultural concept of noninterference.[2] There is a great need for social workers to examine carefully those techniques they plan to use in treating their Native American clients. If the worker discovers any that might be in conflict with the cultural concepts of the Native American, he should search carefully for an alternative approach. To do this, of course, the social worker must be aware of common Native American cultural traits.

Although there is no monolithic Native American culture—because each tribe's culture is unique to that individual tribe, and no social worker could be expected to be familiar with the cultures of some two hundred tribes—the worker should familiarize himself with those customs that are generally characteristic of all Native Americans. Only after a worker has gained at least an elementary knowledge of Native American customs and culture can he proceed to evaluate the various approaches and techniques and choose the most effective ones.

Native American Traits

The concept of sharing is deeply ingrained among Native Americans who hold it in greater esteem than the white American ethic of saving. Since one's worth is measured by one's willingness and ability to share, the accumulation of material goods for social status is alien to the Native American. Sharing, therefore, is neither a superimposed nor an artificial value, but a genuine and routine way of life.

In contrast to the general belief that they have no concept of time, Native Americans are indeed time conscious. They deal, however, with natural phenomena—mornings, days, nights, months (in terms of moons), and years (in terms of seasons or winters).[3] If a Native American is on his way to a meeting or appointment and meets a friend, that conversation will naturally take precedence over being punctual for the appointment. In his culture, sharing is more important than punctuality.

Nature is the Native American's school, and he is taught to endure all natural happenings that he will encounter during his life. He learns as well to be an independent individual who respects others. The Native American believes that to attain maturity—which is learning to live with life, its evil as well as its good—one must face genuine suffering. The resilience of the Native American way of life is attested to by the fact that the culture has survived and continues to flourish despite the intense onslaught of the white man.

One of the strongest criticisms of the Native American has been that he is pessimistic; he is presented as downtrodden, low-spirited, unhappy, and without hope for the future. However, as one looks deeper into his personality, another perspective is visible. In the midst of abject poverty comes "the courage to be"—to face life as it is, while maintaining a tremendous sense of humor.[4] There exists a thin line between pathos and humor.

The Native American realizes that the world is made up of both good and bad. There are always some people or things that are bad and deceitful. He believes, however, that in the end good people will triumph just because they are good. This belief is seen repeatedly in Native American folktales about Iktomi the spider. He is a tricky fellow who is out to fool, cheat, and take advantage of good people. But Iktomi usually loses in the end, reflecting the Native American view that the good person succeeds while the bad person loses.[5] Therefore, the pessimism of Native Americans should instead be regarded as "optimistic toughness."

Those who are unfamiliar with the culture might mistakenly interpret the quiet Native American as being stoical, unemotional, and vulnerable. He is alone, not only to others but also to himself. He controls his emotions, allowing himself no passionate outbursts over small matters. His habitual mien is one of poise, self-containment, and aloofness, which may result from a fear and mistrust of non-Native Americans. Another facet of Native American thought is the belief that no matter where any individual stands, he is an integral part of the universe. Because every person is fulfilling a purpose, no one should have the power to impose values. For this reason, each man is to be respected, and he can expect the same respect and reverence from others. Hence, the security of this inner fulfillment provides him with an essential serenity that is often mistaken for stoicism.

Native American patience, however, can easily be mistaken for inactivity. For instance, the Kiowa, like other Native American tribes, teach their young people to be patient. Today, when the young Native American has to go out and compete in another society, this quality is often interpreted as laziness. The white man's world is a competitive, aggressive society that bypasses the patient man who stands back and lets the next person go first.

The foregoing are only a few of the cultural traits that are common to most Native American tribes, but they represent important characteristics about which the effective social worker must be informed. The concepts of sharing, of time, acceptance of suffering, and optimism differ significantly from the white man's concepts. In dealing with a Native American client, the social worker must realize this and proceed accordingly. He must be familiar with the Native American view that good will triumph over evil and must recognize that Native Americans are taught to be patient and respectful. If the worker fails to do this, he is liable to make false assumptions, thus weakening his ability to serve his client effectively.

Client-Worker Relations

A social worker's ability to establish a working relationship with a Native American will depend on his genuine respect for his client's cultural background and attributes. A worker should never think that the Native American is primitive or that his culture and background are inferior.

In the beginning, the Native American client might distrust the worker who is from a different race and culture. He might even view the worker as a figure of authority, and as such, the representative of a coercive institution. It is unlikely that he will be impressed with the worker's educational degrees or his professional title. However, this uncompromising attitude should not be interpreted as pugnacity. On the contrary, the Native American is gregarious and benevolent. His willingness and capacity to share depend on mutual consideration, respect, and noncoercion.

Because their culture strongly opposes and precludes interference with another's affairs, Native Americans have tended to regard social work intervention with disfavor. Social workers usually are forced to use culturally biased techniques and skills that are insensitive to the Native American culture and, therefore, are either detrimental to these clients or, at best, ineffective.

In an effort to communicate more fully, a social worker is likely to seat himself facing the client, look him straight in the eye, and insist that the client do likewise. A Native American considers such behavior—covert or overt—to be rude and intimidating; contrary to the white man, he shows respect by not staring directly at others. Similarly, a worker who is excessively concerned with facilitating the display of inner feelings on the part of the client should be aware of another trait. A Native American client will not immediately wish to discuss other members of his family or talk about topics that he finds sensitive or distressing. Before arriving at his immediate concern (the real reason he came to the worker in the first place), the client—particularly the Native American—will test the worker by bringing up peripheral matters. He does this in the hope of getting a better picture of how sincere, interested, and trustworthy the worker actually is. If the worker impatiently confronts the client with accusations, the client will be "turned off."

Techniques of communication that focus on the client—that is, techniques based on restating, clarifying, summarizing, reflecting, and empathizing—may help a worker relate to the client who sometimes needs a new perspective to resolve his problem. It is important that the worker provide him with such information but not coerce him to accept it. The worker's advice should be objective and flexible enough so that its adoption does not become the central issue of a particular interview.

For the Native American, personal matters and emotional breakdown are traditionally handled within the family or extended family system. For this reason, the client will not wish to "burden" the worker with detailed personal information. If the client is estranged from his family and cultural group, he may indirectly share such personal information with the worker. To determine the appropriate techniques for helping a Native American client deal with personal and psychological problems, the worker should carefully observe the client's cultural framework and his degree of defensiveness. The techniques of confrontation traditionally associated with the psychoanalytic approach and the introspective and integrative techniques used by the transactional analysts tend to disregard differences in culture and background between a client and worker.

Family Counseling

In view of the close-knit family structure of Native Americans, along with the cultural emphasis to keep family matters inside the family, it is doubtful that many social workers will have the opportunity to render family counseling services. In the event that a Native American family does seek the worker's help, the family worker should be reminded that his traditional role of active and manipulative go-between must be tempered so that family members can deal with their problems at their own pace.[6] Equally important is the worker's awareness of and respect for the resilience of Native American families, bolstered in crisis by the extended family system. The example of the Redthunder family serves as illustration:

> The Redthunder family was brought to the school social worker's attention when teachers reported that both children had been tardy and absent frequently in the past weeks. Since the worker lived near Mr. Redthunder's neighborhood, she volunteered to transport the children back and forth to school. Through this regular but informal arrangement, the worker became acquainted with the entire family, especially with Mrs. Redthunder who expressed her gratitude to the worker by sharing her homegrown vegetables.
>
> The worker sensed that there was much family discomfort and that a tumultuous relationship existed between Mr. and Mrs. Redthunder. Instead of probing into their personal and marital affairs, the worker let Mrs. Redthunder know that she was willing to listen should the woman need someone to talk to. After a few gifts of homegrown vegetables and Native American handicrafts, Mrs. Redthunder broke into tears one day and told the worker about her husband's problem of alcoholism and their deteriorating marital relationship.
>
> Realizing Mr. Redthunder's position of respect in the family and his resistance to outside interference, the social worker advised Mrs. Redthunder to take her family to visit the minister, a man whom Mr. Redthunder admired. The Littleaxe family, who were mutual friends of the worker and the Redthunder family, agreed to take the initiative in visiting the Redthunders more often. Through such frequent but informal family visits, Mr. Redthunder finally obtained a job, with the recommendation of Mr. Littleaxe, as recordkeeper in a storeroom. Mr. Redthunder enjoyed his work so much that he drank less and spent more time with his family.

Obviously, treating a family more pathogenic than the Redthunders might necessitate that the social worker go beyond the role of mediator. Nevertheless, since Native Americans traditionally favor noninterference, the social worker will not find it feasible to assume the active manipulative role that he might in working with white middle-class families. The social work profession needs new and innovative approaches to family counseling that take into account social and family networks and are sensitive and responsive to the cultural orientation of Native American families.[7]

Group Work

Groups should be a natural and effective medium for Native Americans who esteem the concept of sharing and apply it in their daily lives. Through the group process, members can share their joy, intimacy, problems, and sorrows, and find a means of improving their lives. Today's society tends to foster alienation, anomie, disenfranchisement, dissociation, loneliness, and schizoid coolness.[8] People wish for intimacy but at the same time fear it.[9] The new humanistic approaches to counseling and psychotherapy have developed a wide variety of powerful techniques for facilitating human growth, self-discovery, and interpersonal relations.[10] The effectiveness of these approaches in cutting through resistance, breaking down defenses, releasing creative forces, and promoting the healing process has been amply demonstrated. However, such approaches are highly insensitive to the cultural orientation of Native Americans. These people consider such group behavior to be false; it looks and sounds real but lacks genuineness, depth, and real commitment.

As the worker uses his skills in forming the group, diagnosing the problems, and facilitating group goals, he may inevitably retain certain elements of manipulation. However, if he is committed to recognizing individual potential and to capitalizing on the group model of mutual assistance, he should come close to meeting the needs of Native Americans who value respect and consideration for oneself as well as for others.[11]

To avoid manipulation and coercion, a group worker needs to utilize indirect and extra-group means of influence that will in turn influence the members. Thus the worker may act upon and through the group as a mediating structure, or through program activities, for the benefit of his clients.[12] The success of the worker's influences and activities is related to his knowledge and acceptance of Native American culture, its formal and informal systems and norms.

Regardless of whether the purpose of the group is for effecting interpersonal change or social action, such Native American virtues as mutual respect and consideration should be the essential components of the group process. Using the group to pressure members who are late or silent will not only jeopardize and shorten the group's existence, but will cause alienation and withdrawal from future group activities.

In view of the vast cultural difference between Native Americans and other ethnic groups, especially whites, it is doubtful that a heterogeneous grouping of members will produce good results. Similarly, group activities that are action oriented may be contradictory to Native Americans who view the compulsion to reduce or ignore suffering as immaturity.

Community Work

Because of the Native Americans' experience of oppression and exploitation—along with their emphasis on noninterference and resolute acceptance of suffering—it is doubtful that a social worker, regardless of his racial identity, could bring about any major change in community policies and programs. The only exception might be the social worker who is accepted and "adopted" by the community and who agrees to confine himself to the existing system and norms. A worker's adoption by the Native American community will depend on his sincerity, respect, and genuine concern for the people. This concern can best be displayed through patience in daily contact with the community as well as through his efforts to find positive solutions to problems.

A worker who uses the strategy of trying to resolve conflict as a means of bringing about social change will undoubtedly encounter native resistance and rejection. On the other hand, a worker who shows respect for the system, values, and norms of the Native American eventually places himself in a position of trust and credibility. Only through mutual respect, and not through his professional title and academic degree, can the worker produce meaningful social change.

Obviously, social work with Native Americans requires a new orientation and focus on attitudes and approaches. The term Native American encompasses many tribes, and within these there are intratribal differences; furthermore, individuals within each subtribe may react differently to problems or crises. Therefore, it is impossible for a social worker always to know precisely how to respond to a Native American client or group. The worker must be willing to admit his limitations, to listen carefully, to be less ready to draw conclusions, and to anticipate that his presuppositions will be corrected by the client. The worker must genuinely want to know what the problem or the situation is and be receptive to being taught. Such an unassuming and unobtrusive humanistic attitude is the key to working with Native American people.

The social worker who can deal most effectively with Native Americans will be genuine, respectful of their culture, and empathic with the welfare of the people. By no means does the Native American social worker have a monopoly on this type of attitude. In fact, the Native American social worker who has assimilated the white man's culture to the extent that he no longer values his own culture could do more harm than good.

Recognizing the distinct cultural differences of the Native American people, those who plan social work curricula and training programs must expand them to include specific preparation for workers who will be dealing with Native American clients. Literature on the subject is almost nonexistent, and researchers and educators would do well to devote more study to how social workers can serve Native Americans. More Native Americans should be recruited as students, faculty, and practitioners in the field of social work. All persons, regardless of race, should be encouraged to develop a sensitivity toward Native Americans whom they may have the opportunity to serve. Social work agencies that deal primarily with Native American clients should intensify and refocus their in-service training programs.

A worker has the responsibility of acquiring knowledge that is relevant to the Native American culture so that he is capable of providing this effective treatment. A joint effort on the part of all those involved is required to give the service to Native Americans that they justly deserve.

Reference Notes

1. Vine Deloria, Jr., *Custer Died for Your Sins: An Indian Manifesto* (New York: Macmillan Co., 1969), p. 45.
2. For a detailed discussion of noninterference, *see* Rosalie H. Wax and Robert K. Thomas, "Anglo Intervention vs. Native Noninterference," *Phylon,* 22 (Winter 1961), pp. 53–56; and Jimm G. Good Tracks, "Native American Noninterference," *Social Work,* 18 (November 1973), pp. 30–34.
3. Good Tracks, op. cit., p. 33.
4. Clair Huffaker, *Nobody Loves a Drunken Indian* (New York: David McKay Co., 1967).
5. *See* John F. Bryde, *Modern Indian Psychology* (Vermillion, S. Dak.: Institute of Indian Studies, University of South Dakota, 1971), p. 15.
6. *See* Gerald Suk, "The Go-Between Process in Family Therapy," *Family Process,* 6 (April 1966), pp. 162–178.
7. Ross V. Speck and Carolyn L. Attneave, "Social Network Intervention," in Jay Haley, ed., *Changing Families* (New York: Grune and Stratton, 1971), pp. 17–34.
8. Rollo May, "Love and Will," *Psychology Today,* 3 (1969) pp. 17–24.
9. Edward A. Dreyfus, "The Search for Intimacy," *Adolescence,* 2 (March 1967), pp. 25–40.
10. *See* Bernard Gunther, *Sense Relaxation: Below Your Mind* (New York: Macmillan Co., 1968); Abraham Maslow, "Self-Actualization and Beyond," in James F. Bugental, ed., *Challenges of Humanistic Psychology* (New York: McGraw-Hill Book Co., 1967); H. Oho, *Explorations in Human Potentialities* (Springfield, Ill.: Charles C. Thomas, 1966): Carl Rogers, "Process of the Basic Encounter Group," in James F. Bugental, ed., op. cit.
11. For further discussion of a reciprocal model, *see* William Schwartz, "Toward a Strategy of Group Work Practice," *Social Service Review,* 36 (September 1962), pp. 268-279.
12. For further discussion of indirect and extra-group means, *see* Robert Vinter, *Readings in Group Work Practice* (Ann Arbor: Campus Publishers, 1967), pp. 8–38.

The American Indian Client

Cases and Questions

1. Assume you are an elementary school counselor for several rural elementary schools that enroll about twelve American Indian students each year (approximately 5 percent of the total enrollment). Although the American Indian children perform as well as the Anglo children in kindergarten, by fourth grade it is clear they are less advanced to reading, writing, and computational skills. The district in which these schools are located is quite poor, and you are one of the few specialists available to supplement the resources of the classroom teacher.

   a. Upon entering a teacher's lounge in one school, you hear the English teacher, in conversation with several other teachers, relate the American Indian students' poor performance to their family/ cultural background in rather uncomplimentary terms. How would you react?
   b. What responsibility, if any, would you accept for attempting to offset the deficiencies in academic skills these Native American students have?
   c. What response would you expect to receive from American Indian students and their parents to your attempts to improve the students' academic performance (assuming you accept responsibility for doing this)?

2. Assume you are a community social worker employed by the BIA to work with reservation Indian families in which one or both of the parents have a history of chronic alcoholism.

   a. What are some of the factors you believe may contribute to alcoholism among American Indians, and how would your assumptions about the etiology of alcoholism affect your role as a social worker?
   b. What personal and professional qualities that you possess would be helpful in your work with American Indians? What qualities might be detrimental?
   c. Would you attempt to work with several families at once through group counseling? If so, how would you structure the group experience?

3. Assume you are a counselor in an urban high school that enrolls a small number of Native American students whose parents have left reservation life for the employment opportunities of a big city. Johnny Lonetree, an artistically gifted junior who regularly makes the honor roll, has just informed you that he is contemplating returning to the reservation to live with his grandparents. Johnny knows that for all practical purposes this will mean an end to his scholastic education, but he is intensely interested in being immersed in the tribal culture, specifically tribal art work.

   a. How can you best assist Johnny in his decision-making process?
   b. How might some of your own values affect how you proceed with Johnny?
   c. What are some of the social pressures (exerted by administrators, colleagues, Johnny's parents) that are likely to be exerted upon both you and Johnny if he decides to return to the reservation?

The American Indian Client
Role Playing Exercise

Divide into groups of four or five. Assign each group member to a role and the responsibilities associated with the role as follows:

Role	Responsibilities
1. Counselor	1. Assume role as a counselor or mental health worker who encounters an American Indian. Attempt to build rapport with the client.
2. Client	2. Assume role of an American Indian. To play this role effectively, it will be necessary for the student client to (a) identify cultural values of the American Indian group, (b) identify sociopolitical factors which may interfere with counseling, and (c) portray these aspects in the counseling session. It is best to select a few powerful variables in the role play. You may or may not be initially antagonistic to the counselor, but it is important for you to be sincere in your role and your reactions to the counselor.
3. Observers	3. Observe interaction and offer comments during feedback session.

This exercise is most effective in a racially and ethnically mixed group. For example, an American Indian student can be asked to play the American Indian client role. However, this is probably not possible in most cases. Thus, students who play the client role will need to thoroughly read the articles for the group they are portraying.

Identifying the barriers that could interfere with counseling is an important aspect of this exercise. We recommend that a list be made of the group's cultural values and sociopolitical influences prior to the role playing.

Role playing may go on for a period of 5–15 minutes, but the time limit should be determined prior to the activity. Allow 10–15 minutes for a feedback session in which all participants discuss (within the group) how they felt in their respective roles, how appropriate were the counselor responses, what else they might have done in that situation, etc.

Rotate and role play the same situation with another counselor trainee *or* another American Indian client with different issues, concerns, and problems. In the former case, the group may feel that a particular issue is of sufficient importance to warrant reenactment. This allows students to see the effects of other counseling responses and approaches. In the latter case, the new exposure will allow students to get a broader view of barriers to counseling.

If videotaping equipment is available, we recommend that the sessions be taped and processed in a replay at the end. We have found this to be a powerful means of providing feedback to participants.

Part 3
The Asian American Client

The Asian American population has doubled since 1970 and now comprises 2 percent of the U.S. population (3.5 million): 806,000 Chinese Americans, 775,000 Filipino Americans, 701,000 Japanese Americans, 355,000 Korean Americans, 170,000 Hawaiian Americans, 42,000 Samoan Americans, 32,000 Guamian Americans, and 400,000 of other Asian ancestry (S. Sue and Morishima, 1982). Since 1975, over 300,000 Indo Chinese refugees have been admitted to the U.S., and as of this writing, the U.S. admits more than 250,000 Asian immigrants yearly. With the continued admission of refugees from Asia, there is no doubt that the Asian American population is changing. Yet despite the fact that Asian Americans are comprised of such diverse groups, each with its own language and cultural heritage, they continue to be perceived as possessing the same or similar characteristics.

One of the most prevalent and contemporary images of Asian Americans is that of a highly successful minority that has "made it" in society. For example, the popular press has often portrayed Asian Americans as a "model" minority, using such headlines as "Success Story: Outwhiting the Whites," "Success Story of One Minority Group in the U.S.," "The Oriental Express," and "Asian Americans Making the Grade" (*Newsweek*, 1971; *U.S. News and World Report*, 1966; *Psychology Today*, 1986; *U.S. News and World Report*, 1984). The view that Asian Americans are a successful minority is based upon observations of this group; upon studies consistently revealing that Asian Americans have low *official* rates of delinquency, psychiatric contact, and divorce; upon apparently higher levels of educational attainment; and upon apparently higher levels of family income. The conclusion one can draw from all of these statistics is that Asian Americans and Indo-Chinese refugees have never been victims of prejudice and discrimination.

Yet a review of the Asian experience in America indicates the massive discrimination directed at them. Assaulted, murdered, denied ownership of land, denied rights of citizenship, and placed in concentration camps during World War II, Asian Americans have been subjected to some of the most flagrant forms of discrimination ever perpetrated against an immigrant group.

A closer analysis of the status of Asian Americans does not support their success story. Reference to the higher median income does not take into account (a) the higher percentage of more than one wage earner in the family, (b) an equal incidence of poverty despite the higher median income, (c) lower poverty assistance and welfare than the general population, and (d) the fact that salaries are not commensurate with the education levels of Asian American workers (lower salaries despite higher educational level). Statistics on educational levels are also misleading. Asian Americans present a picture of extraordinarily high educational attainment for some, while a large number remain uneducated. The impression that Indo-Chinese refugees are a homogeneous, privileged group is also not supported by data.

For example, the Vietnamese who evacuated were probably the most homogeneous group ever to immigrate to the U.S.

There is also recognition that, apart from being tourist attractions, Chinatowns, Manilatowns, and Japantowns in major metropolitan cities represent ghetto areas. Unemployment, poverty, health problems, and juvenile delinquency are major facts of life. For example, San Francisco's Chinatown has the second greatest population density next to Harlem. It not only has a high tuberculosis rate but a suicide rate three times the national average. Juvenile gangland warfare has also caught the public eye. Underutilization of mental health facilities by Chinese Americans in San Francisco is now recognized to be due to cultural factors inhibiting self-referral (shame and disgrace associated with admitting to emotional problems, reliance on the family to prevent it from becoming public, etc.), and/or to inappropriate institutional policies and practices. Furthermore, Indo-Chinese refugees seem to differ from White Americans in what they regard as mental health problems requiring treatment. As a result, we are now beginning to understand why groups like the Vietnamese are reluctant to seek traditional mental health services in the U.S.

In his leadoff article, "Ethnic Identity: The Impact of Two Cultures on the Psychological Development of Asians in America," D. Sue describes the psychological development of two Asian groups with respect to stereotypes, unique cultural values, and the experience of racism. Personality characteristics, academic abilities, and vocational interests of both Chinese and Japanese Americans are described. These descriptions provide important information for counselors who work with Asian Americans and who need to look behind the "success myth" and understand the Asian experience in America.

It is increasingly recognized that traditional counseling approaches must be modified to fit the life experiences of minority clients. M. Root suggests how such modification in counseling can be made by taking into account such factors as cultural values and the experience of racism. Specific concrete strategies are presented and discussed. Although this article deals only with certain Asian clients, it presents an example of how different approaches might be used for other Asian Americans as well.

In the last article, Brower provides specific information that counselors need to have if they are to be successful when working with one of America's newest immigrant groups, the Vietnamese. Brower suggests that the relationship dynamics of rapport building, interview structure, transference and countertransference, and communication barriers are of particular concern when counseling Vietnamese. She further suggests that counselors need to be sensitive to Vietnamese attitudes toward self-disclosure and sex roles in order to develop a productive counseling relationship. Brower concludes her article by examining mental health problems that counselors who work with Vietnamese are likely to encounter.

References

Are they making the grade? (1984). *U.S. News & World Report.* April

Success story of one minority group in the U.S. (1966). *U.S. News & World Report.* December

Success story: Outwhiting the whites. (1971). *Newsweek.*

Sue, S., and Morishima, J. K. (1982). The mental health of Asian Americans. San Francisco: Jossey-Bass.

The new Americans. (1975). *Newsweek.*

The oriental express. (1986). *Psychology Today.*

7 Ethnic Identity
The Impact of Two Cultures on the Psychological Development of Asians in America
Sue, Derald Wing

Among the many determinants of Asian-American identity, the cultural influences (values, norms, attitudes, and traditions) are of considerable importance. While social scientists agree that psychological development is not an isolated phenomenon apart from socio-cultural forces, most theories of personality are culturally exclusive. Furthermore, empirical studies tend not to deal adequately with the impact of cultural racism on the behavior of ethnic minorities. To understand the psychological development of Chinese- and Japanese-Americans, the cultural and historical forces of racism which serve to shape and define the Asian-American's identity must be examined.

Most studies which focus on the effects of culture on Asian-Americans tend to be highly compartmentalized. For example, one can find research investigating the relationship of culture to (a) personality characteristics (Abbott, 1970; Fong & Peskin, 1969; Meredith, 1966; Arkoff, Meredith & Iswahara, 1964; 1962; Fenz & Arkoff, 1962), (b) child-rearing practices (De Vos & Abbott, 1966; Kitano, 1964), (c) the manifestations of behavior disorders (Marsella, Kinzie, Gordon, 1971; Kitano, 1970; 1969a; Arkoff & Weaver, 1966; Sommers, 1960; Kimmich, 1960), (d) the ineffectiveness of traditional therapy (Sue & Sue, 1972a; 1971; Yamamoto, James & Palley, 1968), (e) acculturation (Matsumoto, Meredith & Masuda, 1970; Meade, 1970; Weiss, 1969; Fong, 1965; Kitano, 1962; Arkoff, 1959), and (f) use of English (Meredith, 1964; Smith & Kasdon, 1961; Smith, 1957). Few attempts integrate these findings into a global description of how cultures influence the socio-psychological functioning of the "whole" person.

Cultural impact is clearly demonstrated in the study of Chinese- and Japanese-Americans, where remnants of Asian cultural values collide with European-American values. The historical meeting of these two cultures and their consequent interaction in a racist society have fundamental importance in understanding the personality characteristics, academic abilities, and vocational interests of Asians in America.

Reprinted by permission of the editors and the publisher from D. W. Sue "Ethnic Identity: The Impact of Two Cultures on the Psychological Development of Asians in America." In S. Sue and N. N. Wagner (Eds.), *Asian-Americans: Psychological Perspectives.* Palo Alto, CA: Science and Behavior Books, 1973.

Asian Cultural Values

Although it is acknowledged that the Asian-American family structure and its subcultural values are in transition, they still retain their many values from the past. Because the primary family is generally the socializing agent for its offspring and because parents interpret appropriate and inappropriate behavior, a description of traditional Asian families will lead to greater understanding of their cultural values.

Chinese and Japanese family interaction patterns have been described as being similar by many social scientists (Sue & Sue, 1971; Abbott, 1970; Kitano, 1969a; 1969b; De Vos & Abbott, 1966; Kimmich, 1960). The Asian family is an ancient, complex institution, the fundamental unit of the culture. In China and Japan, it has long been more or less independent of political alliances; its form has survived political upheavals and invasions of foreigners.

The roles of family members are highly interdependent. Deviations from traditional norms governing behavior are suppressed to keep the family intact. Independent behavior which might upset the orderly functioning of the family is discouraged. The family structure is so arranged that conflicts within the family are minimized; each member has his own role to play which does not interfere with that of another. If a person has feelings which might disrupt family peace and harmony, he is expected to hide them. Restraint of potentially disruptive emotions is strongly emphasized in the development of the Asian character; the lack of outward signs of emotions has given rise to the prevalent opinion among Westerners that Asians are "inscrutable."

The Chinese and Japanese families are traditionally patriarchal with communication and authority flowing vertically from top to bottom. The father's behavior in relationship to other family members is generally dignified, authoritative, remote, and aloof. Sons are generally highly valued over daughters. The primary allegiance of the son is to the family, and obligations as a good father or husband are secondary. Asian women are expected to carry on the domestic duties, to marry, to become obedient helpers of their mothers-in-law, and to bear children, especially males.

The inculcation of guilt and shame are the principal techniques used to control the behavior of family members. Parents emphasize their children's obligation to the family. If a child acts independently (contrary to the wishes of his parents), he is told that he is selfish and inconsiderate and that he is not showing gratitude for all his parents have done for him. The behavior of individual members of an Asian family is expected to reflect credit on the whole family. Problems that arise among Asian Americans such as failure in school, disobedience, juvenile delinquency, mental illness, etc., are sources of great shame. Such problems are generally kept hidden from public view and handled within the family. This fact may explain why there are low *official* rates of juvenile delinquency (Abbott & Abbott, 1969; Kitano, 1967) and low utilization of mental health facilities among

Asians (Sue & Sue, 1972a; Kitano, 1969a; Yamamoto, James & Palley, 1968; Kimmich, 1960). On the other hand, outstanding achievement in some aspect of life (especially educational and occupational success) is a source of great pride for the entire family. Thus, each family member has much at stake in the behavior of others.

In summary, traditional Asian values emphasize reserve and formality in interpersonal relations, restraint and inhibition of strong feelings, obedience to authority, obligations to the family, high academic and occupational achievement, and use of shame and guilt to control behavior. These cultural values have a significant impact on the psychological characteristics of Asians in America.

Historical Experience: Cultural Racism

Kovel (1970) believes that White racism in America is no aberration but an ingredient of our culture which serves as a stabilizing influence and a source of gratification to Whites. In defining cultural racism, Jones (1972) states that it is ". . . the individual and institutional expression of the superiority of one race's cultural heritage over that of another race. Racism is appropriate to the extent that racial and cultural factors are highly correlated and are a systematic basis for inferior treatment." (p. 6) Any discussion concerning the effects of racism on the psychological characteristics of minorities is necessarily fraught with hazards. It is difficult to distinguish the relevant variables which affect the individual and to impute cause-effect relations. However, a historical analysis of Asians in America suggests that cultural racism has done great harm to this ethnic group.

Unknown to the general public, Asian-Americans have been the object of much prejudice and discrimination. Ironically, the American public is unaware that no high walls of prejudice have been raised, historically, around any other ethnic minority than those around the Chinese and Japanese. Asians have generally attempted to function in the existing society without loud, strong, or public protest (Sue & Sue, 1972a).

The first Chinese immigrants came to the United States during the 1840s. Their immigration from China was encouraged by the social and economic unrest in China at that time and by overpopulation in certain provinces (De Vos & Abbott, 1966). During this period, there was a demand for Chinese to help build the transcontinental railroad. Because of the need for cheap labor, they were welcomed into the labor force (Daniels, 1971). However, a diminishing labor market and fear of the "yellow peril" made the Chinese immigrants no longer welcome. Their pronounced racial and cultural differences from the White majority made them conspicuous, and they served as scapegoats for the resentment of White workers. Although Daniels (1971) mainly discusses the economic aspect for the hostility expressed against the Chinese, he points out that the anti-Chinese movement soon developed into an ideology of White supremacy which was compatible with the mainstream of American racism. Chinese were seen as "subhuman" or "heathens" and their mode of living was seen as undesirable and detrimental to the well-being of America. Laws which were passed to harass the Chinese denied them the rights of citizenship, ownership of land, the right of marriage, etc. At the height of the anti-Chinese movement, when prejudice and discrimination against the Chinese flourished, many Chinese were assaulted and killed by mobs of Whites. This anti-Chinese sentiment culminated in the passing of the Federal Chinese Exclusion Act of 1882 which was the first exclusion act against any ethnic group. This racist immigration law, justified by the alleged need to exclude masses of "cheap Chinese labor" from the United States, was not repealed until 1943 as a gesture of friendship toward China, an ally of the United States during World War II.

Likewise, the Japanese in America faced severe hostility and discrimination from White citizens. Japanese began immigrating to the United States during the 1890s when anti-Chinese sentiment was great. As a result, they shared in the pervasive anti-Oriental feeling. Originally brought in to fill the demand for cheap agricultural labor and coming from an agrarian background, many Japanese became engaged in these fields (Kitano, 1969b). Their fantastic success in the agricultural occupations, coupled with a racist climate, enraged many White citizens. Legislation similar to the anti-Chinese acts was passed against the Japanese, and individual-mob violence repeated itself. Such cries as "The Japs must go" were frequently echoed by the mass media and labor and political leaders. In response to hostility toward members of their race, both Chinese and Japanese formed their own communities to isolate and protect themselves from a threatening racist society.

Within this background of White racism, it became relatively easy for White society to accept the relocation of 110,000 Japanese-Americans into camps during World War II. Their pronounced racial and cultural characteristics were enough justification for the atrocious actions taken against the Japanese. The dangerous precedent created by American reaction to the Japanese is an ever-present threat that racial strains can again result in a repeat of history.

There can be no doubt that cultural racism has been practiced against the Chinese and Japanese. Many people would argue that, today, Asian-Americans face no such obstacles as their ancestors. The myth that Asians represent a "model minority" and are successful and functioning well in society is a popular belief often played up by the press (Newsweek, 1971; U.S. News & World Report, 1966). The 1960 Census reveals that Chinese and Japanese, indeed, have higher incomes and lower unemployment rates than their *non-White* counterparts. A further analysis, however, reveals that Chinese and Japanese are lower in income and higher in unemployment rates than the *White* population. This disparity is even greater when one considers that, generally, Chinese and Japanese achieve higher educational levels than Whites. It can only be concluded that social and economic discrimination are still flagrantly practiced against Asian-Americans.

Thus far, the fact that cultural racism has and is being practiced against Asian minorities has been documented. Attention now will be focused on the psychological costs of culture conflict.

Culture Conflict

Jones (1972) believes that many forms of culture conflict are really manifestations of cultural racism. Although there is nothing inherently wrong in acculturation and assimilation, he believes that ". . . when it is forced by a powerful group on a less powerful one, it constitutes a restriction of choice; hence, it is no longer subject to the values of natural order." (p. 166).

When an ethnic minority becomes increasingly exposed to the values and standards of the dominant host culture, there is progressive inculcation of those norms. This has been found for both the Chinese (Abbott, 1970; Meade, 1970; Fong & Peskin, 1969; Fong, 1965) and Japanese (Matsumoto, Meredith & Masuda, 1970; Kitano, 1962; Arkoff, 1959). However, assimilation and acculturation are not always smooth transitions without their pitfalls. As they become Westernized, many Asian-Americans come to view Western personality characteristics as more admirable qualities than Asian characteristics. Constantly bombarded with what constitutes desirable traits by a society that has low tolerance for differing life-styles, many Asian males and females begin to find members of their own race undesirable social partners. For example, Weiss (1969) found many Chinese-American girls coming to expect the boys they date to behave boldly and aggressively in the traditional Western manner. They could be quite vehement in their denunciation of Asian-male traits. Unfortunately, hostility to a person's minority culture background may cause Asians to turn their hostility inward. Such is the case when Japanese-American females express greater dissatisfaction with their body image than Caucasian females (Arkoff & Weaver, 1966). The individual may develop a kind of racial self-hatred that leads to lowered self-esteem and intense conflicts (Sue & Sue, 1971; Summers, 1960). Among individuals of minority cultural background, we find many instances of culture conflict: the individual finds that he is heir to two different cultural traditions, and he may have difficulty in reconciling their effects on his own personality; he may find it difficult to decide to which culture he owes primary loyalty. Such a person has been called a Marginal Man. Because of his marginal status, he often experiences an identity crisis and feels isolated and alienated from both cultures.

In previous articles (Sue & Sue, 1972a; 1971), three different reactions to this stress were described. A person may remain allied to the values of his own culture; he may attempt to become over-Westernized and reject Asian ways; or he may attempt to integrate aspects of both cultures which he believes are functional to his own self-esteem and identity. The latter mode of adjustment is being advocated by the ethnically conscious Asians on many college campuses. In an attempt to raise group esteem and pride, Asian-Americans are actively exploring and challenging the forces in White society which have served to unfairly shape and define their identity (Sue & Sue, 1972b). No longer are they content to be a "banana," a derogatory term used to designate a person of Asian descent who is "Yellow on the outside but White on the inside."

Psychological Characteristics of Chinese- and Japanese-American Students

The cultural background of both the Japanese and Chinese, the historical and continuing forces of White racism, and the cultural conflicts experienced in the United States have left their mark on the current life styles of Asian-Americans. Although it is difficult to impute a direct cause-effect relationship between these forces and the psychological characteristics of Asian-Americans, the following description, certainly, seems consistent with their past background. The remaining sections will focus upon the personality traits, academic abilities, and vocational interests of Chinese- and Japanese-American college students. Findings presented in these sections will rely heavily on research conducted at the University of California, Berkeley (Sue & Kirk). Three tests consisting of the Omnibus Personality Inventory, the School and College Ability Tests, and the Strong Vocational Interest Blank were administered to an entire entering Freshman class. Chinese-American, Japanese-American, and all other students were compared to one another on these three instruments.

Personality Characteristics

The studies conducted at Berkeley reveal that Chinese- and Japanese-American college students tend to exhibit similar characteristics. This is not surprising in view of their similar cultural and historical backgrounds. Asian-Americans of both sexes tend to evaluate ideas on the basis of their immediate practical application and to avoid an abstract, reflective, theoretical orientation. Because of their practical and applied approach to life problems, they tend to be more intolerant of ambiguities and to feel much more comfortable in well-structured situations. Asian Americans also appear less autonomous and less independent from parental controls and authority figures. They are more obedient, conservative, conforming, and inhibited. In interpersonal relationships, they tend to be cautious in directly expressing their impulses and feelings. In comparison to Caucasian norms, both Chinese- and Japanese-American students appear more socially introverted and will more often withdraw from social contacts and responsibilities. Other investigators have found similar results for the Chinese (Abbott, 1970; Fong & Peskin, 1969; De Vos & Abbott, 1966) and Japanese (Meredith, 1966; Fenz & Arkoff, 1962; Arkoff, 1959).

Asian cultural values, emphasizing restraint of strong feelings, obedience, dependence upon the family, and formality in interpersonal relations, are being exhibited by these students. These values are in sharp contrast to Western emphasis on spontaneity, assertiveness, and informality. Because of socialization in well-defined roles, there is a tendency for Asian students to feel more comfortable in structured situations and to feel uncomfortable in ambiguous ones. As a result, they may tend to withdraw from social contacts with those outside their ethnic group or family. As discussed later, their minority status and sensitivity to actual and potential discrimination from White society may make them suspicious of people. It is possible, also, that their concrete and pragmatic approach was reinforced because it possessed social and economic survival value.

The socio-emotional adjustment characteristics of Asian-Americans also seem to reflect their cultural background and experiences as minorities in America. Meredith (1966), in testing Sansei students at the University of Hawaii, found them to be more tense, apprehensive, and suspicious than their Caucasian counterparts. A study by Fetz & Arkoff (1962) revealed that senior high school students of Chinese and Japanese ancestry possessed significantly higher needs for abasement. This trait indicates a need to feel guilty when things go wrong and to accept personal blame for failure. The Berkeley studies also support the fact that Asian-Americans seem to be experiencing more stress than their Caucasian controls. Both Chinese- and Japanese-American students exhibit attitudes and behaviors that characterize alienated persons. They were more likely to possess feelings of isolation, loneliness, and rejection. They also appeared more anxious, worried, and nervous.

Three factors seem to be operating in these findings. First, cultural elements are obviously affecting these tests. For example, Asian values emphasizing modesty and the tendency to accept blame (guilt and shame) would naturally elevate their abasement score. However, clinical observations and the consistency of personality measures revealing higher experienced stress point to real problems. Second, past and present discrimination and the isolation imposed by a racist society would affect feelings of loneliness, alienation, and anxiety. Last the earlier discussion of culture conflict leading to a negative self-image could be a strong component of these findings.

Academic Abilities

Using the School and College Ability Tests, the Berkeley studies revealed that Chinese- and Japanese-Americans of both sexes scored significantly lower on the verbal section of the test than their control counterparts. In addition, Chinese-Americans of both sexes scored significantly higher on the quantitative section of the test. Although Japanese-American students tended to obtain higher quantitative scores, the differences were not significant.

Although the possibility of inherited racial characteristics cannot be eliminated, greater explanatory power seems to lie in a sociocultural analysis. The Asian-American's lowered verbal performance probably reflects his bilingual background (Smith & Kasdon, 1961; Smith, 1957). The nature of Asian society also stresses filial piety and unquestioning respect for authority. Limited communication patterns in the home (parent to child) and the isolation imposed by a dominant society (one that rewarded silence and inconspicuousness and punished outspoken behavior from minorities) greatly restricted verbal interaction (Watanabe, 1971). The higher quantitative scores may represent compensatory modes of expression. Quantitative activities also tend to be more concrete, impersonal, and structured. These attributes are highly attractive to Asian-Americans.

Vocational Interests

Most educators, pupil personnel workers, and counselors throughout the West and East Coasts have frequently remarked on the abundance of Asian students entering the physical sciences. Surveys undertaken at the University of California, Berkeley, (Chu, 1971; Takayama, 1971) reveal that approximately 75 percent of Chinese and 68 percent of Japanese males enter the physical sciences. Using the Strong Vocational Interest Blank, the Berkeley studies compared the interests of Chinese-Americans, Japanese-Americans, and all other students. Chinese-American men expressed more interest in the physical sciences (Mathematician, Physicist, Engineer, Chemist, etc.) than all other students. Although not statistically significant, Japanese-American men also tended to express more interest in these occupations. Males from both ethnic groups appeared more interested in occupations comprising the skilled-technical trades (Farmer, Aviator, Carpenter, Printer, Vocational-Agricultural Teacher, Forest Service Man, etc.) and less interested in sales (Sales Manager, Real Estate Salesman, Life Insurance Salesman) and the verbal-linguistic occupations (Advertising Man, Lawyer, Author-Journalist). Although Chinese-American males exhibited less interest in the social sciences, this was not true for the Japanese-American males. Generally, both groups expressed more interest in the business fields, especially the detail (Senior Certified Public Accountant, Accounting and Office Man) as opposed to the business contact vocations. They tended to be less interested in the aesthetic-cultural fields (Musician and Artist). Although they did not differ significantly in the biological sciences as a group, they did express more interest in the clinically applied ones (Dentist and Veterinarian).

The Asian-American females had a profile similar to their male counterparts. Both ethnic groups exhibited more interest in business occupations, applied-technical fields, biological and physical sciences, and less interest in verbal-linguistic fields, social service, and aesthetic-cultural occupations. Although Chinese- and Japanese-American females tended to express more interest in the domestically oriented occupations (Housewife, Elementary Teacher, Office Worker, and Stenographer-Secretary), only the Chinese-American females scored significantly higher.

An analysis of the relationship between personality traits, academic abilities, and vocational interests for Asian-Americans reveals a logical consistency among all three variables. Greater interest in the physical sciences and lower interest in sales, social sciences, and verbal-linguistic fields are consistent with the Asian-American's higher quantitative and lower verbal skills. Furthermore, the people-contact professions call for some degree of forceful self-expression. These traits are antagonistic to the Asian-American's greater inhibition, reserve in interpersonal relations, and lower social extroversion. Physical sciences and skilled-technical trades, also, are characterized by more of a structured, impersonal, and concrete approach.

The Asian-American's restricted choice of vocations can be explained by two factors. First, early immigrants came from a strongly agricultural and peasant background. This is especially true of the Japanese who, according to the 1960 Census, were over-represented in agricultural fields. Second, early immigrants may have encouraged their sons and daughters into occupations with potentially greater social and economic survival value. Thus, their concern with evaluating choice of vocations on the basis of pragmatism was reinforced by a racist society. Agricultural fields, skilled-technical trades, and physical sciences can be perceived as possessing specific concrete skills that were functional in American society. Discrimination and prejudice were minimized in these occupations while people-contact professions were wrought with hazards of discrimination. Even though the Chinese and Japanese expressed more interest in the businesses, most of the fields were accounting and bookkeeping activities. Furthermore, business occupations which they have historically chosen tended to be within their ethnic community (import-export, family-owned businesses, restaurants, etc.) rather than within the larger society.

Differences Between Chinese- and Japanese-Americans

The discussion thus far has revealed many similarities between Chinese- and Japanese-American students. In light of their many common cultural values and experiences in America, this is not surprising. However, differences certainly exist. On all three measures (personality, abilities, and interests) administered at the University of California, Berkeley, Japanese-American students consistently fell into an intermediate position between the Chinese-American and the control students. In other words, Japanese-Americans are more similar to the controls than are the Chinese-Americans. This finding suggests two possibilities. It might be assumed that Japanese values are much more similar to European-American values than are those of the Chinese. An analysis of Japanese and Chinese cultural values would dictate against this as the sole interpretation. Additionally, the high rate of industrialization in Japan is a relatively recent phenomenon that may have minimal impact at this time. A more plausible explanation lies in the differential acculturation of both groups.

Arkoff, Meredith, and Iswahara (1962) conclude that Japanese-American females appear to be acculturating faster than their male counterparts. Weiss (1969) feels that Chinese females are much better accepted by American society than males. This leads to greater social contact with members of the host society and acculturation is fostered. If differential acculturation occurs between sexes of the same ethnic group, it might be possible that a similar phenomenon has and/or is affecting both the Chinese and Japanese. An answer to this question may lie in the historical past of both the Chinese and Japanese in America.

Prior to the outbreak of World War II, relations between Japan and the United States became noticeably strained. Many Japanese in America feared that their loyalty would be questioned. Fearing that war would break out between the two nations and bring retaliation against Japanese-Americans, many Japanese-American organizations such as the Japanese-American Citizens League emphasized the need to appear as American as possible. Pro-American proclamations were common, and offspring were encouraged to acculturate and identify themselves with the American people.

With the bombing of Pearl Harbor, war was declared on Japan and the relocation experience of 110,000 Japanese-Americans did much to foster acculturation (Umemoto, 1970; Kitano, 1969b). First, it broke up Japanese-American communities by uprooting their residents. Homes and properties of the Japanese were confiscated and lost. Even today, the Japanese communities (Japantowns) are not comparable to the cohesive Chinatowns in San Francisco and New York, which serve as visible symbols of ethnic identity for the Chinese. Second, the camp experience disrupted the traditional family structure and lines of authority. Elderly males no longer had a functional value as household heads. Control and discipline of children and women became noticeably weakened under these circumstances. Third, many Japanese-Americans chose to migrate to the East Coast and Midwest rather than suffer the humiliation of internment. Even after the termination of the relocation centers, some Japanese-Americans chose not to return to the West Coast because of the strong anti-Japanese feeling there. Their greater physical dispersal increased contact with members of the host society and probably aided acculturation.

Conclusions

The psychological characteristics exhibited by Asian-Americans are related to their culture and the Asian-American's interaction with Western society. Any study of ethnic minorities in America must necessarily deal with the forces of racism inherent in American culture. Since there are no Asian-Americans untouched by racism in the United States to use as a control group, the relationship of racism to psychological development becomes a complex issue that cannot easily be resolved. If an attempt is made to use control groups in Taiwan, Hong Kong, or China, the problem becomes clouded by a whole complex of other social and cultural differences. For these reasons, the analyses presented in this article must be seen as somewhat tentative and speculative. Hopefully, further research will help clarify this issue.

References

Abbott, K. A. *Harmony and Individualism,* Taipei: Orient Cultural Press, 1970.

Abbott, K., and Abbott, E. "Juvenile Delinquency in San Francisco's Chinese-American Community." *Journal of Sociology* 4, 1968, 45–56.

Arkoff, A. "Need Patterns of Two Generations of Japanese-Americans in Hawaii." *Journal of Social Psychology* 50, 1959, 75–79.

————; Meredith, G.; and Iswahara, S. "Dominance-Deference Patterning in Motherland-Japanese, Japanese-American, and Caucasian-American Students." *Journal of Social Psychology* 58, 1962, 61–63.

————; Meredith, G.; and Iswahara, S. "Male-Dominant and Equalitarian Attitudes in Japanese, Japanese-American, and Caucasian-American Students." *Journal of Social Psychology* 64, 1964, 225–229.

————, and H. Weaver. "Body Image and Body Dissatisfaction in Japanese-Americans." *Journal of Social Psychology* 68, 1966, 323–330.

Chu, Robert. "Majors of Chinese and Japanese Students at the University of California, Berkeley, for the Past 20 Years." Project report, AS 150, Asian Studies Division, University of California, Berkeley, Winter, 1971.

Daniels, R. *Concentration Camps USA: Japanese-Americans and World War II.* New York: Holt, Rinehart, and Winston, Inc., 1971.

DeVos, G., and Abbott, K. "The Chinese Family in San Francisco." MSW dissertation, University of California, Berkeley, 1966.

Fenz, W., and Arkoff, A. "Comparative Need Patterns of Five Ancestry Groups in Hawaii." *Journal of Social Psychology* 58, 1962, 67–89.

Fong, S. L. M. "Assimilation of Chinese in America: Changes in Orientation and Social Perception." *American Journal of Sociology* 71, 1965, 265–273.

————, and Peskin, H. "Sex-Role Strain and Personality Adjustment of China-born Students in America: A Pilot Study." *Journal of Abnormal Psychology* 74, 1969, 563–567.

Jones, J. M. *Prejudice and Racism.* Massachusetts: Addison-Wesley Publishing Company, 1972.

Kimmich, R. A. "Ethnic Aspects of Schizophrenia in Hawaii." *Psychiatry* 23, 1960, 97–102.

Kitano, H. H. L. "Changing Achievement Patterns of the Japanese in the United States." *Journal of Social Psychology* 58, 1962, 257–264.

————. "Inter and Intra-Generational Differences in Maternal Attitudes Toward Child Rearing." *Journal of Social Psychology* 63, 1964, 215–220.

————. "Japanese-American Crime and Delinquency." *Journal of Psychology* 66, 1967, 253–263.

————. "Japanese-American Mental Illness." In S. C. Plog and R. B. Edgerton (eds.), *Changing Perspectives in Mental Illness*. New York: Holt, Rinehart, and Winston, 1969a.

————. *Japanese-Americans: The Evolution of a Subculture*. New Jersey: Prentice-Hall, 1969b.

————. "Mental Illness in Four Cultures." *Journal of Social Psychology* 80, 1970, 121–134.

Kovel, J. *White Racism: A Psychohistory*. New York: Vintage Books, 1971.

Marsella, A. J.; Kinzie, D.; and Gordon, P. "Depression Patterns among American College Students of Caucasian, Chinese, and Japanese Ancestry." Paper presented at the Conference on Culture and Mental Health in Asia and the Pacific, March, 1971.

Matsumoto, G. M.; Meredith, G.; and Masuda, M. "Ethnic Identification: Honolulu and Seattle Japanese-Americans." *Journal of Cross-Cultural Psychology* 1, 1970, 63–76.

Meade, R. D. "Leadership Studies of Chinese and Chinese-Americans." *Journal of Cross-Cultural Psychology* 1, 1970, 325–332.

Meredith, G. M. "Personality Correlates of Pidgin English Usage among Japanese-American College Students in Hawaii." *Japanese Psychological Research* 6, 1964.

————. "Amae and Acculturation among Japanese-American College Students in Hawaii. *Journal of Social Psychology* 70, 1966, 171–180.

Smith, M. E. "Progress in the Use of English after Twenty-Two Years by Children of Chinese Ancestry in Honolulu." *Journal of Genetic Psychology* 90, 1957, 255–258.

————, and Kasdon, L. M. "Progress in the Use of English after Twenty Years by Children of Filipino and Japanese Ancestry in Hawaii." *Journal of Genetic Psychology* 99, 1961, 129–138.

Sommers, V. S. "Identity Conflict and Acculturation Problems in Oriental-Americans." *American Journal of Orthopsychiatry* 30, 1960, 637–644.

Success Story: "Out-Whiting the Whites." *Newsweek*, June, 1971.

Success Story of One Minority Group in the U.S. *U.S. News and World Report*. December, 1966.

Sue, D. W., and Sue, S. "Counseling Chinese-Americans." *Personnel and Guidance Journal* 50, 1972a, 637–644.

————, and Sue, S. "Ethnic Minorities: Resistance to Being Researched." *Professional Psychology* 2, 1972b, 11–17.

————, and Kirk, B. A. "Psychological Characteristics of Chinese-American College Students." *Journal of Counseling Psychology* in press (1972).

————, and Kirk, B. A. "Differential Characteristics of Japanese- and Chinese-American College Students." Research in progress at the University of California, Berkeley.

Sue, S., and Sue, D. W. "Chinese-American Personality and Mental Health." *Amerasia Journal* 1, 1971, 36–49.

Takayama, G. "Analysis of Data on Asian Students at UC Berkeley, 1971." Project report, AS 150, Asian Studies Division, University of California, Berkeley, Winter, 1971.

Unemoto, A. "Crisis in the Japanese-American Family." In *Asian Women*. Berkeley: 1971.

Watanabe, C. "A College Level Reading and Composition Program for Students of Asian Descent: Diagnosis and Design." Asian Studies Division, University of California, Berkeley, 1971.

Weiss, M. S. "Selective Acculturation and the Dating Process: The Patterning of Chinese-Caucasian Interracial Dating." *Journal of Marriage and the Family* 32, 1970.

Yamamoto, J.; James, Q. C.; and Palley, N. "Cultural Problems in Psychiatric Therapy." *General Archives of Psychiatry* 19, 1968, 45–49.

8 Guidelines for Facilitating Therapy with Asian American Clients

Maria P. P. Root

Ethnicity is a powerful yet sometimes subtle determinant of an individual's patterns of thinking, feeling, and acting regardless of color or level of acculturation. Cultural patterns associated with one's ethnic heritage guide the individual to determine how to express distress, when to seek help, and from whom to seek help. For Asian Americans, the family can be an extremely important point of reference as a microcosm of cultural heritage and identify. Presenting problems need to be understood, diagnosed, and treated with knowledge of the cultural context of the person presenting for help.

Recognizing the importance of the culture and family as a context for understanding presenting problems, however, does not remove all the barriers which are currently present for Asian Americans seeking therapy. Other factors must be understood to structure therapy as a more beneficial form of treatment for Asian Americans. Both guidelines and suggestions are offered to remove some of the obstacles to help-seeking and to prevent premature termination—both of which have contributed to the underutilization of mental health services by Asian Americans.

Explanations for Underutilization of Services

Compared with other ethnic groups such as Blacks, Asian Americans have underutilized mental health resources (President's Commission on Mental Health, 1978; Sue & McKinney, 1975). The pattern of underutilization is striking given that Asian Americans face the same stressors any minority, immigrant group faces, including racism, immigration, and economic disadvantages. But unlike many other minority populations, the diverse Asian American populations have been viewed as an upwardly mobile population that poses few problems or demands on the mental health systems of this country (Sue & Morishima, 1982).

It is striking, given the expected need of mental health services for the various Asian American populations, that services are underutilized. Sue & McKinney (1975), in a survey of 17 Seattle mental health centers, found

Root, M. P. P. (1985). Guidelines for facilitating therapy with Asian American clients. *Psychotherapy, 22,* 349–356. Copyright 1985 by *Psychotherapy.* Reprinted with permission of the editor.

that only 100 clients of 13,198 clients seeking mental health services were Asian Americans, which is a rate significantly lower and disproportionate with the proportion of Asian Americans making up the greater Seattle area. The significantly lower rate of utilization of mental health services of Asian Americans compared with Whites is of concern given additional studies which suggest that by the time Asian Americans seek treatment they are experiencing a greater level of distress (Sue & McKinney, 1975; Sue & Sue, 1974) and would be expected to need more service or receive service for a longer period of time.

Recent research suggests that the Asian American's pattern of mental health utilization does not necessarily reflect a lack of need. Several explanations are emerging. Morishima (1975) suggests that because of the tendency of many Asian Americans to experience stress psychosomatically, help-seeking may occur from medical professionals rather than mental health professionals. Organic explanations of distress may initially be sought for symptoms such as headaches, loss of appetite, difficulty sleeping, allergies, digestive problems also associated with stress, depression, and anxiety. Tsai et al. (1980) offer several reasons why Asian Americans may underutilize mental health services in a study of Chinese Americans. First, the individual's view of the cause of mental distress and/or emotional problems may encourage him or her to problem solve on their own without letting family members know the true extent of their distress. Sue (1976) surveyed Asian (Chinese, Japanese, and Filipino Americans) and white students' conceptions of mental illness. The results of their survey generally supported the notion that the Asian American students tended to believe that mental health was maintained by the avoidance of morbid thoughts. In 1974, Lum (cf. Sue & Morishima, 1982) presented similar results in a survey of Chinese American residents of San Francisco's Chinatown. Residents commonly believed that mental health was maintained through the avoidance of bad thoughts and exercise of willpower. Such explanations logically guide individuals to attribute their distress to personal weakness. Behaviorally and cognitively, the individual may try to shut down any distressing thoughts or feelings, which may further exacerbate distress. A case illustration is provided.

> Ms. H is a 26-year-old Chinese American woman. It was suggested to her that she seek some counseling because she was crying at work and complaining of feeling as though she was "coming apart at the seams." However, it was noted that although she was feeling extremely distressed and desperate, considering suicide, she had not allowed her family to see that she was so distressed. Around the family she was able to to carry out her responsibilities and act as though everything were normal. However, away from the family she was crying, missing days of work, and starting to experience symptoms of panic at work.
>
> At the first interview, Ms. H revealed that in the last six months her life had changed considerably. Her paternal grandmother, who has lived with the

family since Ms. H was very young, had a stroke which partially paralyzed her. Of the five daughters in the family, it was determined that Ms. H should sleep on the floor of her grandmother's room at night because she was the lightest sleeper. Every night she attends to her grandmother's needs at least once. Three weeks prior to the interview, Ms. H reports that her White American boyfriend of three years to whom she was planning to be married announced that they were incompatible. They had been unable in the last six months to spend much time together because of her responsibilities to her grandmother. Finally, she reports being unhappy with the amount of time she was spending in activities related to her music. Ms. H was able to articulate some of her dilemma as one of feeling conflict over what she wanted to do and feeling that she had obligations to the family which were in direct conflict.

Service providers may not be responsive and sensitive enough to clients' fears and beliefs about the causes of their distress and expectations about recovery. As a result, a client's presentation may appear to be more disturbed than it actually would be in the context of the client's background, or vice versa. Service providers need to have an understanding of cultural proscriptions for the types of symptoms one is likely to manifest given their cultural background. The diagnosis may be difficult, as in the case of Mr. T.

Mr. T is a 33-year-old, married, Korean man who has lived in the United States for seven years. He grew up in a farming village in Korea and moved to the city where he met his future wife. She was studying nursing while he went to college on a scholarship. After the marriage, Mr. T realized that he was not in love with his wife. He felt that she was attracted to him because of his achievements at school. They came to the United States so that he could pursue a graduate degree in engineering. However, six years later he had not finished his degree and had significant requirements left to complete. His wife, on the other hand, had been able to obtain some training to receive her nursing diploma and was working to support their family.

Mr. T. has had contact with the mental health system at least four times in the last three years. At the time that he sought the current consultation his wife had announced two months earlier that she wanted a divorce. Since then they had lived separately and Mr. T's daughter had lived with his wife. Mr. T was without a job and his wife refused to support him. Two months earlier he had reported to a local emergency room because of headaches and nausea but was told that there was no reason to admit him. He was referred to outpatient therapy because it was determined that his distress was psychosomatic. At the time of this consultation Mr. T felt that his distress was the result of psychological weakness in his ability to use his willpower to overcome his distress. He was hesitant to explain why he was leaving his current counseling relationship. He suggested that his current psychiatrist was too young, and that another counselor was unable to be sympathetic to his needs.

Mr. T described a pattern of isolation since he had left his farming community for college. Currently he was isolated from the Korean community, believing that many of the people sided with his wife and were therefore unavailable to him. In college he had felt that class and world experience kept him apart from his peers. Mr. T prided himself on his education and insight into his problems, claiming that he was sophisticated unlike his wife who still retained many "primitive" ideas of Korea.

Stigma and shame may arise over experiencing mental distress. Experiencing psychological distress and changes in the ability to function may lead individuals to feel that they have failed to achieve what their family expects of them. Further disgrace would be called for if the individual were to seek help outside of the family. Prizzia & Villanueva-King (1977) surveyed Chinese, Hawaiian, Japanese, Filipino, and Samoan ethnic groups in Hawaii and found that people sought help from family first. Help-seeking outside the family was still kept close to the cultural community; outside the family, priests were approached first, then public sources, and psychiatrists, last. The case of Ms. C illustrates some of these issues.

> Ms. C, a 36-year-old Filipino, came to the mental health center after discharge from a psychiatric hospital for a suicide attempt by overdose on medication. She was nervous, made little eye contact, and repeatedly asked if she was crazy; she felt that her parents and relatives were treating her as though she were crazy. Upon taking her history, she revealed (and it was later confirmed) that in the past 14 months she had been mugged three times, in all cases by black males. Two of these occasions had occurred as she left different jobs where she worked as an RN. Ms. C had become increasingly suspicious of black males, afraid to walk by herself, and unable to work. She was experiencing dizzy spells and severe lapses of concentration which she felt made it impossible for her to return to work. She had been given medication by a physician to address some of the post-trauma symptoms she was experiencing. During a time of isolation, feeling hopeless that she would ever feel better, and unable to peform her duties as a nurse or daughter, she overdosed on her medication.
>
> Ms. C had immigrated to this country eight years prior, leaving her husband and three children in the Philippines. While studying for her RN license, she worked and supported not only herself, but also sent money back to her parents to support some of her youngest brothers and to provide for her own children. She had recently been successful in helping her parents to immigrate to the United States.
>
> She had recently moved from her aunt's house because she could not pay her rent since she had quit working. She was currently living in the basement of a house she had found for her parents. She was distressed that her savings were running out and that her parents were old (recently immigrated) and she was unable to support them. After the first interview, her parents, aunt, and family friend who Ms. C felt had supplanted her as a daughter and niece in the family were asked to come in.

Similarly, a family may not seek services for the anticipated disgrace or reflection on their parenting skills that the need to go outside the family reflects. This is the case in the family described.

The F family was referred for counseling by the school counselor and vice-principal. They sought counseling for their daughter, Angie, a twin, because of her failing grades, difficulty participating in class, social isolation, and tearfulness. The older twin, Mary Lou, in contrast to Angie, did well in school and had many friends.

Upon providing the consultation for the F family, it became clear that the parents were extremely frustrated. Both Mr. and Ms. F were well educated and held good jobs. Mr. F was Filipino and Ms. F was Chinese. Both families of origin valued education and Mr. and Ms. F had made every effort to provide their daughters with the best educational experiences possible. They discussed all the different ways in which they had tried to motivate Angie to improve her grades, and while counseling had been suggested four years ago because similar behavior was already apparent, it was only at this time that they felt they had exhausted all their personal resources and were following the recommendations of the school counselor whom they had come to trust.

The cost of mental health services may prohibit clients from obtaining treatment. Most private practitioners set fees for service that create barriers to seeking mental health for individuals with lower incomes (Owan, 1975; cf. Sue & Morishima, 1982). Additionally, needing to use the family resources for distress which does not appear to be rational or is a sign of personal weakness may make it even more difficult to seek services as in the case of Ms. M.

Ms. M, a 17-year-old Eurasian (Japanese Caucasian) was referred by her older, married sister when she revealed her suicidal feelings. Her sister referred her to seek help at their family's health-care agency. Ms. M is the youngest daughter of a Japanese mother and Caucasian father who had been divorced for two years. At the time of the consultation, she was unhappy in her current living situation with her mother and an older brother who was now acting as a father. In addition, she had recently terminated a relationship with her boyfriend of two years. She had not told her mother about her depression so that she would not distress her. Ms. M was aware of her mother's suicide attempt prior to the divorce.

Ms. M's mother was contacted by telephone. She expressed wanting to come in with her daughter but that her daughter had not asked her. She worried that Ms. M might feel uncomfortable with her present and might not be able to talk about what was necessary for her to feel better. In talking with the mother, it was apparent that she sensed her daughter's distress, but did not know how to respond to her. Additionally, she revealed that her daughter needed to be strong and come to terms with things within herself and by herself. Ms. M's mother was concerned about the cost of consultation because her income was derived from full-time babysitting that provided barely enough income to meet bills. Ms. M worked as a waitress after school and on weekends.

Services may not be conveniently available due to hours or distance. Language barriers may cut off many individuals or recently immigrated families from being able to obtain services. Language barriers and insufficient income provide a double barrier to the accessibility of services and the availability of problem-solving strategies.

Once the Asian American reaches treatment, additional barriers may contribute to premature termination from therapy. Sue & McKinney (1975) demonstrated that of 100 cases of Asian Americans who had sought psychotherapy services from Seattle area mental health clinics, the majority dropped out of treatment after one session, a rate 60% higher than that of white clients seeking services. In contrast to white clients who averaged almost 8 sessions for treatment, Asian Americans averaged slightly more than 2 sessions for treatment. Shon & Ja (1982) suggest that premature termination from treatment may occur because of communication problems, confusion over how psychotherapy works, conflict over the direction of psychotherapy, or unacceptable values that mental health practitioners may use to determine healthy functioning for the Asian American which do not consider cultural rules.

The Family's Role at Presentation

Shon & Ja (1982) Sue & Morishima (1982) and Sue (1981) provide discussions of Asian American families with attention to cultural diversity among and within ethnic groups. What is valued in the Asian American family varies among the populations which are summarily referred to as Asian Americans and reflects the cultural diversity among the Asian American and Pacific Island populations. Understanding Chinese families will not automatically mean that one will understand Filipino families or Japanese families. In fact, as a literature has emerged on the mental health of Asian Americans, clinicians, sociologists, educators, and researchers are taking the time to elaborate on the important differences between the ethnic groups subsumed under the label Asian American (Le, 1983; Munoz, 1983; Santos, 1983; Sue et al., 1983; Yamamoto & Iga, 1983; Yamamoto & Kubota, 1983; Yu & Kim, 1983).

Kleinman et al. (1978) emphasize that the service provider needs to have knowledge of the individual's culture and level of acculturation to be able to make an assessment of normal versus abnormal functioning. It can be assumed that as one's level of acculturation increases, the influences of cultural heritage may be more indirect and less obvious, but nevertheless are present. When an individual seeks help, the guidelines for facilitating healthy adaptation and functioning must attend both to the larger American culture and the culture of his or her specific ethnic group. As mentioned before, the individual's problems and plans for treatment need to be evaluated in context, specifically, culture and family.

An individual's involvement with the family of origin is not necessarily an accurate indication of how much influence the family or culture has over the beliefs and perceptions an individual has about the world and his or her relationship to it. This observation is important in that many Asian Americans have attempted to deny their cultural and ethnic background in an attempt to come to terms with their own individual identities. (Sue, 1981). The author assumes that the influences of ethnicity are powerful and cross-generational.

The Family's Role in the Referral

The family often seeks intervention or refers the identified patient for treatment when they are at a loss as to how to help. Obviously, the family is expressing their concern and at this point of referral, the person who is symptomatic is likely to be extremely distressed. Most Asian American families will be outwardly willing to come in with the distressed family member and be outwardly supportive in the treatment process. At other times, the individual, an adult, will come in alone self-referred or referred by an agency. The client does not want family members to come in because he or she feels ashamed and does not want to burden them. The belief that recovery rests in the exercise of willpower may explain the tenacity of a distressed individual who needs support, but does not want the family to be involved.

By the case illustrations provided above, it becomes apparent that the presenting problems are not unique to Asian or Pacific American clients. However, ethnicity does play a role in the etiology of the problem, the symptoms, help-seeking behavior, and acceptance of the treatment plan. In the cases of Ms. C and Ms. M it is observed that the families are not functioning normatively given the cultural context and level of acculturation. It would be expected that these families would be more supportive and in Ms. M's case more protective. In order for Ms. C and Ms. M to function more adaptively, their families need to become more available to them to reduce some of their feelings of isolation and to restore family functioning to a more normative system.

Many times the referrals described above are at risk for dropping out of treatment prematurely. The F family was embarrassed to seek help. While they were the most educated siblings in both of their families, none of their brothers or sisters had encountered such difficulties with their children. They came to treatment reluctantly feeling that as parents they were failing. It is important for the therapist to be sensitive to the pressures of the extended families as well as the personal sense of failure the parents were feeling, particularly Ms. F who had major responsibility for their daughters' performance in school as Mr. F made it clear. Ms. C is at risk for dropping out of treatment once she starts to feel the least bit better. To be in treatment may confirm her family's perception that she is weak and crazy. Ms. M is at risk for dropping out so that she does not disappoint or worry her family, particularly her mother. Her family's detachment and her mother's sense of failure as a parent (her mother repeatedly tells her that she must be strong and solve things within herself) are powerful deterrents to continuing treatment. Ms. H is at risk for premature termination so that she does not let her family down. Mr. T is at risk for termination as a result of a pattern of isolation and lack of ability to develop trust and comfort in a relationship besides the cultural factors present.

Two conditions must exist to engage the client or family in the therapy process so that the likelihood of premature termination with Asian American individuals and families can be decreased. First, the family must feel that the therapist understands and accepts their reasons for distress. Second, the therapeutic context must make sense so that there will be positive expectations of the therapy. These two conditions are important for any form of therapy. However, with Asian American clients, the therapist must consider that because of cultural rules for illness and treatment, the "curative factors" associated with the therapy process may differ from those assumed in traditional therapies developed for application to the majority culture. If these two conditions are facilitated, there is a much greater chance that the family will continue treatment.

Facilitating the Therapeutic Process

In this section the two conditions mentioned in the previous section (accepting the clients' view of distress and communicating this understanding, and helping therapy to make sense) are discussed as they are relevant to facilitating the therapeutic process. Therapy with the Asian American family as with the individual client does not require that a therapist necessarily develop new skills. The skills central to being an effective therapist remain the same, such as, being able to hear what the client is trying to communicate, respecting the client, and formulating treatment goals which take into account clients' levels of functioning, their resources, and their environment. Neither the problem situations nor the types of family dysfunction that occur are new. What may be new to the therapist is consideration of the context within which the problems exist. It is necessary that the service provider be willing to acknowledge that his or her prejudices, biases, and definitions of healthy psychological functioning may not be as adaptive for clients within their cultural context. Therefore, the therapist also needs to know what is normative functioning in the different groups of Asian and Pacific American families for which they provide consultation and therapy.

Successful therapy also requires that the therapist be sensitive to the factors which contribute to a client's or family's willingness to cooperate and adhere to a treatment plan. Additionally, the therapist needs to be cognizant of the potential administrative and practical barriers to families' continuing treatment. Each of these contributions to therapy is discussed below.

Understanding and Accepting the Presenting Problem

The first session is extremely important, as it is the point at which the individual or family will determine if therapy can help them. Thus, it is important that the client or family feel that they are understood, that their views of the problems are respected, and that their difficulties in seeking treatment are understood. The therapist's tasks are to join with each person involved in the consultation as he or she attempts to respect each person's reasons for seeking a consultation and goals sought.

Joining with the clients will be central to developing the trust and confidence of clients who may be skeptical about therapy as a means of helping them to feel better. It can be helpful to give the individual or family permission to acknowledge how difficult it may have been to decide to seek therapy or a consultation. Find out how many individuals or agencies the client or family has contacted before they reached the current consultation. Furthermore, the therapist can acknowledge and anticipate what clients may experience during the first appointment, including: looking for a solution, affirmation that they are not crazy, embarrassment over having to seek help from a mental health professional, confusion or puzzlement over how therapy can be helpful.

Oftentimes when an individual or family is referred for treatment, the symptoms are indicative of the trouble that he or she is having in solving problems in a different way. This type of dysfunction usually occurs as the family life cycle reflects required changes in roles and relationships with immigration, births, separation, marriage, retirement, and death. These aspects of the changing family cycle are experienced by all families, who must also accommodate to the stress.

The role of ethnicity in therapy becomes salient in assessing and understanding the presenting problem. The therapist needs to determine what is healthy for this family compared with other families of similar background and generation in the United States, and how the family has responded to this change in the family life cycle in previous generations. For example, how did the parents of a 23-year-old Japanese female (first generation born in the United States) leave their respective families of origin? Is their daughter attempting to leave their home in a very different way, which may be misinterpreted by the parents? The clinician can help the family to understand their differences in interpretation of behavior. By acknowledging each individual's view of the problem, the therapist joins with each member involved and then can offer an alternative view of the problem which may be more readily accepted.

Several questions may be relevant in the therapist's attempt to understand the individual's or family's distress. For example, when families present, the following questions may be relevant:

How has the acceptable and implicit family structure and hierarchy been threatened or changed?

Who has become the symptom bearer?

What are the possible purposes of the symptom?

How do family members understand the symptom?

Who else has been a symptom bearer?

How were their symptoms relieved?

How does the symptom attempt to restore balance in the individual or family system?

How can the therapist aid the family in achieving a change in structure which does not feel so threatening yet respects normative cultural rules?

For the client seeking help individually, several questions are also relevant in understanding the presenting problem. Such questions include:

Why does the client feel therapy will be helpful?

Who has the recommended therapy?

Who knows that they have sought help?

What would significant others think about counseling?

What are the client's reasons for not wanting to include significant others in the therapy process or awareness of their distress?

What has the client tried to do to relieve their distress?

Obviously, the questions that are relevant to understanding the purposes of the client's or family's help-seeking behavior are not unique to Asian American clients. However, if the answers to these questions are assumed, the therapist may be operating under inaccurate assumptions, which will be reflected in their understanding of the problem. Subsequently, the therapist may have difficulty in getting the client or family to return for followup.

Helping Therapy to Make Sense

Many Asian American clients and families will not have previously had contact with the mental health system. They have had contact with the medical system. This is a model of authority which is congruent with some of the structure inherent in Asian American family functioning. It is extremely important to educate the client as to how therapy works differently from medicine, and how your role as a therapist is similar but different from the relationships they are accustomed to with a medical doctor.

Sue (1981) outlines some discrepancies between traditional psychotherapy practice and Asian or Pacific Americans' cultural patterns which may make therapy confusing. First, mainstream Western models of psychotherapy distinguish between physical and mental health. With Asian Americans, physical and mental health may be viewed more synonymously. Second, communication of satisfaction and dissatisfaction may be more indirect by the standards than the therapist is used to. For example, if the client disagrees with the therapist, this may not be expressed openly or strongly; expression of feelings may be restrained, clients may self-disclose minimally, and family members may be protected. Many of the values of families and clients will be observed as a client or family seek advice, expect the therapist to tell them what to do, and look for concreteness and structure. Third, clients may bring in the expectation that they must exercise willpower and discipline in order to change. Fourth, language difficulties make a demand on therapists to make sure they understand clients and how they may use words differently from those of the therapist. Fifth, traditional psychotherapy assumes an individual-centered focus expecting ambiguity as part of the therapeutic process. Such an orientation may confuse the client who may be expecting direction. Sixth, while silence may be a sign of resistance for some clients, in this culture silence may be a sign of respect.

Because of the differences in cultural patterns, traditional assumptions upon which mainstream American psychotherapies are based will be challenged. Furthermore, the standard goals of therapy may be incongruent with cultural values. Guidelines for facilitating the initial therapeutic contact are offered.

1. Find out what clients' beliefs are about mental and emotional problems. Determine how other similar problems in the family have been addressed. This provides information on the implicit rules of the family as well as their level of acculturation.

2. Most clients, because of their cultural context and relationships with other helping systems, will expect the therapist to be an authority and to tell them what they have to do in order to feel better. It is suggested that to facilitate the likelihood of a family's coming back, they need therapy to make sense. They need to have a sense of what they will have to do. Providing an overview of the therapeutic plan, types of changes that may need to occur, and who needs to be involved may enhance the family's trust in the therapist and their view of his or her competence.

3. Many clients will come into therapy hoping to be able to leave with an answer and will look to some concrete methods of approaching problem solving. A brief therapy model is a positive model with Asian Americans as it can be a model of health. It is a model that helps persons and families become unstuck.

4. As in any therapy, it is important to determine the limits in helping the family and how to become a part of the system. As a positive part of the system, the therapist can transfer to appropriate members in the family.

5. Try to anticipate reasons for which the client or family would not come back for a second appointment. Attempt to check these possibilities out in the first session as well as address them with the clients. For example, the therapist may share their concern that if the individual feels better after the consultation he or she may not return to follow-up. Such a pattern would increase the likelihood of a relapse in symptoms in the near future without the individual understanding why or having developed the tools to prevent or remedy such a relapse.

Reducing Barriers to Obtaining and Continuing Treatment

Additional factors are briefly discussed which will facilitate the individual's or family's ability to seek treatment as well as continue in treatment.

1. Clinic or private practice hours may determine whether or not a family can come in even if they are very distressed. It will be difficult for many family members to ask for time off from work and further for them to explain why they need the time off. Evening hours and weekend hours increase the likelihood that a family will be able to obtain help.
2. The cost of private practice fees can be prohibitive to seeking help. Sliding scale fees or barter systems may allow the client to pay for service, since they will often be unwilling to accept free services or have exceptions made for them.
3. If the therapist is not very experienced working with Asian Americans, families, or has difficulty with the language of the family, a cotherapist may provide a solution. A cotherapist can complement the therapist's lack of experience or skills.
4. Many families may need help with other social service systems or legal systems. Many therapists will not see it a fit use of their time to help someone maneuver through the social system. This is a legitimate request for a family or individual, and by helping with this request, stressors may be relieved for the client.

References

Kleinman, A. M., Eisenberg, L. & Good, B. (1978). Culture, illness, and care: Clinical lessons from anthropologic and cross-cultural research. *Annals of Internal Medicine,* **88,** 251–258.

Le, D. D. (1983). Mental health and Vietnamese children. *In* G. J. Powell, J. Yamamoto, A. Romero and A. Morales (Eds.), *The Psychosocial Development of Minority Group Children.* New York: Brunner/Mazel.

Morishma, J. K. (1975). Early History, 1850–1965: The meeting of the twain. *In* J. K. Morishima (Ed.), *Report on the Asian American Assessment Colloquy.* Washington, D.C.: Child Development Associate Consortium.

Munoz, F. U. (1983). Family life patterns of Pacific-Islanders: The insidious displacement of culture. *In* G. J. Powell, J. Yamamoto, A. Romero and A. Morales (Eds.), *The Psychosocial Development of Minority Group Children.* New York: Brunner/Mazel.

President's Commission on Mental Health (1978). *Report to the President,* 4 vols. Washington, D.C.: U.S. Government Printing Office.

Prizzia, R. & Villaneuva-King, O. (1977). *Central Oahu Community Mental Health Needs Assessment Survey. Part III: A Survey of the General Population.* Honolulu: Management Planning and Administration Consultants.

Root, M. P. P., Ho, C. & Sue, S. (19XX). Training counselors for Asian Americans. *In* Harriet Lefley (Ed.), *Cross-Cultural Training for Mental Health Professionals.* Springfield, Ill.: Charles C. Thomas.

Santos, R. A. (1983). The social and emotional development of Filipino-American children. *In* G. J. Powell, J. Yamamoto, A. Romero and A. Morales (Eds.), *The Psychosocial Development of Minority Group Children.* New York: Brunner/Mazel.

Shon, S. P. & Ja, D. Y. (1982). Asian families. *In* M. McGoldrick, J. K. Pearce and J. Giordana (Eds.), *Ethnicity and Family Therapy.* New York: Guilford Press.

Sue, D., Sue, D. W. & Sue, D. M. (1983). Psychological development of Chinese-American children. *In* G. J. Powell, J. Yamamoto, A. Romero and A. Morales (Eds.), *The Psychosocial Development of Minority Group Children.* New York: Brunner/Mazel.

Sue, D. W. (1981). *Counseling the Culturally Different: Theory and Practice.* New York: John Wiley.

Sue, S. (1976). Conceptions of mental illness among Asian and Caucasian-American students. *Psychological Reports.* **38,** 703–708.

Sue, S. & McKinney, H. (1975). Asian Americans in the community mental health care system. *American Journal of Orthopsychiatry,* **45,** 111–118.

Sue, S. & Morishima, J. K. (1982). *The Mental Health of Asian Americans.* San Francisco: Jossey-Bass.

Sue, S. & Sue, D. W. (1974). MMPI comparisons between Asian American and non-Asian students utilizing a student health psychiatric clinic. *Journal of Counseling Psychology,* **21,** 423–427.

Tsai, M., Teng, L. N. & Sue, S. (1980). Mental status of Chinese in the United States. *In* A. Kleinman and T. Y. Lin (Eds.), *Normal and Deviant Behavior in Chinese Culture.* Hingham, Mass.: Reidel.

Yamamoto, J. & Iga, M. (1983). Emotional growth of Japanese-American children. *In* G. J. Powell, J. Yamamoto, A. Romero and A. Morales (Eds.), *The Psychosocial Development of Minority Group Children.* New York: Brunner/Mazel.

Yamamoto, J. & Kubota, M. (1983). The Japanese-American family. *In* G. J. Powell, J. Yamamoto, A. Romero and A. Morales (Eds.), *The Psychosocial Development of Minority Group Children.* New York: Brunner/Mazel.

Yu, K. H. & Kim, L. I. C. (1983). The growth and development of Korean-American children. *In* G. J. Powell, J. Yamamoto, A. Romero and A. Morales (Eds.), *The Psychosocial Development of Minority Group Children.* New York: Brunner/Mazel.

9 Counseling Vietnamese

Imogene C. Brower

The continuing influx of Vietnamese refugees means that increasing numbers of counselors unfamiliar with Vietnamese culture will be called on to build helping relationships with refugee children and their families. This article provides specific information to help the counselor establish rapport, avoid misunderstandings in explicit and implicit communication, minimize transference dangers, and deal with Vietnamese attitudes toward sex roles and the individual/family relationship. It also discusses relevant socioeconomic and ethnic differences among the Vietnamese themselves, as well as some war-related mental health problems. Practical matters, such as the proper use of Vietnamese names, are explained.

The United States has historically been a haven for immigrants seeking a brighter future and freedom from oppression. Since 1975 waves of Indochinese refugees, principally Vietnamese, have added a new thread to the rich tapestry of American society. Totaling approximately 304,000 by January 1980, the refugees continue to arrive at a rate of many thousands each month.

As newcomers, the culturally different Vietnamese are not always understood by either the dominant culture or other minorities. A special issue of the *Personnel and Guidance Journal* (March 1973) devoted to Asian Americans makes many general points that can apply to Vietnamese culture. But the Asian Americans discussed in the special issue have been here for generations, and the newly arrived Vietnamese have suffered 30 years of war and often traumatic refugee experiences.

A goal of counseling is to assist recipients in adjusting to or otherwise negotiating various environments (Vontress, 1976). Increasing numbers of Vietnamese "boat people" are encountering adjustment problems after resettling in the United States. This article suggests ways for counselors to build positive relationships—based on understanding of psychosocial differences and war-related traumas—to help Vietnamese students and their families adjust to American environments.

Brower, I. C. (1980). Counseling Vietnamese. *Personnel and Guidance Journal, 58,* 646–652. Copyright AACD. Reprinted with permission. No further reproduction authorized without further permission of AACD.

The Relationship

Because of their very different backgrounds, experiences, and value systems, developing a helping relationship between a Vietnamese and an American is not easy. It may take persistent efforts to establish rapport, to structure the relationship to gain understanding, to overcome communication barriers, and to eliminate possible interference from unconscious negative feelings. By far the most important ingredient in the counseling relationship is rapport or mutual trust. When a Vietnamese trusts someone, other barriers become less important (Nguyen Ngoc Bich, 1979).

Rapport

Vontress (1980) defines *rapport* as a "mutual bond" or "emotional bridge." How does the counselor establish rapport with a Vietnamese client? Because the Vietnamese are family-oriented, the counseling process should begin with parents or older family members. Sensitivity to the family and its reactions—particularly in the initial interview, which is likely to be the introduction to the school system and the concept of counseling—will lay a foundation for building trust with the student. The basis of this sensitivity is understanding and respect for Vietnamese customs and values.

The first possibility for misunderstanding or showing "ethnic superiority" often arises in the use of Vietnamese names. These names may be difficult for the counselor to pronounce, and they are often confusing to Americans because the family name is seldom used, and when it is written it appears first. In the case of a male teacher named Nguyen Hung Dung, for example, *Nguyen* is the family name, *Hung* the middle name, and *Dung* the given name. His close friends would call him Dung; others would call him Mr. Dung or simply "teacher" (*thay,* an honorific title). A married woman does not take her husband's family name. Instead, she will prefix the title of *Mrs.* to her husband's given name or to her own given name. Children, however, do use the father's family name. Compounding the difficulty, no more than 200 or 300 family names are in use, so that unrelated persons often have the same one. In contrast to family names (which are mostly those of ancient royal dynasties), given and middle names have precise meanings (e.g., *Dung*—brave; *Hung*—powerful; *Ngoc Bich*—blue pearl). For this reason, and because the Vietnamese expect formality in the use of names, nicknames or anglicized pronunciations may be unintentionally offensive. The expectation of formality, moreover, may make it difficult at first for a Vietnamese to call a counselor by a first name.

The Vietnamese family is patriarchal. Therefore, in interviews with the student and family the counselor should remember that according to Vietnamese custom, the father, not the student, is the important person. This will be true even if the meeting concerns decisions that mainstream American children are usually expected to make for themselves, such as what electives to take in school (rare in Vietnam except in experimental schools). In such a case, a direct request to the child to choose from among several subjects might only embarrass the child, who would feel that such decisions should be made by the school or the father. It might also upset the father, who would feel his authority was being questioned. In some conferences, the mother may participate alone, because traditionally she supervises the house and children. However, decisions about placement, curriculum, or other school matters are best deferred to enable her to consult the father (or in the absence of a father, perhaps an older son). Older students, especially those who have been in the United States several years, may wish to make their own decisions, but family approval is often sought.

Establishing rapport with Vietnamese is a dynamic process of building respect and understanding between the counselor on the one hand and the client and family on the other. Because the process is mutual, the counselor should be not only sensitive to Vietnamese customs, but also ready to help the Vietnamese learn about American ones. A good place to begin is with the concept of counseling itself.

Structure

Many minority groups have had limited experience with counseling and are more accustomed to authorities teaching or telling them what to do (Vontress, 1974). Thus, in counseling minorities there is greater need for structure than with the culturally dominant (Sue & Sue, 1972; Vontress, 1974). Counseling and psychotherapy are nearly unknown in Vietnam (Nguyen Duy San, 1969). Vietnamese culture is highly structured, with definite roles ascribed; the school is part of the Confucian authority hierarchy; and officials, including counselors, are expected to be authoritative and directive. Vietnamese clients may perceive counselors who are not authoritative as unconcerned (Alexander, Workneh, Klein, & Miller, 1976).

Many American psychotherapeutic theories stress the client's self-disclosure, active participation, openness, decision making, and growth in independence (Frank, 1961). Although these are dominant American cultural ideals, they are not necessarily appropriate goals in counseling Asian Americans (Sue & Sue, 1977). The ideals are even less appropriate for newly arrived Vietnamese, who are accustomed to a concrete, well-structured society.

Referring to the role of counselor as "school parent" may help both counselor and student focus their expectations in Vietnamese context. According to Trinh Ngoc Dung (1979), school authorities in Vietnam are perceived as school parents. Although such a perception suggests danger of overdependence, it is important to recognize that in Vietnam the student is primarily a passive receiver of knowledge, dispensed by a wise and superior teacher. Learning by rote with few textbooks for individual students (Nguyen Ngoc Bich & Dao Thi Hoi, 1978), young children are taught to listen but not encouraged to ask questions in class (Duong Thanh Binh, 1975). Therefore, it is not surprising that newly arrived Vietnamese students may participate less actively in class, need more direction, and expect more help than typical American students. As acculturation progresses, however, this dependence is likely to change. Any initial overdependence on the counselor or teacher can gradually be lessened as the student develops new support systems.

By encouraging the Vietnamese to discuss their view of the school and their educational expectations and by contrasting these with American educational theory and practice, the counselor can help bridge differences. For example, the traditional Vietnamese view of learning as the way to succeed and bring honor to one's family may result in family pressure for a child's academic success, to the extent of discouraging extracurricular activities (National Indochinese Clearinghouse, 1977). The counselor may have to help the family understand that some nonacademic activities provide excellent opportunities to learn more English and adjust to school. Another difference is that in Vietnam, PTAs and parent-teacher conferences are less common, and active parent participation in school affairs is rare. In the United States, therefore, Vietnamese parents may seem to lack interest—they are actually reluctant to intrude on what they regard as the school's prerogative (Trinh Ngoc Dung, 1979). The counselor will need to clarify the American view that education is every parent's responsibility.

Transference and Countertransference

The highly visible United States presence and involvement in the Vietnam war left a residue of strong feelings in many Vietnamese and Americans. In striving to develop a good relationship, the counselor should be aware of possible interference from such feelings, either negative or positive.

Transference, or projecting feelings that stem from former experiences onto the counselor or counseling relationship, is common. Some Vietnamese clients may have had unpleasant war or refugee experience that may impinge on the counseling relationship (Dinh Phuc Van, 1976). Sullivan (1979) reports that during an initial interview, a Vietnamese male adolescent interpreted the counselor's forward lean as highly threatening. He hypothesizes that negative transference may have triggered this response.

Counselors are usually aware of the danger of countertransference, especially when working with those of a different culture. When counseling Vietnamese, counselors should check their personal feelings about clients, particularly because of the residues of strong and deeply divided emotions that the United States involvement in the Vietnam war created in American public opinion. These residual feelings range from contempt and antagonism to guilt and deep sympathy. Recent media reports of the sufferings of the boat people have created a new wave of sympathy. One possible result is preferential treatment—real or merely perceived—which in turn breeds resentment in other groups. Such resentment has already been voiced by some Blacks and Hispanics. Counselors should remember that an overly protective attitude can create barriers as easily as a latently hostile one. If, in addition, being overprotective gives an impression of favoritism, such an attitude also invites difficulties with other minorities.

Communication Barriers

Explicit Communication. We expect "talk" in a counseling interview. Unfortunately, basic language barriers are great for the newly arrived Vietnamese. The difficult Vietnamese language was rarely studied here before United States' involvement in the war, and there were few Vietnamese college students here. French was the preferred second language for most educated Vietnamese. The refugees of 1975 found no preexistent ethnic community to help with language problems (Vuong Gia Thuy, 1976). Until the student and family learn English, finding an interpreter for basic communication can present difficulties.

The counselor may be tempted to use a Vietnamese student who speaks some English as an interpreter. Nguyen Ngoc Bich (1979) points out, however, that it is a mistake to use a young person for that purpose in a school setting, where the Vietnamese expect adult authority. It is desirable to obtain the help of an older man or woman, especially in an initial parent interview. When this is not possible, it is best to write, asking the new student and parents to bring someone if they wish, or for the counselor to use simple, slow, and, if necessary, written English. If the adults are secondary school or university educated, they will have studied either English, French, or both. But classes were so large (60 to 70 pupils) that conversation practice was not feasible; as a consequence, many Vietnamese can read or write some English but not speak it (Duong Thanh Binh, 1975). In communication with parents, the telephone should be avoided if possible. Except in larger Vietnamese cities, the telephone was rarely used and may be a source of anxiety for many older Vietnamese. The anxiety results not only from unfamiliarity with the equipment, but from difficulty of English comprehension, which is intensified by the absence of visual clues.

When an interpreter is used, two pitfalls must be avoided. First, the counselor must be careful to pay attention to the principal parties, not to the interpreter. Otherwise it will be difficult to note reactions, convey warmth, and create rapport. Second, the interpreter must not be allowed to encroach on the counselor's role by offering amplification or clarification. The interview should remain a dialogue between the principal party or parties and the counselor.

Even when an interpreter is unnecessary, explicit communication can be frustrating because the responses may not be as expected. *Yes* in reply to a question may not be an affirmative but merely a polite acknowledgment. Also, Vietnamese often will say *yes* simply because they believe this is the answer desired or fear a negative reply would be rude (Parsons, 1968). Accordingly, it is wise to avoid direct questions when possible. Later on, the counselor may help the student understand that in English a person may say *no* and still be polite. Until this has been learned, the counselor should be aware that a Vietnamese *yes* may mean *no* or *maybe*.

Implicit Communication. Nonverbal responses amplify explicit communication, sometimes reinforcing and sometimes contradicting it (e.g., Argyle, 1972; Sielski, 1979). One's culture provides specific interpretations for variations in speech and for nonverbal cues. The Vietnamese have several implicit communication patterns that can lead to misunderstandings by one who does not share them. For example, a loud voice and a warm, hearty greeting are often ways in which Americans communicate welcome. To the Vietnamese, however, these actions are rude and unseemly in a person of authority. A quiet, dignified, and restrained voice and manner are expected, and when confronted with the opposite, the Vietnamese will often lapse into embarrassed silence. The counselor may feel rebuffed, and the relationship will suffer.

A smile in American culture usually means happiness, often assent. For the Vietnamese it may communicate not only these sentiments but anger, embarrassment, rejection, and other emotions as well (Duong Thanh Binh, 1975). In certain situations a Vietnamese smile may seem inappropriate to Americans. For the Vietnamese, smiling may reflect stoic behavior in adversity, which is admired, or cover hostile or angry impulses (Bourne, 1970).

Eye contact also sends different messages to the two cultural groups. In general, Americans think of "shifty eyes" or unwillingness to look someone in the face as a negative, even suspicious trait. For the Vietnamese adults and children, to look directly at a person with whom they are speaking is a sign of disrespect and rudeness (Nguyen Van Thuan, 1962). When speaking to an older person or one in authority, Vietnamese will glance up occasionally, but usually keep their eyes down. Eye avoidance is especially noticeable in girls and in the lower class.

Socially acceptable body contact is another area in which the two cultures differ. For example, although an affectionate pat on a small child's arm would generally be understood by the Vietnamese, touching a young person on the head is offensive to them. Also, social touching of the opposite sex is usually not done in the Vietnamese culture except sometimes to family members (Nguyen Van Thuan, 1962). A male counselor's handshake to a Vietnamese male would be better received than a handshake to a female. In fact, the male counselor should be aware that the Vietnamese consider his touching females older than age 12 as threatening or insulting. For the adolescent or older Vietnamese woman, even sitting in a room with a nonfamily male with the door closed creates discomfort. In some cases counselors will have to sacrifice privacy to put a student or parent at ease.

In contrast to opposite-sex touching, touching between persons of the same sex, especially age cohorts, is common in Vietnam. Adolescents of the same sex, and even persons in their early twenties, often walk together holding hands or arm in arm. This is merely a show of friendship and has no sexual meaning. Counselors should instruct the student in acceptable and unacceptable American social behavior, because adhering to social expectations enhances acceptance and adjustment.

Psychosocial Differences

Human beings, Sundberg (1976) points out, comprise similarities and differences—sharing universals with all, sharing specific socializations with their own group, and having individual uniqueness. Counselors aware of the universals and individual uniqueness can still be blocked by those specific socializations that make someone "different from us." Only by understanding these differences can we hope to overcome any barriers they may present.

Unwillingness to Self-disclose and Humilty

Most therapists would agree that in a counseling interview, frank discussion of feelings, problems, and concerns is desirable. This can be inhibited by two Vietnamese traits: unwillingness to disclose problems and feelings, and extreme humility. Vietnamese find it difficult to discuss problems and reveal emotions. As children they were taught to conceal antisocial emotions such as anger and hostility. This helped preserve domestic harmony, which was essential because the family was large, with several generations living together in close quarters. It also helped prevent tension between the family and the community, where individual actions tended to involve the family or reflect on its honor. In addition, children were taught not to question authority, especially the father's. According to Bourne (1970), it is almost impossible for a Vietnamese to express anger, resentment, or frustration toward a parent or authority figure. Suppression—refusal to recognize conflict or anger—or withdrawal, either physical or emotional, are the usual ways of coping with authority conflicts (Nguyen Duy San, 1969). Although an emotional explosion can result from unresolved conflicts, such outbursts are usually turned inward, sometimes by committing suicide or running away (Nguyen Duy San, 1969).

The Vietnamese are taught to adopt a humble, self-depreciating attitude toward their accomplishments and those of their family. They are reluctant to complain to authority for fear of being disrespectful, even when injustice has been done or a mistake made. Because a braggart or an overly assertive person is considered rude, the Vietnamese may find it hard to speak of their own accomplishments, to ask questions in class, to volunteer to answer questions, or to express opinions, lest they appear to be showing off. In America, where assertiveness is valued, Vietnamese who exhibit extreme humility will often find it difficult to sell themselves. The counselor may need to help Vietnamese understand American expectations, and assertiveness may be indicated to aid in future employment or education.

Vietnamese upbringing also teaches young persons to conceal stress as a matter of stoic pride. Although Nguyen Ngoc Bich (1979) suggests that the threshold of pain (physical and mental) may be higher for Vietnamese than for Americans, it is more likely that the Vietnamese simply conceal pain better. Personal matters that embarrass or cause hurt or stress are not usually discussed with anyone except family and very close friends. Openness as a basis of understanding and "talking out problems" in a counseling dyad will not be possible to the same extent as with an American, and accuracy in diagnosis may be affected. Group therapy, which Kaneshige (1973) says presents problems for Asian Americans, would also be difficult for Vietnamese because of their reluctance to verbalize their feelings or confront others.

Sex Roles and Attitudes

Male and female roles and expectations were viewed differently in Vietnam. Both sexes had obligations to bring honor to the family, avoid shame, and be obedient (Hammer, 1966)—however, the male led and the female followed. Beginning in childhood, the boy had more freedom of action and fewer specific tasks. To be male was desirable in itself; to be female was desirable only in the context of how well duties or tasks were performed.

The Vietnamese woman thus tends to be less concerned with equal rights than American women and more inclined to value obedience (Penner & Anh Tran, 1977). On the other hand, she controls the family finances and is responsible for the children. She is thus competent and, although theoretically subservient, actually powerful within her sphere. She has also learned to adapt, adjusting to the requirements of obedience—first to her father, then to her husband, and if widowed, to her sons. Therefore Vietnamese girls in school here may hesitate to assert themselves, particularly with boys and male authorities. Because of their adaptibility, however, they and their mothers may adjust more easily than the male members of the family (Trinh Ngoc Dung, 1979).

Another Vietnamese female trait contributing to adjustment problems is extreme physical modesty. Vietnamese girls in school find showering in locker rooms with other girls, attending a class on human reproduction, or participating in a mixed group discussion of personal matters highly embarrassing. (Information and previous discussion with the girl's family about such activities would be an important step in lessening embarrassment.) Girls also find it difficult to associate with boys. Although boys and girls went to school and had classes together in Vietnam, they sat in separate sections, not even sharing lab partnerships, and their social contacts were minimal; American-style dating was not practiced.

The obverse of female subservience in nondomestic matters is male dominance. This intensifies the problems many Vietnamese men face as a result of war and refugee experiences. Defeat in the war often has undermined male self-esteem (Bourne, 1970). Also, Vietnamese are highly status conscious, for example, a study (Kelly, 1978) of male Vietnamese college students noted their unwillingness to accept janitorial jobs acceptable to American students in the same college. According to the U.S. Department of Health, Education, and Welfare (HEW) (1978), Vietnamese immigration to the United States has usually meant loss of occupational status; 68% of former white-collar workers hold blue-collar jobs here. The resulting tension—especially in families in which the women are also working, often in equivalent jobs—leads to an increase in divorce, a virtually unknown phenomenon in Vietnam.

The counselor working with Vietnamese males may have to help them rebuild their confidence and self-esteem. This can be done by acknowledging traditional male authority in the home, and if a low-status job must be suggested, by giving reassurances that as English is learned and skills mastered, higher status employment can be found (Sullivan, 1979). Career suggestions for either sex should always consider the status of the occupation, particularly for the first-born child.

The Family and the Individual

It is not easy for an American to grasp full the extent of Vietnamese family involvement in the person's past, present, and future plans. In Vietnam, the family—a community in miniature—was the source of financial and personal support, old-age and child care, the keeper of all rituals, and the home of the ancestors. Transplanted to America, the family still provides security and order in an alien world (Vuong Gia Thuy, 1976). By including the entire Vietnamese family in school activities, the American school helps to reinforce this support system.

For the Vietnamese, the family's honor, pride, and traditions are more important than the individual's, and any appeal to self alone tends to fail (McAlister & Mus, 1970). If an individual's wishes for a career or goal are counter to the family's desires, the latter will usually prevail. Discussion of educational or career goals will, therefore, involve more parent consultation and active approval than would be expected or desired for the average American.

The American ideal of independence—its lack viewed as maladjustment—is not a Vietnamese ideal. Unmarried Vietnamese men and women in their twenties with advanced degrees usually continue to live with their parents. Even marriage, while no longer arranged, is still a family concern. The American custom of dating creates problems: a "good" Vietnamese family strongly disapproves of a child's going out, especially with an American, partly for fear that marriage may result.

Differences among Vietnamese

Vietnamese society is heterogeneous, and some of its variations are significant to the adjustment of refugees in the United States. The counselor should be aware of a refugee family's former socioeconomic status (often related to educational level, previous cross-cultural experience, and degree of urbanization) and possible membership in the ethnic Chinese subculture.

Many of the 1975–76 refugees were from the upper or upper-middle class, were well-educated, had urban backgrounds, and had worked with French or Americans. They were prepared to meld portions of Vietnamese and American cultures, and their adjustment progressed well (Montero, 1978). On the other hand, those who came to the United States later encompass a much broader social spectrum, and for many the culture shock has been severe. A female refugee's ignorance of how to use a simple mechanical can opener, described in *Newsweek* (Conrad, 1979), may seem an extreme example but warns effectively against assuming too much sophistication.

To "emphasize with differences, to learn the latent messages in intercultural communications" (Alexander et al., 1976, p. 91), the counselor needs to learn as much as possible about the culturally different client. Were the Vietnamese city or rural dwellers? Were they used to western culture, French, or American? What was the father's former occupation? What is the parents' educational background? The answers to such questions will suggest the probable degree of culture shock and will yield valuable insights into potential adjustment problems.

Many of the current refugees are ethnic Chinese. Residents of Vietnam for generations, they have survived in an often hostile environment by sticking together, and have developed a unique subculture bridging the Chinese and Vietnamese cultures. Most of them speak one of three Chinese dialects: Hakka, Fukinese, or Cantonese. The Chinese in Vietnam maintain their own schools, so that their school placement in America may be different from that of other Vietnamese and their schooling may have been interrupted. They tend to live apart, concentrating in the Cholon section of Saigon. They have more group identification than other Vietnamese, may be more suspicious of strangers, may fear "officials," and may fear forms and written documents. (Forms were often used for tax collection by anti-Chinese authorities.) Because it is very difficult for someone who is not Vietnamese to distinguish the two groups by name or appearance, the counselor should ask whether the family is ethnic Chinese. If so, local Chinese-American organizations may be able to help in language and cultural matters, as there is some feeling of community among overseas Chinese.

If a family is not ethnic Chinese, it is important that the counselor avoid mistakingly referring to them as such. Although indebted to Chinese culture, the Vietnamese tend to be anti-Chinese—a feeling that extends, subtly or blatantly, to their own ethnic Chinese minority (Foreign Area Studies of the American University, 1967).

Where concern is with the overall socialization patterns of the two cultures, these distinctions among Vietnamese may seem oversubtle. They will serve to remind the counselor, however, that there is no stereotypical Vietnamese.

Mental Health Problems

Because the Vietnamese are generally unfamiliar with psychotherapy and mental health facilities (Nguyen Duy San, 1969), an individual with problems usually goes to someone older, preferably in the family. In Vietnam the person might go to a "healer" or Buddhist monk known to be adept in such matters. Many believe that mental or nervous difficulties, and problems in general, are caused by evil spirits and are solved by religious means (Hickey, 1964).

Thirty years of war brought dislocation, loss of loved ones and property, and great stress to the Vietnamese people. For the refugees, this stress has been prolonged in dangerous escapes, often in crowded, leaky boats, followed by many months in squalid refugee camps where rape and robbery were common. Because the Vietnamese lack familiarity with mental health and are hesitant in approaching strangers, counselors need to be alert to evidence of stress and the emotional scars of war and refugee experiences.

Depression and Anxiety

Costello (1976) believes that depression is often caused by a loss of structure and meaning in life. According to an HEW report (1978), severe depression and other mental health problems may be three times more frequent among the refugees than in the population as a whole. This report resulted in the funding of a project to train Indochinese paraprofessionals for community health services; so far only six have been trained.

A Vietnamese suffering from severe depression or anxiety has two special problems: Early diagnosis is made difficult because the Vietnamese are unwilling to self-disclose (noted above), and qualified professionals are few. American psychiatrists have had little success with Vietnamese patients because of the language barrier and unfamiliarity with Vietnamese culture (Trinh Ngoc Dung, 1979). Tom That Toai (1979), one of the few Vietnamese psychologists, points out that a Vietnamese child, confronted by a tall stranger speaking English, is very frightened and finds it difficult to respond, even through an interpreter.

A school counselor is in a good position to observe changes in behavior or appearance that may indicate anxiety or the onset of depression. Also, Vietnamese tend to manifest their emotional disturbances in physical symptoms (Nguyen Duy San, 1969); thus, the counselor, teacher, and school nurse should be especially concerned about the child who displays physical symptoms (e.g., frequent stomach upsets, or unexplained aches and pains). Because of the lack of professionals familiar with Vietnamese language or culture, referrals will be difficult and counselors may find themselves working with problems that they might not have otherwise attempted to solve.

Sullivan (1979) notes that counselors have reported students who are preoccupied with blood, guns, and fears of death and dying. These anxieties are particularly true of children who were in the active war zone and also had terrifying escapes. Dinh Phuc Van (1976) writes that many children from the active war zone "do not believe in anyone or anything" (p. 87). *Newsweek* (Deming, Copeland, Buckley, & Coppola, 1979) quotes one refugee as saying about those who had harrowing escapes: "They are maimed. Despair and frustration saturate their minds" (p. 52). The counselor may wish, as the students' English progresses, to help them talk, write, or perhaps draw pictures about experiences that need to be brought into present focus.

Family Conflicts and School Adjustment Problems

According to Ton That Toai (1979), poor adjustment and low achievement at school, especially after a satisfactory start, may reflect conflict within the family. The child who comes home eager to show off English learned or American ways copied from peers may be rebuffed by a formal, traditional family; a passive, indifferent family; or a family that views adaptation to American culture as a positive threat to its solidarity and eventual return to Vietnam.

Various factors contribute to these family attitudes. To a traditional Vietnamese family, becoming "like an American" may mean loudness, disobedience, disrespect, and lack of concern for the elderly. Too often, students who want to be more like Americans but do not have experience in discriminating between behavioral levels fulfill their parent's fears by modeling themselves after peers whose extreme behavior is unacceptable, even to most Americans. To prevent this, a counselor may need to model acceptable behavior for school, social events, and other situations (Sullivan, 1979). Also, the insecurity they have known in the past makes many Vietnamese reluctant to plan for a future in the United States. The Buddhist philosophy, to which 80% of Vietnamese adhere, instills a passive fatalism rather than active striving to shape the future (Nguyen Thanh Liem, 1976). There is also a widespread belief among some refugees that they are here temporarily. Many fled to the United States only to save their lives, and if the Communist regime adopted different policies, they would return to Vietnam. For all these reasons, some older adults have made only minimal efforts to learn English or adjust to American culture and they may actually resist doing so. The result may be conflict with younger family members who seek to be more bicultural, adopt a more "western" attitude toward the future, and lean increasingly toward permanent residence in the United States.

The family's adjustment to life in America may improve as its socioeconomic status rises and it can begin to look to a more secure future. Less successful adults, however, may prefer to live in the past, which can cause problems for their children. The counselor working with a young person may find that all family members need help in adjusting to their environments.

Summary

In dealing with Vietnamese clients, good relations with the family as well as the student are especially necessary. Rapport may be difficult to establish because of the language barrier or conflicting nonverbal cues. Vietnamese humility and unwillingness to self-disclose may inhibit frank discussion, and transference or countertransference may hinder counseling. The counselor may have to structure the relationship more concretely and adopt a more directive approach than is normal with Americans. Differing attitudes toward sex roles and the family may contribute to adjustment problems, as may the emotional scars of war and refugee experiences. Socioeconomic and ethnic differences among the Vietnamese themselves will also have a bearing on adjustment.
But if the counselor is able to convey a respect for cultural differences, a desire to understand and help, and a flexible approach, a positive helping relationship can be established despite these barriers. The rescue of the boat people is not complete when they reach American shores. Problems often follow, and the counselor can help the Vietnamese overcome them.

Acknowledgment

The author wishes to thank Clemmont E. Vontress, Professor of Education, The George Washington University, for his help and encouragement.

References

Alexander, A. A.; Workneh, F.; Klein, M. H.; & Miller, M. H. Psychotherapy and the foreign student. In P. Pederson, W. J. Lonner, & J. G. Draguns (Eds.), *Counseling across cultures,* pp. 82–97. Honolulu: University Press of Hawaii, 1976.
Argyle, M. Non-verbal communication in human social interaction. In R. A. Hinde (Ed.), *Non-verbal communication,* pp. 243–269. Cambridge, Mass.: Harvard University Press, 1972.
Bourne, P. G. *Men, stress and Vietnam.* Boston: Little, Brown, 1970.
Conrad, P. Living with refugees. *Newsweek,* 13 August 1979, p. 15.
Costello, C. G. *Anxiety and depression.* Montreal: McGill-Queen's University Press, 1976.
Deming, A.; Copeland, J. B.; Buckley, J.; & Coppola, V. Home of brave. *Newsweek,* 2 July 1979, p. 52.

Dinh Phuc Van. A Vietnamese child in your classroom. *Instructor,* 1976, *85,* 86–92.

Duong Thanh Binh. *Vietnamese in the U.S.* Arlington, Va.: Center for Applied Linguistics, 1975.

Foreign Area Studies of the American University. *Area handbook for South Vietnam.* Washington, D.C.: U.S. Government Printing Office, 1967.

Frank, J. *Persuasions and healing.* Baltimore: The John Hopkins University Press, 1961.

Hammer, E. *Vietnam yesterday and today.* New York: Holt, Rinehart & Winston, 1966.

Hickey, G. C. *Village in Vietnam.* New Haven, Conn.: Yale University Press, 1964.

Kaneshige, E. Cultural factors in group counseling. *Personnel and Guidance Journal,* 1973, *51,* 407–412.

Kelly, P. L. *Vietnamese students on a small college campus: Observations and analysis.* Papers presented at the meeting of the National Association of Foreign Student Affairs, Iowa State University, Ames, 1978.

McAlister, J. T., & Mus, P. *The Vietnamese and their revolution.* New York: Harper & Row, 1970.

Montero, D. *The Vietnamese refugees in America: Patterns of socioeconomic adaptation and assimilation.* Paper prepared for the Institute of Urban Studies, University of Maryland, College Park, 1978.

National Indochinese Clearinghouse and Technical Assistance Center. *A manual for Indochinese refugee education in 1976–1977.* Arlington, Va.: Center for Applied Linguistics, 1977.

Nguyen Duy San. Psychiatry in the army of the Republic of Viet Nam. In P. G. Bourne (Ed.), *The psychology and physiology of stress,* pp. 45–73. New York: Academic, 1969.

Nguyen Ngoc Bich. Personal communications. Arlington County, Virginia, Public Schools Intake Center. June, August, & September 1979.

Nguyen Ngoc Bich & Dao Thi Hoi. *The Vietnamese learner: Hints for the American teacher.* Unpublished manuscript, Arlington County, Virginia, Public Schools, 1978.

Nguyen Thanh Liem. *Vietnamese culture kit.* Iowa City: Research Institute for Studies in Education, University of Iowa, 1976. (ERIC Document Reproduction Service No. ED 149 602).

Nguyen Van Thuan. *An approach to better understanding of Vietnamese society.* Saigon: Michigan State University Advisory Group, 1962.

Parsons, J. S. *Americans and Vietnamese: A comparison of values in two cultures.* Arlington, Va.: Human Science Research, Inc., 1968.

Penner, L. A., & Anh Tran. A comparison of American and Vietnamese values system. *Journal of Social Psychology,* 1977, *101,* 187–204.

Sielski, L. M. Understanding body language. *Personnel and Guidance Journal,* 1979, *57,* 238–242.

Sue, D. W., & Sue, D. Barriers to effective cross-cultural counseling. *Journal of Counseling Psychology,* 1977, *24,* 420–429.

Sue, D. W., & Sue, S. Counseling Chinese-Americans. *Personnel and Guidance Journal,* 1972, *50,* 637–644.

Sullivan, W. Personnel communication, student advisor, Arlington County Virginia. Public Schools Career Center. 20 September 1979.

Sundberg, N. D. Toward research evaluating intercultural counseling. In P. Pederson, W. J. Lonner, & J. G. Draguns (Eds.), *Counseling across cultures,* pp. 139–169. Honolulu: University Press of Hawaii, 1976.

Ton That Toai. Personal communication, psychologist, Arlington County, Virginia, Public Schools. 4 October 1979.

Trinh Ngoc Dung. Personal communication. HEW Indochinese Refugee Task Force. June & September, 1979.

U.S. Department of Health, Education, and Welfare. *Report to the Congress, Indochinese Refugee Assistance Program.* Washington, D.C.: U.S. Government Printing Office, 31 December 1978.

Vontress, C. E. Barriers in cross-cultural counseling. *Counseling and Values,* 1974, *18,* 160–165.

Vontress, C. E. Racial and ethnic barriers in counseling. In P. Pederson, W. J. Lonner, & J. G. Draguns (Eds.), *Counseling across cultures,* pp. 42–64. Honolulu: University Press of Hawaii, 1976.

Vontress, C. E. Racial and ethnic barriers in counseling. In P. Pederson, W. J. Lonner, & J. G. Draguns (Eds.), *Counseling across cultures* (Rev. ed.). Honolulu: University Press of Hawaii, 1980.

Vuong Gia Thuy. *Getting to know the Vietnamese and their culture.* New York: Frederick Unger, 1976.

The Asian American Client

Cases and Questions

1. Assume you are a high school counselor in a large suburban high school. A Japanese American student whom you have seen for academic advising on several occasions has just shared with you his involvement as a marijuana dealer. Although attempting to hide his emotions, the student is clearly distraught. He is particularly concerned that a recent arrest of a marijuana supplier will eventually lead authorities to him.

   a. How *might* the student's cultural background affect his feelings as he shares this problem?
   b. What kind of input from you as a counselor do you think this student wants/needs most?
   c. Can you anticipate any prejudicial reaction on the part of the school administration (if the student's behavior is uncovered) as a result of the student's racial/ethnic background?

2. Assume you are a community psychologist employed by a community agency which provides psychological services to a population of middle class Japanese American families, among others. A Young Buddhist Association (YBA) has asked you to speak on "resolving intergenerational conflict" at its next meeting. (Your agency is aware that generational conflict has become a major problem in this community in recent years.)

   a. What do you think are some of the causes of the intergenerational conflict being experienced by these young people and their parents?
   b. Other than your talk, what services do you feel qualified to render these young Japanese Americans and their families?
   c. How do you think these services will be received by the YBA members and their families?

3. Assume you are a high school counselor who has been asked by the dean of Guidance to organize and moderate a number of value clarification groups. You plan to set up six groups of eight students

each from a list of volunteers, although seven students were referred by teachers because they are non-participators in class. Six of the seven students referred by teachers are Asian Americans.

a. Will the composition of your six groups be determined by the fact that six of seven teacher referrals are Asian American?
b. What goals do you have for your six groups and for the individual members of these groups?
c. How will your own cultural/educational background affect the way in which you relate to the six Asian American students?

The Asian American Client
Role Playing Exercise

Divide into groups of four or five. Assign each group member to a role and the responsibilities associated with the role as follows:

Role	Responsibilities
1. Counselor	1. Assume role as a counselor or mental health worker who encounters an Asian client. Depending on the client role, the person may be Chinese, Japanese, or Indo-Chinese. Attempt to build rapport with the client.
2. Client	2. Assume role of an Asian client (Chinese, Japanese, or Indo-Chinese refugee). To play this role effectively, it will be necessary for the student client to (a) identify cultural values of the Asian group, (b) identify sociopolitical factors which may interfere with counseling, and (c)portray these aspects in the counseling session. It is best to select a few powerful variables in the role play. You may or may not be initially antagonistic to the counselor, but it is important for you to be sincere in your role and your reactions to the counselor trainee.
3. Observers	3. Observe interaction and offer comments during feedback session.

This exercise is most effective in a racially and ethnically mixed group. For example, an Asian American student can be asked to play the Asian client role. However, this is probably not possible in most cases. Thus, students who play the client role will need to thoroughly read the articles for the group they are portraying.

Identifying the barriers that could interfere with counseling is an important aspect of this exericse. We recommend that a list be made of the group's cultural values and sociopolitical influences prior to the role playing. For example, how might restraint of strong feelings, preference for structure and activity, and trust/mistrust be manifested in the client?

Role playing may go on for a period of 5–15 minutes, but the time limit should be determined prior to the activity. Allow 10–15 minutes for a feedback session in which all participants discuss (within the group) how they felt in their respective roles, how appropriate were the counselor responses, what else they might have done in that situation, etc.

Rotate and role play the same situation with another counselor trainee *or* another Asian client with different issues, concerns, and problems. In the former case, the group may feel that a particular issue is of sufficient importance to warrant reenactment. This allows students to see the effects of other counseling responses and approaches. In the latter case, the new exposure will allow students to get a broader view of barriers to counseling.

If videotaping equipment is available, we recommend that the sessions be taped and processed in a replay at the end. We have found this to be a powerful means of providing feedback to participants.

Part 4
The Black Client

The United States is among the richest countries in the world. Our advances in science and technology have allowed us to produce more food and material goods than any nation on the face of the earth. Yet millions of Americans are unable to feed, clothe, or house themselves without public assistance.

According to the U.S. Bureau of Census, for the first time in decades poverty has defied racial and social lines to strike nearly 15 percent of all Americans. But despite its pervasiveness, black Americans continue to represent a disproportionate percentage of our nation's poor.

Black Americans are the largest ethnic minority in America. Over the past quarter century the black population has increased from 16.5 million to over 29.4 million and has grown from 10.1 to 12 percent of the nation's population. Along with this rapid growth, a burgeoning group of black poor and impoverished has also evolved (U.S. Census Bureau, 1987).

Although most people have a sense of what is meant by the "poor," considerable disagreement exists among professionals over the exact criteria for defining this group. Some have relied on the limitation of income, others refer to deficiencies of community resources and income substitutes, and still others center on the presence of a "culture of poverty" (Ferman, Kornbluh, & Haber, 1966; Will & Vatter, 1970). If the system accepted by the U.S. Congress is used, four class strata are identified: "upper class," "middle class," "working class," and "poor":

—The upper class is designated by those earning $50,000 or more.
—The middle class is designated by those earning between $20,000 and $50,000.
—The working class is designated by those earning between $10,000 and $20,000.
—The poor are designated by those earning under $10,000.

When black Americans are classified according to this system, the results are often shocking. For example, over 64 percent of black Americans earn $20,000 or less. Even more alarming, over 35 percent are classified as "poor" and earn less than $10,000 a year. But these statistics tell only part of the story.

More than any other class, the black poor experience a higher rate of unemployment, female-headed families, undereducation, and victimization in multiple crimes (U.S. News & World Report, 1986). Moreover, many Americans still associate poverty with black stereotypes, asserting that an inherent black "laziness," "thriftlessness," and "immorality" are responsible for "their poverty" (Ferman, Kornbluh, & Haber, 1966).

But, of course, not all black Americans are classified as "poor." The black middle class, for instance, is one of the fastest growing segments of American society, accounting for 29 percent of the black population. It is estimated that their combined incomes represent 45 percent of all black earnings, a financial growth rate of 16 percent over that of poor blacks (Brimmer, 1987). As the black middle class gets richer, the black poor get poorer. With each successive middle-class gain, the gap broadens, leaving the general impression that the black poor are separated not only from the dominant society but from members of their own group as well.

But despite differences in classes, the black middle class and the black poor may not be as far apart as once theorized (Frazier, 1939). A recent survey conducted by the Urban League (Hill, 1987) revealed that the black middle class and the black poor rank racial discrimination and unemployment as the most pressing issues facing black Americans. Similar findings were echoed by Thomas (1986) and other psychologists working with the black client in therapy.

Clearly, America's black poor are caught in a double bind. On the one hand they are viewed and treated in terms of racial biases, and on the other hand discriminated against in terms of distorted views held of the poor. Counselors and other helping professionals, when properly trained, are in a unique position to help.

In the first article in this section, "External Crosscurrents and Internal Diversity: An Assessment of Black Progress, 1960–1980," F. Jones provides an excellent historical background to a period of American history which continues to shape the lives of black Americans today. Jones explores the key battles waged by black Americans to obtain social, economic, and political equality. Each step of the black struggle up to the decade of the 1980s is retraced to explain current gains and losses experienced by blacks at various levels of the class system. The insight Jones offers to counselors working with the black client is invaluable.

The second article in this section, "The Role of the Family Therapist with Low-Income Black Families," addresses the counseling needs of the low-income black family. Carole Grevious confronts the various stereotypes often held toward the poor in general and the black poor in particular. She explores several helpful roles with which the neophyte counselor should be familiar.

In the final article in this section, "Dimensions of the Relationship between the Black Client and the White Therapist," A. Jones and Seagull focus on "self-perception" as it relates to the white counselor working with the black client. They emphasize the importance of the white counselor becoming familiar with his/her own racial values and attitudes as well as those of the client. They explore such concepts as countertransference and the detrimental effects of counselor guilt on counseling.

References

Brimmer, A. F. (1987). Income and wealth. *Ebony,* August, 46–48.
Ferman, L. A., Kornbluh, J. L., & Haber, A. (1966). *Poverty in America:* A Book of Readings, Ann Arbor, The University of Michigan Press.

Frazier, F. E. (1939). *The Negro family in the United States,* Chicago: Chicago Press.

Hill, R. B. (1987). The black middle class defined. *Ebony,* August, 30–31.

A Nation Apart. (1986). *U.S. News and World Report,* March 17, 18–25.

Thomas, M. (1986). Black gain, but far from satisfied. *Psychology Today,* July, 72.

U.S. Bureau of Census, Current Population Report, Series P–60, No. 157, Money, Income, and Poverty Status of families and persons in the U.S., 1986 (Advance data from the March 1987 Current Population Survey) U.S. Government Printing Office, Washington, D.C. 1987.

Will, R. E., & Vatter, H. G. (1970). *Poverty in Affluence,* 2nd Edition, Harcourt, Brace and World, Inc.

10 External Crosscurrents and Internal Diversity:

An Assessment of Black Progress, 1960–1980
Faustine C. Jones

This essay focuses on the past twenty years; it seeks to define and evaluate black progress in the United States during that period. It is assumed that most of those who will read this paper will know something of the vast literature that analyzes white/black-dominant/minority relationships in this country in the years preceding 1960.[1] Present-day black/white inequalities and difficulties are rooted in this earlier period of American history.[2]

Historical Background

Blacks have lived in the United States for 362 years; the first Africans brought to this country in 1619 came as indentured servants, a status that proved to be short-lived. It was supplanted very early by legal slavery, a more onerous status that ended formally only with the passage of the Thirteenth Amendment to the Constitution on December 18, 1865. The slave status was unique to blacks in the United States; no other race was comparably treated.

During the more than two hundred years when most blacks lived in enforced bondage, an elaborate system of laws, social codes, customs, traditions, attitudes, and beliefs developed that were used principally to rationalize and justify the institution of slavery. In the *Dred-Scott* decision of 1857, explicit reference was made to the fact that blacks enjoyed no rights that whites were required to respect.[3] It was during this period that human intergroup relationships became rooted in racial differences[4] characterized by the ascribed superiority of whites and assigned inferiority of blacks. Public policy was formulated wholly in terms of group characteristics, without reference to individual attributes, needs, or interests.

From 1865 to 1877 blacks enjoyed a brief release from certain of these more onerous conditions. Citizenship conferred on blacks by the Fourteenth Amendment (1868) was given ever more concrete expression by the Fifteenth (1870), which guaranteed blacks the right to vote. The Freedmen's Bureau, established by the federal government in 1865, made

Jones, F. (1981). External crosscurrents and internal diversity: An assessment of black progress, 1960–1980. *Daedalus, 110*(2), 71–101. Reprinted by permission of the American Academy of Arts and Sciences.

major efforts to help the recently liberated slaves, especially in the area of education. Blacks now enjoyed specific civil rights, including the right to vote and to be elected to public office. The extent of the federal concern is perhaps most eloquently reflected in the passage of a major civil rights bill in 1875.

Reaction to this kind of progress came swiftly. In 1883 the Supreme Court declared the Civil Rights bill unconstitutional. The majority of blacks, who lived in Southern states, found themselves disempowered through denial of the ballot by "grandfather clauses," and other devices such as the poll tax. The *Plessy v. Ferguson* decision in 1896 institutionalized the separate and unequal conditions legally imposed upon blacks until 1954, when it was overturned by *Brown v. Board of Education of Topeka, Kansas.*[5] From 1896 to 1954 Northern and Southern state policies and practices confirmed the prediction made by Justice Harlan in his dissenting opinion in *Plessy* that the decision would place "in a condition of legal inferiority a large body of American citizens."[6]

Jim Crow laws were passed, segregating blacks under unequal conditions in schools, courtrooms, and churches; public transportation was segregated, as were most other public accommodations and facilities. Fewer employment opportunities existed for blacks in general; the jobs available to them were paid lower rates than those generally offered whites in comparable positions.[7] Housing and health care conditions were deplorable. Although some black individuals and families were able to prosper despite this system of imposed inequality and racism,[8] most blacks were severely hindered by these institutionalized restrictions.

Blacks chose not to accept their castelike status without resistance. Through their own sustained organizational efforts, often with the help of concerned and sympathetic white citizens, they created such institutions as the National Association for the Advancement of Colored People (NAACP) in 1909 and the National Urban League in 1910. These organizations, and others, began systematic resistance against racism. Through the NAACP particularly, white attorneys joined blacks in a step-by-step, case-by-case legal challenge against state and local segregation laws, policies, and practices. These efforts culminated in the *Brown* decision of 1954, which overturned *Plessy,* formally ending the legal disempowerment of black citizens.

The organized efforts of blacks and whites were assisted by demographic and political changes that imposed new pressures on national leaders and served to create a societal climate more conducive to change. From 1915 to 1918 half a million blacks moved north, migrating from small rural Southern communities to work in the war-related industries that were established during World War I.[9] This internal migration put blacks in wholly new settings, especially in Northern industrial centers, where they found new opportunities for employment, better housing, and chances for education and participation in politics greater than any common in the Jim Crow South. The New Deal policies of Franklin D. Roosevelt were beneficial to blacks; equal pay clauses, introduced with the Tennessee Valley Authority legislation, soon became common in all federal agencies. Such policies challenged economic aspects of Southern employment practices at a time when other legal efforts were being made to overturn Southern segregation laws. Roosevelt, in response to A. Philip Randolph's planned March on Washington for equal employment opportunity, issued Executive Order 8802, which created the first Fair Employment Practices Commission (FEPC). As a result of this action, federal contract funds would be made available only to companies hiring black and white workers on an equal basis. Although enforcement was weak, this signaled the beginning of efforts by blacks to effect change through the use of the power of the Executive Office.[10]

In the Fair Deal era of Harry S. Truman, such policies were maintained and, indeed, strengthened. The President's Committee on Civil Rights in 1947 recommended the "elimination of segregation, based on race, color, creed, or national origin, from American life,"[11] and in 1948 Truman issued an executive order desegregating the armed forces. He also recommended that Congress establish a permanent FEPC. The judicial branch of government began to make similar decisions in this period. Segregation in interstate transportation was outlawed in 1944 as was the Democratic white primary in 1947. The federal government increasingly supported the efforts of black individuals and organizations to end institutionalized discrimination.

Meanwhile, demographic changes continued, with very substantial impacts on the black population. From 1940 to 1960 more than 3 million blacks migrated from the South, moving principally to Northern and Western cities. Remunerative employment in war-related industries was important for some. Many others came to participate in politics in cities, counties, and states; blacks began to have a voice in state legislatures as well as in Congress. More than a million blacks served in the armed forces during World War II, and with their reentry to civilian life, these veterans sought to forge domestic changes that would create greater democracy in the United States.

The international scene was also changing. With the beginning of decolonization in the 1940s and 1950s, Africa became gradually a continent of independent black states. The United Nations, formed to monitor world peace and pledged to stimulate friendly reciprocal relations among nations "based on respect for the principle of equal rights and self-determination of peoples," imposed subtle pressures on the United States. To continue to tolerate second-class citizenship for millions of its own citizens would place the United States in an untenable position and, of course, be inconsistent with its international commitments. The United States had assumed a position of world leadership and could ill afford to continue its historic domestic policy of separatism and discrimination. In the late 1940s and during the 1950s, responsible leaders of American labor organizations, religious groups, and civic associations joined with influential newspaper editors and publishers and with political leaders in insisting that the United States move closer toward realizing the justice and necessity of equal rights for its black citizens. New black organizations emerged to join the struggle for recognition of human rights both at home and abroad; this was a time when the Southern Christian Leadership Conference (SCLC), the Congress of Racial Equality (CORE), and the Student Nonviolent Coordinating Committee (SNCC) all came into being.

After the *Brown* decisions in 1954 and 1955, blacks and whites worked together within the system, moving the fight for racial equality and justice from the courts to the buses to the lunch counters, the streets, and even to the jails. This was the era of the Montgomery, Alabama, bus boycott (1955–56) and the Central High confrontation in Little Rock, Arkansas (1957). In the 1950s black efforts to effect change were concentrated in the South, where most blacks lived. It was also the region where segregation was most visible and where discrimination was most blatant and harsh. The movement for change did not take on a national character until the 1960s.

The 1960s were a time of progress for black Americans. By comparison, the 1970s were a time of retrogression for most black citizens. Gains and losses may be measured in three ways: (1) how much blacks had gained by 1980 as compared with their status in 1960, as measured by certain key social indicators—voting rights, education, employment, income, housing, longevity, and the like; (2) how they have fared in comparison, and how their relative position vis-à-vis whites has changed, since 1960 or 1970; (3) what progress they have made in moving steadily toward their ultimate goals, equality and justice. Have blacks, in short, made continuous gains from 1960 to 1980 as they have sought full citizenship rights and an end to their historic castelike status? While these are not mutually exclusive ways of examining the relevant data, those who are most concerned to dwell on "what has been accomplished" are generally white social scientists who perceive "enormous progress" and "marked improvement" for blacks, particularly in the 1960s.[12] Black social scientists and the U.S. Commission on Civil Rights, by comparison, are more inclined to reflect on "what remains to be done"; they generally found "steady progress" in the 1960s, retrogression in the 1970s.[13]

General Principles

Present-day inequalities of blacks in the United States are directly traceable to the historic castelike structures that were created in black/white interrelationships from the seventeenth century to 1865. These inequalities were maintained from 1883 to 1954 through the disempowerment of blacks in a society that continued to accept the basic idea that blacks were inferior beings. Long-standing inequalities in education, economic opportunity, housing, social status, and discretionary choices have been the most salient features of black life in the United States. Progress toward eliminating these inequities was made from 1865 to 1877 and from 1961 to 1968, but each of those periods has been followed by retrogression and retrenchment. Blacks at the bottom of the economic and social scale were not largely affected in either of these periods. Personal ability and individual performance, coupled with family background and the region they live in, have enabled some blacks to overcome structural limitations, especially since 1964. For more than 60 percent of the black population, however, structural arrangements based on racial status continue to be limiting factors, despite the individual attempts of many of these persons to succeed by their own efforts.[14]

Five major questions will be addressed in this paper: What have blacks achieved in the last twenty years? What strategies have they used, and why, to achieve specific purposes? What conceptions of social justice have prevailed as blacks have sought to change their historic castelike societal positions? How have particular strategies adopted by the federal government, political parties, or major special interest groups contributed to the formation and realization of black objectives? Do we now live with substantially new criteria for judging equality?

Crosscurrents and Diversity, 1960–1980

The 1960s were shaped fundamentally by the *Brown* decision, which overturned the concept that separate-but-equal was just and made possible the lifting of the castelike status that had been imposed on black Americans. This was a decade of sustained economic growth, when diverse public efforts were encouraged, especially to aid citizens previously excluded from full political participation. In the early years of the decade, there was a seriousness of purpose coupled with a spirit of optimism and hope on the part of blacks; they sought through various strategies to realize the goal of full integration promised by the *Brown* decision. This was also a time of militancy, marked by "black pride," where "black power" was thought useful in negotiations with the dominant power structure for those policies and programs that were essential to total integration.

The decade began with a continuation of the black self-help efforts that were evident at the end of the fifties. Some of the strategies implemented were based on the principle of direct nonviolent action: sit-ins, wade-ins, and freedom rides in the South; a March on Washington; and an intense drive to register blacks to vote. All this activism was directed toward specific goals: equal access to public accommodations; the right to vote; desegregated elementary and secondary schools; increased access to state-supported institutions of higher learning. Concerned individuals, participating in organized group efforts of SNCC, CORE, and SCLC worked to achieve these goals. At the same time, the NAACP continued its litigation and lobbying strategies designed to eliminate any and all legal barriers to full citizenship.

Not all blacks were satisfied with these strategies, nor was the choice of complete integration as the ultimate goal satisfactory to all. By 1963 and 1964 thousands of discontented blacks, tired of waiting to have their civil rights recognized, showed their disappointment by participating in more than two thousand mass demonstrations and protest movements. From 1964 to 1967 the struggle took on nationwide proportions; major uprisings and revolts occurred in poverty-stricken Northern and Western ghetto areas where fundamental economic needs had long been ignored. The Black Panthers emerged as a new politcal force, insisting that their fight was against police brutality. Increasingly, individuals and groups argued for various kinds of separatism, claiming that continued white resistance to full civil rights for blacks justified such a course. Still others opted for the philosophy and goals of the Nation of Islam (Black Muslims).

Reactions to the civil rights struggle were not slow in coming; there were evidences of concern and support in prestigious intellectual quarters. *Daedalus,* for example, in 1965–66 devoted two full issues to a detailed exploration of the problems, concerns, and goals of the Negro American.[15] Public sensibilities were stirred by televised newscasts, but also by well-planned film documentaries that depicted the condition of the poor in America, the unemployed, migrant workers, and others who lived in misery. At the other end of the spectrum, individuals and groups, who were now seen to be a part of a "blacklash," demanded that Chief Justice Earl Warren be impeached. For them, the Supreme Court appeared as the villain, responsible for giving impetus and legitimation to the black civil rights movement. Also, the cry for "black power" alienated many whites. However, the reactions generally were more positive than negative. White Americans, on the whole, supported the ending of legal barriers that perpetuated discrimination and were indignant about the violence and chicanery perpetrated by extremists against black citizens and their white supporters. Those who sought to restore the *status quo ante* received little encouragement.

In the sixties at least two, and sometimes all three, branches of the federal government showed a measure of support for black efforts to attain civil rights. The judicial branch, exemplified by the Warren Court, assumed a leadership role. Basing its decision on a concept of social justice that recognized low-income individuals and minority groups as Americans protected by constitutional guarantees, the federal courts were used to attack social inequities that were being addressed neither in the state courts nor through the political process.[16]

The executive branch, headed by John F. Kennedy early in the decade, was galvanized into action. Kennedy's small margin in electoral votes was provided by the solid support he received from certain minorities, especially the blacks.[17] The civil rights thrust of his administration suggests that he placed no small value on these black votes. He was influenced also by pressures that resulted from the civil disobedience of blacks and the almost continuous media coverage of the black protest movement. As a result of all these and other factors, he was moved in 1963 to ask Congress for legislation to support court decisions mandating an end to segregation as public policy. Although the desired legislation was not forthcoming until the Johnson years, Kennedy used the resources of the Justice Department to stop certain of the more overt resistance efforts of white Southerners.[18]

Lyndon B. Johnson emerged as an equally strong Chief Executive. His views about social justice were made explicit in his Commencement Address at Howard University, Washington, D.C., in June 1965. In that speech Johnson made unprecedented commitments to interracial reform, promising substantive redress for long-imposed inequalities. Arguing that the solution to continuing interracial problems must exceed "the bounds of legalistic and procedural reform,"[19] Johnson used his influence to promote the enactment of over a hundred bills designed to overcome state and local obstruction of civil rights for blacks. The Johnson legislation included the 1964 Civil Rights Act, the 1964 Economic Opportunity Act, the 1965 Elementary and Secondary Education Act, the Higher Education Act of 1965, the 1965 Voting Rights Act, the 1968 Fair Housing Act, and the Higher Education Amendments of 1968. Also, his Executive Order 11246, issued on September 24, 1965, provided for affirmative action to "ensure that applicants are employed without regard for race, color, religion, or national origin." This was a concrete expression of his "substantive redress" commitment to bring about social justice. Affirmative action became public policy; it was a strategy intended to correct undeserved inequalities that could not be remedied by traditional means. The Vietnam War brought an end to this expanded social concern; many insisted that "guns and butter" could not be secured simultaneously. Domestic programs designed to improve the life chances of minorities were given a lower priority as "butter" gave way to "guns" and as domestic issues generally receded. If the Vietnam War deflected the president's attention from civil rights issues, it also eroded his relationship with the electorate. In 1968 Johnson chose not to seek reelection. His immediate successors came to office with quite different beliefs both about social justice and race relations, beliefs that were not calculated to support black objectives in respect to civil rights or justice.

From 1957 to 1965 Congress passed three major civil rights acts, a voting rights act, and significant legislation affecting education and poverty issues. The civil rights legislation was the first of its kind passed since 1875.[20] One immediate result of this legislation was to strengthen and reinforce the judicial decisions and executive actions taken by the other branches of government; another was the opening of new educational and employment opportunities for blacks. When the three branches of government act in concert, they are a powerful force for social change. In the 1960s they contributed greatly to realizing the objectives that blacks had insisted on: to alter their castelike position and to move toward equal civil rights and justice. The effects of federal action were quickly evident in the South, for example, where it became too expensive for public school systems to discriminate against black children. Since federal funds would be withheld from discriminating districts, such a threat was enough to end practices that had become traditional in the region. The Administration was not equally successful in the North; Johnson, for example, backed down before the objections of Mayor Richard Daley, fearing political reprisals if he insisted on withholding school funds because of discriminatory practices.

The legislation of the 1960s was impressive; so, also, was the fact that the Twenty-fourth Amendment to the Constitution, which outlawed the poll tax, was ratified in 1964. This tax had long served to disfranchise black voters. Black gains during the Johnson years resulted from what Gunnar Myrdal has called a cumulation of social forces. Judicial decisions and pressures from the civil rights movement were principal catalysts; so, also, were Johnson's personal commitments to change, the placement of blacks in important decision-making positions, and the black presence in the Civil Service.[21] Enforcement of the newly minted laws and establishment of systematic means of handling violations and grievances were additional factors contributing to the progress of the 1960s.

There were, of course, certain negative crosscurrents. The federal sector did not always support black efforts to secure equal rights. J. Edgar Hoover, the powerful director of the FBI, for example, was openly antagonistic both to the black movement and its leaders.[22] Congress showed a continued reluctance to pass legislation and to fund at appropriate levels specific social programs designed to provide remedies or compensation for inequalities that originated in racism.[23] A number of Cabinet officials, concerned about civil rights strategies, worried also about the philosophical implications of such a vastly expanded role for government. Many lower-level judges were not inclined to share the liberal viewpoint of the Warren Court.

In short, blacks, together with their white supporters in the 1960s using direct action strategies, both nonviolent and violent, worked within the system through specific group organizational efforts to gain abolition of legal barriers to full citizenship rights; voting rights, which are basic to participation in the political system; and access to education at all levels, since learning is the primary means for entry into the job market and for all subsequent upward mobility. Gains were achieved in all these areas, though certain unintended negative consequences also resulted. In removing legal barriers to full citizenship rights and guaranteeing voting rights, specific goals were achieved across the whole nation; obstructions could be declared unconstitutional and eliminated. But the educational goal proved more difficult to achieve, not least because educational authority is vested in the fifty states and their political subdivisions; it is a costly, time-consuming process to challenge effectively the discriminatory practices of local school boards or officials at the state level.

The black civil rights movement served to give form, shape, and substance to domestic politics during the 1960s. The enormous efforts of blacks and their allies to achieve equal citizenship rights succeeded in awakening the conscience of the nation. As a result, the promise of *Brown* was brought closer to reality; court decisions, executive orders, legislative acts, and public sentiment worked for the same general purposes. The similarities to what had happened in the country a hundred years earlier were striking.

In the 1860s blacks were freed from the bondage of slavery. In the 1960s blacks were freed from the bondage imposed by the "separate-but-equal" doctrine; civil rights acts gave federal enforcement muscle to the judicial decisions of the 1950s. In the 1860s blacks received the right to vote. The right was reconferred in the 1960s on blacks in the South, where the majority of blacks lived. Black officials were elected to local and state offices in the South from the 1860s to the 1890s; their successors began to reappear almost a hundred years later. From 1868 to 1895 twenty-three blacks served in Congress;[24] similar numbers did not sit there again until a century had passed. Educational opportunity for blacks was a major concern of the federal government in the 1860s and 1870s; a major function of the Freedmen's Bureau was to build schools, train teachers, and educate disadvantaged children. Educational opportunity became a major federal concern again in the 1960s.

At the end of the decade, blacks had benefited from many of these societal changes. Major economic and educational gains were made, particularly by a growing middle-income group that enjoyed greater access to jobs and higher earnings. They came closer to some sort of parity with their white counterparts. In 1964 the median income of black families was $3,724—54 percent of that of white families; in 1969 it stood at $5,999— 61 percent of the white median. Economic expansion, significant civil rights legislation, social consciousness, and increased educational attainment made it possible for a certain number of talented, ambitious, trained blacks to advance. Housing options were greater, particularly for middle-income families; so, also, was the availability of good health care.

There was, however, a negative side to the picture. The majority of black Americans remained victimized by unsolved systematic problems— unemployment, a more subtle kind of prejudice, segregation (especially in housing), inferior education, lack of opportunity, and increasing isolation from the rising black middle-income group, as well as from whites. For these blacks, problems of income, employment, education, housing, and health care remained acute. In 1969 the unemployment rate for blacks and other races was twice that of whites—6.4 and 3.1 percent, respectively.[25] These official figures do not adequately reflect the condition of discouraged workers who no longer sought work, or the plight to involuntary part-time workers who failed to find full-time jobs. Thirty-eight percent of blacks were homeowners in 1960 as compared with 65 percent of whites; those proportions changed only slightly in the period 1960–70, when 42 percent of blacks were listed as owners compared with 65 percent of whites.[26] Again, the statistics tell only part of the tale; housing units occupied by blacks, whether as owners or renters, are generally more overcrowded than those occupied by whites, this being especially true in the South.[27] Also, more housing units occupied by blacks lack some or all plumbing facilities; this was as true in 1970 as in 1960, particularly in the South.[28] In 1968, 21.6 percent of the black population age fourteen to twenty-four years old were school dropouts; this compared with 11.9 percent of whites of comparable ages.[29]

To make matters worse, there were evidences of a growing conservative mood in the nation. The rapidity of social change, as well as its breadth and depth, frightened many Americans. The sheer complexity of events confused many others. The recession of 1969–70 created new economic insecurity, contributing to fresh concern about employment. In the sixties a whole series of national and international crises did a great deal to disturb the equilibrium of the country.[30] In these circumstances, the public's concern about the plight of black Americans was considerably reduced.

For the black population, it was also a time of growing uncertainty. Where so many had been genuinely optimistic at the decade's beginning, at its end there were expressions of disappointment both with the pace of change and with its pervasiveness. Bitterness was felt also because of the violent deaths of those black and white leaders who had been major initiators of, and spokesmen for, change. Also, an awareness that the gains had occurred largely in the public sector gave many a new sense of the limits of the purported black progress. The decade ended on a note of ideological debate, at least among black intellectuals, who asked whether integration ought to remain the ultimate goal for American blacks.[31]

By 1970 the civil rights movement clearly had changed, as had its leadership. Organizations such as the Black Panthers that had come into existence in the sixties were obviously in decline; older organizations like the NAACP and the National Urban League seemed to enjoy a new opportunity. It was increasingly evident that black progress had been very uneven. Talented, educated individuals had made gains; the hard-core impoverished had scarcely been touched by the strategies of the 1960s. Techniques that worked well for the smaller sector of the black population did not appear to operate at all successfully for the larger sector. The abolition of legal barriers and the elimination of overtly racist discriminatory policies had not been sufficient to help those blacks at the lower end of the income spectrum. New emphases would need to be considered in the 1970s if life conditions were to improve for the majority.

The black goal remained full inclusion in the society; that term, however, came to mean "cultural pluralism" for many rather than simply "assimilation."

Strategies employed by black organizations and individuals tended to turn away from public confrontations, massive rallies, demonstrations, and boycotts toward the more effective use of the vote. Other strategies were also advocated, the most important of which were greater participation in education at every level—designed to secure enlarged employment opportunities—and the pressuring of labor unions, corporations, and the federal government to expand training and employment opportunities. In the 1970s protest took a back seat to the newer strategies of utilizing electoral politics to influence public policy, participation in education, lobbying for black interests, and renewed efforts at enlarging and equalizing employment opportunities.

A major thrust of black efforts in the seventies was the use of the vote gained in 1965. Many blacks felt that political power was their greatest lever to change the system in their interest; by electing blacks and favorably inclined whites to decision-making positions, they hoped to achieve their ends. By July 1979 those efforts had placed 4,607 blacks in elective offices nationwide, about 66 percent of those being in the South.[32] The greatest gains were at local and state levels; in 1979 there were 191 black mayors, 313 state legislators and executives, 17 Congressmen.[33] This was a marked increase from the 103 elected officials in these categories in 1964,[34] immediately prior to the passage of the Voting Rights Act. Few blacks, in fact, had been elected or appointed to public office between Reconstruction and 1965. Still, elected black officials today constitute less than 1 percent of all elected officials nationally. The Joint Center for Political Studies in Washington estimates that if blacks continue to be elected at the present rate, they would hold only 3 percent of all elective offices by the year 2000. This is far below the almost 12 percent of blacks in the national population. If the goal is to achieve a representative proportion of black people in political decision-making positions, including appointive office, that end remains very distant.

Registration and voting behavior of blacks have been generally disappointing since 1972; blacks have failed to register and vote in the proportions they did in the years 1966–72.[35] Some argue that this is because the tradition for voting in the black community is weak; others suggest that blacks understand instinctively that nothing will be changed by their votes. Whatever the explanation, it is obvious that the full potential power of the black electorate has not been realized.

Traditional belief in the worth of education and its possibilities remained characteristic of the black population throughout the 1970s. It was especially discernible at the higher education levels, where there was continued black progress in gaining access to college. Although blacks were only about 6 percent of the undergraduate population in the mid-sixties, they were slightly over 10 percent in 1976–77, approximating more closely the proportion of blacks in the general American population. Also, black students were more widely distributed among the major institutions, both public and private. Special admissions procedures, increased financial assistance, and supportive tutorial programs made it possible for a greater number of blacks to enter and remain in college.

This is not to say, however, that racial parity has been achieved. A greater number of blacks than whites are in two-year institutions; many of their diplomas or certificates will not allow them to go on to four-year degree-granting colleges.[36] Blacks received only 6.4 percent of bachelor's degrees awarded in 1975–76; 37 percent of the recipients were from the historically black colleges.[37] Clearly, then, far fewer blacks graduate from college than enter; larger proportions of those who enter predominantly black colleges graduate than those who enter other institutions. The situation is graphically rendered in the fact that "in 1978, about 1 out of 10 black men and women 25 to 34 years old had completed 4 or more years of college as compared with 1 out of 4 white men and women in this age group."[38] While there have been substantial gains at the higher-education level, the lag between blacks and whites remains conspicuous.

Equality eludes blacks,[39] and this is particularly apparent at the graduate and the professional levels. Of all the doctorates awarded in 1975–76, blacks received only 3.6 percent. They numbered only 6 percent of the graduate school enrollment in the fall of 1976, and were a mere 4.5 percent of the professional school enrollment. There has been a consistent decline since 1971 in both law school and medical school admissions.[40] There is also a downward trend in Ph.D. recipients, from 1,180 in 1976–77 to 1,100 in 1977–78.[41]

The explanations for these phenomena are not entirely clear, but it appears that several factors are at work, including, very importantly, a more limited use of affirmative action criteria for admissions; increased tuitions, which restrict the number of blacks who can afford to seek such education; and the cost of food, housing, transportation, and the like, which is often quite beyond the means of many potential black students, especially at the graduate and professional levels. Also, job opportunities are fewer, and this affects the decisions of blacks who seek further education.

At the elementary and secondary levels, *de facto* has replaced *de jure* segregation. Although mandatory segregation by law is a thing of the past, segregation itself has not ended. Indeed, segregation has become harder to combat as "segregative intent" needs now to be demonstrated. "White flight" to the suburbs had made school integration wholly impossible in certain communities by the 1970s. At the beginning of the decade, the population of the District of Columbia was 91 percent black, whereas the black public school enrollment stood at 93 percent; in Newark, New Jersey, the black population was 54 percent, whereas 72 percent of that city's public school children were black. Atlanta showed the same configurations in this period: 51 percent of the population were black; 65 percent of the public school children were black.[42] Thousands of poor black children continued to experience substandard education in central city elementary and secondary schools that were for all practical purposes segregated.

The expectation that desegregation would create equal educational opportunity has faded; the foes of integration have found new ways to subvert both the spirit and the letter of the law.[43] Ironically, while desegregated schools became more common in the South in the 1970s, racial isolation became the norm in many Northern public schools. Private schools flourished both in the North and the South; white children abandoned public school systems, and in many central cities, black parents, particularly in the middle class, pulled their children out of public schools, especially at the secondary level, believing them to be inferior and declining institutions. Busing plans came under severe attack in Northern cities as different as Detroit and Boston. Academic achievement records of black children across the nation showed that they were generally below those of whites.[44]

A primary reason for black support of education has been the belief that this would increase employment opportunities. Blacks for a hundred years have been very sensitive to the issues of employment, underemployment, and unemployment. Blacks have little control over the economy, yet the state of the economy—whether it is healthy and growing, or turbulent and faltering—is critical for black employment.[45] Blacks, like whites, benefited from economic growth in the 1960s; the recession of 1969–70 caused a slowdown in these economic gains, and the high rate of inflation, beginning in 1973, worsened their economic plight. More severe recessions in 1974–75 and 1979–80, accompanied by double-digit inflation and large-scale unemployment, have been a catastrophe for blacks. The state of the economy spelled turbulence for blacks throughout the 1970s.[46] As their economic problems became more acute, with the majority of blacks experiencing severe distress, individuals and groups focused on questions of economic opportunity; black organizational efforts shifted their goals—equity in employment opportunity as well as in income potential became prime purposes.

Rampant inflation and recession have been devastating for blacks; reduced opportunities for employment, more limited purchasing power, and underemployment and unemployment have been the common conditions. Two-thirds of blacks earn less than $15,000 annually for a family of four. In 1978 black teenage unemployment rates stood at 52.5 percent; in some central city areas, the unemployment of the young approached 90 percent. Almost half of those who were officially unemployed were age sixteen to twenty-four,[47] who needed not only the income from employment, but an opportunity to begin assuming adult responsibilities. Single-parent families headed by black women were hit especially hard by the high unemployment rates; the small earnings of many of these heads-of-households exacerbated the problem.[48] In the rural South, "where many blacks remain on the fringes of the economy, AFDC (Aid to Families with Dependent Children) is often the only means of survival."[49]

AFDC is synonymous with welfare to many in the larger society, and hostility to blacks "on welfare" is manifest. Although the data show that in absolute numbers most AFDC recipients are white—to be expected, given the size of the white population—many Americans continue to believe that most beneficiaries are black and that they ought to "go to work." That there would not be any economic benefit in their doing so, and that such a nonremunerative choice thus militates against poorly paid work as a solution to the welfare problem, are rarely acknowledged. Isabel Sawhill's research on potential annual earnings for mothers on welfare indicates that "half the welfare mothers could not earn as much in the labor market as they were receiving on AFDC, and only a fourth . . . could increase their income by as much as $1,000 by going to work full time."[50] Their economic problems are systemic, quite beyond their individual capacity to resolve. In a time of skyrocketing living costs, when industry is free to export its jobs to other countries where greater profits are anticipated, and where government policies to control and correct economic forces, including wages and prices, are limited, the individual's control of his own economic destiny is minimal.

Charles Benson noted in 1979 that "many central city areas serve as storage bins for people who have no productive role to play in the market economy."[51] Black unemployment rates are consistently double those of whites, and have been so since 1948 at least.[52] They have not fallen significantly even in the best economic times, as for example during the 1960s. The earnings gap widened in the 1970s not only between blacks and whites, but between the middle-income black minority and the much larger black underclass as well. But large segments of the black middle class feel extremely vulnerable to economic shifts; industrial cutbacks, nonenforcement of the law, and a declining commitment to affirmative action efforts—both public and private—cause great anxiety among them.[53]

The black elderly feel themselves especially vulnerable. Their plight is described in a recent publication of the National Center for Black Aged:

> There exists in America today a generation of Black people who are too old to work, too undereducated to qualify for work and who, during their productive years, were relegated to menial and low-paying work. This gives them, in their twilight years, the lowest of the low-income-related retirement incomes and benefits.
>
> Their incomes are substandard. Their housing is substandard. Health services available to them are far less adequate than those available to whites. Worse yet, the burdens they have carried throughout their lifetime have reduced their potential lifespan to an average of 6 to 7 years less than that of their white counterparts.

The problem will not die with that generation. Even today, 7 out of every 8 Black males between the ages of 55 and 64 have less than a high school education. One out of every three Black families has an income below the federally set poverty level. The median income of Black families headed by persons between 45 and 64, with both parents working, is less than two-thirds that of white families in the same age group.

The translation is simple: less savings, less home ownership, less wage-related retirement income in years to come.

And so the problems of the Black aged grow as their numbers grow. As inflation and unemployment grow, the resources potentially available to meet their problems shrink.[54]

At the end of the 1970s, economic concerns were foremost in the minds of blacks. Social justice now means greater equity in employment, income potential, housing, education, and health care. These economic and social goals are far more difficult to attain than were the legal and political goals of the 1960s. They require far more cooperation from the private sector and a continued willingness by government to implement and enforce existing legislation. They depend on something more than legislation, however; they presume a greater equality of income than now exists. Further, they are all the more difficult to achieve in a time of relative "scarcity," when government protests that it lacks the means to finance social expenditures. Also, achievement of such social goals is complicated by current public policy that permits the entry of waves of immigrants, legal and illegal, who, of necessity, compete with low-skilled and unskilled blacks for jobs that require a minimum of education and experience.

The social climate of the 1970s, so substantially different from that of the 1960s, was accompanied by a no less remarkable change in the political climate. The country moved in a conservative direction from 1969;[55] even the election of Jimmy Carter in 1976 did not alter that situation. Fear intensified and good will declined as Americans found no solutions to certain of the more pressing problems: the international arms race; the energy crisis; escalating housing, food, and transportation costs; the unfinished business of racial justice. New social movements—for women's rights, the rights of ethnic groups, gay rights, and the like—demanded time and attention as these groups also insisted on a greater sensitivity to their demands for social justice. Watergate, which resulted in the first resignation of an American president, was a great shock to the country. Trust in government declined as the American people grew increasingly disillusioned with their leaders. Angry voters showed their displeasure by passing bills such as Proposition 13 that called for substantial relief from the high levels of taxation that had resulted from high levels of government spending. Yet the voters seemed also to want the government to continue to provide them with adequate schools, libraries, parks, and recreational facilities, not to speak of garbage collection and other such services. Voting patterns and demands seemed strangely contradictory and obscure in the 1970s.

Still, the evidences of conservatism and retrenchment were everywhere; they were accompanied by an inward-turning on the part of many in the society. Confronted with so many pressing problems beyond their own control, many accepted the idea that the only reasonable course was to look out for themselves. A philosophy of "me first," "do you own thing," or "looking out for number one" does not lend itself readily to a concern for social justice for the less advantaged. This inward-turning reduced the commitment of many to continue their work for social justice for blacks. When inward-turning was joined to a new ethos of permissiveness, as seemed to be the case in the 1970s, there was little time for involvement in social causes, especially those that seemed to defy equitable solution—as is the case with black/white-dominant/minority relationships. Most of the decade was dominated by the leadership of Presidents Nixon and Ford, whose political behavior was scarcely supportive of black objectives to attain equal civil rights and social justice. As for President Carter, although he made many conspicuous black appointments to high office, he never formulated policies or programs calculated to help the black majority. None of these presidents assumed positive leadership roles in inspiring the American people to live up to their highest societal ideals, or even to the best in themselves, with respect to social justice for blacks. Indeed, Nixon and Ford, in their pronouncements against "forced busing," assumed a public posture of playing to the fears and negative mind-sets of the majority. Such presidential behavior helped to legitimize the conservative mood that was enveloping the nation; it served to arrest the forward progress of blacks who depend on the executive branch of government to enforce the law and on the Chief Executive to serve as a role model for the white majority. The image projected by Nixon is exemplified by his statement on open housing: "I can assure you that it is not the policy of this government to use the power of the Federal Government . . . for forced integration of the suburbs."[56] Such sentiments were not expressed so overtly by either of Nixon's successors—Carter, indeed, made positive efforts to avoid them—but none kept the idea of racial justice and racial equality to the fore.

Nixon's most devastating actions affecting blacks probably occurred with respect to his Supreme Court appointments. His campaign pledge to replace the societal commitment to "justice in our time" with a commitment to "law and order" was realized when he appointed men of conservative views to the Supreme Court. The Burger Court, in reaffirming traditional values and principles in the law, in declining to expand the area of civil and individual rights, and in its decisions on criminal procedure and education, has reinforced state autonomy and judicial restraint. Yet, although it is a far more traditional court than the Warren Court, the Burger Court has not been as conservative in its opinions as Nixon probably expected it to be.

Two of the more controversial cases decided by the Court in the 1970s tested the constitutionality of affirmative action, which was intended to equalize opportunity for blacks and other minorities (including women) in gaining access both to higher education and employment. The first of the cases, *University of California v. Allan Bakke* (1978), was of such moment to its protagonists that sixty-nine *amicus curiae* briefs were filed, a record number for the Supreme Court. When the sharply divided decision was rendered, there was considerable confusion: both sides appeared to have won; both sides appeared to have lost. Although the University of California was ordered to admit Allan Bakke, the Court held that race could be a determining factor in the selective admissions process. How race was to be counted as a "determining factor" was left unclear; Harvard's admissions plan was cited as an acceptable model. The Court's ruling, while cloudy in terms of implementation, left considerable room for interpretation with each admissions committee. Although some blacks and others were disappointed, some looked at the decision positively. Daniel C. Maguire wrote, "While Bakke the man won, Bakke the symbol of invidious individualism lost."[57] The Court had not ruled that affirmative action was unconstitutional, a decision it might have rendered had the evidence warranted such a conclusion.

The second case, *United Steelworkers of America v. Weber* (1979), tested the legality of a Louisiana employment training program with a 50:50 ratio of blacks to whites. Some believed this case to be even more vital to black progress than *Bakke,* since its concern was directly with employment. The legality of the program was upheld, making it a landmark decision in the black struggle for equal employment opportunity.

The Court's clearest decision with respect to affirmative action was rendered on July 2, 1980, in *Fullilove v. Klutznick.* In a 6 to 3 opinion, the Court ruled that Congress may impose a proportional share by race in its allocations of federal funds. More specifically, the ruling upheld a 1977 law that set aside 10 percent of federal public works contracts for minority contractors. In voting with the majority, Chief Justice Burger said:

> Congress had before it, among other data, evidence of a long history of marked disparity in the percentage of public contracts awarded to minority business enterprises. This disparity was considered to result not from any lack of capable and qualified minority businesses, but from the existence and maintenance of barriers to competitive access which had their roots in racial and ethnic discrimination, and which continue today, even absent any intentional discrimination or other unlawful conduct. . . .When effectuating a limited and properly tailored remedy to cure the effects of prior discrimination, such "a sharing of the burden" by innocent parties is not impermissible.

This latest decision is important not only for its clarity, but also because it recognizes that historic barriers based on racial discrimination continue to condition the position and opportunities of today's minorities. Further, even though mandatory legal discrimination has ended officially (*de jure*), its effects continue to be felt (*de facto*) by minorities because of ongoing discriminatory practices. Because the effect on minorities is the same from *de facto* as from *de jure* discrimination, remedies are permissible for those "who still suffer from the effects of identifiable discrimination," and, if necessary, nondiscriminating parties must share the burden of justice.

Black leaders, elated by this decision, felt at once its far-reaching implications. They believe it may be applied to housing, employment, education, and other areas where Congress has evidence of past discrimination for which individuals currently seek a remedy. Collectively, these decisions offer substantial promise to those concerned with racial justice. Thus blacks are greatly concerned about the composition of the Supreme Court, for its structure will affect the course of all future decisions.

Although it is always rash to generalize about Congress, or to predict its future behavior, it is obvious that Congress in recent years has reflected the growing tide of conservatism in the society. There is a clear erosion of social commitment, observable in what must be described as antibusing, antiaffirmative action, and antipoverty legislation. Certain legislators, once liberal, find it necessary now to move toward the political center. Their seats are in jeopardy, and they feel that to save them they must busy themselves with the narrow interests of their own constituencies. But the extension of the Voting Rights Act and very significant legislation in education are evidence that the Congress is not wholly conservative.

In the last twenty years, federal intervention has been recognized as an important follow-up strategy to give substance to the more formal equality obtained by blacks in the 1950s through court decisions and overt protest behavior. When that federal intervention has faltered, black gains have slowed. Blacks believe it is the proper role of government to enact programs that will enhance the economic, educational, social, and political welfare of the underprivileged. This is done to provide opportunities for many to develop their potential so that they can become equal to those citizens who start from a more privileged social position. It is done also to promote the general welfare; there is a compelling national interest in improving the lot of the whole of its citizenry.

The aim of the civil rights movement was never merely to achieve a superficial integration of the classes, as exemplified by the right to dine in the same restaurants, travel on the same planes, or even occupy the same prestigious corporate boardroom positions. The purpose was always to include the black masses—to open new opportunities for them; to obtain jobs that pay living wages, with security in their tenure; to buy houses; to meet the costs of living, even when they escalate rapidly; to educate the children; to enjoy recreation and pleasure; and to prepare for old age and retirement. Those results have not been achieved. Two-thirds of the black population are as far from those goals as they were in 1960.[58] Continuous progress for blacks toward the ultimate goals of equality and justice was not a characteristic of the 1970s.

Gains and Losses from 1960 to 1980

The clearest gains remaining from the civil rights activities of the 1960s include the abolition of mandatory legal segregation, access to public accommodations, voting rights, increased educational opportunity, and a reduction in overt hostility from whites. The historic castelike status of blacks has been altered, though it is by no means eliminated. Conversely, the economic gap between blacks and whites is widening,[59] and there is a widespread opinion that blacks have had as much societal help as they need or deserve. That opinion is fed by an illusory view of black progress,[60] by the highly visible presence of a small number of blacks in prestigious positions not previously held by blacks, and by the presence of some blacks who live in integrated urban and suburban areas.

There are several prominent black social scientists who hold with William Wilson that the gains made by blacks in the 1960s are reflected in greater opportunities available to blacks in 1980, and that the growing number of successful blacks is evidence that race is a factor of declining significance in American society. Since class differences are widening in the black population, they say that class is becoming a more critical factor than race in determining the fate of black Americans.[61] This is a controversial and much-disputed thesis within the black community.[62]

Political System

Blacks continue to feel that participation in electoral politics is essential to the realization of their goals to share more fully in decisions that affect life chances of people in the United States. The Joint Center for Political Studies, believing that election to public office is a major device for achieving certain purposes in the political arena, sees the existence of such institutions as the Congressional Black Caucus as absolutely essential to effective black political action. Voter registration, membership in political parties and other political organizations, service in appointive office, and active support of (or opposition to), issues and candidates, as well as running for public office, are all seen as vitally important.[63]

The research the Center has done confirms that although formal barriers to black political participation have been largely removed, many informal obstacles remain. These include racial gerrymandering, which dilutes the black vote; social and economic forces in most disadvantaged communities that necessarily limit and undercut effective political participation; and the reluctance of white voters to support black candidates. The Center estimates that a significant increase in black elected officeholders will occur only when a great variety of social, economic, political, and attitudinal problems have been resolved.[64] Charles Hamilton, believing that voting occurs only when the process is related to a specific end, suggests that participation will increase when blacks believe that voting will accomplish particular goals.[65]

Until 1918 the greatest part of the black electorate voted Republican because they believed that the "party of Lincoln" was more likely to be sympathetic to their needs and interests than any other. Black loyalty shifted to the Democratic party in 1936 when the policies and programs of Franklin D. Roosevelt were thought to be more conducive to the specific goals that blacks deemed important. Despite these major voting trends, the black vote never has been monolithic. In 1956 it divided 60/40 between Stevenson and Eisenhower. In 1960 the black vote went 70/30 for Kennedy/Nixon, a proportion of some consequence to both. By 1980 black leaders believed disproportionate commitment to the Democratic party to be unwise because it limits effectiveness in political negotiations.

Surveying the current political situation, the Joint Center for Political Studies sees at least two potential threats to black political gains. First, there is great concern over the results of the 1980 census, which will require the redrawing of many congressional districts and the reapportionment of congressional seats among the states. The congressional districts of all fifteen black members of the House of Representatives are likely to be affected, as will certain of the other sixty-six congressional districts in which blacks are 20 percent or more of the total population.[66] If many of these districts are merged into adjoining districts, black representation and influence could be reduced appreciably. This is only one reason for the great concern about the potential black undercount in the 1980 census. Blacks were undercounted by 7.7 percent in the 1970 census; a black undercount in 1980 threatens to compound this error. State officials, required to make congressional districts relatively equal under the Supreme Court's "one-man one-vote" ruling, understand the import of the 1980 census. Black congressional representation, no less than black influence on other legislators, will be influenced by this count.[67]

The Center is concerned also that the ruling of the Supreme Court in April 1980 on at-large elections may be a setback for black political aspirations.[68] In *City of Mobile et al. v. Bolden et al.,* the Supreme Court, in a 6 to 3 decision, dramatically limited the scope of the Voting Rights Act. Though the constitutionality of the act itself was upheld the same day by a 6 to 3 vote,[69] the majority opinion in the Mobile, Alabama, case held that proof of exclusion of blacks and other minorities from electoral schemes at the state and local levels is not enough to warrant federal court action on their behalf. Proof must be established that such exclusion was intentional. This decision follows the pattern set by the Burger Court in school desegregation and employment cases, where the victim is required to prove segregative intent on the part of the other party. Proof of intent is always difficult to establish; it presumes knowledge of the state of mind operative at the time of the action. Since there are no criteria for judging the state of mind, except in the results of specific actions, the Court appears to be building a structure of "intent" that will be hard to crack as blacks and other minorities continue to seek equal justice under law.

Many blacks perceive the decision as part of an effort to effect a "Second Post-Reconstruction Period." So do many whites, who look upon it as the beginning of a "Second Redemption," analogous to the return to power of whites during Reconstruction after the Civil War. While whites seek to retain power and control, blacks seek a larger share of power and control, and their interests necessarily collide. An equitable, just resolution of these competing claims can only be based on a respect for individual rights guaranteed under the Constitution. As the Center makes explicit, "Local governments can hardly be expected to articulate unambiguously any intent they may have to dilute black votes."[70] Moreover, the Voting Rights Act comes up for renewal in 1982; that renewal could be imperiled by the *Mobile* decision.

Voting rights are fundamental to achieving equal rights for blacks. Strong resistance to black voting rights calls for more assertive efforts from blacks, including increased voter participation and developing coalitions with other groups. Section 2 of the Fourteenth Amendment provides that states that restrict voting can have their representation in Congress reduced, a penalty never invoked. However, if political strategies fail to safeguard black voting rights, pressure must be exerted to enforce this constitutional guarantee.

Legal System

Mandatory segregation by law has ended; this is an important achievement. However, it has been replaced by *de facto* segregation in most metropolitan areas. The effect is much the same; segregation has clearly not ended for most of the black population. Those who wish to discriminate find subtle ways to do so, either by manipulating the law or evading its intent. Such subtle forms of discrimination are less easily dealt with than the overt, blatant "massive resistance" schemes of white Southerners in the 1950s and 1960s; they are harder to prove, more difficult to resist.

As the Joint Center for Political Studies has demonstrated, Supreme Court decisions give a "signal" to the country; a decision such as *City of Mobile et al. v. Bolden et al.* transmits the message that black rights can be eroded. Although the adverse effects may be somewhat reduced because the judgment was made by a divided court, such decisions probably do slow the drive to correct inequities.

Also, blacks continue to face serious problems in their encounters with police departments. The summer 1980 uprisings of blacks in Miami, Orlando, and Chattanooga were in part protests against police brutality.

Blacks are more likely than whites to be arrested or jailed; they tend to get longer sentences when convicted. Because blacks are less affluent than whites, they are less likely to be able to employ the services of the best lawyers when legal problems arise. Also, it is common for higher bail to be set for blacks than for whites. All-white juries are again common in the South. They are not at all representative of Southern populations, and they frequently return verdicts unfavorable to blacks.

On the other side of the coin, President Carter appointed more blacks, women, and Hispanics to federal judgeships than all other previous presidents combined. Thurgood Marshall is the first black justice to serve on the Supreme Court. No less important gains have been made in the lower courts.

Still, the continuing assaults on affirmative action and on voting rights, coupled with renewed attacks on proposed housing and education legislation, make it evident that black gains are not secure. Blacks have not attained equal justice under the law, though some progress has been made in their legal status.[71]

Education

Meanwhile, education at all levels remains "a matter of grave concern."[72] What black parents and the NAACP fought for in 1954 was equality: equal per pupil expenditures; equal length of school terms; equal buildings, equipment, facilities, and books; equal curriculum; equally prepared teachers—in short, an equal chance to learn, an equal opportunity for their children to be known as persons of worth and to know other such people. There has been some progress in certain areas where measurement is possible and quantifiable; per pupil expenditures, length of school terms, equipment, books, curriculum, and facilities do appear to be more equal now than they were a quarter of a century ago. Pressures from black organizations and parents, coupled with court decisions, have produced this progress, especially in the South. However, there has been less progress in qualitative improvements, in the quality of schooling provided, and in the opportunity to know individuals of diverse backgrounds. These insufficiencies are evident North and South; there is a continued white flight from public schools, while at the same time many black middle-income students have abandoned the public school systems to attend private schools.

All this is true, yet it is also a fact that at the elementary and secondary level there has been a steady improvement in rates of black participation and in the median years of schooling that blacks complete. This improvement is now very visible in the educational attainments of younger black adults. In 1978, 73 percent of blacks twenty to twenty-four years of age had completed high school; this compared with 85 percent of whites in the same age group. In 1960 only 33 percent of blacks and 61 percent of whites of similar ages had a comparable educational achievement. At the higher education level, participation has increased no less dramatically over the last twenty years. In 1960 only 4 percent of blacks and 12 percent of whites twenty-five to thirty-four years old had completed four years of college or more. By 1978, 11 percent of blacks and 25 percent of whites of the same ages had attained this level.[73] The gains are obvious, but parity remains the goal. One of the results of increased levels of schooling is that larger proportions of blacks are now employed in occupations requiring higher levels of education.

Dropout rates also have declined. The rate for black dropouts fourteen to twenty-four years old was 21.6 percent in 1968, compared with 11.9 percent for whites. By 1978 the rates were 16.5 percent for blacks, compared with 11.3 percent for whites. Improvement is considerable, though black dropout rates remain high. One fifth of black young adults have not completed high school.[74] In a society as credential-oriented as ours, this leads to an enormous reduction in life chances.

The problems that persist affect adversely the possibilities for black children to learn, grow, and develop in ways that are desirable. Attitudinal support for public education is declining; because most black children continue to depend on public education, the health of that system is of the greatest importance to them.[75] Absenteeism and tardiness within schools, coupled with vandalism, crime, and drugs outside, make for a poor learning environment.[76] Cities continue to spend smaller proportions of their total budgets on schools than do suburban communities.[77] It remains common for some prestigious intellectuals to ask whether black children have the native ability to learn as well as do white children.[78] Such ideas can have considerable influence with local school boards, taxpayers, and federal officials, who perhaps may ask whether it is not futile to expend large sums of money to educate disadvantaged blacks, given their supposed inferior mental abilities.

Within far too many urban schools, tests suggest a decline in educational achievement. Many black students do not appear to be mastering reading, writing, and mathematical skills in a way that suggests they will be able to perform competently at work or in college.[79] They are not expected to be effective competitors with higher-achieving students, and their own self-confidence cannot grow until they improve the overall quality of their academic performance.

Competency-testing, approved by some thirty-six states as a measure to guarantee minimum performance levels of high-school graduates, is accompanied today by a back-to-basics trend that has the same purpose in mind. There is considerable controversy about these programs and about the ways they are implemented and the publicity they draw to themselves. Black parents, who have asked for years that schools be held accountable for the competence of their children, sought "community control" in Ocean Hill-Brownsville, in New York City, in Washington, D.C., and in other cities in the late 1960s precisely with such interests in mind. Their efforts, however, were fought by teachers' unions, particularly in New York City, where they were perceived as a threat to the unions, which emerged victorious in the battles that ensued.

At the higher education level, the "open door" of predominantly white colleges tends to be a "revolving door" for a disproportionate number of black students; they end up feeling defeated, and resent the stigma that attaches to them because of their failure. More of the black students who do remain in college and graduate need to be counseled and encouraged to major in fields where blacks are now underrepresented, such as the sciences, mathematics, engineering, architecture, and business, because the traditional fields (the social sciences and the humanities), which offered high employment opportunities in the past, now offer fewer opportunities. Also, disproportionately fewer talented blacks, as compared with talented whites, are able at this time to pursue and complete graduate and professional training.

The existence of a group of historically black colleges, both public and private, since Reconstruction has given young blacks a supportive intellectual environment conducive to learning and to maturity. Most blacks earned undergraduate degrees in these colleges until the 1970s; they were the principal training grounds for black leaders in all fields and remain today a major resource for the black community. The private black colleges, however, are now threatened by fiscal disaster. Many are experiencing severe shortages of students as a growing number of blacks seek higher educational opportunities in integrated colleges. The public black colleges are also threatened; the *Adams* decision, which ruled that dual educational systems violated the law, has been interpreted by some states as an excuse for diminishing their support of black colleges. President Carter, however, in August 1980 signed an executive order to "expand the capacity of black colleges to provide quality education and overcome any discrimination that might keep black educational institutions from taking full part in federal programs."[80] This order reinforces an earlier one in which the president asked heads of federal agencies to facilitate black college and university participation in federally sponsored programs. Black educators have been enthusiastic in their response to such support for black colleges.

Educational institutions have been a primary employer of professional blacks in the past. However, school integration, as it has been implemented, has made the black principal a "vanishing American"; it has also had certain negative effects on black teachers, who suffer from continuing discriminatory practices at state and local levels in employment, promotion, and retention.[81] A number of school boards and local authorities resist the idea of having white teachers work under black principals. It is not uncommon for white parents to object to having their children taught by black teachers. Such resistance is encouraged by socialization patterns that govern authority/power relationships of whites and blacks in the United States today; they are encouraged also by false beliefs about the mental abilities of blacks, even those who have acquired the requisite degrees and teacher/principal certification.

Education is an obviously necessary, though not sufficient, means for blacks to attain the economic, political, and racial goals they seek. They must continue to use education as "an active catalyst for the attainment of equality."[82] Efforts to reverse recent educational gains by limiting legislation at the national level, defeating school bond issues at the local level, and initiating tuition tax-credit schemes, education vouchers, and the like must be counteracted by individuals and organizations through lobbying efforts, voting patterns, and caucuses and coalitions with other individuals and groups equally committed to public schools. The maintenance of a public system of quality education to enhance the general welfare of all by providing equal opportunity remains a prime objective.[83]

Economic System

The economic system is complex and intricate; its inequities are harder to combat than those in the political or legal system precisely because only a small part of it is directly controlled by government. Other forces intrude to make themselves felt; a market economy is not always an economy free of prejudice and special interests, even of the rankest variety. Such an economy is heavily influenced by public mores, which may at times be retrograde and racist. Its values and goals have centered around profits, not improving the quality of human life. Concepts of social justice that operate in the public sector are not automatically accepted in the private sector. Three centuries of discrimination effectively conditioned attitudes, policies, and practices of both public and private employers. Such discrimination has not declined significantly except where federal regulations and enforcement efforts have made it impractical or unprofitable.[84]

To complicate matters, blacks are today seeking economic advancement in a declining economy. While most job-seeking blacks live in central cities, many factories and businesses have moved from the cities to the suburbs and, increasingly, from the industrial Northeast to the Sunbelt areas of the country. Those who most need jobs do not often live in the areas where employment opportunities are the greatest. While the service sector is growing, highly educated professional help is the type that is most sought. At the same time, American corporations have exported a great many jobs to foreign countries where costs are lower; foreign workers, including political refugees, are entering the country in very substantial numbers. All these conditions contribute to a tight employment situation in the United States.

There are other complexities. Lester Thurow has written:

> Historically, one of the interesting things about our economy and political structure is that we find it much easier to set up welfare programs to give

people money than we do to set up work programs to give people jobs. Transfer payments stood at $224 billion in 1978 while only $10 billion was spent in subsidized jobs. Yet public rhetoric would lead one to believe the opposite. If an equitable distribution of economic resources is ever to be achieved, it will require the provision of jobs for everyone who wants to work.[85]

The public welfare system ought to be seen as a substitute for full employment, which is no longer even aimed for. In 1977, 53.6 percent of recipient families in AFDC programs were white; 43.0 percent were black.[86] This evidence notwithstanding, the prevailing public myth is that the welfare system exists primarily to support lazy blacks who refuse to work. Although public subsidies to agribusiness, aircraft and automobile manufacturers, and others encounter little resistance from the public, federal and state subsidies to individuals and families, through the welfare system, are thought by many to be intolerable. Unfortunately, it is true that these subsidy systems have the unhealthy effect of creating a dependence on government on the part of the recipients, corporate and individual. Because the business cycle "has a profound impact on the status of black workers,"[87] any discrimination in either the private or the public sector has an immediate impact, and this is particularly evident in times of recession.

Most of the literature extolling the economic progress made by blacks describes conditions in the 1960s, not the 1970s.[88] The economic gains of the late sixties eroded under the pressure of recession, inflation, and large-scale unemployment. Analyzing black human resources, Barbara Jones wrote:

> The underutilization of blacks as workers has reached crisis levels. Unemployment is twice as high among blacks as whites and three times as high among black teenagers. The high unemployment must be considered in tandem with declining labor force participation rates. Thus, joblessness among black males approaches 40 percent. Occupational shifts are moving many black workers into jobs with higher wages and less unemployment, but these shifts in labor demand are also leaving another group of workers jobless.[89]

The situation is particularly critical in respect to young workers age sixteen to twenty-four. Norman Bowers, examining historical trends and racial differentials between blacks and whites, shows that unemployment has increased continuously for black males both absolutely and relatively since 1954.[90] For black women, the unemployment rate has rarely been less than twice that of white women; also, black women are concentrated in low-paying jobs that offer small opportunity for upward mobility. Bowers concludes:

> Racial unemployment differences have widened; . . . racial disparities in male labor force participation rates and employment-population ratios are increasing; . . . the female-male unemployment differential has increased

moderately; and . . . after lagging behind black female participation for many years, the participation rates of young white women are now generally significantly higher than those of blacks.[91]

When these economic facts are linked to demographic data, the picture becomes truly frightening. The Census Bureau has projected a 1980 return that will show 59 percent of the black population to be twenty-nine years of age or younger.[92] These young people, requiring educational and employment opportunity, find limited opportunities for work. Even their improved educational attainments are no longer sufficient. All this creates the possibility of serious disorder. To make matters worse, although census data show also that in 1980, 33.2 percent of blacks will be between thirty and sixty-four, in what ought to be their most productive years, many will find little opportunity to realize their employment ambitions.[93] Many in this age group are highly educated; many are still searching for their first rewarding employment. The age group includes also a large body of mature adults who were barred from equal employment opportunity and adequate income possibilities as young adults when their careers were beginning. Most of them will need to remain in the labor force until they reach the mandatory retirement age; few have alternative sources of income. Using official figures, known for their undercount, it is obvious that in 1980 and for the rest of this century more than half the black population will be seeking educational opportunity; at the same time, from 33 to 43 percent will be seeking economic opportunity through employment so that they are able to provide for themselves and their families, and to contribute to the society.

To meet the human needs of blacks, other minorities, and the poor, the United States urgently needs a change in social values. We have not even begun to analyze why the failures in the 1970s have been so glaring, why so many Americans remain locked in poverty.

The income that results from employment is a primary factor in all individual decision-making. It determines to a very great extent whether one will marry and have children, where one will live, what one will be able to save or invest, what health care will be available, what educational options will exist, and how one will prepare for retirement. Blacks are today far below whites in both income and income expectations. Thurow's study of poverty and discrimination reveals that the average black family income has consistently remained near 55 percent of white income.[94] The median income ratio was up to 0.61 in 1969, compared with 0.55 in 1960, but dropped to 0.58 in 1974, was at 0.59 in 1976, and was 0.57 in 1977.[95] Managing with such incomes is proving exceedingly difficult for most black families. Energy costs and food expenses consume a higher proportion of black family income than of white family income. The inflated costs of housing, utilities, transportation, health care, and education cannot be met by many so long as these differential income ratios prevail. Since these differences cannot be explained simply by educational inadequacies, skill mismatches, or job-search difficulties, attention must be given to the continuing racial discrimination that afflicts so many blacks.

In his study of poverty and discrimination, Thurow said that "Negro losses and white gains from discrimination amount to approximately $15 billion per year." He states further that "discrimination causes a large reduction in the potential level of output of the American economy. Negro economic resources are not fully utilized and white resources are inefficiently utilized as a result of discrimination. Efficiency losses amount to approximately $19 billion per year."[96] Bowers's analysis of youth employment in 1980 reveals continuing "evidence of a persistent and chronic racial differential for virtually all labor market indicators."[97]

Thurow offers an explanation for the cause of the problem and its solutions:

> Much discrimination is based on the monopoly powers of whites. Without such powers racial prejudices would have less impact on Negro incomes. With monopoly powers, however, whites may gain financially and enforce discriminatory practices that substantially lower Negro incomes. Functionally, monopoly can be reduced without changing the attitudes of the whites who discriminate. Equality need not wait until man has good will toward all races or until the government is willing to bribe him to be nice to his neighbor. . . .The institutions of government are an important link in implementing discrimination. Either directly through legal restrictions or indirectly through harassment and expenditure decisions, the coercive powers of the white community flow through local, state, and federal government institutions. Eliminating discrimination in all levels of government may be one of the most effective means of eliminating the effects of discrimination through the economy.[98]

Elimination of discrimination in government must be a principal aim of the Chief Executive. However, it demands also greater involvement by blacks in the political process, in the making of public policy, and in the planning of the budget.

Continuing discrimination and economic adversity spell disaster for blacks as they seek housing in today's market. The Fair Housing legislation of 1968 has been weakly and unevenly enforced in the country; it provides few remedies for those who have experienced discrimination.[99] Realtors have maintained their traditional steering practices; lending institutions and insurance agencies have continued their "red-lining" policies. These practices and others determine to a very large extent where blacks live and why the Fair Housing Act has not provided the relief anticipated. Housing choices continue to be closely related to skin color. For blacks who have below-average incomes, purchase of a home has become almost an impossibility in 1980. Meanwhile, rental options decline in major cities like Washington, D.C., where apartments, rapidly converted to condominiums, sell at prices far beyond the means of any but the most affluent.

Congress needs to provide through new legislation an effective enforcement mechanism for the Fair Housing Act of 1968. Without such protection, housing discrimination will continue; blacks will continue to suffer major disadvantages in their access to rental housing or to home ownership.

*   *   *

To analyze the black condition in terms of progress or regression calls for an analysis of the larger American society, since the gains and losses of blacks are inextricably bound in with the way society functions. Those forces that seek to retain the *status quo* for blacks continue to encounter those that are working for modification and change; blacks have an interest in seeking greater control of this process through the use of power, exercised selectively.

To analyze the black condition today is to become acutely aware of the growing diversity within this population over the last twenty years. For the first time in American history, about one-third of all blacks live at what may be described as a moderate level of comfort or above. Black progress toward equal opportunity, however tenuous, is a clear gain; it draws on efforts that go back to the 1930s. The most tangible effects are perhaps most evident for blacks who are well-educated intact married couples in which the head of the household is thirty-five or younger.

The remaining two-thirds of the black population still suffer acutely from past and present discrimination. Although there is heated debate on whether the primary cause of this condition is ongoing racism or social-class constraints, those who are forced to live in this condition have no interest in such discussions. For them, the effects are the same; what they most seek are policies and programs that will improve their living conditions and enhance the life chances of their children.

Blacks are divided also about the utility of affirmative action as a policy calculated to give substantial benefits. Although most black intellectuals support the policy, a minority express very serious misgivings. Thomas Sowell and Walter Williams, for example, hold that the stigma that results from the application of affirmative action principles reinforces the notion of black inferiority; in the long run, in their view, the potential harm outweighs the possible good. Charles Hamilton gives somewhat qualified support to affirmative action, believing it to be a corrective policy justified by the substantial national interest involved. He looks for a policy that would combine protecting the public interest with providing equality of opportunity, and recommends that atttention be focused primarily on those constituencies that could be served by individuals trained for specific needs under affirmative action programs. For example, he sees good reason to train individuals to provide health-care services to poor people. Whatever the disagreement among blacks about affirmative action, there is none about the public obligation to affect the conditions under which blacks live, so that they can in fact achieve equality and justice.

The achieving of equal opportunity remains a prime concern. There is an enormous gap between publicly mandated goals of equal access to employment, housing, health care, education, income, and justice, and their actual attainment. Many forms of inequality exist, with complex and varied patterns.[100] While opportunities shift, with industry moving increasingly to the Sunbelt, blacks today seek to accommodate themselves to these changes. In the 1970s, for example, black "reverse migration" to the South came close to the numbers moving from the South.[101] This demographic change could have important political and economic consequences in the future; it remains to be seen, however, what the results of this new pattern may be.

Bold, decisive action is mandatory if this nation is to continue to progress toward its ideals and goals of liberty, equality, and justice for all. The pervasive philosophy of gradualism that has been operative recently must change; the number of blacks now included as full participants in American society is grossly inadequate. Greater efforts must be made by the executive branch of the federal government to assume a new and determined leadership role to shape positively the pattern and pace of change. Legislatures on every level—federal, state, and city councils—share equally in this responsibility, as do local school boards. And it is the responsibility of blacks and their allies to increase both their political consciousness and their efforts to shape the membership and affect the decisions of these legislative bodies. Most of all, policies and programs are needed to move the economy toward full employment. The "cycle of progress," once so useful to blacks, must be reinstituted; the "vicious circle," created in the 1970s by the erosion of forces working for modification and change, must be arrested. Tocqueville saw the situation correctly when he wrote:

> A natural prejudice leads a man to scorn anybody who has been his inferior, long after he has become his equal; the real inequality, due to fortune or the law, is always followed by an imagined inequality rooted in mores; but with the ancients this secondary effect of slavery had a time limit, for the freedman was so completely like the man born free that it was soon impossible to distinguish between them.
>
> In antiquity the most difficult thing was to change the law; in the modern world the hard thing is to alter mores, and our difficulty begins where theirs ended. This is because in the modern world the insubstantial and ephemeral fact of servitude is most fatally combined with the physical and permanent fact of difference in race. Memories of slavery disgrace the race, and race perpetuates memories of slavery.

And,

> The nations of our day cannot prevent conditions of equality from spreading in their midst. But it depends on themselves whether equality is to lead to servitude or freedom, knowledge or barbarism, prosperity or wretchedness.[102]

It is our national obligation to make those choices that will lead us as a citizenry to freedom, knowledge, and prosperity.

Reference Notes

This paper has benefited from the insight and advice of Dr. Benjamin Bowser, Dr. Edmonia W. Davidson, Dr. John E. Fleming, Dr. Robert B. Hill, Dr. Willie T. Howard, Dr. Barbara A. P. Jones, Dr. Charles Long, Dr. Lorenzo Morris, Dr. Louise Taylor, Dr. Kenneth S. Tollett, Dr. Darwin Turner, Dr. Ronald Walters, Dr. Bernard C. Watson, Dr. Emory West, and Dr. Michael Winston. I am grateful for their willingness to share their special knowledge with me. Any shortcomings or errors are my own.

[1]Selected references from this prolific literature are: John Hope Franklin, *From Slavery to Freedom: A History of American Negroes,* 5th ed. (New York: Knopf, 1978); Carter G. Woodson and Charles H. Wesley, *The Negro in Our History,* 11th ed. (Washington, D.C.: Associated Publishers, Inc., 1966); Saunders Redding, *They Came in Chains* (Philadelphia: J. B. Lippincott, 1950); C. Vann Woodward, *The Strange Career of Jim Crow,* 3d rev. ed. (New York: Oxford University Press, 1974); Richard Kluger, *Simple Justice* (New York: Knopf, 1976).

[2]For a succinct, yet complete, explanation of this situation, see John Hope Franklin, "The Two Worlds of Race: A Historical View," *Daedalus,* Fall 1965, pp. 899–920.

[3]Dred Scott v. Sandford (1857) 60 U.S. (19 How.) 393.

[4]Other human intergroup relationships based on *religious* differences, for example, are of longer-standing duration and just as troubling and difficult to resolve justly and humanely. Think of the Catholic/Protestant intergroup conflicts in Ireland, for example.

[5]Brown v. Board of Education of Topeka, Kansas et al. 349 U.S. 483, 74 S. Ct. 686 (1954). This decision was followed in 1955 by Brown v. Board of Education of Topeka 349 U.S. 294.

[6]Plessy v. Ferguson (1896) 163 U.S. 537, at 563.

[7]Public school teachers' salaries are a case in point. Black teachers at Dunbar High School in Little Rock, Arkansas, early in the 1940s won a court action to equalize the salaries of black and white teachers in that city. There were several such suits for equal salaries in Virginia in the late 1930s and early 1940s, beginning in Norfolk and spreading to other cities such as Newport News, Danville, and Richmond. For a more detailed explanation, see Doxey A. Wilkerson, "The Negro School Movement in Virginia: From 'Equalization' to 'Integration,' " in *The Making of Black America,* August Meier and Elliott Rudwick (eds.) (New York: Atheneum, 1969), pp. 261–63.

[8]Such people are W. E. B. DuBois, Booker T. Washington, Carter G. Woodson, Mary McLeod Bethune, Mary Church Terrell, and such families as that of Horace Mann Bond. Successful individuals and families were to be found primarily in cities, North and South.

[9]Faustine C. Jones, "Black Americans and the City: A Historical Survey," *Journal of Negro Education* 42 (3) (Summer, 1973): 261–82.

[10]Dorothy K. Newman et al., *Protest, Politics, and Prosperity: Black Americans and White Institutions, 1940–75* (New York: Pantheon Books, 1978), pp. 11–13.

[11]*To Secure These Rights, The Report of the President's Committee on Civil Rights* (New York: 1947), p. 166.

[12]Richard M. Scammon and Ben J. Wattenberg, "Black Progress and Liberal Rhetoric," *Commentary*, April 1973, pp. 35–44; Herman P. Miller, *Rich Man, Poor Man* (New York: Crowell, 1971), p. 53; Nathan Glazer, *Affirmative Discrimination: Ethnic Inequality and Public Policy*, rev. ed. (New York: Basic Books, 1978), pp. 127–28. Penn Kemble supported this viewpoint in a presentation on Panorama, Metromedia, October 14, 1977.

[13]Outstanding examples are Robert B. Hill, *The Illusion of Black Progress* (Washington, D.C.: National Urban League Research Department, 1978); Robert B. Hill, *The Widening Economic Gap* (Washington, D.C.: National Urban League Research Department, 1979); and U.S. Commission on Civil Rights, *Social Indicators of Equality for Minorities and Women* (Washington, D.C.: U.S. Government Printing Office, 1978).

[14]Useful theoretical explanations for inequality of blacks can be found in Gunnar Myrdal, *An American Dilemma: The Negro Problem and Modern Democracy*, 2 vols. (New York: Harper & Row, 1944, 1962), sponsored by the Carnegie Corporation. A follow-up to that study, also sponsored by Carnegie, is Newman et al., *Protest, Politics, and Prosperity*. See also Robert A. Rothman, *Inequality and Stratification in the United States* (Englewood Cliffs, N.J.: Prentice-Hall, 1978).

[15]"The Negro American," *Daedalus*, Fall 1965 and Winter 1966.

[16]Kluger, *Simple Justice*.

[17]Theodore H. White, *The Making of the President, 1960* (New York: Atheneum, 1961), p. 323.

[18]Under orders by the attorney general, Robert F. Kennedy, federal troops were sent to guard James Meredith, the first known black entrant to the University of Mississippi; several hundred troops had to remain until Meredith graduated. Kennedy also ordered the desegregation of bus depots and airports in the South after the freedom rides had ended. He saw that voting rights were secured in many Southern counties. He met with black spokesmen to learn more about black concerns that needed to be acted upon, and participated in public school desegregation efforts in Memphis, Atlanta, Dallas, and New Orleans.

[19]Albert P. Blaustein and Robert L. Zangrando, *Civil Rights and the American Negro: A Documentary History* (New York: Washington Square Press, 1968), pp. 558–66.

[20]Woodson and Wesley, *The Negro in Our History*, pp. 786–87.

[21]Newman et al., *Protest, Politics, and Prosperity*, pp. 118–19.

[22]Jack Anderson reported in *The Washington Post* that the FBI kept secret files on the leaders of the black movement. The material in the files was obtained through FBI spying and was alleged to be derogatory. J. Edgar Hoover, the director of the FBI, had hoped to use the materials to discredit the leaders, such as Martin Luther King, Jr., and the movement—which he tried to label "communist." Anderson has published the file numbers of these secret files. Also, the FBI tapped King's phone, with the approval of Robert F. Kennedy, then attorney general.

[23]Congressional committees at this time were dominated by the traditional seniority system. Crucial committees were chaired by long-term white Southerners who had spent their entire careers blocking legislation designed to assist blacks by any means at their disposal, primarily through the filibuster. But Lyndon B. Johnson had been their colleague and peer for many years; he was respected by these powerful congressmen, and they responded to his urgings to pass civil rights legislation. This, together with the passage of the Voting Rights Bill in 1965 and with the seniority system under attack from younger, forward-looking congressmen, made the powerful Southern congressmen more willing to pass liberal legislation and to fund it.

[24]Woodson and Wesley, *The Negro in Our History,* p. 403.

[25]U.S. Bureau of the Census, Current Population Reports, Series P-23, no. 80, *The Social and Economic Status of the Black Population in the U.S.: An Historical View, 1790–1978* (Washington, D.C.: U.S. Government Printing Office, 1979), Table 47, p. 69.

[26]Ibid., Table 96, p. 137.

[27]Ibid., Table 102, p. 141.

[28]Ibid., Table 99, p. 139.

[29]U.S. Bureau of the Census, *Statistical Abstract of the U.S.,* 100th ed. (Washington, D.C.: U.S. Government Printing Office, 1979), Table 238, p. 148.

[30]Among these were the space and arms races with the Russians; the Cuban missile crisis; the civil rights struggles, deterioration of the cities and white flight to the suburbs, urban riots, hard-core poverty, the war in Vietnam, youth rebellion, marches on Washington, the assassinations of John F. Kennedy, Martin Luther King, and Robert F. Kennedy, and the women's movement.

[31]See *Black World* (*Negro Digest*) from 1963 to 1966 for commitment to the civil rights movement; 1966 to 1969 for commitment to black power and nationalism; 1969 to 1973 for interest in Pan-Africanism; and 1973 to 1976 for movement to the left, when *Black World* ceased publication. *Freedomways* began in 1961 as a direct result of the intensification of the civil rights struggle, but always had a Third World focus. *The Black Scholar* began publication in 1969 with a militant focus that has continued.

[32]U.S. Bureau of the Census, *Social and Economic Status of the Black Population in the U.S.,* Tables 131 and 132, pp. 179–180.

[33]All of the data come from the Joint Center for Political Studies, Washington, D.C. See their *National Roster of Black Elected Officials,* vol. 9, July 1979.

[34]U.S. Bureau of the Census, *Social and Economic Status of the Black Population in the U.S.,* Table 109, p. 156.

[35]Ibid., Table 130, p. 179; see also Table 103, p. 150.

[36]See Michael A. Olivas, *The Dilemma of Access: Minorities in Two Year Colleges* (Washington, D.C.: Howard University Press, 1979).

[37] *Higher Education Equity: The Crisis of Appearance Versus Reality,* National Advisory Committee on Black Higher Education and Black Colleges and Universities, U.S. Office of Education, Department of Health, Education and Welfare (Washington, D.C.: U.S. Government Printing Office, 1978), p. 22.

[38] U.S. Bureau of the Census, *Social and Economic Status of the Black Population in the U.S.,* p. 168.

[39] Lorenzo Morris, *Elusive Equality: The Status of Black Americans in Higher Education* (Washington, D.C.: Howard University Press, 1979).

[40] Ibid., chapter 7. See also *Access of Black Americans to Higher Education: How Open Is the Door?* National Advisory Committee on Black Higher Education and Black Colleges and Universities (Washington, D.C.: 1979), pp. 24–33.

[41] *Civil Rights Update,* U.S. Commission on Civil Rights (Washington, D.C.: U.S. Government Printing Office, 1979).

[42] Edmonia W. Davidson, "Education and Black Cities: Demographic Background," *Journal of Negro Education* 42 (3) (Summer 1973): 233–60.

[43] Nancy L. Arnez, "Implementation of Desegregation as a Discriminatory Process," *Journal of Negro Education* 47 (1) (Winter 1978): 28–45.

[44] These achievement levels most commonly are ascertained by use of standardized tests. This testing process is very controversial. See Sylvia T. Johnson, *The Measurement Mystique* (Washington, D.C.: Institute for the Study of Educational Policy, 1979). Ralph Nader and Allan Nairn severely criticize the use of standardized achievement tests in *The Reign of ETS: The Corporation that Makes Up Minds* (Washington, D.C.: 1980).

[45] Newman et al., *Protest, Politics, and Prosperity,* pp. 5–7. See also Barbara Becnel, "Black Workers: Progress Derailed," *AFL-CIO American Federationist,* January 1978.

[46] Robert B. Hill, *Black Families in the 1974–75 Depression* (Washington, D.C.: National Urban League Research Department, July 1975). See also U.S. Bureau of the Census, *Social and Economic Status of the Black Population in the U.S.,* Table 133, p. 189; Table 134, p. 190; Table A-25, p. 250.

[47] Lester C. Thurow, *The Zero-Sum Society: Distribution and the Possibilities for Economic Change* (New York: Basic Books, 1980), p. 63. Thurow used official U.S. Labor Department statistics, correcting for the number of black teenagers who have dropped out of the system, not at school, at work, or looking for work.

[48] Robert B. Hill, "Black Families in the 1970s," *The State of Black America 1980* (New York: National Urban League, 1980), pp. 29–58.

[49] Marc Levinson, "Aid to Families with Dependent Children in Georgia," *The Crisis,* January 1980, pp. 31–33.

[50] Isabel Sawhill, "Discrimination and Poverty among Women Who Head Families," in *Crisis in American Institutions,* 4th ed., Jerome H. Skolnick and Elliott Currie (eds.) (Boston: Little, Brown, 1979), pp. 187–97.

[51] Charles S. Benson, "Investment and Disinvestment in Public Education," *Cross Reference* 2 (4) (July/August 1979).

[52] U.S. Bureau of the Census, *Social and Economic Status of the Black Population in the U.S.,* Table 47, p. 69. See also *Social Indicators 1976: Selected Data on Social Conditions and Trends in the United States* (Washington, D.C.: U.S. Government Printing Office, 1977), Chart 8/12a, p. 339; Table 8/12, p. 379.

[53] Barbara A. P. Jones, "Utilization of Black Human Resources in the U.S.," *Review of Black Political Economy* 10 (Fall 1979): 79–96.

[54]Cited in Louis Stokes, "Keynote Address," *Winning the Rights and Entitlements of the Black Elderly,* Sixth Annual Conference of the National Caucus/Center on Black Aged, Washington, D.C., 1978, p. 263.

[55]Faustine C. Jones, *The Changing Mood in America: Eroding Commitment?* (Washington, D.C.: Howard University Press, 1977).

[56]*Nixon: The Second Year of His Presidency,* Congressional Quarterly (Washington, D.C.: U.S. Government Printing Office, 1971), p. 164A.

[57]Daniel C. Maguire, *A New American Justice: Ending the White Male Monopolies* (New York: Doubleday, 1980), p. 39.

[58]Employment, income, and unemployment figures, coupled with inflation rates, support this point. See U.S. Bureau of the Census, *Social and Economic Status of the Black Population; Statistical Abstract of the U.S.,* 100th ed.; also, *The State of Black America 1980.*

[59]Hill, *The Widening Economic Gap.*

[60]Hill, *The Illusion of Black Progress.*

[61]William J. Wilson, *The Declining Significance of Race: Blacks and Changing American Institutions* (Chicago: University of Chicago Press, 1978).

[62]See the two papers on class and race in this issue: Joan W. Moore, "Minorities in the American Class System," and Thomas F. Pettigrew, "Race and Class in the 1980s: An Interactive View." Gerald R. Gill also addresses the race versus class controversy in *Meanness Mania: The Changed Mood* (Washington, D.C.: Howard University Press, 1980), pp. 31–35.

[63]Joint Center for Political Studies, *National Roster of Black Elected Officials,* vol. 9 (Washington, D.C.: 1979).

[64]Ibid.

[65]Charles V. Hamilton, "On Politics," in *The State of Black America 1980,* p. 211. See also Eddie N. Williams, "Black Political Participation in 1978," in *The State of Black America 1979* (New York: National Urban League, 1979), p. 41–77.

[66]Eddie N. Williams, "Perspective," *Focus* 8 (2) (February 1980): 2.

[67]Ibid.

[68]Joint Center for Political Studies news release, April 25, 1980.

[69]Fred Barbash, "Justices Limit Scope of Voting Rights Act," *The Washington Post,* April 23, 1980, A-14; and Fred Barbash, "High Court May Have Derailed Voting Drive by Blacks in South," *The Washington Post,* April 24, 1980, A-1.

[70]Joint Center for Political Studies news release.

[71]Harry A. Ploski and Warren Marr, III, *The Negro Almanac: A Reference Work on the Afro-American* (New York: The Bellwether Co., 1976), pp. 257–92.

[72]Bernard C. Watson, "Education: A Matter of Grave Concern," in *The State of Black America 1980,* pp. 59–93.

[73]U.S. Bureau of the Census, *Social and Economic Status of the Black Population in the U.S.,* Table 124, p. 174; Figure 8, p. 85; Table 71, pp. 94–95.

[74]*Statistical Abstract of the U.S.,* 100th ed., Table 238, p. 148. See also National Center for Education Statistics, *The Condition of Education,* 1979 ed. (Washington, D.C.: U.S. Government Printing Office, 1979), Table 5.5, Chart 5.5, pp. 184–5.

[75]Gill, "Attacks on American Public Education," pp. 36–40.

[76]This is a general phenomenon, not peculiar to blacks. However, there seems to be more of it in low-income black neighborhoods where the children already have more than their share of obstacles to surmount in environmental conditions.

[77]See Table 4.13, Chart 4.13, Table 4.14, Chart 4.14 in *The Condition of Education,* pp. 166–69.

[78]The work of Arthur Jensen, Richard Herrnstein, H. J. Eysenck, and William Shockley on this point is well known. Jensen's most recent book on the subject is *Bias in Mental Testing* (New York: The Free Press, 1979).

[79]Because of public concern about minimum competencies of high-school graduates, thirty-six states have developed and are using minimum competency tests in some way. See *The Condition of Education,* pp. 47–69.

[80]*The Washington Post,* August 9, 1980, A-9. Jeremiah O'Leary provides a more complete account in "Carter Orders Help for Black Colleges," *The Washington Star,* August 9, 1980, A-3.

[81]*NEA News: Press, Radio, and Television Relations,* a National Education Association press release (Washington, D.C.: May 19, 1972). See also J. C. James, "The Black Principal: Another Vanishing American," in *The New Republic,* September 26, 1970, pp. 17–20; and Arnez, "Implementation of Desegregation as a Discriminatory Process," pp. 28–45.

[82]Watson, "Education: A Matter of Grave Concern," p. 61.

[83]Supportive evidence for this statement is provided in John E. Fleming, Gerald R. Gill, David H. Swinton, *The Case for Affirmative Action for Blacks in Higher Education* (Washington, D.C.: Howard University Press, 1978).

[84]Lester C. Thurow, *Poverty and Discrimination* (Washington, D.C.: The Brookings Institution, 1969), p. 153. See also Special Labor Force Report 233, "Young Workers and Families: A Special Section," U.S. Department of Labor, Bureau of Labor Statistics (Washington, D.C.: U.S. Government Printing Office, 1980), p. 5.

[85]Lester C. Thurow, *The Zero-Sum Society,* p. 206.

[86]U.S. Bureau of the Census, *Statistical Abstract of the U.S.,* 100th ed., Table 574, p. 357.

[87]Jones, "Utilization of Black Human Resources in the U.S., pp. 93–94.

[88]Hill, *The Widening Economic Gap,* p. 10.

[89]Jones, "Utilization of Black Human Resources in the U.S.," pp. 94–95.

[90]Norman Bowers, "Young and Marginal: An Overview of Youth Employment," *Young Workers and Families: A Special Section,* Bureau of Labor Statistics, U.S. Department of Labor, Special Labor Force Report 233, 1980, pp. 5–6.

[91]Ibid., p. 16.

[92]U.S. Bureau of the Census, *Social Indicators 1976: Selected Data on Social Conditions and Trends in the United States* (Washington, D.C.: U.S. Government Printing Office, 1977), Table 1/3, p. 23.

[93]Ibid.

[94]Thurow, *Poverty and Discrimination,* chapter 2, pp. 9–25.

[95]U.S. Bureau of the Census, *Social and Economic Status of the Black Population in the U.S.,* Table 14, p. 31; Table 135, p. 191; p. 186.

[96]Thurow, *Poverty and Discrimination,* pp. 158–59.

[97]Bowers, "Young and Marginal," p. 5.

[98]Thurow, *Poverty and Discrimination,* pp. 158–59. His complete analysis is in chapter 7, pp. 111–38.

[99]There are two options for persons who experience discrimination in housing. The first is appeal under state fair-housing laws. Only New York, Massachusetts, Minnesota, Connecticut, Colorado, Michigan, Pennsylvania, and Kentucky have

good records for penalizing violators, according to Martin Sloane of the National Committee against Discrimination in Housing, and William Taylor, director of the Center for National Policy Review. The second is to file a complaint with the Department of Housing and Urban Development in Washington, D.C. HUD invites conflicting parties to resolve their differences, but if the discriminating party does not appear for conciliation, HUD lacks power to do more. The victim then has no option but to file a private lawsuit, if he can afford it; that lawsuit might not be settled for years.

[100]U.S. Commission on Civil Rights, *Social Indicators of Equality for Minorities and Women* (Washington, D.C.: U.S. Government Printing Office, 1978). See also U.S. Commission on Civil Rights, *The State of Civil Rights: 1979* (Washington, D.C.: U.S. Government Printing Office, 1980).

[101]U.S. Bureau of the Census, *The Social and Economic Status of the Black Population in the U.S.,* Table 9, p. 16.

[102]Alexis de Tocqueville, *Democracy in America,* J. P. Mayer, (ed.)(Garden City, N.Y.: Doubleday, Anchor Books, 1969), pp. 341, 705.

11 The Role of the Family Therapist with Low-Income Black Families

Carole Grevious

ABSTRACT: The family therapist working with low-income black families is called upon to assume various roles, such as educator, director, advocate, problem solver, and role model. A few of the barriers to effective therapy and several strategies to overcome them are discussed. Case examples are presented.

INTRODUCTION

Differences between blacks and whites in their experiences with the mental health system have been discussed by several researchers (Gross & Herbert, 1969; Griffith, 1977; Jones & Seagull, 1977; Jones & Korchin 1982; Sager, Brayboy, & Waxenberg, 1972). The professional literature suggests that black families have not fared well in comparison. Gwyn and Kilpatrick (1981) found significant variation in the persistence in therapy. They examined the effectiveness of a family treatment center located in a southern state and found that among black families, the dropout rate was 81 percent. The significance of this figure becomes clearer when one considers that the rate for middle-income, nonblack families was less than 50 percent. In addition, the rate for low-income families (black and white) was 66 percent. It is also significant that black families constituted a relatively small percentage of all families who were utilizing counseling services. Other research indicates that black clients are not as likely as white clients to continue therapy (Sue & McKinney, 1974; Yamamoto, James, Bloombaum, & Hallem, 1967). Foley (1975) described family therapy as being in the "incubator stage" with poor blacks. In general, family therapists' track record with black families—particularly low-income families—is less than impressive.

Barriers to successful therapy stem from a number of sources. Since most black clients are seen by white therapists, differences between blacks and whites in language patterns and cultural traditions may inhibit interaction. In addition, many blacks harbor negative feelings about therapeutic assistance and approach it reluctantly. Once therapy begins,

Grevious, C. (1985). The role of the family therapist with low-income black families. *Family Therapy, 12*, 115–122. Copyright by Libra Publishers. Reprinted by permission of the publisher.

these attitudes may be manifested through tardiness, lack of active participation, or premature termination. To some extent this reluctance arises from a tradition of turning to the family—either nuclear or extended—for help (Hines & Boyd-Franklin, 1982; McAdoo, 1977). Preference for assistance from family stems partially from negative experiences with institutions.

To explain the poor record of family therapy with black families, it is equally important to identify therapist variables that may interfere with treatment. Negative perceptions of low-income black families prevail in this society. Stereotyping may affect therapists' views of black families (Griffith, 1977; Yamamoto, James, & Palley, 1968). Boyd (1977) shed additional light on the subject. In questioning family therapists to determine their perceptions of black families, she found that nearly 50 percent described blacks as more resistant than whites to therapy. Some therapists commented that therapy was a new experience for blacks. Such racial preconceptions pose serious impediments to therapy.

Although the majority of therapists are white and are members of the middle class, there is no guarantee that black therapists will always be more effective than their white counterparts. As a result of their backgrounds and attitudes, some black counselors may have difficulty working with black families, as this author has observed. However, it may be surmised that greater familiarity with the black experience will facilitate successful outcomes.

Even in recent years, family therapy has not placed much emphasis upon the significance of ethnicity. For the most part, professional training in this area is seriously lacking. An analysis of seventy-six American clinical psychology training programs (Bernal & Padilla, 1982) showed that only six offered cross-cultural clinical courses, twelve offered minority courses, and ten offered courses which included minority-group topics. Also, Bradshaw (1978) showed that there is an absence of cross-cultural training in psychiatry. This author's preliminary examination of training programs in marital and family therapy indicates the same pattern. This lack of training severely limits the likelihood that therapists will possess the knowledge that facilitates productive outcomes. This is unfortunate, since many black families are in need of assistance, and there are indications that family therapy is a treatment mode particularly appropriate for blacks. Throughout their history, both in Africa and in America, the family has constituted the most important institution for maintaining personal well-being (Billingsley, 1968; Gutman, 1976; Hill, 1972).

Counseling black families with low incomes requires a workable approach. Emphasis must be placed on clarifying the therapist's role. This paper discusses several key aspects of that role.

When beginning therapy with low-income black families, it is imperative to recognize the importance of race. "In the case of the black family, it is color and not poverty that is the critical issue. This is why the black experience is qualitatively different from that of Hispanics, Europeans, or Orientals who have been subjected to extreme instances of poverty" (Foley, 1983, p. 242). However, black cultural patterns have not been adequately investigated, yet knowledge of black culture is necessary for the development and implementation of appropriate treatment plans (Boyd, 1982; Foley, 1975; Gwyn & Kilpatrick, 1981; Hines & Boyd-Franklin, 1982). In addition, therapists must become aware of their feelings about their own ethnicity, as well as those regarding the group with which they are working (Pinderhughes, 1982). This is not to suggest that all family problems center around race. Such a statement would of course be a gross oversimplification. However, racial issues must be recognized and included in therapy.

The ecostructural approach advocated by Aponte (1979) and adopted here, views clients as more than individuals or members of families. They are also members of communities. Under this approach, the therapist's role expands considerably. He or she does not confine interventions to the family system. Interventions with external systems that interact with the family are viewed as part of the therapist's terrain. As the therapist moves toward that end, the odds are increased that he or she will be able to accept the family as more than a center of pathology. However, if a therapist is unable to identify any strengths within a family, this message will be conveyed to them, creating an atmosphere that is unconducive to successful therapy.

Once the family presents for counseling, the therapist must begin the process of engaging its members. Promoting a successful outcome starts as soon as the family enters the treatment facility. Receptionists must treat all clients with respect and courtesy regardless of race or socioeconomic status. Families must be made to feel welcome. For example, the waiting room can include black-oriented magazines such as *Ebony, Black Family, Essence,* or *Black Enterprise.* In addition, posters, pictures, and calendars depicting black themes can be displayed. If toys are kept in the waiting room and treatment rooms, black dolls and games should be included.

The initial session is critical for engaging the family. The fact that many black families who present for therapy are not self-referred has implications for therapists (Boyd, 1982; Foley, 1975). Many blacks who go for counseling are forced to do so by schools, courts, or the police. If they are to be engaged, it is necessary for therapists to clarify their role in relation to the referring agency. Self-disclosure is essential, but is hindered when family members are uncertain about how much of what they discuss will become available to other agencies. Black and white counselors must recognize this if trust is to develop.

In the initial session, clients should be told what to expect. Thoroughly explaining the nature of therapy to the family can help prevent early termination. Hines and Boyd-Franklin (1982) suggest that when families seek counseling, orientation should be handled at the time of referral. Nevertheless, therapists should provide orientation whether or not it has been handled elsewhere. It provides an opportunity for the counselor and family to discuss and clarify issues which might interfere with therapy.

In order to gain a better understanding of the client, it is usually advisable to observe the entire family in its own environment. The value of a home visit is illustrated in the following example.

Mrs. B., 30, presented for counseling with her 11-year-old son, Todd, because he was experiencing difficulty in school. He was acting out and falling behind in his work. She complained of feeling overwhelmed and out of control, and cited her son's behavior as proof of that. Later, during the home visit, the therapist observed that the family lived in a very run-down building in a declining neighborhood. Despite this, the apartment was immaculate. In addition, Mrs. B. had gone to great lengths to set aside sleeping and working space for Todd in the tiny apartment. The family's deep religious convictions also were evident.

The home visit also yielded important information about the maternal grandmother's role in the family. Until recently, the grandmother had worked and maintained her own apartment. But an operation (amputation of a leg) had made her completely dependent upon her daughter and grandson. Also, her chronic diabetic condition added considerable stress to the household environment. The home visit allowed the therapist to meet the grandmother and observe the power struggle that was occurring. Despite her ill health, the grandmother appeared to be the power broker in the family. The information obtained during the visit proved invaluable in clarifying problem areas as well as family strengths. The therapist was able to identify dysfunctional patterns and move to change them. Identifying family strengths helped the client mobilize the energy necessary for change.

Further evidence as to the utility of home visits is demonstrated by the success of an experimental program in which paraprofessional parent aides worked with families having multiple problems (Epstein & Shainline, 1974). The paraprofessionals' approach differed from the more traditional one in that much of the therapy was conducted in the home. Though some therapists would resist the incorporation of such a strategy on numerous grounds (including but not limited to monetary and time considerations), positive results suggest that this approach, even if modified, should be explored further. Several therapists support its use (Boyd, 1982; Gwyn & Kilpatrick, 1981), and therapists should consider the regular use of home visits as a part of both assessment and treatment.

Helping families to make better use of community resources is another approach that promotes successful treatment. For example, in the above case, Mrs. B. had stopped attending church despite her religious convictions. The therapist encouraged her to begin attending church again. Once she did, Mrs. B. found that participating in church activities lifted her spirits. In addition, the grandmother joined a senior citizens program that transported her to the center three times a week and to church two Sundays a month. These outside activities had a significant beneficial impact on the entire family.

Therapists' difficulty with low-income families extends even to deciding which issues should be addressed (Boyd, 1982; Foley, 1975). Many therapists tend to avoid socioeconomic issues in their work with black families. Boyd (1977) reported that only 53 percent of black psychologists and 7 percent of white psychologists addressed such issues in therapy with blacks. This is unfortunate, since problems with welfare, housing, food stamps, and clinics are pressing concerns for many low-income families.

The importance of offering concrete assistance to families facing multiple problems has been emphasized by Foley (1975). The educational director of the Harlem Interfaith Counseling Service (an agency servicing a large number of black clients) confirms this. The director reported that many black parents clamor for concrete help more than insight-directed therapy. The agency provides both. When a parent-child issue has been identified as requiring therapy, the clients may elect to participate in a parent training program which helps them to develop parenting skills. The results indicate that parents who enroll in the program persist in individual counseling significantly longer than those who do not. The agency interprets this finding to mean that the concrete assistance which the parents receive motivates them to continue counseling.

At times, therapists may find it necessary to educate families about the social services system and the difficulties they may encounter when using it (Pinderhughes, 1982). In some instances, therapists must function as advocates for their clients. Therapists providing concrete assistance must be careful not to take over the clients' tasks. It is important for clients to actively participate in the resolution of their problems (Foley, 1975), as this is essential to the development of feelings of competence.

Empowerment is an extremely important issue for black families in general and for low-income families in particular. The sense of powerlessness or impotence that characterizes many blacks must be addressed, as shown in the following case.

A couple with two children presented for therapy. An intervention which included the family and school was used (Aponte, 1979). Parental inability to control situations was a recurring theme. During therapy, the fact that their daughter was being prevented from applying to a local college because the high school had misplaced her records became a significant issue. The therapist had the parents and daughter make an appointment with a school official, and accompanied them to the meeting. Her function at the interview was to reinforce the parents' sense of power. She was successful. The parents stood up to the school officials and took them to task for their irresponsible behavior. Afterward, the parents felt proud of themselves and reported that in the future they would stand up for themselves.

Therapists may proceed in several other ways to accomplish the goal of promoting empowerment. Weaver (1982) suggests that the therapist acknowledge the client as having specific areas of expertise. Early in therapy these areas are identified and integrated into the sessions. Lerner (1972) reports that the depth of therapists' commitment to democratic values and respect for the autonomy of their clients are positively related to effectiveness. "Democratic values" refers to the extent to which therapists are accepting of therapy directed by the client as well as nontraditional therapeutic approaches. Lerner suggests that clients interpret therapists' attitudes as indicative of the level of respect for them. She views this as playing a significant role in the development of feelings of competence.

Although Foley (1983) does not specifically refer to the concept of empowerment, his justification for the use of multiple family therapy with low-income families is relevant. To a great extent, his belief in this therapy's usefulness stems from his assumption that it reduces the therapists' importance. In light of the oppressed position historically occupied by blacks in this country, a strategy which alters that position has a good probability of facilitating success between a white therapist and a black family. Existing research indicates that multiple family therapy does work with low-income black families. The problems of premature termination and the need for intensive education before meaningful involvement by the clients were not encountered by therapists using this approach (Powell & Monahan, 1969). Success was attributed to the use of behavioral examples and to the group identification process.

Therapists may also facilitate the development of empowerment by direct efforts to enhance racial pride. This can be accomplished in the course of interventions designed to change family structure. During a session with a black family in therapy because of the youngest son's acting out behavior at school, the issue of discrimination arose. The boy was being bused to a predominantly white school. The youngster felt very uncomfortable being one of only a few blacks. This was exacerbated by the boy's absence of black pride. Although his parents were fairly knowledgeable about black heroes, the boy seemed to know very little. To address this, the son was assigned to read a book about any black person and to discuss it with his parents. The father was instructed to assist the boy in selecting the book. The son read it without prodding from his parents. In addition, the other two children joined the family discussions of the book, and their education into black history and pertinent issues continued. By way of the assignment, the parents and children came together to solve a problem, and the children were able to observe their parents in competent behavior. Moreover, all felt an increase in racial pride and competency. In this case, the therapist was black and was knowledgeable about black history. However, that is not a prerequisite for effective therapy. It is much more important that the therapist recognize black achievements and if necessary assist black families to do likewise.

As role models, black therapists can be more successful than their white counterparts in promoting racial pride. The author has found that positive feelings about blackness emerge in families following interactions with a black professional. Often, clients mention the fact that the therapist is a "successful" black person—one whose achievements demonstrate that blacks are able to succeed in the system.

CONCLUSION

The therapist for low-income black families has a multiplicity of roles, such as educator, director, advocate, problem solver, and role model. Despite these diverse roles, the underlying task of the therapist is to provide structured help; yet, he or she also must be flexible enough to alter his or her approach should the clients' needs require it. Given the variety of roles required for effective therapy, it is evident that rigorous demands are being placed upon family therapists, black and white, to achieve greater success with low-income black families.

References

Aponte, H. Family therapy and the community. In M. S. Gibbs, J. R. Lachenmeyer, & J. Sigal (Eds.), *Community psychology: Theoretical and empirical approaches.* New York: Gardner Press, 1979.

Bernal, M., & Padilla, A. Status of minority curricula and training in clinical psychology. *American Psychology,* 1982, *37*(7), 780–787.

Billingsley, A. *Black families in white America.* Englewood Cliffs, N.J.: Prentice-Hall, 1968.

Boyd, N. *Clinicians' perceptions of black families in therapy.* Doctoral dissertation, Teachers College, Columbia University, 1977.

Boyd, N. Family therapy with black families. In E. Jones and S. Korchin (Eds.), *Minority mental health.* New York: Praeger, 1982.

Bradshaw, W. Training psychiatrists for working with blacks in basic residency programs. *American Journal of Psychiatry,* 1978, *135*(12), 1520–1524.

Epstein, N., & Shainline, A. Paraprofessional parent-aides and disadvantaged families. *Social Casework,* 1974, *55,* 230–236.

Foley, V. Family therapy with black disadvantaged families: Some observations on roles, communications, and techniques. *Journal of Marriage and Family Counseling,* 1975, *1,* 29–38.

Foley, V. Can a white therapist deal with black families? In C. Obudho (Ed.), *Black marriage and family therapy.* CT: Greenwood Press, 1983.

Griffith, M. S. The influence of race on the psychotherapeutic relationship. *Psychiatry,* 1977, *40*(1), 27–40.

Gross, H., & Herbert, M. The effect of race and sex on variation of diagnosis and disposition in a psychiatric emergency room. *Journal of Nervous and Mental Diseases,* 1969, *148*(6), 638–642.

Gutman, H. *The black family in slavery and freedom: 1750–1925.* New York: Pantheon Books, 1976.

Gwyn, F., & Kilpatrick, A. Family therapy with low-income blacks: A tool or turn-off? *Social Casework,* 1981, *62,* 259–266.

Hill, R. *The strengths of black families.* New York: Emerson Press, 1972.

Hines, P., & Boyd-Franklin, N. Black families. In M. McGoldrick, M. J. Pearce, & J. Giordano (Eds.), *Ethnicity and family therapy.* New York: Guilford Press, 1982.

Jones, A., & Seagull, A. Dimensions of the relationship between the black client and the white therapist: A theoretical overview. *American Psychologist,* 1977, *32*(10), 850–855.

Jones, E. E., & Korchin, S. Minority mental health perspectives. In E. Jones and S. Korchin (Eds.), *Minority mental health.* New York: Praeger, 1982.

Lerner, B. *Therapy in the ghetto: Political impotence and personal disintegration.* Baltimore: Johns Hopkins University Press, 1972.

McAdoo, H. Family therapy in the black community. *American Journal of Orthopsychiatry,* 1977, *47,* 75–79.

Pinderhughes, E. Afro-American families and the victim system. In M. McGoldrick, M. J. Pearce, & J. Giordano (Eds.), *Ethnicity and family therapy.* New York: Guilford Press, 1982.

Powell, M., & Monahan, J. Reaching the "rejects" through multifamily group therapy. *International Journal of Group Psychotherapy,* 1969, *19,* 35–43.

Sager, C., Brayboy, T., & Waxenberg, B. Black patient, white therapist. *American Journal of Orthopsychiatry,* 1972, *42,* 415–423.

Sue, S., & McKinney, H. Delivery of community health services to black and white clients. *Journal of Consulting and Clinical Psychology,* 1974, *42,* 794–801.

Weaver, D. Empowering treatment skills for helping black families. *Social Casework,* 1982, *62,* 100–105.

Yamamoto, J., James, Q., Bloombaum, M., & Hallem, I. Racial factors in patient selection. *American Journal of Psychiatry,* 1967, *124,* 630–636.

Yamamoto, J., James, Q., & Palley, N. Cultural problems in psychiatric therapy. *Archives of General Psychiatry,* 1968, *19,* 45–49.

12 Dimensions of the Relationship between the Black Client and the White Therapist

A Theoretical Overview

Alison Jones
Arthur A. Seagull

ABSTRACT: The psychological issues involved in having white therapists treat black clients are explored. The topics examined are the importance of the white therapist understanding his or her own feelings, countertransference, the detrimental effect of therapist guilt, and the impact of the therapist's need to be powerful. Also explored are the need for awareness of client-therapist interpersonal similarity and the need for an understanding of our social system for effective psychotherapy. Concrete suggestions are offered for helping therapists deal more effectively with black clients. The white-therapist–black-client relationship is proposed as a paradigm of how people with differing values learn to help each other.

The issue of white therapists treating black clients is complicated by the fact that blacks in this country have been systematically oppressed economically, politically, educationally, and socially for hundreds of years by whites (Frazier, 1965; Kardiner & Ovesey, 1951); that is, racism is deeply embedded in our predominantly white culture (Clark, 1965). Against that background, questions about how and in what capacity whites can help blacks in a counseling situation are extremely relevant, especially since white persons far outnumber black persons in the helping professions, and blacks are going to request their fair share of mental health resources. So, white therapists are going to have black clients to counsel. Given this reality, in this article we examine the conditions under which white counselors can be of most assistance to black clients and make concrete suggestions about ways of understanding and handling areas of difficulty.

White Feelings

First, the white therapist working with black clients must examine and understand his or her feelings about blacks. Quite obviously, a white

Jones, A., & Seagull, A. A. (1977). Dimensions of the relationship between the black client and the white therapist, *American Psychologist, 32,* 850–855. Copyright 1977 by the American Psychological Association. Reprinted by permission of the publisher.

therapist who has blatantly racist attitudes toward blacks should not counsel blacks. (In fact, people with this pathology should be in therapy themselves.) However, for the therapist not in this category, introspection regarding his or her own racial attitudes is still essential. Rosen and Frank (1962), two white psychiatrists, state, "Few of us are entirely free from race prejudice; with some, this is overt; with others it may be below the level of conscious awareness" (p. 456). Further, according to Sager, Brayboy, and Waxenberg (1972), "This latent reserve of racism, this submerged sense that the black man is 'different,' not governed by the white's warm, human emotions or worthy motivations, is part of our American heritage" (p. 417).

The prejudiced, ill-trained, or inexperienced may stereotypically see blacks as nonverbal, concrete, and hence ill-suited for psychotherapy. They may see blacks as a group as untrusting and with character disorders that are unchangeable (Pinderhughes, 1973). But such preconceived notions may elicit these very responses as self-fulfilling prophesies.

Furthermore, white therapists who view all blacks as "culturally deprived," "disadvantaged," "underprivileged," etc., are demonstrating the subtle form of racism inherent in the use of these labels and are simply misinformed. For example, although black culture differs from white culture and has different forms and assumptions, it would be ethnocentric to label it deprived. According to Vontress (1969),

> The problem is not that certain population segments are without culture; rather it seems to be that the powerful dominant cultural group rejects subcultural groups in society. By their rejection, they convey the notion that those unlike themselves are inferior, deprived, or disadvantaged. (p. 12)

If the therapist views blacks stereotypically, she or he neither sees nor treats an individual (Kagan, 1964). As Calia (1966) warns, "Such generalizations lead to categorical prescriptions and the attendant loss of the client's uniqueness and worth" (p. 102). Tolson (1972) adds, "Some of these adjectives, such as 'black,' have become so culturally powerful that they control our perceptions and thereby limit our ability to apply what we know to be good counseling techniques" (p. 735). One must accept that such stereotypical attitudes are held by most whites toward blacks, and it is important that these feelings be understood and "owned" so that one does not unknowingly let them interfere in the therapeutic process.

This is not to say, however, that these stereotyped client behaviors may not sometimes be manifested by fearful blacks (or whites) in therapists' offices. But, we insist, "nonverbal," "mumbling," "unsophisticated," "nonconceptualizing" clients may be responding with a 300-year-old method called "shuckin," which was used by field slaves as a defense against their masters (Foster, 1974). It has been successfully utilized by other groups that feel oppressed and powerless, such as adolescents (Foster, 1974), incarcerated prisoners, who call it "dummying up" (Spewack & Spewack, 1953), and concentration camp inmates (Bettelheim, 1960; Frankl, 1963).

One fights the oppressor with the weapons one has. If weakness is what one has, one uses that. For example, Gandhi forced the British to give up India through nonviolent resistance, the limiting case of powerlessness used as a power maneuver (Ghandi, 1960). Haley (1971) made the same point in his provocative essay "The Power Tactics of Jesus Christ."

The issue in therapy should not be that the client acts as if she or he had no power, but that she or he cannot exhibit other behaviors when she or he wishes, even though the old pattern has proved ineffective, demeaning, and ultimately destructive and leads to a loss of positive self-concept. The task of the therapist is to help the client distinguish when the use of powerlessness is to his or her advantage, and when other forms of interaction seem more efficacious, such as self-disclosure, retreat, confrontation, distraction, or flattery.

As to the alleged "lack of verbal skills" of the black, lower-socioeconomic-level client, the problem may lie in the situation or in the examiner's lack of skill. What are the verbal skills of a black youth who composes the following poetic insult?

> Aw, man, you trying to show you grandma how to milk ducks. Best you can do is to confidence some kitchen-mechanic out of a dime or two. Me, I knocks de pad with them cack-broads up on Sugar Hill and fills 'em full of melody. Man, I'm quick death and easy judgement. Youse just a home-byoy [sic], Jelly, don't try to follow me. (Foster, 1974, p. 220)

Now imagine how this same black person would speak if sent to a white therapist by his parole officer!

It is interesting to note that therapists who would reject a client's complaints that he can "do nothing" about an inability to argue with a friend or maintain an erection, tend to accept without further investigation a client's seeming inability to verbalize feelings. Yet the differences between a black client and a white therapist can be enormous. They may differ in color, sex, socioeconomic level, vocabulary, accent, syntax, mores, religion, and attitude toward time. They meet, perhaps, in the therapist's well-appointed business suite, within a posh office building, in an unfamiliar part of town for an appointment exactly 50 minutes long! And the therapist then wonders why the client doesn't express his deepest feelings.

Clients may also seem "nonverbal" because one does not speak their language (Bernstein, 1958; Foster, 1974), one fears their rage (Grier & Cobbs, 1969), one exhibits countertransference (Vontress, 1971), one lacks knowledge and skill (Foster, 1974), or because of a subtly racist assumption that blacks are inherently less intelligent (Jensen, 1969). So there may be reluctance to challenge the client's use of lack of verbal clarity as a defense (Foster, 1974).

Countertransference

Countertransference occurs when a therapist does not fully understand and acknowledge his or her own feelings and it influences the therapy. Stereotypic reactions toward blacks are also countertransference. According to Vontress (1971), "Countertransference refers to the counselor's reacting to the counselee as he has reacted to someone else in his past. It means that the white counselor unconsciously perceives the black counselee as he always has perceived other blacks" (p. 9). Since many white counselors have middle-class values and mores, they may well bring with them certain feelings about and attitudes toward blacks, which may influence the process of therapy negatively. Because therapy is ambiguous and unstructured, it is possible for the therapist to influence its process by the emotional reactions she or he has toward the client.

Bloch (1968), in "The White Worker and the Negro Client in Psychotherapy," discussed the symbolic value of black persons for whites in America and its influence on the course of therapy. She observed that whites have projected their own unacceptable drives and impulses on to blacks, who are then seen as being supersexual or more aggressive than the white norm. An uninsightful white therapist may feel threatened by his or her own repressions in treating a black client and may thus tend to protect his or her own comfort in the setting at the expense of the client (see Pinderhughes, 1973).

The white therapist must understand his or her motivation for working with black clients if he or she seeks them out. According to Vontress (1971),

> Productive counseling depends on the ability of the counselor to permit himself to become a part of the total counseling situation. . . . The counselor must know what he is doing and why, and this is not possible unless he understands to some degree his own psychodynamics and his cultural conditioning. (p. 12)

Therapists must understand their own feelings to deal effectively with minority clients or those differing from them on other powerful dimensions such as age, sex, religion, politics, sexual mores or preferences, wealth, or education.

Guilt and the White Conscience

Guilt about their own racism motivates some whites who want to counsel blacks and seek them as clients. Such a therapist is likely to be quite *in*effective. First, according to Heine (1950), a person acting from feelings of guilt is likely to identify with the client and to be too sympathetic to be of much assistance. This type of counselor is likely to fear a realistic confrontation and try to be ingratiating, so that the chance to use the therapy relationship as a springboard for reality testing is lost.

Second, feelings of guilt on the part of the therapist are likely to communicate to the client that the therapist is anxious, which will cause the client to strengthen his or her defenses and cease to explore certain areas either in deference to or from compassion for the therapist, or because the client correctly senses that the therapist will not be helpful for that problem.

Third, guilt feelings on the therapist's part can cause the therapist to become overzealous in helping the black client. "Trying too hard" can defeat therapy. If the therapist is working very hard to help, and the client chooses not to respond to the therapist's efforts to help him or her, the therapist can become angry with the client and, through lack of self-awareness, thwart the client's progress.

Fourth, the guilt-ridden therapist may tend to react defensively or to misperceive the black client's rage (Grier & Cobbs, 1969) and hence, rather than encouraging the expression of anger, discourage it. Or the therapist may waste time trying to prove to the client that he or she is different from other whites.

Fifth, the therapist who is motivated by a sense of guilt may easily become unrealistic about the client's real-life problems. He or she will not be respected by the client, and hence will be of little value to the black person.

Any of the above could make therapy ineffective, since the dishonest relationship on which the therapy would be based would make the interaction essentially "duplicitous," in Kaiser's phrase (Fierman, 1965). That is, the therapist would be saying through his or her behavior, "I will appear empathetic, but I am motivated by my own sense of guilt rather than by true concern for the client."

The Need to Be Powerful

Some whites counseling blacks exhibit a need to be powerful and to be in a dominating role. According to Pinderhughes (1973),

> One problem area for many patients lies in the unconscious needs of many psychotherapists to be in helping, knowledgeable, or controlling roles. Unwittingly they wish to be initiators and have patients accommodate to them or to their style or approach. More black patients than white perceive in this kind of relationship the basic ingredients of a master-slave pattern. (p. 104)

The therapist trying to meet this need is likely to behave in a paternalistic, patronizing fashion toward the client. For example, the therapist might see all of the client's problems as stemming from his or her blackness rather than being able to see him or her as a human being who has racial concerns. Needing to help the black client for one's own power needs constitutes "the great white father syndrome" (Vontress, 1971) and is condescending, paternalistic, and ultimately enraging.

The counselor must communicate to the black client that he is not only somewhat omnipotent (probably because he is white) but that he literally guarantees the black counselee that he can "deliver," if he will only put himself in his hands. Simultaneously, he communicates, albeit unconsciously, the implication that if the black client does not depend on him, he will be doomed to catastrophe. (Vontress, 1971, p. 9)

The dangers stemming from the "great white father syndrome" are apparent. If the counselor assumes an omnipotent, all-knowing role, the chances of the client feeling helpless and at his or her mercy are increased. This role parallels the client's problem vis-à-vis society and hence is counterproductive.

Those who counsel blacks should be familiar with and understand black culture, life-styles, and heritage. The counselor should have some feel for what the client's environment and experiences are like if he or she is going to be of help. According to Sager et al. (1972),

It is essential that the therapist know and, more importantly, want to know and to understand the living conditions, cultural patterns, and value systems of the people he seeks to help. Without this appreciation it may be difficult for persons removed from the ghetto to accept the style of life of those who are part of it and to refrain from attempting to impose a Puritan-ethic-tinged morality upon it. (p. 417).

The Role of Client-Therapist Similarity

Real awareness of interpersonal similarity between client and therapist is essential. It increases the ability of the counselor to accept, understand, and emphathize with clients and permits unconditional positive regard, genuineness, and empathy, which are emotional ingredients required for effective, growth-promoting relationships (Rogers, 1962). According to Calia (1966), the qualities of unconditional positive regard and empathy correlate positively with perceived similarity between counselor and counselee. Although a white person can never become black, certainly his or her familiarity with blacks and black culture will help to decrease the interpersonal differences between them.

The issue is even more complex. Hollingshead and Redlich (1958) found that counselors had better feelings toward clients of their own social class, a finding that supports the importance of perceived similarity for acceptance by a therapist. When therapists have an understanding of themselves and their clients, they will try to be open and honest, which means taking the risk of not being accepted by their clients. If therapists present therapeutic facades or personae, they will most likely be seen as insincere and will have trouble establishing relationships.

The establishment of trust, which is essential for self-disclosure in therapy, also increases as the similarities between the therapist and client increase (Jourard, 1964). According to Vontress (1971), "People disclose themselves when they are fairly sure that the target person (the person to whom they are disclosing) will evaluate their disclosures and react to them as they, themselves, do" (p. 10). (See also, for example, Bienenfeld and Seagull [Note 1], for a case study illustrating the resolution of culturally determined misunderstandings between a middle-class, white therapist and a tough, black, welfare client.) Thus, a therapist with a knowledge of a client's culture and background will be perceived as being more similar to the client and hence will be better able to establish an effective, productive relationship.

There is experimental support for the position that prejudice is a function of perceived differences in belief systems (Rokeach, 1960; Stein, Hardyck, & Smith, 1965). "The prejudiced person does not reject a person of another race, religion, or nationality because of his ethnic membership per se, but rather because he perceives that the other differs from him in important beliefs and values" (Stein et al., 1965, p. 281). Having the white counselor learn about the black perspective can help dispel his or her stereotypes. In doing so, he or she will gain a better understanding of black society and help bridge the gap between himself or herself and the client. She or he will become realistic about the problems presented.

Understanding Our Social System

Understanding our social system and the ways in which blacks in this country have been oppressed, discriminated against, and systematically denied equal opportunity is essential for a white therapist working with black clients. It is no service simply to fit black people back into the society that has trapped them. According to Gladwin (1968), "The clinic does the walking wounded of the Negro community no favor by patching them up and sending them back into battle against a system everyone knows they cannot beat" (p. 479). Psychotherapy can be oppressive rather than constructive, according to Pinderhughes (1973):

> Many pschotherapists have value systems which encourage them to help patients to adjust to oppressive conditions rather than to seek changes in the conditions. . . . This is one reason why psychotherapy has sometimes been labeled as an opiate or instrument of oppression. (p. 99)

Instead of merely helping the black client adjust to a destructive social system, goals for therapy should include helping the client work for change in that system if the client so desires. Further, Kincaid (1969) emphasizes that the counselor who is truly working in the black client's best interests will encourage him or her in making choices that may be alien to the values of mainstream, middle-class America. She says,

> If the counselor is committed to his client's freedom, then he must see his task as one of helping black clients understand the discrepancy between their

values and those of the larger society and make choices based on their own values, free of the threat of external evaluation and condemnation by the counselor for "wrong choices." (p. 887)

And finally, the white therapist working with black clients should be sensitive to the clients' needs, rather than working within his or her own rigid framework and imposing his or her own goals. The counselor should discover the clients' needs and wants. For example, the therapist does a grave disservice to any client by insisting on approaching the client in a traditional manner when the client comes in with questions about how to live in the slums with rats and roaches, how to make ends meet on a welfare budget, where to take the children when both parents go to work, etc. The therapist owes it to the client to deal with these more immediate real-life problems, either directly or through referral, before dealing with intrapsychic issues. In the statement, "I'll talk about my father if you want me to, but you have to know that there's no food to feed my kids tonight," lies a real dilemma. However, it can also be destructive for a therapist, white or black, to insist that the black client become more politically aware and fight for racial or social betterment if this is not what the *client* perceives as his or her problem. (See Foster, 1974, especially p. 245). This is not to say that the aims of the therapist may not be moral or valid, but only that the client must set the goal with the therapist. There is a contradiction inherent in having the client blindly follow the dictates, however well-meaning, of the therapist, and that is that the client must be completely dependent in order to learn autonomy! (See Seagull and Johnson [1968] for a discussion of this issue, which we termed "the problem of form and function.")

If the therapist is to help the client meet his or her own needs and grow, it is essential that the therapist understand what the client is saying or asking for before working for change. For example, the counselor who interprets the black client's expression of anger toward whites as displacement, transference, or a defense against dealing with other issues, as does Adams (1950) in his article "The Negro Patient in Psychiatric Treatment," both undermines the client's trust and interferes with his or her reality testing. According to Gochros (1966), "In denying the validity of just complaints or by seeing the mere voicing of anger as an end in itself . . . workers may appear to the client as either insincere or ineffectual" (p. 34). Further, Sager et al. (1972) state,

> It can be disastrous for the therapist either to deny the suspicion and hostility of the black patient or to feel guilty that these negative sentiments exist. The therapist works with these powerful negative feelings as distortion and resistance when they are unfounded, and, conversely, accepts them when they are accurate. (p. 417)

It is essential for the therapist to understand the client and to work toward having black clients gain pride in themselves, their culture, and their identity just as he or she would for any other clients. Wilson (1971) sums up the direction in which we feel therapy should move when he says,

> Counselors should relate to clients with cultural differences in ways that will enhance the cultural identities of their clients. Counselors should relate to clients in ways which will permit the cultural identities of their clients to become positive sources of pride and major motivators of behavior. To do less is to denigrate a client's identity. To do less is to ask a client to give up his values in order to participate in the dominant culture. To do less is to contribute to the destruction of life; and our mission is not to destroy life but to enhance life. (p. 424)

The White Therapist—Alternatives

So what can be done by white therapists who want to help those who come to them yet who feel that they lack the requisite skills or harbor some racist feelings of which they are not proud but which are real none the less? Clearly the first step is self-knowledge, just as it would be for any therapist who found that she or he harbored irrational or potentially destructive feelings. Talking to colleagues, white and black, about it, playing tapes for colleagues, or organizing discussion groups and arranging speakers on the topic through professional groups would be useful.

Second, the issue of color difference should be brought up early in the relationship, certainly not later than the second session, preferably in the first. "I wonder if the fact that I'm white and you are black is affecting our working together?" "How do you feel about that?" The therapist must be willing to explore the issues in depth, including being willing to verbalize nonverbal cues indicating that the client is telling the therapist what she or he feels the therapist wants to hear. The white therapist should model such openness by examining his or her own feelings if they are relevant to the relationship.

Third, books can be read that give one a view of black culture, aspirations, and mores. And fourth, a willingness to accept one's own fallibility with some humor and wry grace is helpful. Therapists are not perfect, but their openness to change is the one attribute they possess that allows them to try to help others.

Foster (1974, pp. 243–245) writes of the traits necessary for the "natural inner-city teacher" to teach black children successfully. We think the concepts are relevant to the white therapist who genuinely wants to help black clients. The assumptions underlying these traits are honesty, interpersonal/personal integrity, and a respect for others as human beings, which includes the belief that people can learn to change. In a larger sense, these issues of black-white interaction are really the most salient example of the constant, basic issue in therapy—namely, How do we treat with dignity and positive regard those who differ from us on some major dimension such as age, color, wealth, sex, politics, religion, sexual mores, or personal beliefs? This is the task of the "helping professions" and a task, basically, for the whole country.

Reference Note

1. Bienenfeld, S., & Seagull, A. A. *Treating a difficult black client: Some observations by a white therapist in supervision.* Manuscript submitted for publication, 1977.

References

Adams, W. A. The Negro patient in psychiatric treatment. *American Journal of Orthopsychiatry,* 1950, *20,* 305–310.

Bernstein, B. A. Some sociological determinants of perception—An inquiry into subculture differences. *The British Journal of Sociology,* 1958, *9,* 159–174.

Bettelheim, B. *The informed heart; Autonomy in a mass age.* Glencoe, Ill.: Free Press, 1960.

Bloch, J. B. The white worker and the Negro client in psychotherapy. *Social Work,* 1968, *13*(2), 36–42.

Calia, V. F. The culturally deprived client: A re-formulation of the counselor's role. *Journal of Counseling Psychology,* 1966, *13,* 100–105.

Clark, K. *Dark ghetto.* New York: Harper & Row, 1965.

Fierman, L. B. (Ed.). *Effective psychotherapy: The contribution of Hellmuth Kaiser.* New York: Free Press, 1965.

Foster, H. L. *Ribbin', jivin', and playin' the dozens: The unrecognized dilemma of inner city schools.* Cambridge, Mass.: Ballinger, 1974.

Frankl, V. E. *Man's search for meaning; An introduction to logotherapy.* Boston: Beacon Press, 1963.

Frazier, E. F. *Black bourgeoisie.* New York: Free Press, 1965.

Gandhi, M. K. [*An autobiography; The story of my experiments with truth*] (M. Desai, Trans.). Boston: Beacon Press, 1960.

Gladwin, T. The mental health service as conspirator. *Community Mental Health Journal,* 1968, *4,* 475–481.

Gochros, J. S. Recognition and use of anger in Negro clients. *Journal of Social Work,* 1966, *11,* 28–34.

Grier, W. H., & Cobbs, P. M. *Black rage.* New York: Bantam Books, 1969.

Haley, J. *The power tactics of Jesus Christ, and other essays.* New York: Avon, 1971.

Heine, R. W. The Negro patient in psychotherapy. *Journal of Clinical Psychology,* 1950, *6,* 373–376.

Hollingshead, A. B., & Redlich, F. C. *Social class and mental illness.* New York: Wiley, 1958.

Jensen, A. R. How much can we boost IQ and scholastic achievement? *Harvard Educational Review,* 1969, *39,* 1–123.

Jourard, S. M. *The transparent self.* Princeton, N.J.: Van Nostrand, 1964.

Kagan, N. Three dimensions of counselor encapsulation. *Journal of Counseling Psychology,* 1964, *11,* 361–365.

Kardiner, A., & Ovesey, L. *The mark of oppression.* New York: Norton, 1951.

Kincaid, M. Identity and therapy in the black community. *Personnel and Guidance Journal,* 1969, *47,* 884–890.

Pinderhughes, C. A. Racism and psychotherapy. In C. Willie, B. Kramer, & B. Brown (Eds.), *Racism and mental health.* Pittsburgh: University of Pittsburgh Press, 1973.

Rogers, C. R. The interpersonal relationship: The core of guidance. *Harvard Educational Review,* 1962, *32,* 416–429.

Rokeach, M. (Ed.). *The open and closed mind.* New York: Basic Books, 1960.

Rosen, H., & Frank, J. D. Negroes in psychotherapy. *American Journal of Psychiatry,* 1962, *119,* 456–460.

Sager, C. J., Brayboy, T. L., & Waxenberg, B. R. Black patient—white therapist. *American Journal of Orthopsychiatry,* 1972, *42,* 415–423.

Seagull, A. A., & Johnson, J. H. ". . . But do as I preach": Form and function in the affective training of teachers. *Phi Delta Kappan,* 1968, *50,* 166–170.

Spewack, S., & Spewack, B. *My three angels.* New York: Random House, 1953.

Stein, D. D., Hardyck, J.A., & Smith, M. B. Race and belief: An open and shut case. *Journal of Personality and Social Psychology,* 1965, *1,* 281–289.

Tolson, H. Counseling the "disadvantaged." *Personnel and Guidance Journal,* 1972, *50,* 735–738.

Vontress, C. E. Cultural differences: Implications for counseling. *Journal of Negro Education,* 1969, *38,* 266–275.

Vontress, C. E. Racial differences: Impediments to rapport. *Journal of Counseling Psychology,* 1971, *18,* 7–13.

Wilson, M. E. The significance of communication in counseling the culturally disadvantaged. In R. Wilcox (Ed.), *The psychological consequences of being a black American.* New York: Wiley, 1971.

1. Assume you have just been hired by a social service agency that has contracted to provide home-liaison services between the local schools and the parents of students attending these schools. Although a large number of the students are black (approximately 35 percent), your agency to date has hired only one black home-liaison counselor (of a staff of twelve counselors). As a home-liaison counselor, your responsibilities include home visits to acquaint parents with community services available to them and to establish rapport between the parents and the schools.

    a. What expectations would you have for your first home visit with a black family?

    b. What are some examples of "small talk" you might use to "break the ice" with the parents of a fourteen-year-old black student who is consistently truant from school?

    c. Assuming none exists when you are hired, what courses and experiences related to black culture would you recommend that the school district offer to students?

2. Assume you have just accepted a counseling position in a correctional facility where a large number of black inmates are incarcerated, most of whom come from nearby urban centers.

    a. What expectations do you have for your own performance as a counselor in this setting?

    b. Do you anticipate black inmates will avail themselves of your services as a counselor? Why?

    c. What psychological needs can you anticipate black inmates may have that you as a counselor might attempt to fulfill? How will you attempt to fulfill them?

3. Assume you are a counselor in a small midwestern college that is predominantly white but recruits black athletes. One of the black athletes (Bill) has been dating a white cheerleader (Mary) you have seen before for counseling. Mary, seeing you alone, has just informed

you that Bill has moved in with her and she fears her parents will disown her when they find out. She has also asked you if she may bring Bill for an appointment the next day.

a. How do you feel about Mary and Bill's cross-racial living arrangement?
b. What are some of the issues you will want to explore with Mary and Bill when they come to see you together?
c. What do you suppose Mary and Bill each want to get out of meeting with a counselor?

The Black Client
Role Playing Exercise

Divide into groups of four or five. Assign each group member to a role and the responsibilities associated with the role as follows:

Role	Responsibilities
1. Counselor	1. Assume role as a counselor or mental health worker who encounters a black. Attempt to build rapport with the client.
2. Client	2. Assume role of a black. To play this role effectively, it will be necessary for the student client to (a) identify cultural values of the black group, (b) identify sociopolitical factors which may interfere with counseling, and (c) portray these aspects in the counseling session. It is best to select a few powerful variables in the role play. You may or may not be initially antagonistic to the counselor, but it is important for you to be sincere in your role and your reactions to the counselor trainee.
3. Observers	3. Observe interaction and offer comments during feedback session.

This exercise is most effective in a racially and ethnically mixed group. For example, a black student can be asked to play the black client role. However, this is probably not possible in most cases. Thus, students who play the client role will need to thoroughly read the articles for the group they are portraying.

Identifying the barriers that could interfere with counseling is an important aspect of this exercise. We recommend that a list be made of the group's cultural values and sociopolitical influences prior to the role playing.

Role playing may go on for a period of 5–15 minutes, but the time limit should be determined prior to the activity. Allow 10–15 minutes for a feedback session in which all participants discuss (within the group) how they felt in their respective roles, how appropriate were the counselor responses, what else they might have done in that situation, etc.

Rotate and role play the same situation with another counselor trainee *or* another black client with different issues, concerns, and problems. In the former case, the group may feel that a particular issue is of sufficient importance to warrant reenactment. This allows students to see the effects of other counseling responses and approaches. In the latter case, the new exposure will allow students to get a broader view of barriers to counseling.

If videotaping equipment is available, we recommend that the sessions be taped and processed in a replay at the end. We have found this to be a powerful means of providing feedback to participants.

Part 5
The Latino Client

As with the labels "Asian American," "Black," and "American Indian," there is a danger that by identifying a group of people as "Latino" (Hispanic), we tend to overlook very real differences that exist within the group. Yet these labels serve an important purpose. Individuals within each group share a common cultural heritage, knowledge of which can enhance the counselor's effectiveness when working with clients from each group. Latinos primarily consist of those Americans with ancestral roots in Mexico, Puerto Rico, Central and South America, and Cuba who, on the whole, share a similar heritage with regard to language, traditional values, and customs. Important similarities and differences within and across these groups will be discussed in some detail in several of the chapters that follow.

Latino Americans are the fastest growing ethnic minority in the United States (Hunt, 1987). Accounting for over 7 percent of the total U.S. population, their numbers are expected to double in the next 35 years, rivaling that of blacks as the largest ethnic minority in the country (*U.S. News and World Report*, 1987). What makes this particularly noteworthy is the fact that Latinos are nearly 90 percent urban dwellers. Thus, many of the problems that commonly plague the inner city potentially affect a larger percentage of this group.

According to a recent report in *U.S. News and World Report* (1987), schools in Latino communities are already feeling the pressures of overcrowding. Between 1968 and 1984, the number of pupils in Latino public schools rose by 80 percent. The immediate effects have been crammed classrooms and fewer resources to go around, but the long-term effects have been far more devastating. Twenty-five percent of Latino children between the ages of fourteen and twenty enroll two or more years below the expected grade levels for their age (*Phi Delta Kappan*, 1985). Moreover, fewer than 51 percent of Latino eighteen- and nineteen-year-olds complete high school compared to 75.6 percent of whites and 59.1 percent of blacks (*Phi Delta Kappan*, 1985).

Growing numbers of Latinos are also joining the poverty ranks. Today, 5.1 million Latinos live in poverty, an increase of 500,000 during the past three years of economic recovery for the nation as a whole. Among Puerto Rican families, 2 in 5 are poor or headed by a single woman. While Latinos captured a record 19 percent of new jobs created in the 1980s, many of these positions represented the lowest-paying jobs of the market (*U.S. News and World Report*, 1987).

This situation can be accounted for to a large degree by a cycle of poverty set in motion with the early migration of Latinos to this country. Ancestral immigrants of many present-day Latinos came to the United States from nonindustrial, agrarian-based countries and, for the most part, were unskilled and spoke little or no English. (A major exception was the Cuban population, many of whom were middle class and skilled when they migrated.) Their life-style, customs, and language set them apart from the dominant society, making them the objects of stereotyping, prejudice, and discrimination. Thus hamstrung, Latinos were forced to join the millions of other American ethnic minorities in competition for scarce jobs and low pay. Hence the pattern was set, and each new generation has been condemned to the perpetual cycle of poverty and group discrimination. Often the result of this process is loss of hope and motivation and an increase in mental health related problems.

In Chapter 13, Padilla, Ruiz, and Alvarez suggest that although Latinos are subject to conditions that foster mental health related problems, they tend to underutilize existing mental health service facilities. The authors examine several reasons for this underutilization and conclude that discouraging institutional policies are largely responsible. Three models of mental health services are discussed that are designed to meet the special needs of the Latino community. The chapter concludes with a number of recommendations for the delivery of mental health services to the Latino population.

In the second article in this section, "A Language Minority: Hispanic Americans and Mental Health Care," Laval, Gomez, and Ruiz provide a wealth of information on how to work effectively with the Spanish-speaking client. Language and class-bound barriers which commonly plague counselors working with the Hispanic client are thoroughly discussed. Special attention is also given to the importance of good rapport development, culturally sound evaluations, appropriate use of standardized tests, and the role of language in the treatment of the Spanish-speaking client.

In the final article to this section, "Counseling Puerto Ricans: Some Cultural Considerations," Christensen provides a brief introduction to the Puerto Rican in America. Important differences between native-born Puerto Ricans and Neo-Ricans are discussed, as well as the values and traits linked to the Puerto Rican ethos. Most helpful to the counselor is a section in which Christensen offers a number of specific suggestions that apply directly to counseling Puerto Ricans.

References

For Latinos, a growing divide. (August 10, 1987). *U.S. News and World Report,* 47–49.
Hunt, G. H. (1987). Making something happen. *America, 152,* 57.
Staff. (1985). Hispanic children are less well-educated and more likely to drop out. *Phi Delta Kappan, 67,* 242.

13 Community Mental Health Services for the Spanish-Speaking/Surnamed Population

Amado M. Padilla
René A. Ruiz
Rodolfo Alvarez

In the United States, the Spanish-speaking/surnamed (SSS) population receives mental health care of a different kind, of a lower quality, and in lesser proportions than any other ethnically identifiable population. Demographers consistently agree that ethnic minority group members, and particularly minority group members who are poor, receive less health care than the rest of the population. Studies surveyed confirm the demographic findings; in fact, some indicate that the problem may be more serious in mental health care (e.g., see Abad, Ramos, & Boyce, 1974; Cobb, 1972; Hollingshead & Redlich, 1958; Kolb, Bernard, & Dohrenwend, 1969; Padilla & Ruiz, 1973; Srole, Langer, Michael, Opler, & Rennie, 1962; Padilla, Note 1). This article delineates why the SSS receive poorer mental health care than other U.S. citizens and offers some recommendations for remedying this situation.

It should be clear from the onset that by SSS we are referring to the more than nine million residents of the United States who have been identified by the U.S. Bureau of the Census (1971a, 1971b) as people of "Spanish origin." The three largest groups of U.S. residents include more than five million Mexican Americans, approximately one-and-one-half million Puerto Ricans, and more than 600,000 Cubans. The remaining two million SSS members include Central or South Americans and "other" people of Spanish origin. In all, the SSS represent the second largest minority group in the United States. Further, in spite of geographic and in some cases racial differences between the SSS subgroups, all share cultural and socioeconomic similarities that allow us to speak here with relative ease of the SSS as a homogeneous group.

Padilla, A. M., Ruiz, R. A., & Alvarez, R. (1975). Community mental health services for the Spanish speaking/surnamed population *American Psychologist, 30,* 892–905. Copyright 1975 by the American Psychological Association. Reprinted by permission of the publisher and author.

Use of Available Services

A review of the scant literature available indicates that the SSS population has been seriously underrepresented among the clientele of existing mental health service facilities. For example, Karno and Edgerton (1969), using California census figures, estimated that Mexican Americans made up 9%–10% of the state's population in 1962–1963. They found that during this same period, the percentages of Mexican Americans receiving treatment in California were as follows: 2.2% admissions to the state hospital system, 3.4% to state mental hygiene clinics, .9% to the Neuropsychiatric Institute, and 2.3% to state or local facilities. The resident inpatient population was 3.3%. Thus, underrepresentation ranges from 6.6% to 9.1%. Although these data emanate from one state only, other localities also report high degrees of underrepresentation. For example, Jaco (1960), after surveying the incidence rate of mental disorders during a period from 1951 to 1952 in the state of Texas, also reported a lower frequency of the use of private and public mental hospitals by Mexican Americans. More recently, Abad et al. (1974) have reported that statistics available at the Connecticut Mental Health Center indicate that from July 1, 1971, to March 1, 1972, admissions and readmissions of Puerto Ricans were at least 3.5 times lower than that of blacks, a group comparable in terms of poverty and minority status.

Several investigators have suggested that although the SSS receive comparatively less mental health care than the general population, they actually need more. One reason for this is that the SSS as a group are only partially acculturated and marginally integrated economically and, as a consequence, are subject to a number of "high-stress" indicators. These indicators, known to be correlated with personality disintegration and subsequent need for treatment intervention, include: (a) poor communication skills in English; (b) the poverty cycle—limited education, low income, depressed social status, deteriorated housing, and minimal political influence; (c) the survival of traits from a rural agrarian culture that are relatively ineffectual in an urban technological society; (d) the necessity of seasonal migration (for some); and (e) the stressful problem of acculturation to a society that appears prejudicial, hostile, and rejecting (see also Abad et al., 1974; Karno, 1966; Karno & Edgerton, 1969; Torrey, 1972). These authors all concluded that demographic data *underestimate* the frequency and severity of mental health problems among the SSS, and that the underutilization of mental health services by the SSS is therefore even greater than we know. The latter conclusion is particularly telling because a wide range of mental health modalities does not seem available for the SSS as it does for other U.S. citizens.

Type and Quality of Treatment

If referred or committed to a mental health service facility for treatment, what type of assistance is extended to SSS clients? In an effort to answer this question, Yamamoto, James, and Palley (1968) reported data on the psychiatric care of 594 men and women from four groups: 387 Caucasians, 149 Negroes, 53 Mexican Americans, and 5 Orientals. Each of these persons had applied for treatment at the Los Angeles County General Hospital Outpatient Clinic. Yamamoto et al. reported that compared to Anglo controls, SSS patients were referred for individual or group psychotherapy less often and received less lengthy and intensive treatment (e.g., terminated sooner or were not recommended for continued sessions). Karno (1966) reviewed case records of Negro, Mexican-American, and Caucasian patients of the psychiatric outpatient clinic of the Neuropsychiatric Institute, UCLA, and his findings corroborated the Yamamoto et al. findings. Karno stated:

> The prospective ethnic patients are less likely to be accepted for treatment than are the nonethnic patients. Ethnic patients who are accepted for treatment receive less and shorter psychotherapy than do nonethnic patients of the same social class characteristics. Ethnicity tends to be avoided by clinic personnel. (p. 520)

In an extensive review of the quality of treatment delivered to ethnic minority group and lower-socioeconomic-status patients, Lorion (1973) stated explicitly that "psychiatrists refer to therapy persons most like themselves, that is, whites rather than non-whites and those in the upper rather than in the lower income range" (p. 266). Continuing further, Lorion stated that the proportion of ethnic minority group patients receiving treatment at the Manhattan mental health clinics was, in proportion, "far below the general population rate for that area" (p. 266). He further maintained that in the review of a number of studies, "socioeconomic status correlates significantly and negatively with acceptance for and duration of individual psychotherapy, with experience level of assigned therapists, but not with a patient's diagnostic category or source of referral" (p. 266). These findings take on greater significance because the data were drawn from clinics in which ability to pay was not a condition for treatment.

In a related article, Lorion (1974) discussed the expectations of members of the lower socioeconomic classes toward psychotherapy. Such a person typically hopes for advice rather than reflection and for the resolution of "social" rather than "intrapsychic" problems. Thus, if a psychotherapist naively approaches such a patient with an extensive and historical view of childhood, the patient is confused and the therapist frequently experiences frustration when treatment is terminated "prematurely." On the other hand, if the psychotherapist is sophisticated and sensitive enough to recognize that his patient needs to learn the discrimination between personal and social problems, and better ways of responding to both, then treatment has a much greater potential of achieving the success toward which both patient and therapist are striving. This point is supported by Abad et al. (1974), who stated:

> They [Puerto Ricans] expect to see a doctor who will be active in his relationship with them, giving advice, and prescribing medication or some form of tangible treatment. The more passive psychiatric approach, with reliance on the patient to talk about his problems introspectively and take responsibility for making decisions about them, is not what the Puerto Rican patient expects. This discrepancy between the patient's expectations and his actual experience may well determine whether he continues in treatment. (p. 590)

Thus far we have documented the fact that the SSS underutilize existing mental health services; further, when they do present themselves for service, they tend to receive less frequent care or treatment that is not addressed to their needs or expectations. To understand how these problems have come about and, more importantly, to develop practical means of circumventing them, it is necessary to turn our attention to several explanations that have been used to account for the lower use of mental health facilities by the SSS.

Basically two minor formulations and one major formulation explain why SSS subgroups receive proportionately less mental health care than the general population and why, when delivered, such care tends to be less relevant to patient needs and expectations.

Lower Frequency and Severity of Mental Illness

Some evidence exists for the point of view that certain aspects of SSS subcultures protect members against mental breakdown or provide continued familial support after a breakdown (Jaco, 1959, 1960; Madsen, 1964). Jaco, after finding that Mexican Americans are underrepresented in residential care facilities for the mentally ill, argued that the social structure of Mexican Americans provides protection against stress for its members. Madsen generally concurred with this "stress resistance" formulation but added an elaboration of the protective role of the extended family system. He suggested that Mexican Americans discourage the referral of family members to mental health centers—as they would to any other majority group institutional structure—because the centers are perceived as alien and hostile.

The argument that SSS members are better prepared to tolerate stress or to require less support from social institutions must be interpreted with caution. Both Jaco and Madsen have predicted an increase in emotionally related problems once the SSS undergo a lessening of their traditional social structure (i.e., acculturation). As noted earlier, Karno and Edgerton (1969) and Torrey (1972) identified five sources of massive psychological stress for the SSS that are detrimental to adaptive psychological functioning, including the problems associated with acculturation as one of these. Because the literature on the inadequate mental health treatment delivered to the lower socioeconomic classes essentially corroborates these points, it seems reasonable to conclude that the explanation for the underutilization of mental health resources by the SSS poor must be sought elsewhere.

Use of "Folk" Medicine and/or "Faith" Healers

A small and steadily growing literature exists on the use of folk medicine and the practice of faith healing among the SSS (e.g., Creson, McKinley, & Evans, 1969; Edgerton, Karno, & Fernandez, 1970; Garrison, 1975; Kiev, 1968; Leininger, 1973; Lubchansky, Ergi, & Stokes, 1970; Garrison, Note 2). These investigators either argue or imply that such practices are sometimes selected as alternative solutions for the types of emotional problems for which most majority group members would probably seek more commonplace psychiatric treatment.

One reason why many SSS subgroups may prefer folk healers to more conventional psychiatric treatment may rest in a conceptual difference between lower-class patients and middle-class therapists as to what constitutes mental health or illness. For example, Hinsie and Campbell (1970) defined "mental health" or "psychological well-being" as "adequate adjustment, particularly as community-accepted standards of what human relations should be" (p. 388). This emphasis on adjustment implies a distinction between "mental" and "physical" health, a concept that does not exist among SSS subcultures. The state of well-being is usually conveyed in Spanish as *estar saludable* ("to be healthy"), *ser feliz* ("to be happy"), *sentirse o estar como un cañon* ("to feel or be like a cannon," i.e., the Spanish equivalent of "fit as a fiddle"), or *estar sano y fuerte* ("to be healthy and strong"). All of these Spanish idioms imply that physical and psychological "well-being" are inseparable.

These Spanish phrases reflect the cultural truism that some SSS who "do not feel well" *(que no se sienten sanos)* may consult a physician for help but are quite unlikely to approach a mental health professional for help with an "emotional" (i.e., nonphysical) problem. In support of this, Karno and Edgerton (1969) commented on the active role of the family physician in their study of mental illness among Mexican Americans in Los Angeles. If a problem should be perceived as nonphysical and "spiritual," for example, guilt, shame, a sense of sin, disrespect for elders or family values, then it seems eminently probable that a religious leader would be consulted for solace. It is equally predictable that fellow members of the extended family system, who share the same cultural values, would probably either recommend or support a referral to a physician or a priest or minister. Thus, problems perceived by the Anglo majority as "emotional" in nature and as requiring psychotherapeutic intervention might be perceived differently by the SSS subculture, that is, as subtle problems in physical health or as spiritual malaise.

It should be pointed out that the literature discussing folk psychiatry among Mexican Americans documents the use of such methods among a wide spectrum of the Mexican-American population. Creson et al. (1969) presented data from interviews with 25 Mexican Americans who were receiving treatment in either a pediatric or a psychiatric outpatient clinic. Five subjects admitted having used a faith healer at least once, 7 reported that at least one family member had used one, and 20 demonstrated familiarity with the concepts or language of faith healing. These data imply a substantial degree of recourse to faith healers among Mexican Americans, even among patients receiving conventional medical treatment. A second interpretation is that among this particular SSS group, these beliefs were highly stable. To quote the authors, "the concept of folk illness was deeply entrenched and resistant to the influence of the Anglo culture and its scientific medicine" (Creson et al., 1969, p. 295). Thus, it may be that recourse to faith healing is frequent enough to inhibit self-referrals to mental health centers.

The article by Leininger (1973) illustrated folk illness in depth, using the case-history approach with Spanish, Mexican-American, and lower-class Anglo families. In addition to providing a theoretical model to explain why the families embraced the "witchcraft" model of mental illness, the author outlined a series of therapeutic interventions that were effective in reducing personal and familial stress.

In an attempt to answer why the SSS underutilize mental health services, Torrey (1972) observed that Mexican Americans in California's San Jose and Santa Clara Counties have "their own system of mental health services." He described how this SSS group seeks improved health from self-referral to faith healers. In spite of this community-oriented health system, however, Torrey posited that when and if relevant health services staffed by professionals are available, this will become the preferred mode of health care sought by Mexican Americans.

Similarly, the Karno-Edgerton group recognized the existence of faith healing and described its practice. However, these investigators pointed out that use of the system is minimal and that its existence cannot be used to explain the underutilization of conventional health services (see especially Edgerton, Karno, & Fernandez, 1970).

Similarly, Lubchansky, Ergi, and Stokes (1970) and Garrison (1975: Garrison, Note 2), in studies of Puerto Rican spiritualists in New York City, reported that although spiritualists are consulted, Puerto Ricans also seek professional mental health services. Thus, among Puerto Ricans who believe in folk medical practices, more conventional mental health services are also sought, when available. For this reason, these authors concluded that the efficacy of professional treatment practices is confounded by the existence of this alternative system of mental health.

In sum, the underutilization of traditional mental health services cannot be explained because of the substitution of either folk medicine or faith healing by substantial numbers of the SSS. This conclusion seems warranted despite the seemingly valid conclusion by Leininger (1973) that a limited number of rural and/or migrant peoples still adhere to "witchcraft" beliefs.

Discouraging Institutional Policies

Certain organizational factors and institutional policies are primarily responsible for the use patterns of mental health facilities exhibited by the SSS. A review of the literature by Gordon (1965), concerned with characteristics of patients seeking treatment at child guidance clinics, suggested that the needs of minority group children are not being met (cited by Wolkon, Moriwaki, Mandel, Archuleta, Bunje, & Zimmerman, 1974). Primary factors responsible for this situation are defined as "inflexible intake procedures and long waiting lists." A study of a specific child guidance clinic confirmed the inference based on the literature review (Wolkon et al., 1974). The period between the initial self-referral for service and the intake interview ranged from 1 to 52 weeks, with a median of 28 weeks. The four Mexican-American families seeking treatment had a median wait of 28 weeks, with a range of 24.5–42.5 weeks. In case of "emergency," patients were seen "immediately." At the same clinic, while the median waiting period for Caucasians was only 4.5 weeks, the Mexican Americans had to wait 5.5 weeks. Although these differences failed to achieve statistical significance, it is clear that an "emergency" telephone contact is not generally honored for more than a month in the case of Caucasians but takes almost 6 weeks in the case of Mexican Americans. The inference that delays for ordinary and emergency treatment are discouraging is confirmed by the finding that "77% of the total initial request for services did not receive treatment" (Wolkon et al., 1974, p. 711).

A study even more directly relevant to treatment of the SSS (Torrey, 1972) described mental health facilities located in a catchment area of one million persons, of whom approximately 100,000 were Mexican-American. Torrey evaluated these facilities as "irrelevant" for Mexican Americans because 10% of the local population generated only 4% of the patient referrals. The basis of his judgment was that the bilingual poor should be expected to generate a larger proportion of referrals because they are subject to many stresses known to bring on mental breakdown. His explanation for this discrepancy was based primarily on the following four variables:

1. Geographic isolation is an important casual factor. Mental health services are "inaccessible" to the SSS because they are often located at the farthest distance possible from the neighborhood of the group with the highest need. All too often community mental health services are attached to schools of medicine or universities located outside of the barrio and accessible only by a half-hour, or more, bus ride. Not only does the distance impede the frequency of self-referrals, but both the cost of transportation and the lack of adequate child care during the absence of the mother also serve to decrease the use of mental health facilities by the SSS.

2. Language barriers are a second explanatory factor. Torrey described the "majority" of local Mexican Americans as bilingual. Nevertheless, only 4 members of a professional staff of 120 studied by Torrey spoke any Spanish at all, and none of the directional and/or instructional signs were in Spanish. The interpretation that referrals will decrease if patient and therapist cannot communicate is shared by Edgerton and Karno (1971; Karno & Edgerton, 1969), among others.

3. Class-bound values are a third causal factor. Here the reference is primarily to therapist variables, that is, to personal characteristics of the professional staff that dissuade the patient from continued mental health treatment. Abad et al. (1974), Yamamoto et al. (1968), and Torrey (1972) all indicated that therapists conduct treatment in accord with the value system of the middle class, that is, a system in which the client is seen by the therapist for 50 minutes once or twice a week or in a group therapy in which the client is seen in a group once or twice a week. This approach was proven ineffective with, and discouraging to, lower-class patients. When frustrated because clients fail to respond to this approach, psychologists are more likely not to encourage the SSS client to seek therapy after the first meeting. These points have also been noted by the Karno-Edgerton group as well as by Kline (1969).

4. Culture-bound values are a fourth explanatory factor. Again, Torrey attended to therapist variables. His point was that whenever therapists from one culture diagnose and prescribe treatment for patients from another culture, there is an inherent probability of professional misjudgment. To illustrate, he cited data (p. 156) indicating that 90% of Anglo residents in psychiatry associate the phrase *hears voices* with the word *crazy*, whereas only 16% of Mexican-American high school students make the same association. The concept of intrinsic culture conflict was also advanced by Bloombaum, Yamamoto, and Evans (1968), the Karno-Edgerton group, Kline (1969), and Phillipus (1971).

Although all four factors operate to minimize self-referral to mental health centers by the SSS, the last three (language, class, and culture) seem to interact in such a way that the SSS are actively discouraged from using mental health services. A review of studies of low-income patients, both white and nonwhite, who apply for mental health services (Lorion, 1973) is particularly relevant here. One major conclusion that emerges from this review is that middle-class therapists are typically members of a different cultural group than their lower-class patients. As a consequence, patient and therapist experience all the difficulties in communication that occur whenever members of two cultures interact. This "culture conflict" was described in much greater detail in a second article by the same author (Lorion, 1974). Therapists, and particularly therapists in training, tend to be "turned off" by low-income patients because they perceive the patients as hostile, suspicious, using crude language, and expecting *merely* "symptomatic relief." Studies reviewed by Lorion reveal that the success of a therapist in working with low-income patients bears a closer relationship to the therapist's personal characteristics than it does to his experience level or treatment approach. Lorion also reported that therapists from low socioeconomic backgrounds are equally successful with patients from all social classes. The reverse does not seem to be true, that is, that upper-class therapists can deal with equal effectiveness across social classes. More interesting is the fact that "low-income patients engage in significantly more self-exploration early in treatment if matched with their therapist on race and/or socio-economic background" (Lorion, 1974, p. 346). Cobb (1972), in a review of similar literature, supported an earlier argument made in this article that therapeutic expectations vary to some extent as a function of social class. Low-socioeconomic-status patients seem to expect therapists to assume a more active role, as physicians typically do in dealing with medical problems, as opposed to a passive or "talking" role. As a result, Cobb concluded that such patients will probably respond better to therapists who are more active. Taken together, the reviews of Cobb (1972) and Lorion (1973, 1974) lead to two major conclusions: First, race and social class of the therapist seem to affect the patient's response to treatment; and second, an effective and appropriate "solution" to a problem based upon middle-class values may be totally inappropriate and ineffective for a patient returning to his lower-class environment.

Three Models for Improved Services to the SSS Population

Having reviewed the panorama of complex explanations for the underutilization of mental health services by the SSS population, let us now examine three emerging models for service to this population.

Two points seem relevant here: First, our perusal of the literature suggests that these are the *only* programs designed specifically for the SSS (though there may be others which have not been described in the literature); and second, these programs seem to have been designed primarily for the treatment of adult self-referrals. We return at a later point in this article to the need for child-guidance clinics or similar organizations providing treatment programs for younger patients.

Professional Adaptation Model

The major characteristic of the *professional adaptation model* is that the professional and paraprofessional staff of the community mental health center receive some form of specialized nonstandard training or in some way "adapt" themselves to the specific requirements of serving the SSS population. Two examples of the professional adaptation model follow.

First, Karno and Morales (1971) described the effort in east Los Angeles to design a community mental health service that would attract local Mexican Americans. Major innovations were implemented in staffing, service quarters, and treatment programs. At the end of a 2½-year recruitment program, the medical director had attracted 22 full-time professional, paraprofessional, and clerical personnel. Of these 22, 15 were "completely fluent," 4 were "conversant," and 3 had a "rudimentary knowledge" of Spanish. Ten were natives and/or residents of the area. More interesting is the fact that 12 were of Mexican-American and 2 were of other Latin (Cuban and Peruvian) descent. Service quarters selected were "in the heart of the . . . community, convenient for . . . transportation, and comfortable . . . and inviting" (p. 118). The treatment program was based on the philosophy of prevention. Thus, the major thrust was upon mental health consultation to a wide variety of community service agencies. As a backup, the center offers short-term crisis-oriented treatment using individual, family, group, and chemical therapy. The center seems to be fulfilling the objective of providing appropriate treatment for Mexican Americans because the first 200 patients matched local population figures.

A second, but somewhat similar, example of the professional adaptation model has been created for the Hispanic population of Denver (Phillipus, 1971). Three of the eight team members are Spanish-speaking, and the center is located in the neighborhood of the target population. It is in a building designed so that the prospective patients enter a reception area furnished to resemble a living room. The initial contact person is usually a secretary-receptionist, who is always Spanish-speaking. The patient is referred immediately to a team member to begin whatever action seems necessary. The rationale is that treatment is directed toward crisis resolution that, by definition, is incompatible with rigid adherence to the traditional 50-minute-hour schedule. The staff began to refer to each other and to the patients on a first-name basis when it became apparent that the use of more formal address was estranging some members of the Hispanic group. Unequivocal data bearing on the appropriateness of the program for the SSS are difficult to obtain because of its recency. Nevertheless, new referrals increased to a point that proportional representation of the target population relative to the general population was soon reached. When certain specific elements of the program were eliminated, Hispanic self-referrals began to decline but returned to former levels when reinstituted.

Family Adaptation Model

Under the conception of the "family" (i.e., a strong sense of an extended network of primary social relationships) as an important cultural feature that helps to provide emotional support against stresses experienced by the SSS population, a variant of group psychotherapy appears to be evolving into what we call the *family adaptation model*.

Maldonado-Sierra and Trent (1960) described a "culturally relevant" group psychotherapy program for chronic, regressed, schizophrenic, Puerto Rican males based on assumptions about the Puerto Rican family structure. The father of these families is typically described as a "dominant, authoritarian" figure, and the mother as submissive, nurturant, and loving. The older male sibling is perceived as a figure whom the other siblings respect, admire, and confide in. In this article and in a second (Maldonado-Sierra, Trent, & Fernandez-Marian, 1960), the authors described how these observations were translated into action.

First, three groups of eight patients each spent several weeks together in a variety of activities under the supervision of an individual who represented the older male sibling. A few days before group sessions were initiated, the group was introduced to an older male therapist who represented the father figure. He maintained dignity, remained aloof, and restricted social interaction to brief interchanges. The third therapist was an older female who fulfilled mother-figure expectations by distributing food and chatting informally.

The complexity of the group psychotherapy process of this type is too extensive to describe here. Suffice it to state that this analogy of the Puerto Rican family permitted patients an opportunity to identify their common problems and to resolve them therapeutically.

Although this section is thus far limited to the work of Maldonado-Sierra and his associates with hospitalized schizophrenic patients, the family adaptation model deserves further exploration with less severely disturbed SSS patients. The use of cultural themes such as *machismo, respecto, comadrazco-compadrazco,* the role of women, and *personalismo* in therapy, especially family therapy, could prove extremely valuable in effecting more adequate therapeutic models. Limitations of space preclude a refined definition of these terms, but the basic concepts are that sex roles of SSS men and women are much more rigidly defined: Males value highly the virtues of courage and fearlessness *(machismo);* respect is given elders and there is an adherence to cultural norms and values *(respecto);* extended family relations, especially between godfather-godmother and godchildren, are ritualized and have a religious connotation *(comadrazco-compadrazco);* and interpersonal relations are based on trust for people mingled with a distaste for institutions or organizations that operate on a formal and impersonal basis *(personalismo).*

Barrio Service Center Model

By virtue of the conclusion that the vast majority of the sources of stress experienced by the SSS population are of economic origin, the barrio service center model is emerging and rapidly gaining legitimacy. This model seems to fit particularly well with the "health services catchment area" concept, in which a community center is staffed with personnel who can effectively intervene on behalf of the surrounding population to get jobs, bank loans, and many other basic economic services. Four examples of the barrio service center model exist in the literature:

1. First, Lehmann (1970) described the operation over a two-year period of three storefront neighborhood service centers in New York City as follows:

> [The] typical client [is] a Puerto Rican woman in her mid-30's with two or three children and there is no father present. She is usually an unemployed housewife . . . on welfare . . . with income less than $3,000 a year. She is almost certainly born in Puerto Rico . . . and there is only about one chance in three she speaks English well. (p. 1446)

Lehmann admitted that "their [i.e., the centers'] record for problem solving was less than brilliant" (p. 1454) but attributed whatever successes achieved by the centers to their accessibility, informality, and open-door policy with respect to problems and people, and their use of community residents as staff.

2. A second example of the barrio service center model was described by Abad et al. (1974) in an article identifying demographic and subcultural characteristics of a Puerto Rican sample of residents of New Haven, Connecticut. The "Spanish clinic," or *la clinica hispana* as it is called by the Spanish-speaking community, provides walk-in coverage five days a week and includes psychiatric evaluations and follow-up treatment, medication groups, individual counseling, couple and family therapy, referral services, home visits, and transportation. The staff is bilingual-bicultural and includes a Spanish psychiatrist, a part-time Puerto Rican social worker, and a paraprofessional indigenous staff including community leaders with public visibility. The clinic is prepared to intervene in a variety of problem situations, even if the situations are not of a "clinical" nature. For example, one of the "most frequent roles within the Spanish community is that of intermediary between Spanish-speaking clients and other agencies" (p. 592). The article concluded that everyone benefits from such an arrangement: the clientele receive help with problems and this help permits them to function more effectively within their environment; the barrio agency gains the reputation of being a "helpful" institution; and community support of the clinic is enhanced.

3. A third example of the barrio service center model was reported by Burruel (Note 3), who described the creation of *La Frontera,* a mental health outpatient clinic situated in south Tucson, Arizona, designed specifically to provide care for the Chicano community. Burruel described

the ongoing services of the clinic, including "diagnosis and treatment for adults and children with emotional or personality problems and general problems of living" (p. 27). Treatment modalities include "individual therapy, conjoint, family and group therapy" (p. 27). Community representation was originally excluded from planning and administration of the center until "pressure was applied" (p. 29). Currently, the administrative board is a "policy-making board which incorporates representatives from the community" (p. 29). Under the leadership of a Chicano full-time director, deliberate effort was expended "to make the services relevant to the Chicano community . . . by searching for bilingual and bicultural mental health professionals" (p. 29). A deliberate effort to attract patients from the catchment area was implemented by announcing services on the Mexican radio stations and by eliminating the "waiting list" that is typical of traditional mental health clinics. It is stated that patients may be seen "immediately, hours later, or at the latest, the next day" (p. 32). The response to this innovative program is described as follows: "underutilization of mental health services by Mexican Americans has not been the case at *La Frontera;* 61.5% of the total patient population consists of Mexican Americans" (p. 28).

4. The fourth and final example of the barrio service center model was described by Schensul (1974), who brought the insights of an applied anthropologist to the creation of a new mental health center specifically for an SSS subgroup. Schensul described how a group of young Chicanos working in Chicago's west side developed the idea in the summer of 1971 to create a community-controlled youth facility to be called *El Centro de la Causa.* The original operating budget of $1,800 was raised by a community fiesta. According to Schensul, the activist group had, within months, convinced a church organization to provide $40,000 for staff and seed money. Within three years, the operating budget was over $400,000. This funding was used to train community residents as paraprofessionals in mental health and to support mental-health-training and reading-improvement programs, English classes, recreation and youth activities, and programs to prevent drug use. Schensul concluded that whatever success was achieved by *El Centro de la Causa* was primarily because of the youthful Chicano activists and their consistent efforts to maintain community involvement.

The major conclusion is that successful therapeutic models for SSS groups are possible when cultural and social variables are made part of the therapeutic setting. It would be misleading to conclude this discussion without noting that some of the successful programs described here no longer exist (e.g., that described by Phillipus). These programs are only highlighted because they represent the very small number that are described in the literature.

General Conclusions and Recommendations

The preceding review and analysis of the extant literature on the delivery of mental health services to the SSS population clearly reveal a crisis situation. What, then, is to be done? While we are not at this time prepared to generate totally novel institutional mechanisms for the maximum delivery of high-quality mental health services to the SSS population, we are prepared to make a number of recommendations designed to encourage speedier evolution of three promising avenues for improvement of service to this target population. The three models described in the preceding section of this article appear to us to offer considerable promise. Our objective is to focus on their essential distinguishing characteristics and to make compatible recommendations designed to enhance their potential for success.

The recommendations we make here may be viewed as stemming from the intellectual perspective of the community mental health movement. Before proceeding to our recommendations, a word about the community mental health movement is in order. Although there is no exact and technically precise definition of what is still an evolving concept of "community mental health," it can be differentiated from the traditional, exclusively *medical* approach to mental health by four of its major characteristics: First, the community mental health movement seeks an empirical, research-based understanding of the interconnectedness between the family, community, social, economic, and cultural structures, as well as biological and psychic structures, as sources of pressures that directly affect the mental health of individuals. Second, the community mental health movement seeks to promote an improved general state of mental health through intervention techniques in which the recipients of health care have had a measure of knowledge of and participation in the process of development and implementation. Third, the prime objective is positive and preventive, in that it seeks to promote and maintain *health* rather than to dwell on an exclusive concern with the treatment of *illness* that has become too great to be ignored. Fourth, the target of the community mental health movement is the entire population of a defined community in its collective sense, and not simply those individuals whose mental condition has become so acute as to be identified as mentally ill. These, then, are the four intellectual perspectives guiding our recommendations for the improvement of the three models that appear to be making a start toward effective mental health service delivery to the SSS population.

Despite a variety of reasons advanced to explain why the SSS receive proportionately less mental health care, the literature reviewed supports the conclusion that mental health centers across the country are failing to meet the needs of the SSS, with a few notable exceptions. One explanation for this failure is that mental health centers and related agencies are so overly committed to traditional models of health care delivery that they ignore other problems troubling the SSS that are of much greater severity. Occasionally, centers and agencies offer chemotherapy combined with some variation of individual or group counseling to deal with emotional conflicts of an allegedly intrapsychic nature. These treatment services completely deny, of course, the bona fide problems of a "social" nature that are anxiety provoking, depressing, frustrating, enraging, debilitating, and potentially disruptive to adaptive psychological function. These problems include premature termination of education among the young, elevated rates of arrest and incarceration, widespread abuse of alcohol and illegal drugs, and high rates of unemployment, to cite only the most obvious and destructive.

With regard to treatment programs, a number of investigators have commented that many current modalities, especially those based on majority culture and/or middle-class values, have proven ineffective. Encouraging results have been reported, however, from some centers that emphasize some combination of (a) community consultation as a preventative measure, (b) crisis intervention as a matter of course, and (c) "back-up" treatment with individual, group, family, and drop-in therapies. The literature supports the recommendation that more innovative programs be created and applied on a more widespread basis.

A recommendation for "innovative" treatment programs is self-defeating unless validating research is conducted. Even more critically, demographic and survey research is needed to guide the development of programs with the greatest probability of success. Schensul (1974) spoke of developing "research expertise" among community representatives who lack formal academic, scientific training. Basically, Schensul described an interaction between community activists and researchers that both educates and enhances the quality of the findings that emerge.

In addition, a wide range of innovative programs is necessary to deal with the social problems besetting the SSS (e.g., remedial education, vocational guidance and retraining, drug abuse and crime prevention programs, and possibly even college counseling). The problem of providing appropriate services and attracting clientele can be resolved somewhat by using the agency as a multipurpose center. In addition to providing treatment for a wide range of human problems, the facilities could be used for youth activities (e.g., sports, dances, etc.), for culturally relevant events (e.g., Spanish-language films, fiestas, etc.), or for the satisfaction of any variety of community needs. It makes eminent sense to involve the community in a center in their neighborhood which is situated there to satisfy their needs. The literature supports the contention that the community can be penetrated more effectively, and the quality of services increased, if community representation is involved in the administration. Even more specifically, Burruel (Note 3) and Schensul (1974) agreed that the use of the community mental health center for a variety of purposes has the beneficial effects of attracting more clienetele and delivering services of higher quality.

We also recommend a "business model" approach to attract clientele. There may be some value in using advertising media, in both Spanish and English, to disseminate information to the target population concerning available facilities, therapeutic services, and related activities. Boulette (1974), for example, advocated the use of television to inform clientele of the availability of appropriate services. If one is offended by the "unprofessional" aspects of advertising to provide needed services to an oppressed people, one should reflect upon the extensive publicity suggesting examinations for breast cancer following the illness and surgery of the wives of internationally prominent politicians.

Only slight modifications in existing treatment methods can be created if one is only marginally aware of the nature of the social problems that plague the SSS. Individual psychotherapy, conducted on a once-a-week basis and for the purpose of uncovering alleged unconscious conflicts, is obviously highly ineffective with problems of a social nature. To encourage an SSS youngster to remain in school, it makes much more sense to exploit some modification of family counseling techniques. Peer group psychotherapy has achieved some modest success in reducing delinquency rates among the young. Such an approach will probably be highly unsuccessful, however, if the group is conducted by a non-SSS therapist who attempts to encourage introspection based on psychodynamic formulations. Because many members of SSS subgroups conceptualize "treatment" as something they receive while remaining passive, it makes much more sense to encourage discussion groups among potential drug users, possibly including adults who have "kicked the habit." When a patient has the expectation that he will be helped by "doing something," rather than by just talking, it makes sense to involve potential counseling clients in some form of activity therapy (Cobb, 1972). We turn now to recommendations for improvement of each of the three specific community mental health models.

There is the obvious problem of communication with the professional adaptation model. Potential clients whose predominant language is Spanish will certainly feel unwelcome in settings where they cannot read signs, where they are greeted by clerical personnel to whom they cannot communicate their needs, and where they are subsequently referred to majority-group, monolingual, English-speaking professionals. The use of translators is uneconomical, may not communicate nuances successfully, and seems to possess a vast potential to offend and estrange both patient and professional.

Crash programs in Spanish-language acquisition for monolingual, English-speaking professionals are a partial solution to this problem. But language skill is not enough. As we have indicated at several points, the mental health professional must be knowledgeable about the culture of a particular SSS subgroup he works with in order to be effective. Mental health centers may remedy such educational deficits on the part of their professional staff by presenting lectures, seminars, and films on the particular subgroup being treated. In this context, the use of community representatives as teachers and/or consultants who impart insight to a particular subculture can be invaluable.

Federal legislation is currently under consideration (S. 3280, Note 4) which bears directly on the resolution of this problem. Applicants seeking federal funding for programs of health delivery and health revenue sharing to a catchment area in which "a substantial proportion of the residents of which are of limited English-speaking ability" will be *required* to:

> (a) make arrangements for providing services to the extent practical in the language and cultural context most appropriate to such individuals and (b) identify an individual on its staff who is bilingual and whose responsibilities shall include providing for training for members of the applicant's staff, and of the staff of any providers of services with whom arrangements are made, regarding the cultural sensitivities related to health of the population served and providing guidance to appropriate staff members and patients in bridging linguistic and cultural differences. (pp. 151–152)*

Every article describing the delivery of mental health services to SSS subgroups agrees on essentially two major points (Abad et al., 1974; Lehmann, 1970; Schensul, 1974; Burruel, Note 3). First, it is generally agreed that the problem of poor communication between patient and therapist may be partially resolved by the employment of local community representatives who are bilingual and bicultural and their subsequent training at the paraprofessional level in the delivery of mental health services. The consequences of hiring and training community residents appear to benefit everyone. The agency achieves a more positive image in the community when local residents are hired, and the quality of services for the SSS is enhanced when patient and therapist can communicate. The second point on which there is consistent agreement is that community involvement in the administration of the mental health center is critical for success. These articles attest that the SSS refuse to refer themselves for treatment to agencies that are perceived as alien institutions intruding into their community and staffed by non-SSS personnel. It is impressive how closely these recommended practices, based upon empirical evidence, matched the letter and spirit of the suggestions that emerged from the 1974 APA conference held in Vail, Colorado.

The training of paraprofessionals to deliver treatment services and to conduct research leads to an ethical dilemma. Speaking practically, if paraprofessionals are *not* trained, then the SSS will receive essentially no services from anyone who shares their bilingual, bicultural background.

---

*Since the writing of this article, S.3280 was passed by the Senate committee and forwarded to the joint House-Senate conference committee. The bill was passed by the joint conference committee, but pocket vetoed by President Ford at the end of the congressional session in December 1974. Similar legislation has been reintroduced by both the House and the Senate during the present 94th session of Congress.

Whenever paraprofessionals are used for these purposes, however, it is clear that they lack the education, training, and experience of the professionally trained members of the helping professions. But as Ruiz (1971) has indicated, no such cadre of SSS professional mental health specialists exists. Thus, unless professional organizations such as the American Psychological Association and the American Psychiatric Association intervene, a significant number of SSS Americans will receive little or no mental health care. We strongly urge the membership of these two organizations to instruct their elected representative to assume a posture of moral leadership by working to increase the number of students from SSS subgroups in the mental health professions. Organizations that remain passive and apathetic in the face of problems of this nature and severity can no longer describe themselves as created "to promote human welfare."

A cadre of SSS professionals is needed to provide treatment and to conduct research in the mental health area. Without such SSS professionals, the national problem of underutilization of mental health services by the SSS will probably continue indefinitely. In a survey of selected mental health personnel, Ruiz (1971) identified 58 SSS psychologists from a pool of approximately 28,500, and 20 psychiatrists out of 16,000. Despite the tremendous underrepresentation these data denote, the situation is, in fact, even worse: 30 of the 58 psychologists were Spaniards, a group not ordinarily thought of as a disadvantaged minority group.

Regardless of why the SSS are underrepresented in the mental health professions, it is reasonably certain that this situation will remain essentially unchanged without constructive intervention. Recommendations are for programs to identify those SSS high school students with academic promise, to encourage continued school attendance, to subsidize educational expenses, and to motivate career choices in mental health fields. Implementation of these recommendations will require funding, legislation, and possibly legal pressure on high school counselors and on admission boards at colleges and universities. But a partial solution could be achieved at minimal expense and without new laws if the membership of the American Psychological Association, as well as that of the American Psychiatric Association, would take a more active role in the training of SSS students in the mental health professions as suggested above.

Family Adaptation Model

As we noted earlier, there has been little exploration of SSS family roles as a method of therapeutic entry in working with SSS clients. Such an approach would appear to be sucessful especially in those situations where several of the family members must be counseled. Therapists knowledgeable about the family dynamics of SSS clients could, for example, use family therapy to better understand the ways in which family members conform to their culturally ascribed roles in times of stress. Moreover, this technique could be used to analyze how the entire kinship network of an SSS person responds as a support system during periods of extreme mental stress. Weaknesses in the kinship support system could be detected and remedied. Concomitant with this, the knowledgeable therapist could get the SSS client to act out situations demanding elaboration of cultural traits such as *machismo* or *personalismo* in order to better understand points of conflict between the SSS client's cultural values and those of the dominant majority culture. To illustrate this point, Abad et al. (1974) noted that conflict with the *respecto* concept is particularly common in parent-child relationships among Puero Ricans on the mainland. As Abad et al. stated:

> Influenced by their Anglo peers, children, especially adolescents, strive to be more independent and rebel against restrictions that they might well accept if living on the island. An unknowing therapist in such a situation may too quickly conclude that the adolescent is acting appropriately against rigid expectations, and in so doing, the therapist may alienate himself from the parents, make them defensive, and ruin any chance for further family intervention. (p. 588)

In addition, the family adaptation model would extend to the architectural design of community mental health centers. There is evidence suggestive of the fact that centers with "living room" reception areas appear to be the most attractive to SSS clientele (e.g., Phillipus, 1971). This homelike informality becomes even more attractive, of course, when the SSS patient is greeted by someone who can speak his own language, who can evaluate the problem rapidly, and who can implement immediate disposition. This kind of action based on *personalismo* is similar to the kind of brokerage system employed in Latin America and to which many SSS clients are accustomed.

Barrio Service Center Model

New centers should be situated in the appropriate neighborhoods. Centers established at a distance from the target population must "attract" clientele, perhaps by following a business model. Possibilities include arranging transportation (e.g., a busing service or a patient share-a-ride system), providing child-care facilities for parents (e.g., at the center or home-visit "babysitters"), and encouraging regular attendance at therapy sessions (e.g., through reduced fees or by remaining open "after hours").

Two clinics located in high-density-population urban areas (Abad et al., 1974; Schensul, 1974) report remarkable success by "word-of-mouth" advertising among their Spanish-speaking clientele. While this informal communication network generated self-referrals in a more sprawling geographic area with a smaller population (south Tucson, Arizona), Burruel (Note 3) described a "tremendous" response to an announcement of services on the Mexican radio stations. The inference of significance is clear. If mental health centers for the SSS are to fulfill the purposes for which they are designed, they must exert effort to contact the target population.

The next consideration involves the selection procedure of community representatives to serve as paraprofessionals and the nature of the training program designed for them. Both Abad et al. (1974) and Burruel (Note 3) agree that faith healers and other practitioners of folk medicine are highly qualified as students for paraprofessional training programs. These individuals already enjoy some degree of community acceptance and probably possess skill in responding appropriately to human problems. This statement should not be misconstrued as indicating that ethnic-minority group membership is a necessary condition for therapeutic effectiveness. As Sue (1973) has demonstrated, it is possible to develop highly sophisticated and effective training programs to train ethnic minority group students to serve as counselors for clients from their own ethnic minority group. Programs of equivalent validity must be developed for the SSS, and it is assumed that the efficacy of any paraprofessional will be related to the quality of whatever program is created for training pruposes.

At this point, we shall expand on some of the recommendations presented above dealing with treatment programs. "Crisis intervention" may be defined and applied in a number of ways helpful, or even crucial, to the continued well-being of patients, but which fall well outside the optimal (or even usual) models of mental health care. Imagine, for example, a widow whose sole source of support is her monthly welfare check. If this check were delayed only a few days, the family might be literally in a "crisis." A center sensitive to the needs of the target population in this hypothetical instance might furnish emergency funding, might contact tradesmen requesting credit, might implore creditors to wait a "few more days," or might ask the welfare agency for immediate reimbursement. Because this type of crisis intervention does not require professional education, the patient could be rendered a tremendous service by a paraprofessional who spoke her language, grasped her plight, was knowledgeable concerning other community agencies, and responded immediately.

This type of "crisis intervention" represents the flexibility that community mental health centers must adopt if they are to respond appropriately to the human problems of the SSS. This point is elaborated in great detail by several writers (see especially Martinez, 1973) who agree that intrapsychic conflict represents only a small portion of the numerous human and social problems that trouble the SSS.

Reference Notes

1. Padilla, A. M. *Special report to the Planning Branch of the National Institute of Mental Health on the mental health needs of the Spanish speaking in the United States.* Unpublished manuscript, 1971. (Available from author, Department of Psychology, University of California, Los Angeles, California 90024.)

2. Garrison, V. *Social networks and social change in the "culture of poverty."* Paper presented at the meeting of the American Association for the Advancement of Science, Philadelphia, Pennsylvania, December 1971.

3. Burruel, G. *La Frontera,* a mental health clinic in the Chicano community. In *Report on the Southwest States Chicano Consumer Conference* (DHEW Publication No. HSM 73–6208). Washington, D.C.: U.S. Department of Health, Education, and Welfare, 1972.

4. S. 3280. 93rd Congress, second session, September 5, 1974. *A bill to amend the Public Health Service Act to revise and extend programs of health delivery and health revenue sharing.*

References

Abad, V., Ramos, J., & Boyce, E. A model for delivery of mental health services to Spanish-speaking minorities. *American Journal of Orthopsychiatry,* 1974, *44,* 584–595.

Bloombaum, M., Yamamoto, J., & Evans, Q. Cultural stereotyping among psychotherapists. *Journal of Counseling and Clinical Psychology,* 1968, *32,* 99.

Boulette, T. R. *Problemas familiares:* Television programs in Spanish for mental health education. *Hospital and Community Psychiatry,* 1974, *25,* 282.

Cobb, C. W. Community mental health services and the lower socioeconomic class: A summary of research literature on outpatient treatment (1963–1969). *American Journal of Orthopsychiatry,* 1972, *42,* 404–414.

Creson, D. L., McKinley, C., & Evans, R. Folk medicine in Mexican American subculture. *Diseases of the Nervous System,* 1969, *30,* 264–266.

Edgerton, R. B., & Karno, M. Mexican American bilingualism and the perception of mental illness. *Archives of General Psychiatry,* 1971, *24,* 286–290.

Edgerton, R. B., Karno, M., & Fernandez, I. Curanderismo in the metropolis: The diminishing role of folk-psychiatry among Los Angeles Mexican Americans. *American Journal of Psychotherapy,* 1970, *24,* 124–134.

Garrison, V. *Espiritismo:* Implications for provision of mental health services to Puerto Rican populations. In H. Hodges & C. Hudson (Eds.), *Folk-therapy.* Miami, Fla.: University of Miami Press, 1975.

Gordon, S. Are we seeing the right patients? Child guidance intake: The sacred cow. *American Journal of Orthopsychiatry,* 1965, *35,* 131–137.

Hinsie, L. E., & Campbell, R. J. *Psychiatric dictionary.* New York: Oxford University Press, 1970.

Hollingshead, A. B., & Redlich, F. C. Social class and mental illness. New York: Wiley, 1958.

Jaco, E. G. Mental health of the Spanish American in Texas. In M. F. Opler (Ed.), *Culture and mental health: Cross-cultural studies.* New York: Macmillan, 1959.

Jaco, E. G. *The social epidemiology of mental disorders: A psychiatric survey of Texas.* New York: Russell Sage Foundation, 1960.

Karno, M. The enigma of ethnicity in a psychiatric clinic, *Archives of General Psychiatry,* 1966, *14,* 516–520.

Karno, M., & Edgerton, R. B. Perception of mental illness in a Mexican-American community. *Archives of General Psychiatry,* 1969, *20,* 233–238.

Karno, M., & Morales, A. A community mental health service for Mexican Americans in a metropolis. *Comprehensive Psychiatry,* 1971, *12,* 115–121.

Kiev, A. *Curanderismo: Mexican-American folk psychiatry.* New York: Free Press, 1968.

Kline, L. Y. Some factors in the psychiatric treatment of Spanish Americans. *American Journal of Psychiatry, 1969, 125,* 1674–1681.

Kolb, L. C., Bernard, V. W., & Dohrenwend, B. P. *Urban challenges to psychiatry.* Boston: Little, Brown, 1969.

Lehmann, S. Selected self-help: A study of clients of a community social psychiatry service. *American Journal of Psychiatry, 1970, 126,* 1444–1454.

Leininger, M. Witchcraft practices and psychocultural therapy with urban U.S. families. *Human Organization, 1973, 32,* 73–83.

Lorion, R. P. Socioeconomic status and traditional treatment approaches reconsidered. *Psychological Bulletin. 1973, 79,* 263–270.

Lorion, R. P. Patient and therapist variables in the treatment of low-income patients. *Psychological Bulletin, 1974, 81,* 344–354.

Lubchansky, I., Ergi, G., & Stokes, J. Puerto Rican spiritualists view mental illness: The faith healer as a paraprofessional. *American Journal of Psychiatry, 1970, 127,* 312–321.

Madsen, W. Value conflicts and folk psychiatry in South Texas. In A. Kiev (Ed.), *Magic, faith and healing.* New York: Free Press, 1964.

Maldonado-Sierra, E. D., & Trent, R. D. The sibling relationship in group psychotherapy with Puerto Rican schizophrenics. *American Journal of Psychiatry, 1960, 117,* 239–244.

Maldonado-Sierra, E. D., Trent, R. D., & Fernandez-Marian, R. F. Cultural factors in the group-psychotherapeutic process for Puerto Rican schizophrenics. *International Journal of Group Psychotherapy, 1960, 10,* 373–382.

Martinez, C. Community mental health and the Chicano movement. *American Journal of Orthopsychiatry, 1973, 43,* 595–601.

Padilla, A. M., & Ruiz, R. A. *Latino mental health: A review of literature.* Washington, D.C.: U.S. Government Printing Office, 1973.

Phillipus, M. J. Successful and unsuccessful approaches to mental health services for an urban Hispano-American population. *Journal of Public Health, 1971, 61,* 820–830.

Ruiz, R. A. Relative frequency of Americans with Spanish surnames in associations of psychology, psychiatry, and sociology. *American Psychologist, 1971, 26,* 1022–1024.

Schensul, S. L. Commentary: Skills needed in action anthropology: Lessons from El Centro de la Causa. *Human Organization, 1974, 33,* 203–209.

Srole, L., Langer, T. S., Michael, S. T., Opler, M. K., & Rennie, T. A. C. *Mental health in the metropolis: The Midtown Manhattan study.* New York: McGraw-Hill, 1962.

Sue, S. Training of "Third World" students to function as counselors. *Journal of Counseling Psychology, 1973, 20,* 73–78.

Torrey, E. F. *The mind game: Witchdoctors and psychiatrists.* New York: Emerson Hall, 1972.

U.S. Bureau of the Census. Persons of Spanish origin in the United States: November 1969. In *Current population reports* (Series P-20, No. 213). Washington, D.C.: U.S. Government Printing Office, 1971. (a)

U.S. Bureau of the Census. Selected characteristics of persons and families of Mexican, Puerto Rican, and other Spanish origin: March 1971. In *Current population reports* (Series P-20, No. 224). Washington, D.C.: U.S. Government Printing Office, 1971. (b)

Wolkon, G. H., Moriwaki, S., Mandel, D. M., Archuleta, Jr., Bunje, P., & Zimmermann, S. Ethnicity and social class in the delivery of services: Analysis of a child guidance clinic. *American Journal of Public Health,* 1974, *64,* 709–712.

Yamamoto, J., James, Q. C., & Palley, N. Cultural problems in psychiatric therapy. *Archives of General Psychiatry,* 1968, *19,* 45–49.

14 A Language Minority:

Hispanic Americans and Mental Health Care

Ramon A. Laval, Ph.D.
Efrain A. Gomez, M.D.
Pedro Ruiz, M.D.

Hispanic Americans constitute an ethnic minority in the United States who experience various degrees of discrimination and lack of opportunity in such important areas of life as housing, employment, education, health and mental health care. The minority status Hispanics occupy in such diverse realms of life has made itself particularly evident in the area of mental health care, where Hispanics have consistently been found to be seriously underrepresented and to experience a variety of difficulties that serve as impediments to treatment.[1]

The term "Hispanic" has generally been used to refer to individuals of Spanish origin or descent. While a large number of these individuals are bilingual, for many English is not the preferred language, and for a large percentage of them, Spanish is their only language. Thus, whether bilingual or monolingual, Hispanics constitute a language minority in the United States. This is particularly evident when we consider the Hispanic patient in relation to the mental health care systems, where communication is of paramount importance as a vehicle for rendering services, and where Spanish-speaking mental health professionals also constitute a minority.[2] The 1980 U.S. Census Bureau estimated the population of Hispanics residing in this country at 14.6 million. Although representing approximately 6.5% of the total U.S. population, this figure excludes a large number of undocumented illegal aliens.[3]

It should be noted that the Hispanic population is not a homogeneous group, but rather is composed of subgroups that differ in terms of their geographic origin, the length of time they have resided in this country, and the degree of assimilation and acculturation they have achieved. The extent to which they were forced to migrate to this country also varies, and therefore the motivation to leave their countries may reflect different factors, such as political persecution or socioeconomic pressures. Based on their geographic area of origin, Hispanics can be subgrouped into four main categories: Hispanics from 1) Mexico comprise the largest; followed by 2) Puerto Ricans; 3) Cubans; and 4) Central and South Americans. With Hispanics the fastest growing minority in this country, (with an annual

Laval, R. A., Gomez, E. A. & Ruiz, P. (1983). A language minority: Hispanics and mental health care. *The American Journal of Social Psychiatry, 3*(2), 42–49. Reprinted by permission of Brunne/Mazel, Inc.

increase rate ranging between 1.8 and 3.5%,)[4] one would expect a parallel increase in their demand for mental health services. Yet, they tend to participate only minimally in mental health care systems and are at a serious disadvantage when they compete with the rest of the American population for these types of services. Even when Hispanics do link themselves with the mental health care system, they tend to terminate treatment at much higher rates than their Anglo counterparts.[5]

Attempts to account for this perceived underutilization have at times demonstrated a tendency to "blame the victim"; thus, it has been thought that it is the Hispanic's own attitudes and perceptions regarding mental illness and care that act as an impediment to treatment and account for this underutilization. Although it appears that the degree of acculturation minimizes the potential for early termination of treatment by Hispanics,[6] this reasoning has not always been supported by empirical research. For example, Karno and Edgerton[7] found that Mexican Americans and Anglo Americans residing in the area of Los Angeles were markedly similar in their perceptions of, and attitudes toward, mental illness and treatment. Other explanations for the underutilization of mental health care services by Hispanics have also been offered. For instance, Keefe and Casas[8] critically reviewed the evidence underlying a number of such assumptions as they relate to Mexican Americans. They considered the following aspects in this regard: 1) Mexican Americans have few emotional problems; therefore, they make less use of mental health services; 2) Mexican Americans have strong extended families, which support members with emotional problems; 3) Mexican Americans make use of a folk medical system and consequently avoid modern mental health care; 4) Mexican Americans are unfamiliar with traditional mental health services; 5) Mexican Americans have negative attitudes toward majority-group institutions in general, and mental health services in particular; and 6) institutional policies at mental health clinics discourage utilization by Mexican Americans. After critically reviewing the pertinent literature, Keefe and Casas found full support for only two of these assumptions, namely that the existence of the extended family is a particularly important source of support for the emotionally troubled Mexican Americans, and that this population is generally discouraged in seeking care by the institutional policies prevalent in the mental health programs. The fourth assumption received only partial support; Mexican Americans who are Spanish-speaking, undereducated, and recent migrants to this country are unfamiliar with traditional mental health care services. These results probably generalize to other Hispanic groups, although research is needed to explore intragroup differences.

Three major factors have been identified as being potential sources of conflict, and thus acting as impediments in the treatment of Hispanics: language barriers between therapists and patients; class-bound values characterizing traditional forms of treatment; and culture-bound values underlying such treatments.[9] The notion of *language barrier* refers to the use of the English language as the main vehicle for communication, which tends to discriminate against Spanish-speaking individuals. As we will discuss later, language barriers have a significant effect in both the evaluation of psychopathology and in the psychotherapeutic process. Traditional forms of treatment have been considered to be class and value bound, and thus they discourage Hispanic patients to seek out or to continue with their treatment. In this context, behavior is often judged as normal or deviant within the frame of the majority culture, and treatment is generally performed within the value system of the middle class. While investigating the perceived underutilization of mental health care services by the Spanish-speaking population is of critical importance, evaluating such issues as establishment of a therapeutic alliance, clinical assessment, psychological testing and treatment interventions as they relate to Hispanic patients who do utilize such services, is equally relevant. Without disregard for the uniqueness of each individual patient, and acknowledging that Hispanics do constitute a heterogeneous group of people who at times demonstrate important differences in their sociocultural characteristics, it is felt that they share enough commonalities to allow us to use flexible generalizations that can guide us in rendering appropriate mental health services.

This paper will try to provide relevant information based on clinical and research data, which would help minimize the barriers encountered by both clinicians and the Hispanic patient in the area of mental health care. Four topics pertinent to the service-delivery aspects will be covered. A particular emphasis will be given to the factor of language as it relates to assessment of psychopathology and psychotherapy. First, we will discuss a number of factors that are of importance in the development of rapport and the establishment of a therapeutic alliance; second, we will focus on the area of clinical assessment with particular attention to differences in the presentation of psychopathology; third, we will discuss the role and use of psychological testing when working with Hispanics; fourth, we will focus on treatment considerations pertinent to the Hispanic patient.

Developing a Working Alliance

Since Hispanic Americans tend to terminate treatment after only one visit at rates much higher than Anglo-Americans,[5] an increased awareness of the factors that can foster the development of a working alliance is particularly important. Professional workers sensitive to the unique linguistic, social and cultural characteristics of Hispanic patients have provided a number of recommendations geared toward the development of a therapeutic alliance. For instance, physical expressions of greeting, such as hand shaking or placing a hand on the shoulder of the person being greeted may be optional with Anglo Americans; however, such expressions are highly recommended when greeting Hispanics. Studies in the field of proxemics have provided useful information applicable to the interview and treatment process; for example, Hispanic-Americans not only allow, but also seek a greater degree of personal closeness compared to other ethnic groups, particularly Anglos.[10] Thus, in order to foster a greater degree of intimacy and closeness, the therapist may seat the Hispanic patient closer than he or she generally would with other patients from other ethnic groups. Also, Hispanics, by in large, prefer to reflect the family lineage by including both the paternal and maternal last names; thus, when first meeting the patient, an attempt should be made to mention both names. If not available in the records, asking the patient in an informal manner for his or her maternal name will usually reflect an attitude of interest and reverence toward both the patient and his or her family. The use of small talk, or what many Hispanics call "la platica," at the onset of the interview process has been found to be of particular importance when interviewing Hispanic patients.[11] Clinicians who are not sensitive to what Hispanic patients consider proper manners in a social context, may construe the Hispanic patients' need for "la platica" as suggestive of evasiveness or unwillingness to confront problems. However, allowing a few moments for such interactions can facilitate the establishment of rapport, and consequently induce a greater level of self-disclosure later in the session. Although Hispanic patients may display a lower tendency to self-disclosure in comparison to Anglo patients, their willingness to do so is still rather high.[12] Hispanic patients may reveal themselves at a slower pace than other ethnic groups; this can be explained as a normal process reflecting different cultural norms and does not imply an unwillingness to provide relevant personal information. Interpretations suggesting resistance or defensiveness on the part of the Hispanic patient can only create tension and misunderstanding.

There may be a number of inconsistencies between the demands of certain conversational patterns characteristic of the interview or therapeutic situation, and those which exist within the cultural tradition of some Hispanics. We have already mentioned how an emphasis on directness of speech or on "getting to the point" may place Hispanic patients, who value the use of "la platica," at a disadvantage. Also, rules governing the progression of communication in the Hispanic group may be different from those Hispanic patients are expected to follow in the interview or therapy situation. This is perhaps most evident in insight-oriented psychotherapy, where the patient is expected to assume responsibility and spontaneously to initiate conversations in the absence of specific questions from the therapist. Such action may run counter to a tradition that the sanction is to speak after one has been spoken to, particularly before an authority figure, and thus may result in misinterpretations on the part of the therapist, as well as increased apprehension and confusion on the part of the patient. While some groups, particularly Anglos, may heavily depend on eye contact to monitor the extent to which others are paying attention, Hispanics on certain occasions may consider eye contact disrespectful and may tend to avoid gaze holding in the clinical situation.[9] To attach meaning other than that the patient displayed a certain degree of reverence and respect toward the clinician when a Hispanic patient avoids eye contact, may result in misunderstanding. Clinicians are therefore advised to be cautious in attempting to maintain eye contact with Hispanics who are actively trying to avoid it, or in interpreting such behavior as reflecting resistance or evasiveness.

Evaluation

The language issue can present a number of evaluative problems for both the Spanish-speaking patient and the clinician. Depending on the degree of language barrier, such problems could range from an inability to render services to the Hispanic patient to misunderstanding and consequently misevaluation of the patient's condition. As an attempt to extend mental health services to the Hispanic patients in the U.S.A., clinicians may often have to rely on bilingual translators. Making a clear distinction between what constitutes a direct translation of the patient's reports, and what reflects a personal interpretation on the part of the translator, is a complex task. Even when the clinician is provided with a complete and correct translation, subtleties in the patient's process of speech may be generally lost. Some authors[13] have suggested that the use of a translator does not impose difficulties for the establishment of rapport, and that in fact it appears to evoke positive reactions from many patients. The particular effects of the translator-mediated interview on the assessment of pathology have not received enough attention, and are therefore limited to descriptions of the interview process and two case studies of Spanish-speaking patients evaluated and treated by English-speaking clinicians via a translator.[14,15] Marcos[16] conducted a more systematic study on the effects of the use of lay translators on the evaluation of psychopathology in Spanish- and Chinese-speaking patients. He found three major sources of distortions that interfered with the clinicians' ability to assess patients appropriately, namely, distortions associated with the interpreter's language competence and translation skills, distortions that reflected the interpreter's lack of psychiatric knowledge, and distortions associated with the translator's personal attitudes toward either the patient or the clinician.

There is general agreement that bilingual Hispanic patients will convey different clinical information depending on the language they use during the evaluation process. There are, however, some discrepant views regarding the direction in which language will influence the patient's reports and the clinician's perception and assessment of psychopathology. In one nonexperimental report, Del Castillo[17] described several clinical experiences with Hispanic patients in which they appeared more psychotic when interviewed in their native tongue and evidenced less psychopathology when interviewed in English. The author suggested that the use of a foreign language resulted in an increased vigilance or guardedness on the part of the patient, thus leading to a filtering of information suggestive of psychopathology. More recently, in a study with bilingual Mexican American schizophrenic patients, Gonzalez[18] found qualitative and quantitative differences between interviews conducted in Spanish and in English; according to him, however, such differences did not imply greater or lesser evidence of psychopathology. However, Marcos et al., [19,20] using a standard psychiatric format to interview in both English and Spanish a group of 10 Hispanic bilingual schizophrenic patients, found a number of consistent differences in each patient during these interviews. In one report,[19] the findings indicated that, with respect to the content of the English interview, there were a number of changes in the sense of the response, usually suggesting greater psychopathology. The content also changed drastically due to differences in the length of the responses; answers in English were shorter, sometimes consisting of only a word, and with greater use of silence. Translation difficulties were also frequent, affecting the content of the interview and suggesting greater pathology. Noncontent differences also emerged when comparisons were made between the English and Spanish interviews. Such variables as speech disturbance, speech rate and silent pauses were all suggestive of more pathology, particularly anxiety and depression, when the interview was conducted in English. Another report[20] indicated that bilingual Hispanic patients were judged to demonstrate significantly more overall psychopathology when they were interviewed in English. When a structured psychiatric rating was used to judge the Spanish and English interviews, results indicated that the subscales most influenced by the English language were tension, depressed mood, hostility, anxiety, emotional withdrawal and somatic concern. This was true even for patients who reported a preference for being interviewed in the English language. All these studies suggest that there may exist an interaction between language and severity of illness on assessment of psychopathology. Definitely, further research is needed to explore this possibility.

From another angle, perceptions regarding mental illness and psychiatric care may also influence the patient's clinical presentation during evaluation. For example, Spanish-speaking and English-speaking Hispanic patients differ in their perceptions of symptoms as they relate to mental illness. In a comprehensive survey of Mexican Americans in the Los Angeles area, Edgerton and Karno[21] found a number of differences between those individuals who preferred to be interviewed in Spanish and those who expressed a preference for English. Spanish-speaking respondents showed a tendency to adhere to a more somatic, nonpsychological conception of mental illness than the English speaking ones. Puerto Rican patients have also been found to present an unusually high degree of somatic problems upon evaluation. For example, Abad and Boyce[22] found that Puerto Rican patients evidenced a significantly higher frequency of physical and somatic complaints than either White or Black patients. Although some of the most common complaints among the Puerto Rican groups were depression, anxiety, and feared loss of control, such problems were rarely reported directly, but rather in terms of symptoms of insomnia, eating problems, fatigue, headaches, body aches, feelings of weakness, heart palpitations, dizziness and fainting. Along these lines, certain folk syndromes recurrent among some Hispanic groups (such as "empacho," "susto," and "mal de ojo" among low-socioeconomic Mexican American patients and "ataques de nervios" among Puerto Rican patients) can create difficulties for the evaluator, which could affect both diagnosis and treatment. Also, the degree of psychopathology ascribed to such experiences as hallucinations should take into consideration the cultural background of the patient. For example, hallucinations, especially visual and tactile ones, are significantly more frequent among Puerto Rican patients than Black or White patients. For the Puerto Rican patient, hallucinations tend to be more vivid and detailed than those experienced by other ethnic groups. While they represent a common experience in the presentation of the psychotic, borderline, and neurotic illnesses among Puerto Rican patients, they are also present among normal individuals, for whom hallucinations may constitute a rather meaningful and positive experience.[22]

Psychological Testing

Differences in test performances between Hispanics and other ethnic groups, particularly Anglos, are well-known factors in the field. These findings may prompt us to conclude that such discrepancies reflect actual differences between these ethnic groups in whatever construct the test is supposed to measure (e.g., intelligence, school achievement, psychopathology). In discussing issues regarding personality testing in Mexican Americans, Padilla and Ruiz[23] have asserted that interpretations of test responses for Mexican Americans "are based on an implicit assumption that this group is somehow 'no different' from the majority group . . . and that cultural differences exert minimal influence upon personality test responses." Projective tests such as the Rorschach and the TAT have traditionally been considered to be "culture free." This contention has been seriously questioned on the grounds that responses to such tests can and do reflect the cultural background of the individual.[23-25] Thus, interpretations regarding the unique psychodynamic functioning of a patient should take into consideration the cultural context of such a patient.

The most frequently used objective personality test by psychologists is the Minnesota Multiphasic Personality Inventory (MMPI).[26] We have no reason to doubt that when Hispanic patients are referred for psychological testing, the MMPI is routinely incorporated as part of the test battery. It should be noted, however, that Hispanics were not represented in the standardization sample; thus, the appropriateness of this sample as a reference group has been seriously questioned. However, very few studies have evaluated the applicability of this test to Hispanic populations. These investigations have generally compared differences in MMPI responses between Mexican Americans and other ethnic groups, particularly Anglo Americans. What is striking about the results of these studies is the frequent lack of significant differences between clinical-scale scores of Mexican Americans and those of Anglos, or the contradictory findings regarding differences between these ethnic groups across studies. Some consistencies do emerge. Mexican Americans score higher on scale 1 (Hypochondriasis),[27,28] possibly indicating a greater concern over bodily functioning and an increased tendency to make use of somatization as a defense mechanism; these differences, however, could also be explained on the basis of socioeconomic factors.[28] Also, Mexican Americans and other Hispanic patients score lower on scales 4 and 5 (Psychopathic Deviance and Masculinity-Femininity),[29,30] suggesting increased rigidity and conventionality and a stronger identification with the traditional masculine role. Noteworthy is the significantly high degree of consistency across studies regarding differences in the MMPI validity scales, particularly in Scale L (Lie). Compared to Anglos, Mexican Americans score higher on this scale as well as on scale K (Correction), suggesting a more defensive test-taking attitude, a tendency to deny psychological problems and an attempt to "look good."[27-31] It should be noted at this point that the concept of statistical differences is not synonymous with that of clinical differences, and that actual MMPI interpretation, which is generally (or should be) based not on single scale elevations but rather on the whole profile configuraton, may not be seriously affected by these findings. Too little research exploring the differences in MMPI responses between Hispanic patients and other ethnic groups has been conducted to allow us to suggest a lack of applicability of this test with Hispanic populations. It would seem, however, that if sociocultural factors are taken into consideration, the Minnesota Multiphasic Personality Inventory can aid in the understanding of the personality functioning of the Hispanic person. To our knowledge, all of the studies reviewed here administered the English MMPI to the Hispanic samples. The extent to which these subjects were proficient in the English language cannot be fully determined from the various descriptions of the target populations. For example, consider the following descriptions: "Mexican Americans who were bilingual and bicultural,"[30] or "Mexican Americans, as defined by Spanish surname and self-report."[27] It is noteworthy that one study[29] did not include in the analysis data from subjects whose F validity scale (Frequency) showed extreme elevations; elevations in this scale are particularly suggestive of languages and conceptual deficits. It should also be noted that in a different study,[27] Hispanics showed significantly higher elevations in the F scale than Anglos. As mentioned before, bilingual Hispanic patients convey different clinical information depending on whether the evaluation is conducted in Spanish or

English. There is clearly a need to assess whether language in which the MMPI is administered also influences the clinical presentation of the Hispanic patient.

Treatment

It has been suggested that one of the most recurrent errors in treatment of the Spanish-speaking patients is the assumption, held by many, that this population is not suitable for traditional psychotherapy.[32] This assumption is based on certain characteristics (such as relative passivity, reverence, inhibited silence, inability to verbalize and be introspective) attributed to the Hispanic patient.[33] It has also been suggested that their strong family loyalty and mistrust toward outsiders are probably important factors that impede their ability to self-disclose in therapy.[34] However, many of these assumptions are not empirically based and, by in large, are not substantiated by research findings. With respect to their unwillingness to self-disclose, for example, early studies did support this contention.[35] More recent research, with greater applicability to the actual therapy situation, indicates that, although Hispanic patients may evidence a tendency to self-disclose less than other ethnic groups, their willingness to do so is rather high and would not act as a barrier to treatment.[12,36] In therapy, it may be necessary for clinicians to allow the Hispanic patient to provide relevant personal and intimate information at a slower pace than they would be accustomed to when working with patients from a different ethnic group.

Although referring primarily to Mexican Americans, Roll et al.[32] have provided a strong argument against the notion that Hispanic patients are not suitable candidates for traditional forms of therapy. In support of their contention, the authors discuss the relatively high interpersonal orientation of the Hispanic culture. This appears in the traditional belief among many Hispanics that sharing intimate fears and secrets with another person will lessen psychological discomfort, in a tradition of "personalismo," and in the inclination to trust persons rather than institutions. Thus, insofar as treatment approaches rely heavily on the therapist-patient relationship as a vehicle for change, as in dynamic psychotherapy, Hispanic patients may in actuality be at a considerable advantage. The success of traditional individual psychotherapy with Hispanic patients has been documented.[37]

Treatment of the poorer members of this population may expose the clinician to witness environmental stress in the areas of work, education and housing. Two possible errors can occur at this point; the first may influence the clinician to decide that the only intervention appropriate for these individuals is in the form of casework designed to alleviate these external problems, thus preventing the use of psychotherapy even when intrapsychic conflicts are evident. The second error may result if the clinician engages the patient in psychotherapy without first guiding him/her in resolving external stress, in which case the patient may drop out of therapy, feeling that the clinician has nothing positive to offer. It has been found that when environmental problems are dealt with in conjunction with intrapsychic conflicts, Hispanic patients not only remain in treatment but also benefit from psychotherapeutic interventions.[34]

Another important issue regarding treatment of the Hispanic patient is the effect of bilingualism on the process of psychotherapy. In this regard, the work of Marcos et al.[38-42] has been invaluable. These authors delineate two major dimensions of bilingualism that influence the process of psychotherapy: language barrier and language independence. The language barrier primarily affects bilinguals classified as subordinate; these are individuals demonstrating differential competence in two languages and who experience difficulties in the processing of information when communicating in their nondominant language. Speaking the second language requires elaborate mental work necessary for translating material from one language to the other. Besides the fact that fewer words are made available to express experiences, the subordinate bilingual also has to struggle with grammatical ordering and articulation of speech.

Language barriers appear to have several major implications for psychotherapy. The patient may tend to engage in splitting or unintegration of affect and experience; this may cause certain experiences to seem vague and unreal to both patient and therapist. Intense feelings that patients may have toward the therapist are difficult to express appropriately, resulting in blocking or displacement of emotions. In extreme cases, the patients will express these emotions in the form of explosive episodes or by acting out in the therapeutic relationship. Language barriers may also facilitate or reinforce the use of obsessive resistances on the part of the patient. Patients tend to capitalize on the extra efforts needed to communicate in a second language, and will therefore invest their attention in how to verbalize their experiences rather than in the content of what they say. This situation maximizes the potential for intellectualization and rationalization and therefore decreases emotional involvement. Language barriers, on the other hand, may permit patients to communicate in the nondominant language information which, because of its emotional impact, was not available in the dominant language. Finally, therapists who are not sensitive to the implications of language barriers in psychotherapy may misinterpret the patient's verbalizations, and may not be able to utilize the potential resources allowed by the language barriers for the benefits of the therapy process.

The second dimension of bilingualism, language independence, affects proficient bilinguals who have learned and maintain a native command of two languages, each with different encoding mechanisms as well as parallel lexical, syntactic, phonetic, semantic, and ideational components. Language independence has two major implications for psychotherapy. First, important experiences in the patient's intrapsychic world may remain unavailable or unexplored due to the fact that they are independent of the language in which therapy is being conducted. Second, as in the case with language barrier, there is evidence of splitting and unintegration of verbalized experience and its emotional component. Thus, bilinguals may choose to speak in one language so as to avoid the anxiety provoked by emotionally charged materials. In this regard, patients may even experience a sense of dual self. They will describe themselves in different ways depending on which language they are using or display a loss of emotionality when communicating in one of the languages. In this regard, splitting is also evident in the way that different mechanisms of defense are linked to each of the two languages, with intellectualization and obsessive defenses being associated with the nonnative language.

When working with Hispanic patients, the therapist should attempt to aid the patient in understanding his/her linguistic experiences and the self-identity associated with each language. Language switching on the part of the patient may provide him/her with a way to avoid dealing with important emotionally charged materials during therapy. An unwillingness to deal with these emotional materials may prompt the patient to use the less affective, more logical second language. On the other hand, if the patient does not desire to achieve a more intellectual, cognitive understanding of certain emotional experiences, he/she may choose to rely on the more emotional native language. Strategic use of language switching may be used by the therapist according to specific characterological traits of the patient. Thus, a patient who relies on obsessive maneuvers and a high degree of intellectualization may be encouraged to speak in his/her native language. On the other hand, a patient with more hysterical tendencies, whose intense affect interferes with attempts to objectify experiences, may be encouraged to speak in his/her nonnative language.

Conclusion

The minority status that Hispanics occupy in such diverse and important areas of American life as housing, employment, education and health care has made itself particularly evident in the area of mental health care. Here, Hispanics have consistently been found to be seriously underrepresented and to experience a variety of problems that serve as impediments to treatment. Although a number of social, cultural, and ethnic factors have been explored, the particular relevance of language barrier as an added obstacle to quality mental health care has not received enough attention. While a large segment of the Hispanic population in the United States is bilingual, for many Spanish is the language of choice, and still for many others Spanish is the only language. Thus, whether bilinguals or monolinguals, Hispanics in this country constitute a language minority. This is particularly evident when we consider the Hispanic patient in relation to the mental health care system, where Spanish-speaking mental health professionals also constitute a minority. Additionally, it is difficult to determine to what extent Spanish-speaking clinicians are willing to or actually spend time treating Hispanic patients.

The implications of bilingualism for mental health service delivery are considerable. Language barriers can create serious difficulties for both the clinician and the Hispanic patient. These difficulties can lead to an incapacity to render services or to misinterpretation and, therefore, to misevaluation of the patient's condition. Language barriers can also lead to a variety of obstacles and impediments to treatment. In an effort to minimize these obstacles, clinicians may often have to rely on bilingual interpreters to evaluate and treat Spanish-speaking patients. The very limited findings, however, seem somewhat pessimistic with respect to the efficacy of mental health services that are mediated via a translator. There is a clear need to train increasing numbers of proficient bilingual Hispanics (and Anglos, for that matter) in the various mental health professions. The current availability of professional resources needs to be further explored, and bilingual clinicians presently working in the field may be encouraged to increase their involvement with Spanish-speaking populations. Concomitant with these efforts, the careful training of interpreters is also indicated. Marcos's findings[16] would suggest that important aspects of this training should be geared toward improving translation skills and psychiatric knowledge and minimizing distortions associated with interpreters' attitudes toward both the patients and the mental health professional.

Likewise, the issue of psychological testing of Spanish-speaking minorities deserves special attention. In addition to considering the cultural appropriateness of different tests, the confounding effects of language factors need to be partialled out. Accurate assessment of language proficiency is of paramount importance, as it will guide the clinician in determining how to evaluate (in what language) other aspects of the individual, such as personality and intelligence functioning, achievement, degree of psychopathology or mental status, among other things.[43] In concluding, although implicit throughout this paper, by now it may appear clear that the implications of language barrier for evaluation, testing, and treatment of Spanish-speaking minorities also applies to other language minority groups in the United States, including groups for whom the use of standard English may not always be of choice, such as Black Americans or American Indians.

Reference Notes

1. Padilla, A. M., Ruiz, R., Alvarez, R.: Community mental health services for the Spanish-speaking/surnamed population. *Amer Psych 30*:892–905, 1975.
2. Ruiz, R. A.: Relative frequency of Americans with Spanish surnames in associations of psychology, psychiatry, and sociology. *Amer Psych 26*:1022–1024, 1971.

3. U.S. Department of Commerce 1980 census population totals for racial and Spanish origin groups in U.S. Washington, DC, 1981.
4. Macias, R. F.: U.S. Hispanics in 2000 A.D. Projecting the numbers. *Agenda* 7:16–19, 1977.
5. Sue, D. W., Sue, D.: Barriers to effective cross-cultural counseling. *J Counsel Psych 21*:420-429, 1977.
6. Miranda, M. R. et al: Mexican American dropouts in psychotherapy as related to level of acculturation. In M.R. Miranda (ed), *Psychotherapy with the Spanish-speaking: Issues in Research and Service Delivery*. Spanish-speaking Mental Health Research Center, University of California at Los Angeles, 1976.
7. Karno, D. T., Edgerton, R. B.: Perception of mental illness in a Mexican American community. *Arch Gen Psych 20*:233–238, 1969.
8. Keefe, S. E., Casas, J. M.: Mexican Americans and mental health: A selected review and recommendations for mental health service delivery. *Amer J Comm Psych 8*:303–326, 1980.
9. LeVine, E. S., Padilla, A. M.: *Crossing Cultures in Therapy: Pluralistic Counseling for the Hispanic*. Monterey, CA, Brooks/Cole, 1980.
10. Padilla, A. M.: Pluralistic counseling and psychotherapy for Hispanic Americans. In A. J. Masella, P. B. Pedersen (eds), *Cross Cultural Counseling and Psychotherapy*. New York, Pergamon, 1981.
11. Moll, R. S. et al: Mental health services in East Los Angeles: An urban community case study. In M. R. Miranda (ed), *Psychotherapy with the Spanish-Speaking: Issues in Research and Service Delivery*. Spanish-speaking Mental Health Research Center, UCLA, 1976.
12. Acosta, F. X, Sheehan, J. G.: Self-disclosure in relation to psychotherapist expertise and ethnicity. *Amer J Common Psych 6*:545–553, 1978.
13. Kline, F., Acosta, F. X. et al: The misunderstood Spanish-speaking patient. *Amer J Psychiat 137*:1530–1533, 1980.
14. MacKinnon, R. A., Michels, R.: *The Psychiatric Interview in Clinical Practice*. Philadelphia, Saunders, 1971.
15. Sabin, J. E.: Translating despair. *Amer J Psychiat 132*:1977–199, 1975.
16. Marcos, L. R.: Effects of interpreters on the evaluation of psychopathology in non-English-speaking patients. *Amer J Psychiat 136*:171–174, 1979.
17. Del Castillo, J. D.: The influence of language upon symptomatology in foreign born patients. *Amer J Psychiat 127*:242–244, 1970.
18. Gonzalez, J. R.: Language factors affecting treatment of bilingual schizophrenics. *Psychiat Annals 7*:68–70, 1978.
19. Marcos, L. R., Urcuyo, L. et al: The language barrier in evaluating Spanish-American patients. *Arch Gen Psych 29*:655–659, 1973.
20. Marcos, L. R., Alpert, M. et al: The effect of interview language on the evaluation of psychopathology in Spanish-American schizophrenic patients. *Amer J Psychiat 130*:549–553, 1973.
21. Edgerton, R. B., Karno, D. T.: Mexican-American bilingualism and the perception of mental illness. *Arch Gen Psych 24*:286–290, 1971.
22. Abad, V., Boyce, E.: Issues in psychiatric evaluations of Puerto Ricans: A socio-cultural perspective, *J Oper Psychiat 10*:28–39, 1979.
23. Padilla, A. M., Ruiz, R. A.: Personality assessment and test interpretation of Mexican-Americans: A critique. *J Person Assess 39*:103–109, 1975.

24. Kaplan, B.: Reflections of the acculturation process in the Rorschach test. *J Project Tech 19*:30–35, 1955.
25. Kaplan, B., Rickers-Ovsiankina, M. A., Joseph, A.: An attempt to sort Rorschach records from four cultures. *J Project Tech 20*:172–180, 1956.
26. Lubin, B., Wallis, R. R., Paine, C.: Patterns of psychological test usage in the United States: 1935–1969. *Professional Psychol 2*:70–74, 1971.
27. Hibbs, B. J., Kobos, J. C., Gonzalez, J.: Effects of ethnicity, sex, and age on MMPI profiles. *Psych Rep 45*:591–597, 1979.
28. McCreary, C., Padilla, E.: MMPI differences among blacks, Mexican-Americans and white male offenders. *J Clin Psych 33*:171–177, 1977.
29. Penk, W. E., Robinowitz, R. et al: MMPI differences of male Hispanic-American, black, and white heroin addicts. *J Consul Clin Psych 49*:488–490, 1981.
30. Plemons, G.: A comparison of MMPI scores of Anglo- and Mexican-American patients. *J Consul Clin Psych 45*:149–150, 1977.
31. Reilley, R., Knight, G. E.: MMPI scores of Mexican-American college students. *J Coll Stud Pers 11*:419–42, 1970.
32. Roll, S., Millen, L., Martinez, R.: Common errors in psychotherapy with Chicanos: Extrapolation from research and clinical experience. *Psych Theory Res Prac 17*:158–168, 1980.
33. Karno, M.: The enigma of ethnicity in a psychiatric clinic. *Arch Gen Psych 14*:516–522, 1966.
34. Heiman E. M., Burruel, G., Chavez, N.: Factors determining effective psychiatric outpatient treatment for Mexican-Americans. *Hosp Comm Psychiat 26*:515–517, 1975.
35. Jourard, S.: *The Transparent Self.* New York, Van Nostrand, 1971.
36. Acosta, F. X.: Preferences and self-disclosure in relation to psychotherapist professional and ethnic identification. *J Psych 103*:129–134, 1979.
37. Gomez, E., Ruiz, P., Laval, R.: Psychotherapy and bilingualism: Is acculturation important? *J Oper Psychiat 13*:13–16, 1982.
38. Marcos, L. R.: Bilinguals in psychotherapy: Language as an emotional barrier. *Amer J Psychother 30*:552–560, 1976.
39. Marcos, L. R.: Linguistic dimensions in the bilingual patient. *Amer J Psychoanal 36*:347–354, 1976.
40. Marcos, L. R., Alpert, M.: Strategies and risks in the psychotherapy with bilingual patients: The phenomenon of language independence. *Amer J Psychiat 133*:1275–1278, 1976.
41. Marcos, L. R., Urcuyo, L.: Dynamic psychotherapy with the bilingual patient. *Amer J Psychother 33*:331–338, 1979.
42. Pitta, P., Marcos, L. R., Alpert, M.: Language switching as a treatment strategy with bilingual patients. *Amer J Psychoanal 38*:255–258, 1978.
43. Olmedo, E. L.: Testing linguistic minorities: *Amer Psych 36*:1078–1085, 1981.

15 Counseling Puerto Ricans
Some Cultural Considerations
Christensen, Edward W.

Puerto Ricans comprise a significant percentage of potential clients for many counselors. The migration of Puerto Ricans to the mainland over the years has created cultural differences between Puerto Ricans raised in Puerto Rico and those raised in the U.S., but both groups are at a disadvantage in the dominant American culture. Migration back to the island in recent years is creating some problems for Puerto Rico, so Puerto Ricans often find prejudice both here and there. In this article the author, who married into a Puerto Rican family, discusses some values and traits that characterize Puerto Ricans and the behaviors that emerge from these traits. He offers practical suggestions for those counselors who have Puerto Rican clients.

In recent years the educational world has become increasingly concerned with students whose cultural backgrounds are different from those of the dominant culture in the U.S. This concern, though belated and still insufficient, has prompted other helping professions to follow the lead. Thus there has recently been increased publication on counseling members of minority groups, writers advocating giving more attention to the needs of clients who are culturally and ethnically different.

One of the outcomes of the increased attention given minority groups has been a tendency on the part of many to lump all minority individuals together. Thus, although early legislation and educational endeavors were designed to help blacks, American Indians, Mexican-Americans, and Puerto Ricans, they often served only to identify them all as having the same needs and disadvantages. Each group has protested this treatment, and all have insisted that their uniqueness be recognized and preserved. This need to understand the uniqueness of clients from specific cultural and ethnic backgrounds motivated the preparation of this article about counseling Puerto Ricans.

Some Facts about Puerto Rico

There is a great deal of ignorance among mainland Americans with regard to Puerto Rico. A few years ago, when I was in the U.S. on sabbatical leave

Christensen, E. W. (1975). Counseling Puerto Ricans: Some cultural considerations. *Personnel and Guidance Journal, 55,* 412–415. Copyright AACD. Reprinted with permission. No further reproduction authorized without further permission of AACD.

from the University of Puerto Rico, I brought my automobile, which had Puerto Rican license plates. A number of people asked if the car had been driven from Puerto Rico! Other typical questions reveal a lack of knowledge concerning this significant group in our society. Mainland Americans have asked: "Aren't all Puerto Ricans dark-skinned?" "Does one need a passport to go there?" "You won't serve me that hot and spicy food, will you?"

Puerto Rico is an island in the Caribbean, about 1,050 miles from Miami and 1,650 miles from New York. The island is about 35 miles by 100 miles and has a population of over 2.8 million. Its population density is greater than that of China, Japan, or India. Puerto Ricans are all American citizens, proclaimed so by the Jones Act of 1917. The population is a mixture of Taino Indians, Africans, and Spaniards, although the Indian influence is much more cultural than biological, as conflicts with the Spaniards practically decimated that group. Skin colors range from as white as any Scandinavian to as black as the darkest African, with all shades and mixtures in between.

It is impossible in this article to clear up all the myths and misunderstandings about Puerto Rico and Puerto Ricans. Indeed, there is currently much study, debate, and conflict regarding many issues of Puerto Rico's culture, identity, and political future. (Readers will find relevant material cited in the list of suggested readings at the end of this article.) These larger issues will not be easily resolved, but the present reality concerning Puerto Ricans is crucial for today's educators and counselors. In order to perform in a helpful and ethical way in assisting clients to grow and make viable decisions, a counselor must recognize personal prejudices and erroneous assumptions.

The problem of understanding Puerto Ricans is confounded by the fact that today there are really two groups of Puerto Ricans. From a crowded island not overly endowed with natural resources beyond its people and its climate, thousands of Puerto Ricans have come to the mainland, especially in the period since World War II. Many have stayed. Scarcely a state is without any Puerto Ricans, and some places, such as New York City, Boston, Hartford (Connecticut), and several areas in New Jersey have large numbers of Puerto Ricans. Many have raised families on the mainland, and these second- and third-generation Puerto Ricans are different in many significant ways from those who were raised on the island.

The mainland-raised Puerto Rican, sometimes called Neo-Rican, is generally English-dominant with respect to language. This Puerto Rican has adapted, as one might expect, to the unique environment of the urban setting but has retained a strong influence from and linkage to a primarily Latin American setting. Thus, having been brought up in another climate, with another language, with different fears and aspirations, and perhaps often with a different reference group, the mainland Puerto Rican is understandably different from the island Puerto Rican. Yet the culturally dominant group in the U.S. defines all Puerto Ricans in the same way, and the Neo-Rican often suffers from the same prejudices inflicted on the recent arrival from San Juan, Ponce, or Ciales.

In many ways, however, Puerto Ricans from the mainland and those from the island do share common cultural characteristics. As dangerous as generalizations can be, it is important for counselors to consider some of the qualities a Puerto Rican client might possess.

Cultural Characteristics

There are certain values and traits that are generally agreed on as being linked to the Puerto Rican ethos. Chief among these are *fatalismo, respecto, dignidad, machismo,* and *humanismo* (Hidalgo undated; Wagenheim 1970). Wells (1972) has added *afecto* to this list. (See the glossary at the end of this article for definitions of Spanish words used.) These cultural attributes are important to any group, and a wise counselor should have some understanding of them. The reader who has difficulty conceptualizing these terms may find it helpful to empathize with what the Puerto Rican experiences on entering an alien culture. The following explanations may help.

There is a certain amoung of overlap in the words used above. *Dignidad* and *respecto,* which have to do with the dignity of an individual and respect for those deserving of it, are interrelated concepts. *Machismo,* generally connoting male superiority, is also part and parcel of the other cultural traits. Because these concepts are so central to the Puerto Rican as an individual and as a representative of a culture that is—at least politically—bound to this country, it is very important that the counselor understand how some of these attributes are translated into behaviors. The behaviors discussed apply in some degree to most Puerto Ricans, but in some instances they may be less typical of second-generation Puerto Ricans on the mainland.

Typically the Puerto Rican is highly individualistic, a person who is not used to working in concert with others, following in single file, and, in general, organizing in ways that Anglos would call "efficient." Whether in a traffic jam or a line of patrons in a bank, a Puerto Rican may break line and take a position ahead of others. But the Puerto Rican will also offer another person the same privilege, being much more tolerant than Anglos of this demonstration of individuality.

Another characteristic of Puerto Ricans is their demonstration of love and tolerance for children. It is rare that a baby or tot, taken down any street in Puerto Rico, is not exclaimed over, chucked under the chin, and generally complimented. This love for children is stronger than its stateside equivalent; generally speaking, in fact, the family unit is stronger among Puerto Ricans. Perhaps because of the love for children, illegitimacy is not frowned on or punished among Puerto Ricans. It is not unusual for families to add to their broods with nephews, nieces, godchildren, and even the children of husbands' alliances with mistresses. It is therefore difficult for the Puerto Rican arriving at a mainland school to understand all the fuss about different last names and shades of skin color and all the confusion about birth certificates among siblings.

The characteristic of gregariousness, a trait common to nearly all Puerto Ricans, often dismays many Americans, who view it as excessive when compared with their own culture. The existence of large families and extended families, the *compadrazgo* (godparent) relationship, and life on a crowded island are probably causes as well as effects of this gregariousness. Puerto Ricans love to talk, discuss, gossip, speculate, and relate. No one needs an excuse to have a fiesta. Music, food, and drink appear instantly if someone comes to visit. Group meetings, even those of the most serious nature, often take on some aspect of a social activity. I remember more than one dull and pedantic committee meeting at the University of Puerto Rico that was saved from being a total loss because refreshments and chatting were an inseparable part of the meetings. A colleague used to reinforce attendance at meetings in her office by furnishing lemon pie and coffee.

"Puerto Ricans are seldom found in professional or managerial jobs; they are usually working in low-paying, menial occupations, to an even greater degree than blacks."

Puerto Ricans' hospitality is related to their gregariousness. In the poorest home in a San Juan slum or in a remote mountain shack, a visitor will be offered what there is or what can be sent out for on the spot. And it is not good manners to refuse this hospitality; it is offered from the heart, and refusal is rejection. The visitor in this situation will give more by partaking of the hospitality than by bringing a gift.

As might be deduced from the preceding comments, Puerto Ricans are sensitive. Social intercourse has significant meaning, and Puerto Ricans typically are quite alert to responses they evoke in others and to others' behavior, even behavior of a casual nature. Often Puerto Ricans avoid a direct confrontation, and they do not like to give a straight-out no to anyone. Marqués (1967) is among those who has described Puerto Ricans as passively docile, and indeed docility is a noticeable Puerto Rican characteristic. Silén (1971), however, has interpreted this characteristic as actually having aggressive overtones, pointing out that historically this docility was simply a refusal to engage in battles that were impractical. Silén has also reminded us of some of the past and present revolutionary stirrings of the "docile" Puerto Rican. Whichever interpretation is accepted, there is evidence that there has been some change in this behavior, especially among younger Puerto Ricans on the island and those Puerto Ricans who have been raised on the mainland.

Puerto Ricans on the Mainland

For most readers of this article, the Puerto Rican living on the mainland is likely to be of greatest interest and relevance. There are approximately two million Puerto Ricans living in the U.S. They come to the mainland primarily for jobs. They generally do not intend to remain here and, as economic conditions for the family improve, increasingly return to the island. In recent years Puerto Rico has made some economic progress and some advances in creating jobs, and thus Puerto Ricans, who typically aspire to live in Puerto Rico, find it increasingly attractive to go back.

This return migration has created some economic, social, and educational problems for Puerto Rico. For example, when younger Puerto Ricans who have been raised in New York City or other areas return to the island, they face certain cultural assimilation problems not at all unlike those their parents faced when they came to the mainland. English-dominant young people must master Spanish for school, work, social life, and participation in family and civic affairs. These youngsters' modes of behavior are often in conflict with the attitudes and values of grandparents, uncles, and the general society. Some efforts are being made to deal with these conflicts, including the establishment of special classes given in English and even the employment of a bilingual counselor or two, but the island's resources are too limited to permit extensive help in this regard. It is fair to say, however, that the Puerto Rican returning to Puerto Rico is treated considerably better than the islander who comes to the U.S. mainland.

Puerto Ricans coming to the mainland often encounter prejudice. Part of this seems to be due to the fact that they are "foreign"; most Americans—even those whose parents were born in another country—are inclined to be cool, to say the least, toward people different from themselves.

"A person's name *is* that person, and a counselor's mispronouncing it—whether through carelessness or laziness—can easily be construed as the counselor's lack of interest in the client."

Certainly racism is another significant element in the prejudice against Puerto Ricans. Senior (1965) has reported:

> Census figures show that fewer non-white Puerto Ricans come to the States than whites, in comparison with their proportion of the population, and a special study indicates that a larger percentage of the non-whites return to their original homes after a sojourn on the mainland. (p. 46)

But problems for the Puerto Rican are not limited to prejudice. For those young people newly arrived in the States or born here of Puerto Rican parentage, the generation gap becomes compounded by what Senior has called "second-generationitis." These youngsters must contend not only with the expectancies and pressures of a different and dominant culture but also with conflicts of values representing two different cultures. Mainland Puerto Ricans may not be able to identify completely with the Puerto Rican culture, but neither are they a part of the dominant mainland culture. Social scientists often refer to this situation as the "identity crisis" of the Puerto Rican in the States.

As has been shown in the tragic treatment of blacks in the U.S., social and personal prejudice against a group is generally accompanied by a lack of economic opportunities for that group. Puerto Ricans are seldom found in professional or managerial jobs; they are usually working in low-paying, menial occupations, to an even greater degree than blacks. There are many causes for this. The low educational levels of Puerto Ricans on the mainland is undoubtedly a significant factor. Prejudice, suspicion, language difficulties, and the familiar self-fulfilling prophecy of low aspirations leading to lowly positions also play heavy roles in maintaining the Puerto Rican on the bottom rung of the economic and vocational ladder.

Practical Considerations for the Counselor

The following suggestions offered for counseling Puerto Ricans are based on my eleven years of experience as a counselor in Puerto Rico and on those human relations tenets to which all counselors presumably subscribe. The suggestions may seem simple and obvious to the reader; they are purposely so. They are intended as exhortations for those who are thoughtless, as reminders for those who forget, and as reinforcements for those who truly attempt to accept and understand their clients.

Examine your own prejudices. Counselors should consider their attitudes toward poor, rural, Spanish-speaking, racially mixed, culturally different clients. Knowledge alone cannot overcome prejudice, and an intellectual understanding expressed with emotional distaste will only serve to exacerbate the situation. If a counselor has negative stereotyped feelings about Puerto Ricans, it is not likely that his or her counseling relationships with them will be open and warm.

Call students by their right names. In Spanish, people are given two last names. The first last name is from the father's side of the family, the second from the mother's. The American custom is to look for the last word, and this becomes the last name. If this logic is followed with Latins, a student named Angel Rodríguez López gets called Angel López, thus dropping his father's family name. Not only might the father and son be understandably insulted by such cavalier treatment, but the boy's identity— in a real as well as a cultural sense—is in question. For those who fervently desire to maintain their cultural and personal identities without being antagonistic to the larger society, acknowledgment of the correct name can be critical.

Another element in this linguistic area is simply pronouncing names in reasonably accurate ways. Even though other students and staff may pronounce names inaccurately, it would seem that a counselor who espouses the establishment of good relationships might make a special effort in this area. A person's name *is* that person, and a counselor's mispronouncing it—whether through carelessness or laziness—can easily be construed as the counselor's lack of interest in the client. Counselors can check with a client about pronunciation. (Spanish, incidentally, is much more consistent in pronunciation than English, because each vowel is pronounced the same way in all words.)

Work with the family. For the Puerto Rican, the family is much more important than it is for the typical American. If possible, the counselor should deal not only with the young person but also with the family, getting to know them as well as the youngster. If this is not possible, the counselor can at least talk with the client about his or her family. Among Puerto Ricans, the family and extended family are often sought out for help more readily than is a counselor; research, in fact, indicates that the family is the source of greatest help (Christensen 1973). The counselor should realize that others are helping and should work with them, understanding that each person has something to offer. Ignoring this fact is equivalent to refusing to recognize that a client is also receiving help from another professional.

Refrain from using the child as an interpreter. In cases where a parent knows little English and the child is reasonably bilingual, it is a temptation to rely on the son or daughter to carry a message to the parent. This should be avoided whenever possible. Even though it might be a source of pride for the child, it might place the parent in a dependent position, preventing the parent from entering into the counseling relationship as a full partner. There is an additional concern: the possibility that the child might twist others' statements. Puerto Rican families are close, but a situation in which a parent continually communicates only through the child can alter relationships and create family strains.

Understand that to the Puerto Rican you are the foreigner. One cannot jump into instant relationships. The counselor must give the client time to know and trust him or her. To facilitate this, the counselor may need to meet the client outside of the school or the counselor's office. The counselor should share and be somewhat self-disclosing, revealing some things about his or her family, ideas, home, and so on, in order to give the client a chance to know the counselor as a person. Counselor self-disclosure can be a sign of trust for any client, but it is even more crucial where some feeling of "foreignness" is present in both counselor and client.

Understand the concept of "hijo de crianza." This term refers to someone other than the child's parents raising the child—either family members (such as an aunt or a grandmother), extended family members (such as a godparent), or even a friend or neighbor. It also may refer to a family's raising the father's children from another marriage or even from outside a legal union. Counselors must not apply their moral values in such situations. The child is the parents' child through love and acceptance, and exact relationships are not that important.

Be patient. This should be a given for all counselors with all clients, but it is especially true when counselors desire to establish any kind of relationship with clients from a different culture. Puerto Ricans have many obstacles to overcome, some of which are not of their own making. In the counseling relationship, counselors have to overcome some of these same hurdles. Counselors must demonstrate their credibility, honesty, and reliability, just as their Puerto Rican clients must do almost daily in an alien society. The difference is that the counselor is in a more advantageous position, and therefore the counselor's initiative is crucial. The Puerto Rican client may expect the counselor to be prejudiced, arrogant, and lacking in knowledge about Puerto Ricans. The burden is on the counselor to demonstrate that these expectations will not be fulfilled.

The Fruits of Labor

The counselor who works with Puerto Ricans of any age and in any setting may find some difficulty in doing so. But counselors who are willing to learn will find the effort rewarding. Puerto Rican clients need counselors as much as—or more than—other clients do. Moreover, in the final analysis, we Americans need them also. For they, along with all people of differing ethnic and cultural backgrounds, offer all of us a richness that even a wealthy country cannot afford to be without.

Glossary of Spanish Terms

afecto   literally means "affect." Refers to the affective side of life—warmth and demonstrativeness.

compadrazgo   refers to the relationship entered into when a person becomes a godfather (*padrino*) or godmother (*madrina*). This person then becomes a *compadre* or *comadre* with the parents of the child and traditionally not only takes on certain responsibilities for the child but also is closely related to the entire family of the other person. In some cases this may also involve even other *compadres,* and then the total relationships derived from this system of *compadrazgo* are complex and far-reaching and form the basis for what sociologists term the extended family, which is so characteristic of many societies.

dignidad   dignity, but of special importance in Puerto Rico and closely related to *respeto.* One can oppose another person, but taking away a person's respect or dignity in front of others is about the worst thing one can do.

fatalismo   fatalism.

humanismo   humanism, especially as contrasted with the more pragmatic set of the typical Anglo.

machismo   related to male superiority and, in its original form, implying the innate and biological inferiority of women. Characterized as an overcompensatory reaction to the dependence-aggression conflict, *machismo* is acted out through fighting and sexual conquest.

respecto   signifies respect, especially respect for authority, family, and tradition.

References

Christensen, E. W. (Ed.) Report of the task force for the study of the guidance program of the Puerto Rican Department of Education, vocational and technical education area. San Juan, Puerto Rico: College Entrance Examination Board, 1973.

Hidalgo, H. A. The Puerto Rican. In National Rehabilitation Association (Ed.). *Ethnic differences influencing the delivery of rehabilitation services: The American Indian; the black American; the Mexican American; and the Puerto Rican.* Washington, D.C.: National Rehabilitation Association, undated.

Marqués, R. *Ensayos (1953–1966).* San Juan, Puerto Rico: Editorial Antillana, 1967.

Senior, C. *The Puerto Rican: Strangers—Then neighbors.* Chicago: Quadrangle Books, 1965.

Silén, J. A. *We, the Puerto Rican people: A story of oppression and resistance.* New York: Monthly Review Press, 1971.

Wagenheim, K. *Puerto Rico: A profile.* New York: Praeger, 1970.

Wells, H. *La modernización de Puerto Rico: Un analisis politico de valores e instituciones en proceso de cambio.* San Juan, Puerto Rico: Editorial Universitaria, 1972.

Suggested Readings

Adams, J. F. Population: A Puerto Rican catastrophe. Address delivered to the Puerto Rican League of Women Voters, Hato Rey, Puerto Rico, February 1972.

Cordasco, F., & Bucchions, E. *Puerto Rican children in mainland schools.* Metuchen, N.J.: The Scarecrow Press, 1968.

Espin, O. M., & Renner, R. R. Counseling: A new priority in Latin America. *Personnel and Guidance Journal,* 1974, *52*(5), 297–301.

Fernández Méndez, E. (Ed.) *Portrait of a society: Readings on Puerto Rican sociology.* San Juan, Puerto Rico: University of Puerto Rico Press, 1972.

Fitzpatrick, J. P. *Puerto Rican Americans: The meaning of migration to the mainland.* Englewood Cliffs, N.J.: Prentice-Hall, 1971.

The Latino Client

1. Assume you are a counselor at a large state university that has publicly stated support for all its federally mandated affirmative action programs. Recently, however, the Sociology Department's graduate admission procedure has been under fire by the campus newspaper for its practice of reserving 20 percent of its new admissions for Chicano students (the state in which the school is located is composed of 20 percent Chicanos).

   a. How do you feel about the selection procedure described?
   b. What action would you take in view of your feelings?
   c. What impact would you expect this to have on your ability to relate to Chicano students?

2. Assume you are a counselor in a state-run rehabilitation agency. A Puerto Rican paraplegic enters your office looking very sullen and begins to question your ability to help her. She points out that you cannot possibly understand her problems since you are not encumbered, as she is, by the forces of multiple oppression.

   a. How will you respond to her charges?
   b. What doubts do you have about your ability to work with this client?
   c. What are some of the cultural factors to which you need to be sensitive in working with this client?

3. Assume you are a counselor in an urban elementary school with a student enrollment that is 60% Anglo, 40% Chicano. Several physical confrontations have occurred in the school cafeteria recently, apparently the result of insult trading between Anglos and Chicanos over "Mex" and "Gringo" food. The school principal has asked you to work with some of the students involved.

   a. How do you plan to work (what is your role) with these students?
   b. Do you anticipate any difficulty in establishing a relationship with either the Anglo or Chicano students? How will you deal with the difficulty?
   c. What community resources might you want to tap in dealing with this problem?

The Latino Client
Role Playing Exercise

Divide into groups of four or five. Assign each group member to a role and the responsibilities associated with the role as follows:

Role	Responsibilities
1. Counselor	1. Assume role as a counselor or mental health worker who encounters an Hispanic. Attempt to build rapport with the client.
2. Client	2. Assume role of an Hispanic. To play this role effectively, it will be necessary for the student client to (a) identify cultural values of the Hispanic group, (b) identify sociopolitical factors which may interfere with counseling, and (c) portray these aspects in the counseling session. It is best to select a few powerful variables in the role play. You may or may not be initially antagonistic to the counselor, but it is important for you to be sincere in your role and your reactions to the counselor trainee.
3. Observers	3. Observe interaction and offer comments during feedback session.

This exercise is most effective in a racially and ethnically mixed group. For example, a Hispanic student can be asked to play the Hispanic client role. However, this is probably not possible in most cases. Thus, students who play the client role will need to thoroughly read the articles for the group they are portraying.

Identifying the barriers that could interfere with counseling is an important aspect of this exercise. We recommend that a list be made of the group's cultural values and sociopolitical influences prior to the role playing.

Role playing may go on for a period of 5–15 minutes, but the time limit should be determined prior to the activity. Allow 10–15 minutes for a feedback session in which all participants discuss (within the group) how they felt in their respective roles, how appropriate were the counselor responses, what else they might have done in that situation, etc.

Rotate and role play the same situation with another counselor trainee *or* another Hispanic client with different issues, concerns, and problems. In the former case, the group may feel that a particular issue is of sufficient importance to warrant reenactment. This allows students to see the effects of other counseling responses and approaches. In the latter case, the new exposure will allow students to get a broader view of barriers to counseling.

If videotaping equipment is available, we recommend that the sessions be taped and processed in a replay at the end. We have found this to be a powerful means of providing feedback to participants.

Part 6
Implications for Minority Group Cross-Cultural Counseling

16 Future Directions in Minority Group/Cross-Cultural Counseling

Counseling Practice

In chapter 2 it was noted that a great deal of criticism by minority individuals has been directed at the traditional counseling role. Time-bound, space-bound, cathartic counseling is rejected by these critics as largely irrelevant to minority life experiences and needs. The counselor, they argue, needs to get out of the office and meet the client on the client's ground. Rather than demanding that the client adapt to the counselor's culture, the counselor should adjust to and work within the client's culture. Furthermore, minority individuals are by definition oppressed, and it is highly unlikely that any minority client problem is ever totally free of this oppression. Providing an empathic ear so that the client can reassess past experiences, or even changing the client's behavior so that he or she can cope better with the environment, does not eliminate the oppression.

Several roles that overcome at least some of the criticisms leveled by minority critics have been proposed as alternatives to the traditional counseling role. For the most part, these roles are not really new, since they have been proposed and to some degree implemented in the past (Pine, in his 1972 article, refers to them as "old wine in new bottles"). They are "new," however, in that they have not gained widespread acceptance by the counseling profession, and the traditional counseling role remains solidly entrenched as the counselor's primary modus operandi.

In general it can be said these alternative roles involve the counselor more actively in the client's life experiences than does the traditional role, and the former often require the counselor to move out of his/her office into the client's environment. They also share a preventative thrust rather than the more traditional remedial focus. Because of this there is considerable overlapping of the role functions, but each includes some aspects that are unique to the role. The alternative roles to be discussed are: (1) facilitator of self-help, (2) outreach role, (3) consultant role, (4) ombudsmun role,

(5) change agent role, and (6) facilitator of indigenous support systems. We also offer a brief discussion of how traditional psychotherapy with ethnically diverse clients may be applied more effectively than it has in the past.

Facilitator of Self-Help

As suggested in Chapter 2, a major criticism of the traditional counseling model is the focus on intrapsychic sources of the client's problem and on psychotherapy as the primary intervention for resolving the problem. As facilitator of self-help, the counselor helps the client identify the external sources of his or her problem as well as methods of resolving the problem. Rather than encouraging the client to "own the problem," the counselor helps the client become aware of the oppressive forces creating the problem. Then together the counselor and client develop a strategy for eliminating or reducing the effect of the oppression on the client's life.

Smith (1985) describes a self-help model of counseling ethnically diverse clients labeled the "Stress, Resistant, Delivery Model" or SRD model. According to Smith (1985), the SRD model "puts emphasis on sources of stress rather than on the symptoms of stress," and the counselor "not only helps the client to become aware of the forces in his or her life but also how to marshal resources to relieve stressful forces" (p. 568). The SRD model involves three steps, the first of which is to identify the sources of stress impinging on the client. The second step is to analyze the internal and external factors that mediate the stress as well as the stress-resistant forces within the individual and his/her culture. The third step is to identify a method of delivering services to the client that emphasizes a self-help approach.

Ponterotto (1987) describes a multi-modal approach to counseling Mexican Americans that appears equally applicable to other ethnic groups. One component of the approach involves identifying the social, environmental, and institutional factors that are oppressing the client but that are external to his/her control. The counselor first acknowledges the oppressive environment and then helps the client organize a plan for confronting the situation directly and/or helps the client identify agencies that could facilitate resolution of the problem.

Outreach Role

The outreach role requires that counselors move out of their offices and into their clients' communities (Weinrach, 1973; Mitchell, 1971a). Minority clients in educational settings are often hesitant to contact counselors (Calia, 1966); and Haettenschwiller (1971) urges counselors to make the initial contact with minority students on the students' home ground, thus establishing the counselor as a person, ". . . to whom the student can turn when confronted by the uncertainty and ambiguity of institutional demands" (p. 31). Grevious (1985) advises that a home visit will help the counselor better understand a Black client. Meeting clients in this manner allows the counselor to divest him/herself of the Establishment association that an office visit can generate. Woods (1977) describes a counseling services program that relies heavily on group counseling and group activities rather than on traditional one-to-one counseling and, in keeping with an outreach philosophy, the group sessions are often, ". . . conducted at students' apartments for potluck dinners, and at local beaches and parks for picnics and games" (p. 417).

By making him/herself available in the client's environment, the counselor is in a better position to respond to client needs at the time they are experienced. Exposure to the client's world may also help the counselor understand the cultural experience of the client and may enhance the counselor-client relationship. Furthermore, the counselor as an outreach worker may be in a position to directly observe the environmental factors that are contributing to the client's problems, and the counselor is thus less likely to attribute deviations from majority norms to pathology. In addition to direct exposure to the environment of minority clients, counselors should become actively involved in community and social programs and activities in their minority clients' communities (Wilson & Calhoun, 1974).

Consultant Role

The goal of consultation is the development of a nurturing ecological system designed to optimize each client's self-growth (Blocker & Rapoza, 1972). In this role the counselor works with teachers, parents, peers, and others who have an impact on the minority client (Maes & Rinaldi, 1974).

Perhaps the most effective way a counselor can function as a consultant vis-à-vis minorities is by designing and implementing a peer-counseling program. Minority-client populations frequently find it easier to trust a peer than a professional, regardless of the professional's membership-group status. Gravitz and Woods (1976) describe a peer counseling program in which Third World students function as liaison between the University and minority students. Peer counselors focus their efforts on the ". . . clinically asymptomatic student who has problems of living in a complex university community" (p. 231). The primary philosophy of this peer-counseling program is to serve a preventative function; to anticipate minority-student difficulties and to alleviate them before they become aggravated. In order to do this, peer counselors often spend much of their time outside the counseling center, meeting minority students in residence halls, student centers, and minority centers. In addition to providing direct services to minority students, one result of the peer-counseling program reported by Gravitz and Woods is that an increased number of minority students make contact with the counseling center's professional staff.

The training of minority peers is an important aspect of any minority, peer or paraprofessional program. D. W. Sue (1973) has described a training program for Third World student counselors; this includes a course on peer counseling of minority students offered for credit. The course stresses six content areas: (1) the cultural backgrounds of the minorities to be served, (2) techniques of counseling, (3) crisis intervention, (4) ethical issues, (5) behavior pathology, and (6) referral sources. In addition, trainees spend 1½ hours a week role playing counselor-counselee interactions in small groups supervised by a professional counselor. In general, the role-playing sessions are aimed at helping trainees develop skills associated with facilitative and action conditions (Carkhuff, 1971) of the helping relationship. Sue reports that an important aspect of the training procedure is the feedback provided by fellow trainees.

Lewis and Lewis (1977) have pointed out that counselors can also serve as consultants with groups of minority people who want to organize in order to improve the conditions under which they live. They describe four ways the counselor can serve in this capacity: the counselor can assess community needs, coordinate activities and resources, provide training in skill building, and advocate change.

Ombudsmun and Change Agent Roles

In both the ombudsmun role and the change agent role the counselor discards entirely the intrapsychic counseling model and clearly views the problem as existing outside the minority client. Economic, political, social, emotional, and other forms of oppression are identified as the underlying causes of minority client problems, and the counselor's role is to combat oppression. The two roles differ slightly, however, in terms of focus.

Ombudsmun. The ombudsmun role (spelled with a *u* to avoid a sexist connotation) originated in Europe where it functions as a protector of citizens against bureaucratic mazes and procedures (Bexelius, 1968). A number of colleges and universities in this country have instituted the ombudsmun role, and recently school counselors have been urged to serve as student advocates (Ciavarella & Doolittle, 1970). In this role the counselor represents a client or group of clients who have brought a particular form of oppression to the counselor's attention. Being an empathic counselor who suggests alternative ways of coping with a particular problem is not enough; the counselor must be willing to pursue actively alternative courses with or for the client, including making "a personal contact for the student who is overwhelmed by the bureaucracy" (Mitchell, 1971, p. 36). Not infrequently the injustice involves the institution employing the counselor, either directly or indirectly, making the counselor somewhat unpopular at times with institutional administrators. If the client's goals are in conflict with those of the institution, "the counselor must decide to represent the student and not the institution or the system" (Williams & Kirkland, 1971, p. 114), presumably within ethical restrictions imposed by the profession. When a minority client is involved, the ombudsmun has the added responsibility for making certain that the minority person can benefit fully from the social and economic resources of the majority culture without losing what is unique and valued in his/her own culture (Maes & Rinaldi, 1974).

Change Agent role. In the change agent role, the counselor assumes an alloplastic counseling position, devoting considerable time and energy to changing the social environment of his/her minority clientele (Banks, 1972). By necessity, this often means changing the social environment of majority peers and superiors in the offending environment. Like the ombudsmun role, counselors in this role must often identify the problem as residing with the very institution that employs them and must be willing to confront their employers (Williams & Kirkland, 1971).

As a change agent, the counselor need not represent a particular client or group of clients known to the outsider. Rather, the entire minority culture experiencing an injustice functions as the client. Furthermore, the counselor serving as a change agent frequently assumes a low-visibility stature, often finding it useful to mobilize other influential persons in the offending institution so as to bring about change (Waltz & Benjamin, 1977).

Anderson & Love (1973) exhort counselors to, ". . . assume responsibility for making efforts to increase positive human relations and fostering development of a multicultural view of the world" (p. 667), and suggest psychological education as a vehicle to aid this process. The Division 17 Professional Affairs Committee of the American Psychological Association agrees that special measures are needed to combat institutional oppression of minority people in this country.

> Problems of institutional racism are paramount on a university campus. Counseling alone on discrimination issues will be ineffective. Counseling psychologists must involve themselves in affirmative action programs, sponsor symposia and workshops on racism in society, and actively involve themselves in programs of cultural awareness. (Ivey, 1976, p. 10–11).

As a change agent, however, the counselor need not necessarily spend his/her time confronting institutional bureaucracy. The counselor can work directly with majority clients in an attempt to move them toward the goal of reducing racism, sexism, and other discriminatory attitudes toward minorities. Katz and Ivey (1977) describe a racism-awareness training program that could easily be adapted to majority attitudes toward nonracial minorities. The program involves a reeducation process designed, ". . . to raise consciousness of White people, help them identify racism in their life experience from which their racist attitudes and behaviors have developed, and move them to take action against institutional and individual racism" (p. 487). The six phases of the program are designed to help participants to:

1. Increase their understanding of racism in society and themselves.
2. Confront discrepancies existing between the myths and reality of American ideology and behavior.
3. Sort through some of their feelings and reactions that were triggered by phases 1 and 2.
4. Confront the racism in the White culture that their own actions support.

5. Understand and accept their Whiteness.
6. Develop specific action strategies to combat personal and institutional racism (p. 487).

The authors' suggestion that racism is a White problem and White counselors should assume a major role in dealing with it, is plausible. Majority counselors are, in some respects, in the best position to confront the majority population with their own stereotypic attitudes and behaviors.

Role as Facilitator of Indigenous Support Systems

Pedersen (1976) has discussed the need for counselors who are engaged in international cross-cultural counseling to be aware of the culture's indigenous mental health care systems. Focusing specifically on the Native American population, Torrey (1970) has suggested that mental health workers should structure their activities to supplement, not supplant, the existing system of mental health services among American Indians and Eskimos. Within most other U.S. minority groups, culturally relevant procedures have evolved to assist the individual who is experiencing a psychological problem. Frequently, counselors are unaware of or are disdainful of these procedures, preferring to engage the client in the very counseling process so heavily criticized by minority representatives. The inevitable result is a mismatch of treatment and need, loss of credibility in the counselor, and the client's disengagement from counseling. We would like to suggest that counselors may be able best to serve their minority clientele by attempting to facilitate rather than discourage use of indigenous support systems. In some cases this may mean understanding, acknowledging, and honoring the folk-belief system to which the client adheres. According to Cayleff (1986), counselors violate the ethical principle of beneficence (doing good by preventing harm) if they fail to honor the client's belief system (p. 345).

The counselor working with a minority client might begin the facilitative process by exploring with the client how he/she has dealt with similar problems in the past. Familiarity with the client's culture will help the counselor understand culturally relevant support systems that may assist the client. For instance, among some Mexicano groups *curanderos* perform many of the functions of a counselor. In numerous minority cultures, the extended family plays an important supportive role. In others (e.g. women, gays), the family may provide little support, but peers provide the reinforcement needed to survive and overcome crisis. The counselor can facilitate problem resolution by encouraging the client to use these support systems where appropriate.

In many cases, minority-client problems can be linked directly to oppression. Depression, for instance, may result from years and years of futile attempts to achieve some measure of social equality. A facilitative counselor might encourage a client experiencing depression of this nature to participate in an organization within the client's culture that fosters minority community pride.

Not all cultural adaptations to psychological problems engender growth, and in some instances the client may be too acculturated to benefit from procedures developed by the minority culture. In these instances, the facilitative process begins with an exploration of processes with which the client feels comfortable. A key distinction in these cases, however, is that the exploration serves to discover a process for resolving the client's difficulty, not as a process for resolving a problem in and of itself.

Traditional Psychotherapy

While the exclusive use of psychotherapy as the intervention of choice with ethnically diverse clients is inappropriate, the elimination of psychotherapy as a counseling tool with special populations would be equally ill-advised. Some ethnically diverse clients do experience psychological problems similar to those afflicting nonminority clients. Further, many ethnically diverse clients are acculturated into mainstream American society to the point that they feel very comfortable with traditional forms of psychotherapy. Thus, counselors need to explore early in their counseling relationships with ethnically diverse clients the role that discrimination and oppression has played in the client's problem and the extent to which the client is acculturated into mainstream American culture.

S. Sue and Zane (1987) have suggested that although knowledge of a client's culture and techniques generated by this knowledge are important when working with ethnically diverse clients, their primary importance in psychotherapy may be to establish therapist credibility. These authors argue that both knowledge of a client's culture and culturally specific forms of intervention may be distal to therapeutic outcome. More directly related to therapeutic outcome, they argue, are therapist credibility and giving, two processes particularly relevant when working with ethnically diverse clients. Credibility is a function of ascribed status and achieved status. Ascribed status is assigned by others; achieved status is primarily a function of the therapist's skills. Sue and Zane (1987) suggest that three factors are significantly linked to achieved status:

1. *Conceptualization of the problem.* If the client's problems are conceptualized in a manner that is incongruent with the client's belief systems, the credibility of the therapist is diminished.
2. *Means for problem resolution.* If the therapist requires from the client responses that are culturally incompatible or unacceptable, the achieved credibility of the therapist is diminished.
3. *Goals for treatment.* If the definitions of goals are discrepant between therapist and client, credibility of the therapist will be diminished. (p. 41).

By giving, S. Sue and Zane (1987) are referring to the need to offer clients a benefit from therapy as soon as possible. Giving does not mean a short-term treatment for the client's problem but rather a meaningful gain early in therapy. The authors suggest that anxiety reduction, depression relief, cognitive clarity, normalization of experiences, reassurance, hope and faith, skills acquisition, a coping perspective, and goal setting are examples of therapeutic giving.

Counselor Education

In response to the negative view minorities have of counseling, some authors have suggested that indigenous and paraprofessional counselors should be trained for minority-group counseling, since it is doubtful whether majority counselors can become truly sensitive to minority needs (Ward, 1970). Yet in view of the multicultural makeup of American society, it seems highly unlikely that counselors being trained today (especially those being trained for educational settings) will escape contact with culturally different clients. It seems imperative, therefore, that counselors of all cultural backgrounds be at least minimally prepared to work with clients who differ culturally from themselves. In our opinion, programs that train counselors need to do a better job both of increasing the number of minority counselors and of preparing all counselors for cross-cultural counseling experiences.

Recruiting, Admitting, and Supporting Minority Counselor Trainees

It is probably safe to say that very few counselor education programs in the 1980s intentionally discriminate against minority applicants in their admission's policies and procedures. Yet surveys of psychology departments and American Psychological Association (APA) members consistently reveal that ethnic minorities are still underrepresented in psychology (Kennedy & Wagner, 1979; Padilla, Boxley, & Wagner, 1973; Parham & Moreland, 1981; Russo, Olmedo, Stapp, & Fulcher, 1981; Strong & Peele, 1977). According to Russo et al. (1981), ethnic minorities make up 3.1 percent of all APA members, 5 percent of all graduate faculty in psychology, approximately 8 percent of those awarded Ph.D.'s in psychology in 1980, and approximately 10 percent of those enrolled in graduate psychology programs in 1981. These data suggest a slight increase in the production of minority psychologists, but an increase so gradual that it will take decades to achieve parity with nonminorities in the field of psychology. Underrepresentation of ethnic minorities has also been documented in counselor-education programs (Atkinson, 1983; Jones, 1976).

Korchin (1981) has identified five reasons, paraphrased below, why the underrepresentation of ethnic minorities in the mental health professions must be eliminated:

1. It is morally right to do so.
2. Minority mental health workers are better able than are their nonminority colleagues to understand minority clients.

3. Minority mental health workers are more motivated than are their nonminority colleagues to work with minority clients.
4. Minority mental health workers are needed as identification figures for minority clients.
5. Minority mental health workers can enrich the knowledge of their nonminority colleagues by sharing their knowledge of human diversity.

One reason that psychology departments and counselor education programs have not enrolled significant numbers of ethnic minority students in the past is that they fail to recognize counselor-trainee selection as a three-phase process involving recruitment, admission, and support (Atkinson, 1981). Even an admission policy designed to increase minority enrollment can have only a limited impact if the applicant pool includes only a few minority applicants. Further, as victims of oppression, ethnic minorities often need economic, social, and emotional support that nonminorities may not need in order to complete a degree in counseling.

In a survey of a representative sample of counselor-education programs, Atkinson and Wampold (1981) found that 57 percent of the respondents stated an interest in enrolling ethnic minorities in the literature describing their program. Slightly less than half (49 percent) indicated that someone from their campus had been identified as an affirmative action recruiter for their program, and only 31 percent said their affirmative action recruiter travels to other colleges or universities to recruit ethnic minorities. Fewer than 3 out of 10 programs (29 percent) responding to the survey said that they send applications to eligible ethnic minorities without request.

A successful affirmative action recruitment effort is designed to identify and solicit applications not only from those minority individuals who already have definite plans to enroll in a counselor education program, but also from those individuals who have ruled out graduate education in counseling for less than valid reasons (e.g., lack of knowledge about financial support available to them), although they have the prerequisite educational and experiential background. Such a recruitment effort is affirmative in the true sense of the word. It reaches out to those who might settle for a less appealing vocation because their oppressive experience has conditioned them to settle for less than what they actually desire. It includes recruitment literature that identifies: (1) the counselor-education faculty's commitment to enroll a diversified student population, (2) aspects of the training program (e.g., course content, field-work settings, research focus) that provide a multicultural experience, and (3) support services (e.g., tutorial, financial, social) that are available to minorities. It includes active recruitment by students and faculty at college career days, professional conventions, and in day-to-day encounters. It also includes personal contacts with interested minority persons by department heads and individual faculty to communicate a real interest in enrolling ethnic minorities.

With regard to admission activities, the Atkinson and Wampold (1981) survey found that fewer than half (42 percent) of the responding programs give credit for ethnicity as part of the selection process. Approximately 4 out of 10 (39 percent) of the respondents indicated that credit is given to applicants who have prior experience working with members of an ethnic minority. Only 34 percent of the respondents employed ethnic minority persons to review application materials and only 31 percent used ethnic minority interviewers when they interviewed applicants.

Counselor-education programs need to develop admission policies and procedures that will admit as many qualified minority applicants as is legally, morally, and ethically possible in order to eliminate the current underrepresentation of minorities in the field of counseling. Traditional admission criteria of undergraduate GPA and graduate aptitude test scores have been found to discriminate against ethnic minorities (Bernal, 1980) and to be unreliable predictors of counseling performance (Rowe, Murphy, & DeCsipkas, 1975). New and/or additional criteria need to be identified by counselor education programs that will insure minorities are adequately represented in their student populations. As most counselor educators are aware, the famous U.S. Supreme Court decision in *Bakke vs. Regents of the University of California* ruled out the use of quotas as a means of ensuring minority admissions. What tends to be overlooked, however, was the court's approval of some admission's procedures designed to ensure minority representation. Citing the Harvard undergraduate admission policy as an example, the Court held that a "representational" admission policy designed to ensure representation from diverse groups was acceptable as long as it did not involve quotas.

An alternative to the "representational" admission policy has been described by Atkinson, Staso, and Hosford (1978); it seeks to identify counseling-related strengths held by minorities and include them as admission criteria. Briefly, the selection process involves three equally weighted criteria: academic index, experiential background, and personal interview. The traditional criteria of undergraduate GPA and graduate aptitude test are included in the academic index but their negative impact on minority applicants is lessened by using only the higher of the two scores (GPA or test score) relative to other applicants and restricting the weight to one-third of the total criteria. Experiential background is measured by a background questionnaire and points are awarded to applicants with multicultural experiences and goals that include working with ethnic minorities. For the personal interview criterion, applicants are asked to respond to videotaped counseling scenarios that involve minority clients and are offered an opportunity to conduct their interview in a second language. The combined effect of this process is to admit increased numbers of minority applicants by structuring the admission criteria around multicultural strengths that anyone may have but which minorities are more likely to possess than nonminorities.

In the area of support, the Atkinson and Wampold (1981) survey found that over half of the respondents (57 percent) offered support groups for ethnic minorities. However, only 39 percent reserved special fellowship, teaching assistantships, or other intramural sources of financial assistance exclusively for ethnic minorities, and only 28 percent provided special tutorial services for these groups. Less than 4 out of 10 respondents (37 percent) provided special advising services for ethnic minorities.

A variety of support services are needed to ensure that ethnic and other minorities, once admitted, are able to complete their graduate education in counseling. Special fellowship funds need to be developed and administered for underrepresented groups that could not otherwise attend graduate school (Bernal, 1980). Whenever feasible, minorities should be employed as research and teaching assistants, since these positions involve not only a financial remuneration but serve as apprenticeships for skills needed as a professional counselor and/or researcher. In addition to financial support, counselor-education programs should provide tutorial support to those individuals who may have experienced an inferior education due to their minority status. Since role models for minorities are often missing from counselor-education faculties, nonminority faculty need to expand their advising role for minority students to include the functions of mentor (Walton, 1979). As a minority-student mentor, the faculty member attempts to minimize the trauma of graduate education and maximize the supportive services for each minority advisee. For emotional/psychological support, many counselor-education programs have arranged to have support groups offered for their minority students.

In summary, counselor-trainee selection involves recruitment, admission, and support. If counselor-education programs are to reduce the underrepresentation of ethnic minorities in the counseling profession, expanded effort in all three areas will be needed in the future.

Rationale and Goals for Cross-Cultural Training

In addition to training more ethnically diverse counselors and psychologists, all mental-health practitioners, regardless of their ethnicity, need to be trained to work with culturally diverse clients. The need to train counselors and psychologists to work with culturally diverse clients has been recognized by the Association for Counseling and Development (AACD) and the American Psychological Association (APA). Both of these professional organizations have developed training standards that include education in cultural diversity as an important component. In order to be accredited by the Council for Accreditation of Counseling and Related Educational Programs (CACREP, the accrediting arm of AACD), a counseling program's goals must reflect (a) "current knowledge . . . concerning the counseling and human development needs of a multicultural society" and (2) "the present and projected needs of a multicultural society for which specialized counseling and human development activities have been developed" (Accreditation procedures, 1988, p. 25). Further, in order to be accredited by CACREP, the curriculum of a counselor training program must provide knowledge and skill in human growth and development "within cultural contexts" and in social and cultural foundations of "societal subgroups" (Accreditation procedures, 1988, p. 25).

Similarly, the APA accreditation manual includes cultural and individual difference as one of the major criteria for psychology-program approval.

> . . . social responsibilities and respect for cultural and individual differences and attitudes . . . must be reflected in all phases of the program's operation: faculty recruitment and promotion, student recruitment and evaluation, curriculum, and field training. . . . Programs must develop knowledge and skills in their students relevant to human diversity, such as people with handicapping conditions; of differing ages, genders, ethnic and racial backgrounds; religions, and life-styles; and from differing social and individual backgrounds. (Committee on Accreditation, 1980).

As suggested in Chapter 2, however, these accreditation requirements have not been translated into specific competencies that counseling and psychology trainees are expected to acquire. Very few counselor training programs to date have developed and offered systematic training in multicultural counseling (Bales, 1985; Bryson & Bardo, 1975). However, the goals and competencies of a cross-cultural training program have been identified by several authors.

S. Sue, Akutsu, and Higashi (1985) have identified three important elements of any cross-cultural counseling training program. Training in cross-cultural counseling should include knowledge of various cultural groups and history of their treatment in this country, experience counseling clients of various ethnic groups, and training in devising innovative treatment strategies. Copeland (1983) listed four components of a cross-cultural training program: a consciousness-raising, a cognitive understanding, an affective, and a skills component (p. 13). Similarly, Bernal (quoted in Bales, 1985) stated that a multicultural training program for psychologists should have the following goals:

> Understanding the social, historical, and cultural background and characteristics of minority groups; conveying a positive attitude toward these groups and a desire to learn from them, gaining theoretical knowledge and expertise in the scientific study of sociocultural variables, as well as in culturally appropriate intervention strategies; and communicating fluently in the appropriate language (p. 7).

According to Bernal and Padilla (1982), a multicultural approach to training psychologists includes certain important components and a particular training philosophy.

The components include a concern for cultural sensitivity, a better understanding of racism and its consequences for mental health, knowledge about the merits and dangers of customs of different cultures as they affect their members in terms of universal standards of mental health, an increase in opportunities for students to work with clients of ethnically similar and dissimilar backgrounds, and enlargements of the numbers of minority students and faculty. The multicultural training philosophy acknowledges that it is vital for trainees to have a broad-based historical and cultural understanding of minority groups, to develop positive attitudes toward them, to gain theoretical knowledge and expertise in the scientific study of sociocultural variables, to become experienced in the application of primary, secondary, and tertiary preventative strategies that are culturally appropriate, and to be able to communicate fluently in their client's language. (Bernal & Padilla, 1982, p. 786).

Perhaps the most extensive discussion of cross-cultural counseling competencies to date has been offered by the Education and Training Committee of Division 17, American Psychological Association. In the position paper, the committee identified consciousness raising (attitudes and beliefs), knowledge, and skills as three important curriculum areas for a cross-cultural counseling program. Under attitudes and beliefs they list four competencies that a cross-cultural counselor should have. The culturally skilled counseling psychologist:

1. is one who has moved from being culturally unaware to being aware and sensitive to his/her own cultural heritage and to valuing and respecting differences.
2. is aware of his/her own values and biases and how they may affect minority clients.
3. is one who is comfortable with differences that exist between the counselor and client in terms of race and beliefs.
4. is sensitive to circumstances that may dictate referral of the minority client to a member of his/her own race/culture.

The Committee also identified four types of knowledge a cross-cultural counselor should have. The culturally skilled counseling psychologist:

1. will have a good understanding of the sociopolitical systems operation in the United States with respect to its treatment of minorities.
2. must possess specific knowledge and information about the particular group he/she is working with.
3. must have a clear and explicit knowledge and understanding of the generic characteristics of counseling and therapy.
4. is aware of institutional barriers that prevent minorities from using mental health services.

Finally, the Committee identified three skills that a cross-cultural counselor should have:

1. must be able to generate a wide variety of verbal and nonverbal responses.
2. must be able to send and receive both verbal and nonverbal messages accurately and "appropriately."
3. is able to exercise institutional skills on behalf of his/her client when appropriate.

The full text of the *Position Paper on Cross-Cultural Counseling Competencies* is reprinted in Appendix A. The position paper has also been published in *The Counseling Psychologist* (D. W. Sue, Bernier, Durran, Feinberg, Pedersen, Smith, & Vasquez-Nuttal, 1982).

Curriculum Controversy

While there is general agreement about the need to teach appropriate attitudes, knowledge, and skills in counselor and psychologist training programs, there is some controversy about how this can best be accomplished. Copeland (1982) has identified four curriculum models that have been employed by cross-cultural counseling programs. The four curriculum models are: (a) separate course, (b) interdisciplinary, (c) integrated, and (d) area of concentration. Briefly, in the separate-course model the goals of cross-cultural training are met in a single course. In the interdisciplinary model, students are encouraged to take courses in ethnic studies and human-service-oriented fields in order to sensitize them to the needs of ethnic and other minority groups. Under the integrated model, the goals of cross-cultural training are integrated into all the counseling courses. And under the area of concentration model, the training program offers several courses that focus on one or several minority groups.

Each of these models has certain strengths and weaknesses. The separate course model is easy to employ but may be viewed as ancillary (Copeland, 1982). Margolis and Rungta (1986) have argued against the inclusion of an indefinite number of specialized courses in the counseling curriculum. Their criticisms include: (1) budget restraints make it impractical to cover all groups, (2) accenting subgroup differences may lead to the advocation of a separate set of standards and strategies (leading to a new form of racism), (3) focus on one characteristic (e.g., being Latino) may result in a failure to understand the person's total experience, (4) counselors who specialize too much may limit their employability as graduate counselors, (5) choosing which groups will receive special courses could be divisive for a counseling program, and (6) focus on separate groups could limit counselors' ability to transfer their learning from one group to another.

Margolis and Rungta (1986) suggest that, ideally, attention to the needs of diverse groups should be infused in all aspects of a counselor-education program. Unfortunately, this is probably an unrealistic goal for the near future since it would require that all faculty members have knowledge and skills for which they have not received training. Instead, these authors argue for a course that

> would include the examination of common client issues associated with membership in a special population, as well as difficulties of counselors in working with populations different from themselves. Opportunities for role play or actual counseling sessions with a variety of clients would be provided. The integrated nature of the course would allow counselors to formulate guidelines that would help them deal effectively with any unfamiliar populations with which they might work in the future. (pp. 643–644).

While the differences among ethnically diverse groups must not be ignored, they do share the common experience of oppression. As a result, many clients from ethnically diverse groups also face the common issues in counseling of identity crisis, poor self-esteem, a need for validation of personal experience, and a need for empowerment (Margolis & Rungta, 1986, p. 643).

The area of concentration and interdisciplinary model provides for an in-depth study of one or several ethnic groups but may not result in the kind of generalized understanding of ethnic and other minority groups that is the goal of cross-cultural training. The integration model meets all the goals of cross-cultural training but may be the most difficult to achieve because it requires that all the counseling faculty be sensitive to cross-cultural issues that relate to the courses they teach and be willing to incorporate these issues into their course content.

We feel that, ideally, cross-cultural issues should be integrated into all counselor training courses. We are aware, however, that most counseling faculty members have never received any training in cross-cultural counseling and that it therefore may be unrealistic to assume that the integrated model can be successful at this time. We therefore advocate that training programs employ a combination of the separate course model and a pseudo-integrated model while working toward a fully integrated model.

We feel a separate course can cover some of the important common experiences of ethnic and other oppressed groups. One of the major objectives of a cross-cultural counseling class should be to acquaint the student with etic and emic qualities of favored counseling approaches. For instance, it seems clear that rapport is a culturally generalizable element basic to all counseling interaction (Vontress, 1971, 1973, 1974, 1979). Techniques to establish rapport, however, may be culturally specific and not capable of generalization. Nondirective techniques presently taught in many training programs as rapport-building responses may actually antagonize some minorities or seem meaningless to others (Sue & Sue, 1972a). As Bryson and Bardo (1975) point out, ". . . it can no longer be assumed that techniques and strategies that are successful with one group of clients will work effectively with another group" (p. 14). Yet it would be a serious error to assume that all concepts associated with counseling theory developed to date must be discarded when working with a minority client. For instance, the learning theory principles upon which behavioral counseling is predicated presumably hold true in any culture. It seems axiomatic that operant conditioning, classical conditioning, and vicarious learning concepts apply to one culture as well as another. The ways in which these principles may manifest themselves in a variety of cultures may differ, however, and what may be a reinforcing stimulus in one culture may prove to be aversive in another.

In addition to courses specifically designated as cross-cultural counseling or multicultural counseling courses, all counselor education offerings should be revised to include minority-relevant topics. Mitchell (1971) offers a model of such a program.

Examples of Experientially Based Training Programs

Vontress (1974) has suggested that, "although a course in counseling racial and ethnic minorities may be another exciting and rewarding cognitive exposure, needed most are affective experiences designed to humanize counselors" (p. 164). The experiences that he and other authors suggest are needed are those designed to increase counselor understanding in two areas: first, to understand themselves and their previous unrecognized biases; second, to gain appreciation for the experiences of someone who is culturally different and to become open to divergent life-styles (Calia, 1966). In order to achieve these goals, "sensitive training", in which the counselor lives and works in the minority community to experience it first-hand, is recommended (Vontress, 1971).

One method for increasing counselors' understanding of themselves and their previously unrecognized biases is the Awareness Group Experience (AGE) described by Parker and McDavis (1979). AGE is a one-day structured workshop for minority and nonminority counselors (the authors recommend 15 members from each group) consisting of five sessions. Session one, *Becoming Aware,* provides for dyadic and large-group sharing of individual cross-cultural experiences. Session two, *Eliminating Stereotypes,* involves a role-played social gathering with each participant wearing an ethnic stereotypic label on his/her back followed by a group processing of the experience. In session three, *Ethnic Lunch,* participants eat together at an ethnic restaurant followed by a tour of an ethnic community. Session four, *Minority Student Perceptions of Counselors,* is designed to make counselors aware of how they are viewed by ethnic minority students. Seven to ten students are interviewed by the group leaders in a "fishbowl" procedure with the participants seated around them. In session five, *Action Plan,* the participants are divided into groups of five to develop plans for changing their negative attitudes toward ethnic minorities.

McDavis and Parker (1977) have described a course designed to help counselor-education students become aware of their attitudes toward ethnic minorities that includes AGE as one component. Other topics/experiences covered are *Facilitating Interracial Groups, Minority Student Panels, Counseling Ethnic Minorities Individually, Class Projects,* and *Ethnic Dinner.* In addition to increasing self-awareness of ethnic biases, the course is designed to help students learn to build rapport and counsel ethnic minorities individually and in groups.

The most recent cross-cultural training program developed by Parker and his associates is called the Ethnic Student Training Group (ESTG; Parker, Bingham, & Fukuyama, 1985). The ESTG is a service and training experience offered for counseling center psychologists, intern trainees, and practicum students to improve their ability to understand and counsel ethnically diverse students. The ESTG meets for one-hour sessions bimonthly and includes the following activities: (a) intercultural interaction; (b) case presentations; (c) panel presentations; (d) ethnic student walk-in; and (d) supervision.

Several authors have proposed that prior to direct experience in a cross-cultural setting, counselors in training should be exposed to simulated cross-cultural encounters. Bryson, Renzaglia, & Danish (1974) describe a simulation-training procedure designed ". . . to assist counselors in training and other human service workers to function successfully with Black citizens" (p. 219), which might be adapted to other cross-cultural situations. A counselor-trainee group is shown a number of videotaped or filmed vignettes in which actors portray the emotions associated with rejection, fear of rejection, intimacy given, and fear of intimacy (p. 219). The trainees are asked to think of the role player as a client and to respond affectively and empathically. The trainees as a group then discuss their reactions to the simulated situation. During the discussion, trainees are asked to (a) identify the role-played emotion, (b) identify their own emotional reaction, and (c) suggest alternative responses to the role-played emotion.

An intriguing simulation procedure referred to as the *Triad Model* has been described by Pedersen (1977), who views counseling as a power struggle between client and counselor and the problem. Counselor trainees are divided into teams of three in which one trainee portrays the counselor, one the client, and one the "anticounselor." The client and "anticounselor" are matched with respect to cultural factors as closely as possible and the "anticounselor's" role is to use ". . . cultural similarity with the client in order to disrupt the counselor-client cross-cultural coalition" (Pedersen, 1977, p. 95). The "anticounselor" may attempt to build a coalition with the client by privately supplying negative feedback to the client about the counselor, or may attempt to destroy a client-counselor coalition by joining the counseling interaction and attacking the counselor openly. Pedersen (1978) has also identified four skill areas (articulate the problems, anticipate resistance, diminish defensiveness, and recovery skills) covered by the *Triad Model*. He reports that this procedure has been successfully employed with both prepracticum training and in-service workshops (Pedersen, 1977, 1978). Pedersen and his associates (Pedersen, Holwill, & Shapiro, 1978) and others (Neimeyer, Fukuyama, Bingham, Hall, & Mussenden, 1986) have provided research evidence that counselors who participate in triad training increase their ability to interact empathically, genuinely, and with understanding of affective communication. A one-hour videotape consisting of four triad interviews and a training manual have been developed for use in any counselor-training program.

Lewis and Lewis (1970) propose a training model in which beginning counselors-in-training are paired with experienced counselors and placed as teams in inner-city schools to work as full-time counselors. While on-the-job experience working with disadvantaged youth would serve as the basic core of this program, didactic course work taught in participating public schools would bridge theory and practice requirements. A major objective of this training model would be to develop counselors ". . . skilled in the processes of consultation and change and group and individual counseling" (Lewis & Lewis, 1970, p. 37).

Mitchell (1971) describes a counselor training program that is similar to the Lewis-Lewis (1970) model. The program is designed to provide for a Black perspective but includes several features that could be generalized to cross-cultural situations. For instance, in implementing the new program, internships were developed in predominately minority-attended schools. Also, in addition to developing new courses aimed at understanding the Black experience, core guidance and counseling courses were designed to include minority-relevant materials. This could conceivably be done in any counselor-education program. Most programs, for instance, include the equivalent of such courses as Introduction to Guidance/Counseling, Test and Measurements, and Vocational and Educational Information. The Introduction course could include a discussion of how the promise of guidance has fallen short for minority students (Russell, 1970). The testing class could devote considerable attention to cultural test biases as well as to problems of validity and reliability (Barnes, 1972). And the Vocational class could focus on the special problems of minorities in obtaining and retaining jobs (Miller & Oetting, 1977).

Arredondo-Dowd and Gonsalves (1980) have proposed that counselor training programs should specialize in bilingual-multicultural education and "assist students in developing basic attitudes, skills, and competencies to be culturally effective counselors" (p. 659). With respect to competencies, the authors specify counseling, cultural, linguistic, and pedagogical competencies needed by counselors who work with a diverse client population.

Arredondo (1985) describes three types of cross-cultural training programs that have been implemented in American universities: (a) specifically funded projects, (b) specializations integral to existing counseling-psychology programs, and (c) continuing-education conferences. She lists the DISC (Developing Interculturally Skilled Counselors) program at the University of Hawaii as an example of the first type. For existing counseling-psychology programs that have integrated a cross-cultural focus, she lists: Boston University; Teachers College, Columbia University; the University of California, Santa Barbara; California State University, Northridge; Syracuse University; The University of Massachusetts at Amherst; and Western Washington University at Bellingham. For universities sponsoring continuing-education conferences on cross-cultural counseling, she lists Teachers College, Columbia University, and Boston University.

Ponterotto and Casas (1987) surveyed eighteen "leading multicultural counseling specialists" to determine their rankings of leading cross-cultural training programs. In order of nominations received, the five leading programs were housed at Syracuse University, Boston University, Western Washington University, University of Hawaii, and University of California, Santa Barbara. The common core elements shared by these four programs were: (1) at least one faculty member seriously committed to cross-cultural counseling research and/or training, (2) at least one course on multicultural issues is offered, and (3) more racial-ethnic diversity on the faculty and student body than is typical at most training programs.

Training for Activist Roles Needed

The major challenge in the future to counselor education vis-à-vis minority group/cross-cultural counseling is the establishment within the profession of activist alternatives to the traditional counseling role. Until such time as counselor-education programs define outreach, consultation, ombudsmun, change agent, and facilitator of indigenous support-systems roles as viable alternatives to time-bound, space-bound, personal-social counseling, it seems unlikely these roles will be accepted and implemented by the profession in general (Atkinson, Froman, Romo, & Mayton, 1977). Counselor education's long-standing love affair with the intrapsychic model of client problems must cool, and the effects of an oppressive society be acknowledged, before counseling as a profession will achieve credibility with a large portion of the minority populations.

Counseling Research

Sattler (1970) reviewed the research concerned with the effect of *experimenter* race on experimentation, testing, interviewing, and psychology, and found only three studies related to counselor-client interaction. While a number of studies have been carried out since Sattler completed his review (see subsequent reviews by Abramowitz & Murray, 1983; Atkinson, 1983b, 1985; Casas, 1984, 1985; Harrison, 1975; Sattler, 1977), empirical research in this area is still generally lacking. Several reasons for the relative paucity of research concerned with minority group/cross-cultural counseling present themselves. One possibility is that a majority-controlled counseling research establishment has simply not viewed minority status as an important factor in counseling. Counselor-educators and researchers who espouse an etic counseling approach may feel cultural factors in counseling play a subordinate role to counseling techniques in affecting counseling outcome.

Another reason may be that majority researchers believe that the topic is a highly controversial issue and prefer to conduct research on less controversial subjects. As Gardner (1971) points out, ". . . many blacks have called for a moratorium on all further efforts by white investigators to study and explain the psychological and social characteristics of blacks" (p. 78). Similar requests have been made by other minority professionals who believe that forays by majority researchers into minority cultures have resulted in reinforced stereotypes rather than enlightened understanding. While aimed primarily at researchers in sociology and psychology who have attempted to explain minority behavior in terms of deviance from majority norms, the attitude that the majority researcher–minority subject combination is destined to produce distorted, biased results has obviously become generalized to counseling psychology.

Furthermore, individual members of various minority groups have grown increasingly resistant to research and refuse to serve as subjects (Sue & Sue, 1972b). Black males are understandably reluctant to participate in any activity that smacks of experimentation. Perhaps the most tragic abuse of research with human subjects in this country occurred when four hundred Black men identified during the 1930s as having syphilis were allowed to suffer its effects without treatment (infamously known as the Tuskegee experiment). At least forty-eight of these men died, and numerous others were permanently maimed as a direct result of the disease. A number of other studies with potentially harmful effects have been conducted on inmates (a majority of whom are members of racial/ethnic minorities) in federal and state prisons either without the subject's knowledge or with direct or indirect coercion.

Proposed Research Model for Minority Group/Cross-Cultural Research

The suggestion has been made that the impacts of the preconceptions or prejudices of the experimenter on cross-cultural counseling research can be minimized when the researcher feels "comfortably polycultural" (Vontress, 1976, p. 2). We feel that the danger of cultural bias on the part of a single researcher, no matter what his/her race, socioeconomic background, sex, sexual orientation, etc., is unavoidable. It seems unlikely that any researcher has totally escaped the impact of cultural stereotyping that may be present as unrecognized bias in the design, implementation, and/or data analysis of a research project.

The possibility of unrecognized bias can be reduced, however, when research teams are composed of at least one representative from each cultural group included in the study. We are proposing, in effect, whenever two or more cultural groups are represented in a research design, that each group have an advocate on the research team who is likely to be sensitive to cultural bias. Objectivity might also be enhanced if the research team included a person whose cultural background was not directly related to the variables under study. Thus, a research team examining the effectiveness of Black or White counselors with Black or White clients might include an Asian American researcher as well as Black and White investigators.

The American Psychological Association hosted a conference on professional training at Vail, Colorado, in 1973; on that occasion one recommendation developed was that ". . . counseling of persons of culturally diverse backgrounds by persons who are not trained or competent to work with such groups should be regarded as unethical" (Pedersen, 1976, p. 35). We would like to recommend that a similar ethical restriction be placed on minority group/cross-cultural researchers.

Other steps that can be taken to reduce cultural bias in cross-cultural counseling research include having a member(s) of the ethnic group(s) be studied on the human subjects committee that reviews the research, the funding review committee if it is a funded study, and the journal editorial board if the study description is submitted for publication. When members of the group(s) being studied do not already sit on these reviewing agencies, the reviewing agency should be required to appoint ad hoc members for the review of cross-cultural studies.

Areas Where Research Is Needed

Some barriers and benefits resulting from cross-cultural counseling were presented in the first chapter. For the most part, these variables have been identified through clinical observation, with little solid research evidence to support their effect on the counseling relationship. Research is needed to establish this effect, then to determine how benefits can be maximized and obstacles minimized. Also, since much of the writing in this area has been done by Black theorists, research is needed to determine if these factors can be generalized and applied to other cultures.

Research is also needed to determine the etic quality of current counseling approaches. What are the underlying assumptions of behavioral counseling, transactional analysis, gestalt therapy, rational emotive therapy, reality therapy, existential approaches to counseling, which apply to all cultures? Which techniques based on these assumptions are equally applicable to all cultures? What assumptions are obviously not applicable to all cultures, and what implications does this have for associated techniques?

What are the emic solutions to psychological problems that have been developed within the various cultures in American society? How can counseling be used to increase the effectiveness of these procedures? Draguns (1976) argues that both etic and emic counseling approaches are needed and that both ". . . are equally valid and complimentary. . . . The crucial thing is to recognize these orientations for what they are; practical and conceptual pitfalls appear only when the etic orientation is mistaken for the emic or vice versa" (p. 3). Research is sorely needed that identifies etic and emic qualities of current counseling procedures.

Research that examines the effect of membership group and attitude similarity on counseling process and outcome also appears promising. The relationship of racial, sexual, socioeconomic, religious, and sexual orientation similarities to counseling effectiveness is yet to be determined. The relationship of membership group and attitudinal similarities to the nature of the client's problems in a variety of dimensions (related or unrelated to client minority status, personal-social-educational-vocational, internal-external locus of problem) needs to be assessed. Given membership group dissimilarity, how can attitudinal similarity be communicated by the counselor? One interesting hypothesis that needs testing is that when the counselor responds with empathy, he/she is perceived by the client as holding similar values. If so, are there more effective ways of communicating attitudinal similarity?

Finally, research is needed to assess the effectiveness of activist counseling roles when dealing with minority clientele. Are counselors who serve as ombudsmuns, change agents, etc., actually perceived by minority clients as more helpful than counselors who function in a more traditional role? More important, what is the actual impact of counselors functioning in these roles?

If this book helps to stimulate research activity in these and other areas related to minority group/cross-cultural counseling, it will have served an important purpose. We are optimistic that the barriers to cross-cultural counseling can be bridged.

References

Abramowitz, S. I., & Murray, J. (1983). Race effects in psychotherapy. In J. Murray & P. R. Abramson (Eds.), *Bias in psychotherapy* (pp. 215–255). New York: Praeger.

Accreditation procedures manual and application. (1988). Alexandria, Va.: Council for Accreditation of Counseling and Related Educational Programs.

Anderson, N. J., & Love, B. (1973). Psychological education for racial awareness. *Personnel and Guidance Journal, 51,* 666–670.

Arredondo, P. (1985). Cross-cultural counselor education and training. In P. Pederson (Ed.), *Handbook of cross-cultural counseling and therapy.* Westport, Conn.: Greenwood Press.

Arredondo-Dowd, P. M., & Gonsalves, J. (1980). Preparing culturally effective counselors. *Personnel and Guidance Journal, 58,* 657–661.

Atkinson, D. R. (1981). Selection and training for human rights counseling. *Counselor Education and Supervision, 21,* 101–108.

Atkinson, D. R. (1983). Ethnic minority representation in counselor education. *Counselor Education and Supervision, 23,* 7–19. (a)

Atkinson, D. R. (1983). Ethnic similarity in counseling psychology: A review of research. *The Counseling Psychologist, 11*(3), 79–92. (b)

Atkinson, D. R. (1985). A meta-review of research on cross-cultural counseling and psychotherapy. *Journal of Multicultural Counseling and Development, 13,* 138–153.

Atkinson, D. R., Froman, T., Romo, J., & Mayton, D. M. II. (1977). The role of the counselor as a social activist: Who supports it? *The School Counselor, 25,* 85–91.

Atkinson, D. R., Staso, D., & Hosford, R. (1978). Selecting counselor trainees with multicultural strengths: A solution to the Bakke decision crisis. *Personnel and Guidance Journal, 56,* 546–549.

Atkinson, D. R., & Wampold, B. (1981). Affirmative action efforts of counselor education programs. *Counselor Education and Supervision, 20,* 262–272.

Bales, J. (1985). Minority training falls short. *APA Monitor, 16*(11), 7.

Banks, W. (1972). The Black client and the helping professionals. In R. I. Jones (Ed.), *Black psychology.* New York: Harper & Row.

Barnes, E. J. (1972). Cultural retardation or shortcomings of assessment techniques? In R. L. Jones (Ed.), *Black psychology.* New York: Harper & Row.

Bernal, M. E. (1980). Hispanic issues in psychology: Curricula and training. *Hispanic Journal of Behavioral Sciences, 2,* 129–146.

Bernal, M. E., & Padilla, A. M. (1982). Status of minority curricula and training in clinical psychology. *American Psychologist, 37,* 780–787.

Bexelius, A. (1968). The ombudsman for civil affairs. In D. C. Rowat (Ed.), *The ombudsman: Citizen's defender.* Toronto: University of Toronto Press.

Blocker, D. H., & Rapoza, R. (1972). A systematic eclectic model in counseling-consulting. *Elementary School Guidance and Counseling, 7,* 106–112.

Bryson, S., & Bardo, H. (1975). Race and the counseling process: An overview. *Journal of Non-White Concerns in Personnel and Guidance, 4,* 5–15.

Bryson, S., Renzaglia, G. A., & Danish, S. (1974). Training counselors through simulated racial encounters. *Journal of Non-White Concerns in Personnel and Guidance, 3,* 218–223.

Calia, V. F. (1966). The culturally deprived client: A re-formulation of the counselor's role. *Journal of Counseling Psychology, 13,* 100–105.

Carkhuff, R. R. (1971). *The development of human resources.* San Francisco: Holt, Rinehart, & Winston.

Casas, J. M. (1984). Policy, training and research in counseling psychology: The racial/ethnic minority perspective. In S. Brown & R. Lent (Eds.), *Handbook of counseling psychology* (pp. 785–831). New York: John Wiley.

Casas, J. M. (1985). A reflection of the status of racial/ethnic minority research. *Counseling Psychologist, 13*(4), 581–598.

Cayleff, S. E. (1986). Ethical issues in counseling, gender, race, and culturally distinct groups. *Journal of Counseling and Development,* 345–347.

Ciavarella, M. A., & Doolittle, L. W. (1970). The Ombudsman: Relevant role model for the counselor. *The School Counselor, 17,* 331–336.

Committee on Accreditation. (1980). *Accreditation handbook.* Washington, DC: American Psychological Association.

Copeland, E. J. (1982). Minority populations and traditional counseling programs: Some alternatives. *Counselor Education and Supervision, 21,* 187–193.

Copeland, E. J. (1983). Cross-cultural counseling and psychotherapy: A historical perspective, implications for research and training. *Personnel and Guidance Journal, 62,* 10–15.

Draguns, J. G. (1976). Counseling across cultures: Common themes and distinct approaches. In P. B. Pedersen, W. J. Lonner, & J. G. Draguns (Eds.), *Counseling across cultures.* Honolulu: The University of Hawaii Press.

Gardner, L. H. (1971). The therapeutic relationship under varying conditions of race. *Psychotherapy: Theory, Research and Practice, 8* (1), 78–87.

Gravitz, H. L., & Woods, E. (1976). A multiethnic approach to peer counseling. *Professional Psychology, 8,* 229–235.

Grevious, C. (1985). The role of the family therapist with low-income Black families. *Family Therapy, 12,* 115–122.

Haettenschwiller, D. L. (1971). Counseling black college students in special programs. *Personnel & Guidance Journal, 50,* 29–35.

Harrison, D. K. (1975). Race as a counselor-client variable in counseling and psychotherapy: a review of the research. *Counseling Psychologist, 51*(1), 124–133.

Ivey, A. E. (1976). *Counseling psychology, the psychoeducator model and the future.* Paper prepared for APA Division 17 Professional Affairs Committee.

Jones, L. K. (1976). A national survey of the program and enrollment characteristics of counselor education programs. *Counselor Education and Supervision, 15,* 166–176.

Katz, J. H., & Ivey, A. (1977). White awareness: The frontier of racism awareness training. *Personnel and Guidance Journal, 55,* 485–489.

Kennedy, C. D., & Wagner, N. N. (1979). Psychology and affirmative action: 1977. *Professional Psychology, 10,* 234–243.

Korchin, S. J. (1981). Clinical psychology and minority problems. *American Psychologist, 35,* 262–269.

Lewis, M. D., & Lewis, J. A. (1970). Relevant training for relevant roles: A model for educating inner-city counselors. *Counselor Education and Supervision, 10,* 31–38.

Lewis, M. D., & Lewis, J. A. (1977). The counselor's impact on community environments. *Personnel and Guidance Journal, 55,* 356–358.

Maes, W. R., & Rinaldi, J. R. (1974). Counseling the Chicano child. *Elementary School Guidance and Counseling, 9,* 279–284.

Margolis, R. L., & Rungta, S. A. (1986). Training counselors for work with special populations: A second look. *Journal of Counseling and Development, 64,* 642–644.

McDavis, R. J., & Parker, W. M. (1977). A course on counseling ethnic minorities: A model. *Counselor Education and Supervision, 17,* 146–148.

Miller, C. D., & Oetting, G. (1977). Barriers to employment and the disadvantaged. *Personnel and Guidance Journal, 56,* 89–93.

Mitchell, H. (1971). Counseling black students: A model in response to the need for relevant counselor training programs. *The Counseling Psychologist, 2* (4), 117–122. (a)

Mitchell, H. (1971). The black experience in higher education. *The Counseling Psychologist, 2* (1), 30–36, (b)

Neimeyer, G. J., Fukuyama, M. A., Bingham, R. P., Hall, L. E., & Mussenden, M. E. (1986). Training cross-cultural counselors: A comparison of the pro-counselor and anti-counselor triad models. *Journal of Counseling and Development, 64,* 437–439.

Padilla, E. R., Boxley, R., & Wagner, N. (1973). The desegregation of clinical psychology training. *Professional Psychology, 4,* 259–265.

Parham, W., & Moreland, J. R. (1981). Nonwhite students in counseling psychology: A closer look. *Professional Psychology, 12,* 499–507.

Parker, W. M., Bingham, R. P., & Fukuyama, M. (1985). Improving cross-cultural effectiveness of counselor trainees. *Counselor Education and Supervision, 24,* 349–352.

Parker, W. M., & McDavis, R. J. (1979). An awareness experience: Toward counseling minorities. *Counselor Education and Supervision, 18,* 312–317.

Pedersen, P. B. (1976). The field of intercultural counseling. In P. Pedersen, W. J. Lonner, & J. G. Draguns (Eds.), *Counseling across cultures.* Honolulu: The University of Hawaii Press.

Pedersen, P. B. (1977). The triad model of cross-cultural counselor training. *Personnel and Guidance Journal, 56,* 94–100.

Pedersen, P. B. (1978). Four dimensions of cross-cultural skill in counselor training. *Personnel and Guidance Journal, 56,* 480–484.

Pedersen, P. B., Holwill, C. F., & Shapiro, J. (1978). A cross-cultural training procedure for classes in counselor education. *Counselor Education and Supervision, 17,* 233–237.

Pine, G. J. (1972). Counseling minority groups: A review of the literature. *Counseling and Values, 17,* 35–44.

Ponterotto, J. G. (1987). Counseling Mexican Americans: A multimodel approach. *Journal of Counseling and Development, 65,* 308–312.

Ponterotto, J. G., & Casas, J. M. (1987). In search of multicultural competence within counselor education programs. *Journal of Counseling and Development, 65,* 430–434.

Rowe, W., Murphy, H. B., & DeCsipkes, R. A. (1975). The relationship of counselor characteristics and counseling effectiveness. *Review of Educational* Research, *45,* 231–246.

Russell, R. D. (1970). Black perception of guidance. *Personnel and Guidance Journal, 48,* 721–728.

Russo, N. F., Olmedo, E. L., Stapp, J., & Fulcher, R. (1981). Women and minorities in psychology. *American Psychologist, 36,* 1315–1363.

Sattler, J. M. (1970). Racial experimenter effects in experimentation, testing, interviewing and psychotherapy. *Psychological Bulletin, 73,* 137–160.

Sattler, J. M. (1977). The effects of therapist-client racial similarity. In A. S. Burman & A. M. Razin (Eds.), *Effective psychotherapy* (pp. 252–290). New York: Pergamon Press.

Smith, E. M. J. (1985). Ethnic minorities: Life stress, social support, and mental health issues. *The Counseling Psychologist, 13,* 537–579.

Strong, D. J., & Peele, D. (1977). The status of minorities in psychology. In E. L. Olmedo & S. Lopez (Eds.), *Hispanic mental health professionals.* Los Angeles: Spanish Speaking Mental Health Research Center.

Sue, D. W. (1973). Ethnic identity: The impact of two cultures on the psychological development of Asians in America. In S. Sue & N. N. Wagner (Eds.), *Asian Americans: Psychological perspectives.* Ben Lomand, Calif.: Science and Behavior Books, Inc., 140–149.

Sue, D. W., Bernier, J. E., Durran, A., Feinberg, L., Pedersen, P., Smith, E. J., & Vasquez-Nuttal, E. (1982). Position paper: Cross-cultural counseling competencies. *The Counseling Psychologist, 10*(2), 45–52.

Sue, D. W., & Sue, S. (1972). Counseling Chinese-Americans. *Personnel and Guidance Journal, 50,* 637–644. (a)

Sue, D. W., & Sue, S. (1972). Ethnic minorities: Resistance to being researched. *Professional Psychology, 3,* 11–17. (b)

Sue, S., Akutsu, P. D., & Higashi, C. (1985). Training issues in conducting therapy with ethnic-minority-group clients. In P. Pederson (Ed.), *Handbook of cross-cultural counseling and therapy.* Westport, Conn.: Greenwood Press.

Sue, S., & Zane, N. (1987). The role of culture and cultural techniques in psychotherapy: A critique and reformulation. *American Psychologist, 42,* 37–45.

Torrey, E. F. (1970). Mental health services for American Indians and Eskimos. *Community Mental Health Journal, 6,* 455–463.

Vontress, C. E. (1971). Racial differences: Impediments to rapport. *Journal of Counseling Psychology, 18* (1), 7–13.

Vontress, C. E. (1973). Counseling: Racial and ethnic factors. *Focus on Guidance, 5,* 1–10.

Vontress, C. E. (1974) Barriers in cross-cultural counseling. *Counseling and Value, 18*(3), 160–165.

Vontress, C. E. (1976). Racial and ethnic barriers in counseling. In P. B. Pedersen, W. J. Lonner, & J. G. Draguns (Eds.), *Counseling across cultures.* Honolulu: The University of Hawaii Press.

Vontress, C. E. (1979). Cross-cultural counseling: An existential approach. *Personnel and Guidance Journal, 58,* 117–122.

Walton, J. M. (1979). Retention, role modeling, and academic readiness: A perspective on the ethnic minority student in higher education. *Personnel and Guidance Journal, 58,* 125–127.

Waltz, G. R. & Benjamin, L. (1977). *On becoming a change agent.* Ann Arbor: Eric Counseling and Personnel Services Information Center.

Ward, E. J. (1970). A gift from the ghetto. *Personnel and Guidance Journal, 48,* 753–756.

Weinrach, S. (1973). Integration is more than just busing. *The School Counselor, 20,* 276–279.

Williams, R. L., & Kirkland, J. (1971). The white counselor and the black client. *The Counseling Psychologist, 2,* 114–116.

Wilson, W., & Calhoun, J. F. (1974). Behavior therapy and the minority client. *Psychotherapy: Theory, Research and Practice, 11* (4), 317–325.

Woods, E. (1977). Counseling minority students: A program model. *Personnel and Guidance Journal, 55,* 416–418.

Appendix A Position Paper
Cross-cultural Counseling Competencies
Education and Training Committee
Division 17, American Psychological Association
January 1981

Derald Wing Sue, Chairperson
California State University-Hayward

Joseph E. Bernier, College of St. Rose
Anna Durran, Columbia University
Lawrence Feinberg, University of California, Berkeley
Paul Pedersen, University of Hawaii
Elsie J. Smith, State University of New York, Buffalo
Ena Vasquez-Nuttall, University of Massachusetts, Amherst

Ever since the 1960s, counseling and psychotherapy have been challenged as to the appropriateness of the services they offer to minority clients. A barrage of criticism have been leveled against traditional counseling practices as being demanding, irrelevant, and oppressive toward the culturally different. Admonitions to develop new methods, concepts, and services more appropriate to the life experiences of minority clients have been plentiful. Yet, many mental health educators continue to argue the merits of including curriculum on ethnic minority groups, and/or incorporating ethnic content into existing courses.

The purpose of this position paper is threefold. First, we would like to outline and challenge some prevalent myths and misunderstandings which have made it difficult to develop appropriate curricula, and relevant counseling/therapy competencies for the culturally different in the United States. Second, we would like to begin the much needed task of defining the term "cross-cultural counseling/therapy" which has been increasingly used in the literature. Last, we would like to recommend the adoption of specific cross-cultural counseling and therapy competencies by the American Psychological Association to be used as a guideline for accreditation criteria.

The Need for a Cross-Cultural Perspective:

Myths and Misunderstandings

One of the main arguments proposed against the need for a cross-cultural perspective in the mental health profession has been *the belief that current research strategies and approaches as well as mental health practices are*

Reprinted with permission from *The Counseling Psychologist,* 1982, *10*(2), 45–52.

adequate and appropriate in application to various minority groups. This assumption can be seriously challenged when a thorough review of the counseling and mental health literature is undertaken. Below are listed documentation that support this point.

1. Many writers have noted that the mental health literature and specifically research have failed to create a realistic understanding of various ethnic groups in America (Bryde, 1971; Sue & Sue, 1972; Thomas & Sillen, 1972; Williams, 1970; Smith, 1973; Padilla & Ruiz, 1974; Sumada, 1975). The social sciences have generally ignored the study of certain ethnic groups in the United States (D. W. Sue, 1975), and/or tended to reinforce a negative view by concentrating on the pathological aspects of minorities (Billingsley, 1970; E. R. Padilla, 1971; Trimble, 1976; D. W. Sue, 1981). When reading the literature, one gets the impression that the difficulties encountered by minorities are due to intrinsic factors such as racial inferiority, incompatible value systems, and/or inherent pathological forces. Thus, the portrayal of the culturally different in literature has generally taken the form of stereotyping them as "deficient" in certain "desirable" attributes. Minorities have generally been perceived as deficient genetically (the genetic deficient model) and/or culturally (the culturally deficient model). That the genetic deficient model still exists can be seen in the writings of Shuey (1966), Jensen (1969), Hernstein (1971), and Shockley (1972). The position of these writers have been used to support the view that Blacks are genetically inferior and that the accumulation of weak or low intelligence genes in the Black population should be seriously curtailed by not allowing Blacks to bear children.

Even more disturbing has been recent allegations that Cyril Burt, imminent British psychologist, fabricated data to support his contention that intelligence is inherited and that Blacks have inherited inferior brains (Dorfman, 1978; Kamin, 1974; Gillie, 1978). To many minorities, the Cyril Burt fiasco may represent another instance of so-called "scientific racism." The question as to whether or not there are differences between races and intelligence is both a complex and emotional one. Besides the difficulty in defining "race," there exists questionable assumptions regarding whether research on the intelligence of whites can be generalized to other groups, whether middle class and lower class minorities grow up in similar environments to middle and lower class whites, and whether instruments are valid for both minority and white subjects. More importantly, we should recognize that the "average values" of different populations tell us nothing about any one individual. Yet, much of the social science literature continues to portray ethnic minorities as being genetically deficient in one sense or another.

It is important to note that even well-meaning social scientists who challenged the genetic deficient model, and who place heavy reliance on environmental factors were victims to their own cultural biases. Instead of an emphasis on genetics, terms such as culturally "disadvantaged," "deficient" or "deprived" were used. What occurred in the social science literature was that the biological differences that were originally proposed to cause the differences were now shifted to the lifestyles or values of various ethnic groups (Baratz & Baratz, 1970; Sumada, 1975; Smith 1977). The term "culturally deprived" was inadequate because it meant to lack a cultural background which is contradictory, because everyone inherits a culture. Such terms tend to cause conceptual and theoretical confusions that may adversely affect social planning, educational policy and research. Even more disturbing is the assumption that cultural deprivation is synonymously equated with deviation from and superiority of white middle class values.

2. Western-based social sciences have generally prided themselves on the objectivity of research and its findings. Yet, it has become increasingly clear that what a researcher proposes to study and how he/she interprets such findings are intimately linked to a personal, professional, and societal value system. As we saw in the previous discussion, these societal values may affect the interpretation of data as it relates to minorities. A similar analogy can be drawn with respect to the counseling profession. For example, the profession's preoccupation with pathology tends to encourage study of deficits and weaknesses rather than strengths or assets. Racist attitudes, biases and prejudices may intensify this narrow view as minorities may be portrayed in professional journals as neurotic, psychotic, psychopathic and/or parolees instead of a well-rounded person.

Additionally, the Western approach in research has stressed the experimental design as the epitome of the "scientific method." Associated with this emphasis are characteristics of control, manipulation, and a linear analytic approach. D. W. Sue (1981) has indicated how these characteristics may oftentimes clash with the world views and cultural perspectives of different ethnic groups.

3. Many mental health professions have noted that racial and ethnic factors may act as impediments to counseling and psychotherapy (Carkhuff & Pierce, 1967; Vontress, 1971; D. W. Sue, 1975; Ruiz & Padilla, 1977). Misunderstandings can oftentimes arise from cultural variations in communications that may lead to alienation and/or inability to develop trust and rapport. This may result in an early termination of therapy (Yamamoto, James & Palley, 1968). In a comprehensive study conducted in the state of Washington, S. Sue and Associates (Sue, McKinney, Allen & Hall, 1974; Sue & McKinney, 1975; Sue, Allen, & Conaway, 1978) have found supporting evidence that Asian Americans, Blacks, Hispanics and American Indians terminate therapeutic services after only one contact at a rate greater than 50%. This is in sharp contrast to a 30% termination rate for Anglo clients. These investigators along with others have concluded that it may be inappropriateness of interpersonal transactions that might

account for the premature termination. D. W. Sue (1981) points out that language barriers which often exist between the counselor and client, classbound values which indicate that counselors conduct treatment within the value system of the middle class, and culture-bound values which are used to judge normality and abnormality seriously hinder and distort the counseling therapy process. That counseling and psychotherapy are handmaidens of the status quo and transmitters of society's values lead many minorities to believe that the mental health profession is engaged in a form of cultural oppression. In reviewing the minority-group literature on counseling, Pine (1972) found the following views to be representative of those held by many minority individuals:

> that it is a waste of time; that counselors are deliberately shunting minority students into deadend nonacademic programs regardless of student potential, preferences, or ambitions; that counselors discourage students from applying to college; that counselors are insensitive to the needs of students in the community; that counselors do not give the same amount of energy and time in working with minorities as they do with white middle class students; that counselors do not accept, respect, and understand cultural differences; that counselors are arrogant and contemptuous; and that counselors don't know how to deal with their own hangups. (p. 35)

These three points are at odds with the myth that current research and mental health practices are adequate for all ethnic groups and that a cross-cultural perspective is not needed. We need a perspective that allows us to present a balanced realistic picture of minorities in the U.S. For example, much can be learned from the current help-giving networks that exist in minority communities, from the manner in which racial/ethnic minorities have dealt with racism, and from the positive aspects of being bicultural. Indeed, since most minorities are bicultural/bilingual, they are in an advantaged position where cross-cultural counseling is needed. It is ironic that in our society, the social psychological forces continue to reward a monolingual/monocultural orientation which would prove limiting to effective cross-cultural interactions.

Another myth that tends to be prevalent in the counseling and mental health profession is that *ethnic cultural issues are only the province of a select few individuals who are considered experts in the field because it applies to a small segment of the population.* Traditionally, counseling and clinical psychology has emphasized the importance of self-understanding as an important component in the development of therapists. Espin (1979) points out how little attention has been given to the importance of the trainee's own ethnicity, cultural biases and prejudices. When these issues are addressed, people believe that they are more appropriate for "minorities" than "Mainstream" counselors/therapists. This position is a fallacy and deprives practitioners and their clients of an understanding of psychological and developmental processes that influence ethnicity.

Ethnicity and culture is a function of every person's development and not limited only to "minorities." Espin (1979) states

> If counselors can acquire a greater understanding of their own ethnicity and its overt and covert influences on their personalities and interpersonal styles, they will be better able to recognize the ways in which ethnic background influence different individual behavior, peer interaction, values and life goals of counselors. (p. 1)

It is also important for us to realize that we live in a multicultural, multilingual and pluralistic society. It is infrequent that we have no contact with people whose cultural backgrounds or lifestyles differs from our own. In one way or another we are bound to interact with individuals who can be classified as "culturally different" and it is our responsibility as practicing psychologists to become more culturally aware and sensitive to our work with different populations. For example, it is estimated that by 1990 over half the population of the state of California will be members of minority groups.

Another reason for a cross-cultural perspective in counseling is the possible scientific contributions it would make to our field (S. Sue, 1980). *The practice of counseling and psychotherapy assumes a universality of psychological theories and concepts.* In many ways, the study of culturally different groups tests the limits and generalities of psychological theories in mental health practices. In traditional assumptions and theories of mental health are valid across cultures and situations, then they constitute "universals." Likewise, means of conducting treatment and or delivering services that are effective with the diverse range of client types would indicate its universal applicability. In the absence of a culturally diverse population of study, it is difficult to know when universals have been found, or when techniques and assumptions are culturally specific. Triandis (1972) indicated the importance of the problems in differentiating etic (universal) and emic (culture specific) phenomena in cross-cultural research. To the extent that the Western theories, assessment procedures, treatment approaches, and research methods are inappropriate for different cultural groups, they must be modified (Brislin, Lonner & Thorndike, 1973).

While we have moved a long way from the "individual centered" approaches of counseling and psychotherapy, the prevalent orientation is still upon the individual. *The belief in "rugged individualism" and that the person is totally responsible for his or her own lot in life* hinders a more realistic understanding of the influence of culture and the sociopolitical influences. As pointed out by D. W. Sue (1981), an overemphasis on the "individual" oftentimes leads to a person-blame orientation while minimizing the contributions of the sociopolitical system. A cross-cultural perspective in mental health work will begin to increase our awareness of the cultural-environmental-contextual perspective on mental health as proposed by Ivey & Authier (1978). It is not enough to study solely different cultural groups in the United States without understanding the sociopolitical history that minorities have undergone. The history and experiences of the culturally different have been the history of oppression, discrimination, and racism (D. W. Sue, 1981). Institutional racism has created psychological barriers among minorities that are likely to interfere with the counseling/therapy process. Feelings of powerlessness, inferiority, subordination, deprivation, anger and rage, and overt/covert resistance to factors in interracial relationships are likely to occur and must be dealt with in the counseling/therapy context. It is inappropriate and a fallacy to consider that these issues can be simply dealt with through study of the individual or just cultural differences. It is precisely the interaction of the cultural apsects with the sociopolitical system which creates many of the dilemmas of oppression, racism, etc.

Definition of Cross-Cultural Counseling/Therapy

Cross-cultural counseling/therapy may be defined as any counseling relationship in which two or more of the participants differ with respect to cultural background, values, and lifestyle. In most cases, the mental health practitioner is generally a member of the majority group and the client is a minority group member or international (a citizen of another country). This definition of cross-cultural counseling also includes situations in which both the counselor/therapist and client are minority individuals, but represent different minority groups (Black-Hispanic, Asian-American–American Indian, Puerto Rican–Black, and so forth). It also includes situations in which the counselor/therapist is a minority person and the client a majority person (Black counselor–white client, Chicano counselor–white client, etc.). Additionally, it may include situations in which the counselor/therapist and client are racially and ethnically similar but may belong to different cultural groups because of other variables such as sex, sexual orientation, socioeconomic factors, religious orientation, and age (white male–white female, Black straight person–Black gay, poor Asian American–wealthy Asian American, etc.) (Atkinson, Morten & D. W. Sue, 1979). In measurement terms, the degree of counselor/therapist–client similarity or dissimilarity in terms of cultural background, values and lifestyles would be the key determinants in discussing cross-cultural counseling/therapy.

The concept of cross-cultural counseling/therapy presented here will no doubt stimulate much debate and discussion. To recognize too many differences might (a) dilute our focus and intent, and/or (b) make all counseling/therapy cross-cultural. However, we recognize that every counseling/therapy interaction is slightly cross-cultural; this recognition may be a source of strength rather than an impediment. What we need to acknowledge is the relative importance and power of each variable in affecting the counseling relationship.

While we do not want to be guilty of focusing upon the negative aspects of a cross-cultural counseling situation, the reality is that in most cases, counseling a person from a culturally different background poses major problems. In a cross-cultural counseling situation, differences between the counselor and client may potentially block, either partially or wholly, a counselor's (a) true understanding of the client's situation, difficulties or strengths; (b) ability to empathize with and understand the world view of the client; and (c) ability to utilize culturally relevant counseling/therapy modes. Cross-cultural counseling problems are most likely to occur when there is a low degree of client-counselor assumed similarity in terms of their respective backgrounds, values and life-styles. Because cross-cultural counseling has been defined in terms of assumed dissimilarity between the counselor and the client, the importance of sociopolitical interpretations of differences must also be an intimate part of the definition. In discussing cross-cultural counseling effectiveness, D. W. Sue (1981) has stated that individuals who share the same world view as their clients are most likely to be helpful. World views are frequently correlated with a person's cultural/racial heritage, ethnic identification and experiences in society. There are many complexities in this statement as many of these variables may conflict with one another. For example, attitudinal/belief similarity tends to facilitate cross-cultural counseling by enhancing counselor credibility and attractiveness. Yet, membership group similarity also tends to facilitate cross-cultural counseling, because it also enhances counselor credibility and attractiveness. Whether membership group similarity is more important than attitudinal similarity in cross-cultural counseling depends on many variables and becomes an empirical question.

Cross-Cultural Counseling Competencies

There is now a growing awareness that the human service professions including counseling and clinical psychology have failed to meet the particular mental health needs of ethnic minorities (Sue, D. W., 1981; Korman, 1973; Dulles Conference, 1978). Most graduate programs give inadequate treatment to mental health issues of ethnic minorities (McFadden & Wilson, 1977). Cultural influences affecting personality formation and the manifestation of behavior disorders are infrequently part of mental health training programs (D. W. Sue, 1981). When minority group experiences are discussed, they are generally seen and analyzed from the "white middle class perspective" (Smith, 1977). As a result, professionals who deal with mental health problems of ethnic minorities lack understanding and knowledge about ethnic values and their consequent interaction with an oppressive society. It is this very issue of cultural encapsulation and its detrimental affects on minorities which have generated training recommendations from the 1973 Vail Conference

(Korman, 1973), Austin conference (1975), and the Dulles Conference (1978). All of these conferences noted the serious lack and inadequacy of psychology training programs in dealing with religious, racial, ethnic, sexual and economic groups. Selected recommendations included advocating (a) that professional psychology training programs at all levels provide information on the potential political nature of the practice of psychology, (b) that professionals need to "own" their value positions, (c) that client populations ought to be involved in helping to determine what is "done to them," (d) that education and training programs include not only the content, but also an evaluation of its graduates, and (e) that continuing professional development occur beyond the receipt of any advanced degree.

A recognition of these serious inadequacies and needs in cross-cultural training of mental health professionals have led to the creation of an APA Board of Ethnic Minority Affairs voted upon by APA members in 1980. The new board is charged with formulating policy recommendations and initiating activities related to issues which impinge directly on American Indians/Alaskan Natives, Asians/Pacific Americans, Blacks and Hispanics. The board is expected to focus on three major areas of research, training, and service delivery, and to conduct several major activities that include the following: (a) increasing scientific understanding of psychology that pertain to culture and ethnicity; (b) increasing the quality and quantity of educational and training opportunities for ethnic minority persons in psychology; (c) promoting the development of culturally sensitive models for the delivery of psychological services; and (d) serving as a clearing house for the collection and dissemination of information relevant to or pertaining to ethnic minority psychologists and students (True, 1980). There are several other recommendations and charges which deal specifically with organizational factors among the various ethnic groups. However, our focus is primarily concerned with those points outlined above.

One of the most important recommendations and themes arising from the numerous conferences listed above and from the formation of the Board of Ethnic Minority Affairs was the importance of identifying and assessing competencies of psychologists as they relate to the culturally different. The importance of providing educational experiences that generate sensitivity to, and the appreciation of the history, current needs, strengths, and resources of minority communities was stressed. Students and faculty members should be helped to understand the development and behavior of the group being studied, thus enabling them to (a) use their knowledge to develop skills in working with minority groups; and (b) develop strategies to modify the effects of political, social and economic forces on minority groups. The curriculum must focus on immediate social needs and problems. It must stimulate an awareness of minority issues caused by economic, social and educational deprivation. The curriculum must also be designed to stimulate this awareness not solely on a cognitive level. It must enable individuals to understand feelings of helplessness and powerlessness, low self-esteem, poor self-concept, and how they contribute to low motivation, frustration, hatred, ambivalence, and apathy. In addition, curriculum should present a balanced positive picture of minority groups. The contributions of various ethnic/racial minorities, their strengths and assets, the legitimacy of their

Table 1
Characteristics of the Culturally Skilled Counseling Psychologist

Beliefs/Attitudes	1. The culturally skilled counseling psychologist is one who has moved from being culturally unaware to being aware and sensitive to his/her own cultural heritage and to valuing and respecting differences.
	2. A culturally skilled counseling psychologist is aware of his/her own values and biases and how they may affect minority clients.
	3. A culturally skilled counseling psychologist is one who is comfortable with differences that exist between the counselor and client in terms of race and beliefs.
	4. The culturally skilled counseling psychologist is sensitive to circumstances (personal biases, stage of ethnic identity, sociopolitical influences, etc.) which may dictate referral of the minority client to a member of his/her own race/culture.
Knowledges	1. The culturally skilled counseling psychologist will have a good understanding of the sociopolitical system's operation in the United States with respect to its treatment of minorities.
	2. The culturally skilled counseling psychologist must possess specific knowledge and information about the particular group he/she is working with.
	3. The culturally skilled counseling psychologist must have a clear and explicit knowledge and understanding of the generic characteristics of counseling and therapy.
	4. The culturally skilled counseling psychologist is aware of institutional barriers which prevent minorities from using mental health services.
Skills	1. At the skills level, the culturally skilled counseling psychologist must be able to generate a wide variety of verbal and nonverbal responses.
	2. The culturally skilled counseling psychologist must be able to send and receive both verbal and nonverbal messages accurately and "appropriately."
	3. The culturally skilled counseling psychologist is able to exercise institutional intervention skills on behalf of his/her client when appropriate.

indigenous help-giving networks, and the advantages of being bicultural need to be recognized. It was felt that the curriculum should contain areas dealing with consciousness raising, knowledge and skills.

With these issues in mind, the Education and Training Committee of Division 17 feels a strong responsibility to bring to the membership's attention the need for developing minimal cross-cultural counseling competencies to be incorporated into training programs. The following pages contain some general guidelines which we hope will aid in the development of more concrete and sophisticated competencies for working with culturally different clients. In light of our earlier review, it seems imperative that we move quickly to challenge certain assumptions which permeate our training program and to critically evaluate not only the practices of the past, but the present as well. For this reason, we advocate the adoption of the following beliefs/attitudes, knowledges and skills by the Executive Committee and the membership of Division 17. Hopefully, these competencies will be incorporated into graduate schools of counseling psychology as well as other mental health training programs.

Beliefs/Attitudes

1. *The culturally skilled counseling psychologist is one who has moved from being culturally unaware to being aware and sensitive to his/her own cultural heritage and to valuing and respecting differences.* Culturally skilled counselors have moved from ethnocentrism to valuing and respecting differences. Other cultures are seen as equally valuable and legitimate as their own. A culturally unaware counselor is most likely to impose his/her values onto a minority client.

2. *A culturally skilled counseling psychologist is aware of his/her own values and biases and how they may affect minority clients.* They constantly attempt to avoid prejudices, unwarranted labeling and stereotyping. They try not to hold preconceived limitations/notions about their minority clients. As a check upon this process, culturally skilled counseling psychologists monitor their functioning via consultation, supervision and continual education.

3. *A culturally skilled counseling psychologist is one who is comfortable with differences that exist between the counselor and client in terms of race and beliefs.* Differences are not seen as being deviant! The culturally skilled counselor does not profess "color blindness" or negate the existence of differences that exist in attitudes/beliefs. The basic concept underlying "color blindness" was the humanity of all people. Regardless of color or other physical differences, each individual is equally human. While its intent was to eliminate bias from counseling, it has served to deny the existence of differences in clients' perceptions of society arising out of membership in different racial groups. The message tends to be "I will like you only if you are the same," instead of "I like you because of and in spite of your differences."

4. *The culturally skilled counseling psychologist is sensitive to circumstances (personal biases, stage of ethnic identity, sociopolitical influences, etc.) which may dictate referral of the minority client to a member of his/her own race/culture.* A culturally skilled counselor is aware of his/her limitations in cross-cultural counseling and is not threatened by the prospect of referring a client.

Knowledges

1. *The culturally skilled counseling psychologist will have a good understanding of the sociopolitical system's operation in the United States with respect to its treatment of minorities.* Understanding the impact and operation of oppression (racism, sexism, etc.), the politics of counseling, and the racist concepts that have permeated the mental health/helping professions are important. Especially valuable for the counselor is an understanding of the role cultural racism plays in the development of identity, and world views among minority groups.
2. *The culturally skilled counseling psychologist must possess specific knowledge and information about the particular group he/she is working with.* He/she must be aware of the history, experiences, cultural values and lifestyle of various racial/ethnic groups. The greater the depth of knowledge of a cultural group and the more knowledge he/she has of *many* groups, the more likely the counselor can be an effective helper. Thus, the culturally skilled counselor is one who *continues* to explore and learn about issues related to various minority groups throughout their professional careers.
3. *The culturally skilled counseling psychologist must have a clear and explicit knowledge and understanding of the generic characteristics of counseling and therapy.* These encompass language factors, culture-bound values and class-bound values. The counselor should clearly understand the value assumptions (normality and abnormality) inherent in the major schools of counseling and how they may interact with values of the culturally different. In some cases, the theories or models may limit the potential of persons from different cultures. Likewise, being able to determine those which may have usefulness to culturally different clients is important.
4. *The culturally skilled counseling psychologist is aware of institutional barriers which prevent minorities from using mental health services.* Such factors as the location of a mental health agency, the formality or informality of the decor, the language(s) which are used to advertise their services, the availability of minorities among the different levels, the organizational climate, the hours and days of operation, the offering of the services really needed by the community, etc., are important.

Skills

1. At the skills level, *the culturally skilled counseling psychologist must be able to generate a wide variety of verbal and nonverbal responses.*

There is mounted evidence to indicate that minority groups may not only define problems differently from their Anglo counterparts but respond differently to counseling/therapy styles (Berman, 1979; Atkinson, Mariyama & Matsui, 1978; D. W. Sue, 1981). Ivey and Authier (1978) state that the wider repertoire of responses the counselor possesses, the better the helper he/she is likely to be. We can no longer rely on a very narrow and limited number of skills in counseling. We need to practice and be comfortable with a multitude of response modalities.

2. *The culturally skilled counseling psychologist must be able to send and receive both verbal and nonverbal messages accurately and "appropriately."* The key words are "send," "receive," "verbal," "nonverbal," "accurately," and "appropriately" are important. These words recognize several things about cross-cultural counseling. First, communication is a two-way process. The culturally skilled counselor must not only be able to communicate (send) his/her thoughts and feelings to the client, but also be able to read (receive) messages from the client. Second, cross-cultural counseling effectiveness may be highly correlated with the counselor's ability to recognize and respond to not only verbal but nonverbal messages. Third, sending and receiving a message accurately means the ability to consider cultural cues operative in the setting. Fourth, accuracy of communication must be tempered by its appropriateness. This is a difficult concept for many to grasp. It deals with communication styles. In many cultures, subtlety and indirectness of communication are highly prized arts. Likewise, directness and confrontation are prized by others.

3. *The culturally skilled counseling psychologist is able to exercise institutional intervention skills on behalf of his/her client when appropriate.* This implies that help-giving may involve out-of-office strategies (outreach, consultant, change agent, ombudsmen roles and facilitator of indigenous support systems) which discard the intrapsychic counseling model and views the problems/barriers as residing outside of the minority client.

A Call for Action

The objectives of the Education and Training Committee of Division 17 have been to provide a rationale for the inclusion of cross-cultural counseling/therapy training in graduate schools of psychology and to briefly outline attitudes/beliefs, knowledges, and skills inherent in such competencies. We have not addressed ourselves to the issue of how to implement these recommendations because they have been covered in detail elsewhere (Korman, 1973; McFadden, Quinn & Sweeney, 1978; Blau, 1970; President's Commission on Mental Health, 1978; Dulles Conference 1978; Society for the Psychological Study of Social Issues, 1973; D. W. Sue & S. Sue, 1972). Among the multitudes of suggestions are (a) offering academic and research courses specifically on ethnic/racial minorities, (b) integrating cross-cultural issues into existing psychology courses, (c) encouraging recruitment and retention of both minority faculty and students, (d) providing practicum and internship experiences in a multi-racial setting, (e) developing resource materials relevant to minority issues, and (f) incorporating such recommendations into current APA and other accreditation criteria. Unfortunately, these strategies and recommendations have made minimal progress partly due to the lack of institutional and professional organizational support beyond the rhetorical level. The Education and Training Committee of Division 17 would like to request that the President in conjunction with the Executive Committee take the following actions:

1. Formal endorsement of the current position paper with respect to the rationale and the delineation of minimal cross-cultural counseling/therapy principles needed outlining the rationale, issues, and need for minimal cross-cultural counseling/therapy competencies.
2. Take whatever steps necessary, to ensure that the current paper receives widespread dissemination among its membership, relevant boards, committees and divisions within APA and in state organizations.
3. Move towards implementing these competencies into current APA accreditation criteria.
4. Establishment of an ongoing process within Division 17 which will continue to develop and define the cross-cultural competencies and issues, and monitor the implementation of these objectives.

Reference Notes

Espin, O. M. Paper on ethno-cultural concerns presented to ACES, May 15, 1979.

McFadden, J., & Wilson, T. Non-white academic training within counselor education, rehabilitation counseling and student personnel programs. Unpublished research, 1977.

Society for the Psychological Study of Social Issues. Document entitled "Graduate programs in psychology, in the sciences, in education, social work, public health, suitable to the needs of minority students," Los Angeles, 1973.

References

Atkinson, D. R., Morten, G., & Sue, D. W. *Counseling American Minorities: A Cross-Cultural Perspective.* Dubuque: Wm. C. Brown Co. Pub., 1979.

Atkinson, D. R., Mariyama, M., & Matsui, S. The effects of counselor race and counseling approach on Asian Americans' perceptions of counselor credibility and utility. *Journal of Counseling Psychology,* 1978, *25,* 76–83.

Baratz, S., & Baratz, J. Early childhood intervention: The social sciences base of institutional racism. *Harvard Educational Review,* 1970, *40,* 29–50.

Berman, J. Counseling skills used by Black and white male and female counselors. *Journal of Counseling Psychology,* 1979, *26,* 81–84.

Billingsley, A. Black families and white social science. *Journal of Social Issues,* 1970, *26,* 127–142.

Blau, T. APA Commission on accelerating Black participation in psychology. *American Psychologist,* 1970, *25,* 1103–1104.

Brislin, R., Lonner, W., & Thorndike, R. *Cross-cultural research methods.* New York: Wiley, 1973.

Bryde, J. F. *Indian students and guidance.* Boston: Houghton-Mifflin Co., 1971.

Carkhuff, R. R., & Pierce, R. Differential effects of therapist race and social class upon patient depth of self-exploration in the initial clinical interview. *Journal of Consulting Psychology,* 1967, *31,* 632–634.

Dorfman, D. D. The Cyril Burt question: New findings. *Science,* 1978, *201,* 1177–1186.

Espin, O. M. Paper on ethno-cultural concerns presented to ACES, May 15, 1979.

Gillie, D. *Phi Delta Kappan,* 1978, *58,* 469.

Hernstein, R. "IQ." *The Atlantic Monthly,* 1971, *228* (3), 43–64.

Ivey, A., & Authier, J. *Microcounseling: Innovations in interviewing training.* Springfield, Ill.: Charles C. Thomas, 1978.

Jensen, A. How much can we boost IQ and school achievement? *Harvard Educational Review,* 1969, *39,* 1–123.

Kamin, L. *The science and politics of I.Q.* Potomac, Md.: Eribaum, 1974.

Korman, M. *Levels and patterns of professional training in psychology.* Washington, D.C.: American Psychological Association, 1973.

McFadden, J., Quinn, J. R., & Sweeney, T. J. *Position paper by Commission on Non-white concerns of ACES.* APGA. Washington, D.C.: 1978.

McFadden, J., & Wilson, T. Non-white academic training within counselor education, rehabilitation counseling and student personnel programs. Unpublished research, 1977.

Padilla, A. M., & Ruiz, R. A. *Latino mental health.* Washington, D.C.: DHEW, 1974.

Padilla, E. R. The relationship between psychology and Chicanos: Failures and possibilities. In N. N. Wagner & M. R. Haug (Eds.), *Chicanos: Social and psychological perspectives.* St. Louis, Mo.: Mosby, 1971, pp. 286–294.

Pine, G. J. Counseling minority groups: A review of the literature. *Counseling and Values,* 1972, *17,* 35–44.

President's Commission on Mental Health. Report to the President. Washington, D.C.: U.S. Government Printing Office, 1978.

Ruis, R. A., & Padilla, A. M. Counseling Latinos. *The Personnel and Guidance Journal,* 1977, *55,* 401–408.

Society for the Psychological Study of Social Issues. Document entitled "Graduate programs in psychology, in the sciences, in education, social work, public health, suitable to the needs of minority students." Los Angeles, 1973.

Shockley, W. *Journal of Criminal Law and Criminology,* 1972, *7,* 530–543.

Shuey, A. *The testing of Negro intelligence.* New York: Social Science Press, 1966.

Smith, E. J. Counseling black individuals: Some stereotypes. *Personnel and Guidance Journal,* 1977, *55,* 390–396.

Smith, E. J. *Counseling the culturally different black youth.* Columbus, Ohio: Charles E. Merrill Book Co., 1973.

Sue, D. W. *Counseling the culturally different: Theory and practice.* New York: John Wiley & Sons, 1981.

Sue, D. W. Asian Americans: Social-psychological forces affecting their life styles. In S. Picou, & R. Campbell (Eds.) *Career behavior of special groups.* Columbus, Ohio: Charles E. Merrill Publishers, 1975.

Sue, D. W., & Sue, D. Barriers to effective cross-cultural counseling. *Journal of Counseling Psychology,* September 1977.

Sue, D. W., & Sue, S. Ethnic minorities: Resistance to being researched. *Professional Psychology,* 1972, *2,* 11–17.

Sue, S. Issues in Asian American psychology curriculum. *Journal of the Asian American Psychological Association,* 1980, *5,* 6–11.

Sue, S., Allen, D., & Conaway, L. The responsiveness and equality of mental health care to Chicanos and Native Americans. *American Journal of Community Psychology,* 1978, *6,* 137–146.

Sue, S., & McKinney, H. Asian Americans in the community mental health care system. *American Journal of Orthopsychiatry,* 1974, *45,* 111–118.

Sue, S., McKinney, H., Allen, D., & Hall, J. Delivery of community mental health services to black and white clients. *Journal of Consulting and Clinical Psychology,* 1974, *42,* 794–801.

Sumada, R. J. From ethnocentrism to a multicultural perspective in educational testing. *Journal of Afro-American Issues,* 1975, *3,* 4–18.

Thomas, A., & Sillen, S. *Racism and psychiatry.* New York: Brunner/Mazel, Inc., 1972.

Triandis, H. *The analysis of subjective culture.* New York: Wiley, 1972.

Trimble, J. E. Value differences among American Indians: Concerns for the concerned counselor. In P. Pedersen, W. J. Lonner, & J. G. Draguns (Eds.), *Counseling across cultures.* Honolulu: East West Center Press, 1976.

True, R. H. APA members vote to create Board of Minority Affairs. *Journal of the Asian American Psychological Association,* 1980, *5,* 3–4.

Vontress, C. E. Racial differences: Impediments to rapport. *Journal of Counseling Psychology,* 1971, *18,* 7–13.

Williams, R. L. Black pride, academic relevance and individual achievement. *Counseling Psychologist,* 1970, *2,* 18–22.

Yamamoto, J., James, Q. C., & Palley, N. Cultural problems in psychiatric therapy. *Archives of General Psychiatry,* 1968, *19,* 45–49.

Author Index

Foreign Area Studies of the American
   University, 139, 142n
Foster, H. L., 201, 202, 207, 208, 209n
Frank, J., 131, 142n
Frank, J. D., 201, 210n
Frankl, V. E., 201, 209n
Franklin, J. H., 185n
Frazier, E. F., 200, 209n
Frazier, F. E., 152, 153n
Freedle, R., 36, 37, 47n
Freeman, D., 62, 69n
Fretz, B. R., 13, 34n
Froman, T., 289, 293n
Fukuyama, M., 287, 295n
Fukuyama, M. A., 288, 295n
Fulcher, R., 18, 32n, 53, 70n, 278, 295n

Gaier, E. L., 21, 32n
Gandhi, M. K., 202, 209n
Gardner, E. A., 14, 30n
Gardner, L. H., 24, 25, 26, 31n, 290, 294n
Garfield, J. C., 14, 31n
Garrison, V., 223, 224, 239, 239n
Gill, G. R., 189n
Gill, Gerald, R., 190n
Gilliam, O. L., 62, 70n
Gillie, D., 298, 310n
Gladwin, T., 206, 209n
Glazer, N., 186n
Gochros, J. S., 207, 209n
Goldenberg, I. I., 7, 9n
Goldstein, G., 58, 70n
Goldstein, G. S., 58, 70n
Gomez, E. A., 242, 255n
Gonsalves, J., 288, 293n
Gonzalez, J., 255n
Gonzalez, J. R., 254n
Good, B., 121, 127n
Good Tracks, J. G., 54, 57, 61, 62, 63, 70n,
   92
Gordon, P., 103, 114n
Gordon, S., 225, 239n
Granberg, L. I., 22, 31n
Gravitz, H. L., 273, 294n
Green, B. E., 53, 70n
Greenson, R. R., 24, 31n
Grevious, C., 192, 272, 294n
Grier, W. H., 17, 31n, 202, 204, 209n
Griffith, M. S., 192, 193, 198n
Gross, H., 192, 198n
Guerney, B. G., 14, 31n
Gunnings, T. S., 17, 31n
Gunther, Bernard, 92n
Gutman, H., 193, 198n
Gwyn, F., 192, 194, 195, 198n

Haase, W., 14, 31n
Haber, A., 151, 152n
Habermann, L., 14, 31n
Haettenschwiller, D. L., 23, 31n, 291, 294n
Haley, J., 202, 209n
Hall, J., 14, 33n, 299, 311n
Hall, L. E., 288, 295n
Hall, W. S., 36, 37, 47n
Halleck, S. L., 13, 31n
Hallem, I., 192, 199n
Hamilton, Charles V., 189n
Hammer, E., 136, 142n
Hardyck, J. A., 206, 210n
Harrison, D. K., 290, 294n
Hatten, J., 14, 34n
Havighurst, R. J., 21, 31n
Heiman, E. M., 255n
Heine, R. W., 203, 209n
Helms, J. E., 35, 36, 47n
Herbert, M., 192, 198n
Hernstein, R., 298, 310n
Hibbs, B. J., 255n
Hickey, G. C., 139, 142n
Hidalgo, H. A., 258, 264n
Higashi, C., 18, 33n, 282, 296n
Highwater, Jamake, 83n
Hill, R., 193, 198n
Hill, R. B., 152, 153n, 186n, 189n, 190n
Hill, Robert B., 188n
Hill Witt, S., 62, 67, 69n
Hines, P., 193, 194, 199n
Hinsie, L. E., 223, 239n
Ho, C., 127n
Ho, Man Keung, 84n, 85
Ho, M. K., 54, 57, 58, 61, 64, 65, 70n
Hollingshead, A. B., 20, 21, 31n, 205, 209n,
   219, 239n
Holwill, C. F., 288, 295n
Hosford, R., 280, 293n
Huffaker, Clair, 92n
Hughes, E. C., 4, 10n
Hunt, G. H., 217, 218n

Ibrahim, F. A., 17, 31n
Iga, M., 121, 128n
Iswahara, S., 103, 112, 113n
Ivey, A., 275, 294n, 301, 310n
Ivey, A. E., 275, 294n

Ja, D. Y., 121, 128n
Jackson, A. M., 24, 25, 26, 31n
Jackson, B., 36, 37, 47n
Jackson, G. G., 16, 31n
Jaco, E. G., 220, 222, 239n

Marques, R., 259, 264n
Marr, Warren, III, 189n
Marsella, A. J., 54, 70n, 103, 114n
Martinez, C., 238, 240n
Martinez, R., 255n
Maruyama, M., 23, 29n
Maslow, Abraham, 92n
Masuda, M., 103, 107, 114n
Matsui, S., 23, 29n, 308, 309n
Matsumoto, G. M., 103, 107, 114n
May, Rollo, 92n
Maykovich, M. H., 36, 38, 47n
Mayton, D. M., II, 289, 293n
McAdoo, H., 193, 199n
McAlister, J. T., 137, 142n
McCreary, C., 255n
McDavis, R. J., 286, 287, 295n
McFadden, J., 17, 31n, 303, 308, 309n, 310n
McFee, M., 68, 70n
McKinley, C., 223, 224, 239n
McKinney, H., 14, 33n, 116, 117, 121, 128n,
    192, 199n, 299, 311n
McNickle, D., 68, 70n
Meade, R. D., 103, 107, 114n
Mercado, P., 14, 32n
Meredith, G., 103, 107, 112, 113n, 114n
Meredith, G. M., 103, 108, 109, 114n
Michael, S. T., 219, 240n
Michels, R., 254n
Millen, L., 255n
Miller, A. G., 65, 70n
Miller, C. D., 288, 294n
Miller, H. P., 186n
Miller, J. D. B., 8, 9n
Miller, M. H., 131, 138, 141n
Miranda, M. R., 254n
Mitchell, H., 32n, 272, 274, 286, 288, 295n
Moll, R. S., 254n
Monahan, J., 197, 199n
Montero, D., 138, 142n
Moore, B. M., 4, 10n
Moore, J. W., 189n
Morales, A., 228, 239n
Moreland, J. R., 18, 32n, 278, 295n
Morey, S. M., 62, 70n
Morishima, J. K., 99, 101n, 116, 117, 120,
    121, 127n, 128n
Moriwaki, S., 225, 241n
Morris, Lorenzo, 188n
Morten, G., 302, 309n
Moss, R. N., 58, 70n
Munoz, F. U., 121, 127n
Murphy, H. B., 280, 295n
Murray, J., 12, 14, 29n, 290, 292n

Mus, P., 137, 142n
Muskrat, J., 69, 70n
Mussenden, M. E., 288, 295n
Mydal, G., 186n

Nader, R., 188n
Naditch, M., 37, 46n
Nairn, A., 188n
National Indochinese Clearinghouse and
    Technical Assistance Center, 132, 142n
Neimeyer, G. J., 288, 295n
Neugarten, B. L., 21, 31n
Newman, Dorothy K., 186n, 188n
Newsweek, 99, 101n, 106, 114n
Nguyen Duy San, 131, 135, 139, 142n
Nguyen Ngoc Bich, 130, 131, 133, 136, 142n
Nguyen Thanh Liem, 140, 142n
Nguyen Van Thuan, 134, 142n

Oetting, G., 288, 294n
Oho, H., 92n
O'Leary, J., 190n
Olivas, Michael A., 187n
Olmedo, E. L., 18, 32n, 53, 70n, 255n, 278,
    295n
Opler, M. K., 219, 240n
Ovesey, L., 200, 210n

Padilla, A., 193, 198n
Padilla, A. M., 17, 19, 30n, 32n, 35, 47n,
    219, 238n, 240n, 253n, 254n, 282, 283,
    293n, 298, 299, 310n
Padilla, E., 255n
Padilla, E. R., 18, 32n, 278, 295n, 298, 310n
Paine, C., 255n
Palley, N., 14, 34n, 103, 105, 115n, 193,
    199n, 221, 226, 241n, 299, 311n
Pambrum, A., 53, 70n
Parham, T. A., 35, 36, 47n
Parham, W., 18, 32n, 278, 295n
Parker, W. M., 286, 287, 295n
Parks, R. E., 47n
Parsons, J. S., 134, 142n
Pedersen, P., 17, 33n, 284, 296n, 297
Pedersen, P. B., 16, 17, 32n, 54, 70n, 276,
    287, 288, 291, 295n
Peele, D., 278, 296n
Penk, W. E., 255n
Penner, L. A., 136, 142n
Peoples, V. Y., 23, 32n
Personnel and Guidance Journal, 129
Peskin, H., 103, 107, 108, 113n
Pettigrew, T. F., 189n

Subject Index

afecto, 258, 263
Aid to Families with Dependent Children (AFDC), 168, 180
alloplastic, 16, 45
alternatives to the traditional counseling role, 271–77
American Association for Counseling and Development (AACD), 17, 281
American Indian Social Work Career Training Program, 81
American Psychological Association (APA), 12, 17, 53, 54, 281
anticounselor, 287
APA Board of Ethnic Minority Affairs, 12, 306
APA Board of Social and Ethical Responsibility for Psychology, 12
APA Minority Fellowship Program, 12
APA Office of Cultural and Ethnic Affairs, 12
APA Society for Psychological Study of Ethnic Minority Issues, 12
ataques de nervios, 248
Austin Conference, 12
Autoplastic, 16
Awareness Group Experience (AGE), 286–87

Bakke vs. Regents of the University of California, 280
barriers to minority group/cross-cultural counseling, 18–26
benefits to cross-cultural counseling, 26–27
Black Identity Development Model, 37
Black Muslims, 160
Black Panthers, 164
black power, 159, 160
black pride, 159, 197
black stereotypes, 151
blame the victim, 243
Brown vs. Board of Education of Topeka, Kansas, 156
Bureau of Indian Affairs, 51
Burger Court, 170

Change agent role, 272, 275
Chinese Exclusion Act of 1882, 6
City of Mobile et al. vs. Bolden et al., 174, 175
Civil Rights Act of 1964, 161
civil rights movement, 11
Civil Service, 162
Class-bound values, 20–21
client expectations, 24, 28
color or culture blindness, 24
Community Mental Health, 232
compadrazco, 229
compadrazgo, 259, 263
Conformity Stage, 39, 44
Congressional Black Caucus, 173
Congress of Racial Equality (CORE), 158, 159
consultant role, 271, 273
controlled schizophrenia, 67
Council for Accreditation of Counseling and Related Educational Programs, 281
counselor-client coalition, 287
countertransference, 24, 28, 203
Cross-Cultural Counseling, 9
cultural assimilation, 6–7
culturally deprived, 5, 21, 299
culturally different, 6
culturally disadvantaged, 5, 299
culturally distinct, 6
cultural pluralism, 6–7
cultural racism, 105–6
culture, 4–6, 8, 21
culture blind, 27
culture-bound values, 19, 21–23
culture conflict, 67, 107
culture free, 248
culture of poverty, 151
curanderos, 276

Declaration of Independence, 11
de facto segregation, 166, 172, 175
de jure segregation, 166, 172
Developing Interculturally Skilled Counselors (DISC), 289

321

dignidad, 258, 263
Dissonance Stage, 40–41, 44, 45
Division 17 Education and Training
    Committee, 17, 297, 283
Division 17 Professional Affairs Committee,
    275
Dred-Scott decision of 1857, 155
Dulles Conference, 12

Economic Opportunity Act of 1964, 161
Elementary and Secondary Education Act of
    1965, 161
emic-etic dichotomy, 18
empacho, 248
Ethnic Heritage Studies Bill of 1973, 7
ethnicity, 4
Ethnic Student Training Group (ESTG), 287
ethnocentrism, 5
Executive Order 11246, 161

facilitator of indigeneous support systems,
    272, 276
facilitator of self help, 271, 272
Fair Deal, 157
Fair Employment Practices Commission, 157
Fair Housing Act of 1968, 161, 182
family adaption model, 229, 236–37
fatalismo, 258, 263
Federal Chinese Exclusion Act of 1882, 106
Fifteenth Amendment, 155
First World, 8
Fourteenth Amendment to the Constitution,
    155
Freedmen's Bureau, 155, 163
Fullilove vs. Klutznick, 171

guilt, White feelings of, 203–4

Harlem Interfaith Counseling Service, 196
He-Who-Kills-With-His-Eyes, 58
Higher Education Act of 1965, 161
Higher Education Amendments of 1968, 161
hijo de crianza, 262–63
humanismo, 258, 263

Indian Child Welfare Bill, 65
Indian Health Service, 56
Indian problems, 51
Indian time, 66
inter-minority group counseling, 26
intra-minority group counseling, 25
intrapsychic model, 15–16
Introspection Stage, 42, 44

Japanese-American Citizens' League, 112
Jim Crow laws, 156
Joint Center for Political Studies, 165, 173,
    174, 175
Jones Act of 1917, 257

la clinica hispana, 230
la Frontera, 230
language barrier, 243–44, 251
la platica, 245

machismo, 229, 237, 258, 264
mal de ojo, 248
Manifest Destiny, 55
March on Washington, 159
Marginal Man, 68, 107
melting pot theory, 6
Minnesota Multiphasic Personality Inventory,
    248–50
Minority, 3, 7–8
minority group counseling, 8, 11
Minority Identity Development Model, 35,
    39–44
minority typologies, 35–36
model minority, 99, 109

National Association for the Advancement of
    Colored People (NAACP), 156, 164, 176
National Center for Black Aged, 168
National Congress of American Indians, 74
National Institute of Mental Health, 12, 54
National Urban League, 164
Nation of Islam, 160
Negro-to-Black Conversion Experience, 37
New Deal policies, 157
noninterference, 62

ombudsmun role, 271, 274
oppression, 7
outreach role, 271, 272

personalismo, 229, 237, 250
Plessy vs. Ferguson, 156
Position Paper on Cross-Cultural Counseling
    Competencies, 283–84, 297–311
potlatches, 72
powwows, 72
President's Commission on Mental Health, 54
President's Committee on Civil Rights, 157
professional adaption model, 228
proposition 13, 169
pseudoetic approach, 18

race, 3–4
racial types, 4
representational admission policy, 280
resistance, 24, 28
Resistance and Immersion Stage, 41–42, 44
respecto, 229, 237, 258, 264

Sansei, 36
second generationitis, 261
Second World, 8
societal subgroups, 282
Southern Christian Leadership Conference
   (SCLC), 158, 159
Special Populations Task Force, 12
stereotypes, 15, 23
stereotyping, 23
Stress Resistant Delivery Model, 272
Student Nonviolent Coordinating Committee
   (SNCC), 158, 159
success myth, 100
super-minority counselor, 26
susto, 248
Synergetic Articulation and Awareness
   Stage, 43, 44

Third World, 8–9, 273
Thirteenth Amendment to the Constitution,
   155
tiers monde, 8
traditional counseling role, 15, 271, 277–78
transference, 24, 28
Triad Model, 287–88
Twenty-fourth Amendment to the
   Constitution, 162

United Nations, 157
United Steelworkers of America vs. Weber,
   171
University of California vs. Allan Bakke, 171
Urban League, 152, 156

Vail Conference, 12, 17
Voting Rights Act of 1965, 161, 172

Warren Court, 160, 162, 170
Wounded Knee, 73

Yellow Peril, 105